P9-CRN-522

MINE EYES HAVE SEEN THE GLORY

MINE EYES HAVE SEEN THE GLORY

The Civil War in Art

BY HAROLD HOLZER AND MARK E. NEELY, JR.

ORION BOOKS
NEW YORK

Endpaper illustration courtesy Museum of the Confederacy, Richmond, Virginia;
photograph by Larry Sherer.

Copyright © 1993 by Harold Holzer and Mark E. Neely, Jr.

All rights reserved. No part of this book may be reproduced or transmitted in any form or
by any means, electronic or mechanical, including photocopying, recording, or by any
information storage and retrieval system, without permission in writing from the publisher.

Published by Orion Books, a division of Crown Publishers, Inc., 201 East 50th Street, New
York, New York 10022. Member of the Crown Publishing Group.
Random House, Inc. New York, Toronto, London, Sydney, Auckland

ORION and colophon are trademarks of Crown Publishers, Inc.

Manufactured in Japan

Designed by Kay Schuckhart

Library of Congress Cataloging-in-Publication Data
Holzer, Harold.
Mine eyes have seen the glory : the Civil War in American art / by
Harold Holzer and Mark E. Neely, Jr.—1st ed.
Includes bibliographical references and index.
1. Painting, American.   2. Painting, Modern—19th century—United
States.   3. United States—History—Civil War, 1861–1865—Art and
the war.   I. Neely, Mark E.   II. Title.
ND210.H66   1993
758'.99737—dc20 92-29547

ISBN 0-517-58448-4
10   9   8   7   6   5   4   3   2   1
First Edition

For Richard Nelson Current

C O N T E N T S

odern military painting began as an American art. At least it began with an American, Benjamin West, who chose to depict the death of General James Wolfe at the Battle of Quebec with the protagonists garbed not in symbolic Roman armor and togas but in historically correct military costume of the eighteenth century. Thus he dignified a contemporary military event with the heroic scale and style previously confined to classical subjects.[1] With that innovation, West launched a revolution in the art of war. The genre did not immediately flower here, however, because of the antimilitary tradition ingrained in the republican ideology of the American struggle for independence from Great Britain. Hatred of standing armies formed a powerful legacy of the American Revolution, and occasional successes in military art, such as John Trumbull's depiction of the Battle of Bunker Hill, may have owed their fame in part to the fact that they showed Americans fighting *against* standing armies. ✹ Antimilitarism kept America's armed forces small and her painters interested mainly in peace-

INTRODUCTION

ful genres, portraits, and landscapes until the outbreak of the Civil War.[2] Then the need for military art exploded. The new national identity that emerged after 1865 was forged in the blood of 620,000 Americans, more of whom died in one battle of the war than in all her previous wars put together. The idea of the nation was now vitally linked to war, and the subject demanded artistic treatment. ✵ The demand came largely from Americans who, as veterans or passionate observers of the conflict, now desired artistic renderings of the conflict for their public buildings, soldiers' homes, and veterans' clubs. Thus patronage was added to public interest to stimulate military painting. This powerful combination helped produce hundreds of canvases in the fifty years that followed the war. The story of how and why they were finally produced, and who produced them, has never before fully been told. ✵ This book offers a substantial sampling of those works—some of the best known and a number of more obscure but arresting images—along with an attempt to explain their meaning. We chose not to include the art of photography or the work of the sketch-

book artists who covered the war for the illustrated newspapers, except as their work influenced the fine arts; both of these popular media have been well documented in past studies. Similarly, we have limited our discussion of popular prints, a subject about which we ourselves have frequently written, to their relationship to the fine arts, which often inspired them. Nor did we include the new generation of Civil War artists working today, though we hope their current popularity will help revive interest in their counterparts who worked before World War I. Instead we focus on the first fifty years of Civil War art, neglected years, the era before the war to end all wars forever ended our romantic view of warfare. ✷ Our book is not an illustrated history of the Civil War, or perhaps one should say *another* such history. Several already exist and they routinely slight paintings in favor of photographs and journalistic illustrations contemporary with the conflict. This is understandable in a way, because the neglected paintings, though numerous and beautiful, do not provide a systematic chronicle of the war. Paintings do not exist—and never did—in quality or quantity exactly proportional to the importance of Civil War battles, events, and leaders. This imbalance is part of the story we hope to tell. ✷ More important, this book is at war with the very idea of "illustration" in Civil War history. Students of American history will no doubt have already seen some of the works reproduced in this book, but these paintings have been more often seen than studied. Their previous use as illustrations has robbed them of the power they once held to provoke responses from their viewers. Paintings, of course, do not "illustrate" anything so much as the viewpoints of their painters. They crackle with controversial content and lively assertion. ✷ Or, rather, they once did. Now they seem mute, mere "illustrations" of this battle or that leader. Avid readers of Civil War magazines will recognize what we mean if they review the "letters to the editor" sections of previous issues. There readers find angry letter after angry letter complaining that one article or another was either too pro-Southern or too pro-Northern, or somehow slighted the contributions of one general to magnify those of another. One looks in vain for similar expressions of indignation about the pictures reproduced in these magazines. After all, visual representations of Civil War events, like verbal ones, inevitably contain a "point of view." But many of today's readers have been desensitized to this by the idea of "illustration." ✺ It is true, of course, that illustrated histories and magazines conduct what they call "picture research." By this, however, they do not mean so much research into pictures as a search *for* pictures. More often than not, such research—difficult enough, to be sure—boils down to a quest for a visual representation of some person, place, or thing mentioned in the text, representations in appealing style and of proper dimensions to fit layouts. The enterprise seems roughly analogous to shopping for pleasant "sofa-sized" paintings for home decoration. The content of the painting so used, the artist's intentions, and the effects it had on viewers when first unveiled remain matters unexamined and without comment in the spare and often inaccurate captions. Readers are seldom told the dimensions of these artworks— are these details or complete works; were the originals giant cycloramas or miniatures?—or their often revealing titles. ✺ When we researched the paintings *after* our own initial search for them revealed their locations, our eyes opened to meanings never before explained. We want to share these revelations with other readers interested in the Civil War—hence this book. ✺ We are not art historians, but there are qualities in these artworks that can be appreciated only by looking at them in a way that art historians customarily do not or would not. We did not encounter the canvases as individual episodes in the career of one painter, or as examples of artistic movements or styles. Rather, we considered them as part of a great effort to comprehend the Civil War, and the opportunity for comparison offered by this approach revealed meanings in the works about which we had never before read. ✺ Coming to this subject as historians and as writers on the popular arts of photography and lithography, we were struck by the difficulty of the painters' enterprise and the gulf that separates these works from the more popular arts. We find ourselves, therefore, not hypercritical but generally appreciative of their achievements. We realize, too, that the artists lacked the room to maneuver artistically that their twentieth-century counterparts enjoy. With virtually no public museums yet in existence, their works had to be fitting for domestic use as "decorations" in private homes or, in the case of public paintings, in essentially celebratory surroundings: government buildings, Grand Army of the Republic halls, Loyal Legion posts, United Confederate Veterans lodges, regimental armories, and the like—anywhere and everywhere that the strategies, charges, and retreats of "the late war" could be debated or refought by proud old soldiers. In a divided postwar society, surely as culturally sectionalized as it had been before Fort Sumter, these survivors launched their organizations to prescrve the wartime spirit of causes lost and won, and to make sure that "the other side" did not dominate the historical landscape. And paintings constituted potent weapons in their war for the collective memory of the American people. ✷ It is useful to remember that few such paintings were produced while the war still raged. "During the war," the *American Cyclopaedia* acknowledged in 1866, "the Fine Arts witnessed a very considerable development" but only along antebellum lines. "To the surprise of most persons, who looked for some higher influence imparted by the late war, pictures identical in character with the last decade continued to be produced...."[3] ✷ Nor did the establishment of wartime Union Leagues in New York, Boston, Philadelphia, and Chicago immediately change matters. In New York's club, "a committee on arts and relics" was by 1863 empowered to procure "works of art...and to make all proper efforts to enlarge and display the collection." But not until 1867 did any exhibition there devote itself exclusively to "Pictures of the War." Until then such depictions were scarcely shown. Union "sanitary fairs," organized to raise funds for sick and wounded soldiers, might have provided another early stage for Civil War art, but with rare exceptions the art exhibits at these events featured genre scenes, portaits, and landscapes—few of which portrayed the wartime events that had inspired these fairs in the first place (only sixteen Civil War works, for example, could be found among the 1,061 paintings at the 1864 Great Central Fair in Philadelphia; only one out of 120 at the Maryland State Fair the same year— Winslow Homer's *Playing Old Soldier*). In 1864, even Winslow Homer, by then selling some of his canvases for as much as $750 at the Brooklyn Art Association, confided that he expected to realize no more than "sixty dollars" for a Civil War sharpshooter scene, complaining that "that was what Harper paid…for a full drawing on the wood." As it turned out, he failed to realize even that much for it; there were as yet no takers.[4] ✤ "The war itself has not inspired many works," *Harper's Weekly* lamented in 1862. In 1864, in a frank article on "Painting and the War," the journal *The Round Table* would concur: "One of the most remarkable circumstances connected with the existing war is the very remote and trifling influence which it seems to have exerted upon American Art."[5] ✤ In the South, meanwhile, the taste for such works developed even more slowly. Viewing a display of E. B. D. Julio's *The Last Meeting of Lee and Jackson* in Memphis in 1869, Jefferson Davis, then the reigning symbol of the Lost Cause, pronounced the painting a "success," and added: "Few offerings could be more acceptable to our people than historical paintings which will transmit to posterity characteristic likenesses of soldiers whose moral character and great deeds have endeared them to their countrymen." But in New Orleans, where the canvas was subsequently exhibited, subscription efforts, lotteries, and raffles all failed to raise enough money to purchase the painting for public display.[6] ✤ Eventually, American painters gave the Civil War serious appraisal, and in evaluating their efforts we have tried not to set an impossible standard. However horrid the true nature of combat, its rendering by the late-nineteenth-century painter had to be somehow beautiful. Thought-provoking shock may be appropriate in modern public museums, but painters in the previous century had to sell their works in different circumstances. Moreover, the nineteenth-century aesthetic demanded that works of art be somehow uplifting and didactic. ✤ Still, historians must always maintain a critical outlook on their sources and subjects, and we attempt to do more here than lead cheers for neglected works. We live in an era in which the grisly nature of war has been a subject emphasized for more than seventy-five years, from the futile assaults at the Somme in 1916 onward. We cannot help but maintain some critical distance from paintings that somehow made war beautiful. ✤ In fact, distance from them is what invariably we must all feel. Increasingly, it is what we feel at any evocation of this bygone era. The most remarkable aspect of the Civil War period was its ability to evoke passionate responses to public events from its ordinary people—hence the 80-percent voter turnout in the national election preceding the war, hence the toll of 620,000 dead in the war, hence the 25-percent death rate among Confederate soldiers. None of this, for better or for worse, seems duplicable in modern society. ❄ The Civil War world is a lost world, and these paintings reveal it to us in a way that properly evokes curiosity and wonder at a civilization with so great a capacity for heroism and individual self-sacrifice. ❄ These works of art have always had this power, and they should not be allowed to lose it in the dim reproductions seen in "illustrated" histories. Even as formidable a critic as the novelist Henry James could not ignore them. Visiting the old White House of the Confederacy years after the war, James found its walls crowded with "not a single object of beauty, scarce one in fact that was not altogether ugly." Among the "sorry objects" that earned his particular scorn were "faded portraits of faded worthies...primitive products of...the crayon [and] the brush." These "daubs of portraiture," he sneered, were mere "echoes" of genuine art. Yet on these walls, he suddenly realized, hung not only objects of "undying rancor" but also of "valuable, enriching, inspiring, romantic legend." Looking closer at the portraits, listening appreciatively as an enthusiastic matron regaled him with "the patriotic unction of her references to the sorry objects about, as no enchanted object could have done," James suddenly understood what the collection revealed:

> *Practically, and most conveniently, one feels, the South is reconciled, but theoretically, ideally, and above all for the new generation and the amiable ladies...it burns like a smothered flame. As we meanwhile look about there, over a scene as sad, throughout, as some raw spring eventide, we feel how something of the sort must, in all the blankness, respond morally and socially to a want.*[7]

That want was not Southern alone, and it eventually inspired a bountiful artistic record of the Civil War for both sides. If this war of art failed to determine a clear winner, it certainly provided a priceless window onto the visions each side treasured of its experience. ❄ The fact that exposure to these pictures could animate, stimulate, and inspire viewers was until the dawn of World

War I obvious—and might have been evident to artists as well as critics as early as 1865, had more people looked closely. That April, New York's National Academy of Design belatedly opened its annual art exhibition, having postponed it for two weeks after Lincoln's assassination, and evoked from at least one visitor a visceral appreciation for the handful of Civil War scenes among the 616 pictures on view. ✹ That visitor, a local customs inspector who, the previous decade, had tried his hand at fiction writing without great commercial success, probably attended the show only because his brother was one of its sponsors. But once inside the Academy's new Gothic-style headquarters on Fourth Avenue, his eyes fell hungrily on scenes that rekindled memories of the thrilling war paintings he once viewed in European museums, known there as "battle-pieces." ✹ Deeply moved by the exhibition, the customs inspector, Herman Melville, began writing the volume of poetry he would pub-

lish the following year under the title that flashed into his mind that day at the Academy: *Battle-Pieces*. Its appearance solved a mystery the *New York Herald* acknowledged in its review, admitting that "for ten years the public has wondered what became of Melville."[8] ✹ What the reviewer did not know was that it took a glimpse of Civil War art to help invigorate Melville's dormant talent and ambition. Rare as such opportunities still remained for most other ordinary Americans— with the war of art only beginning—see the art they eventually would. And Herman Melville would not be the only enthusiast so moved. ✹ The following pages should help explain why. ✹

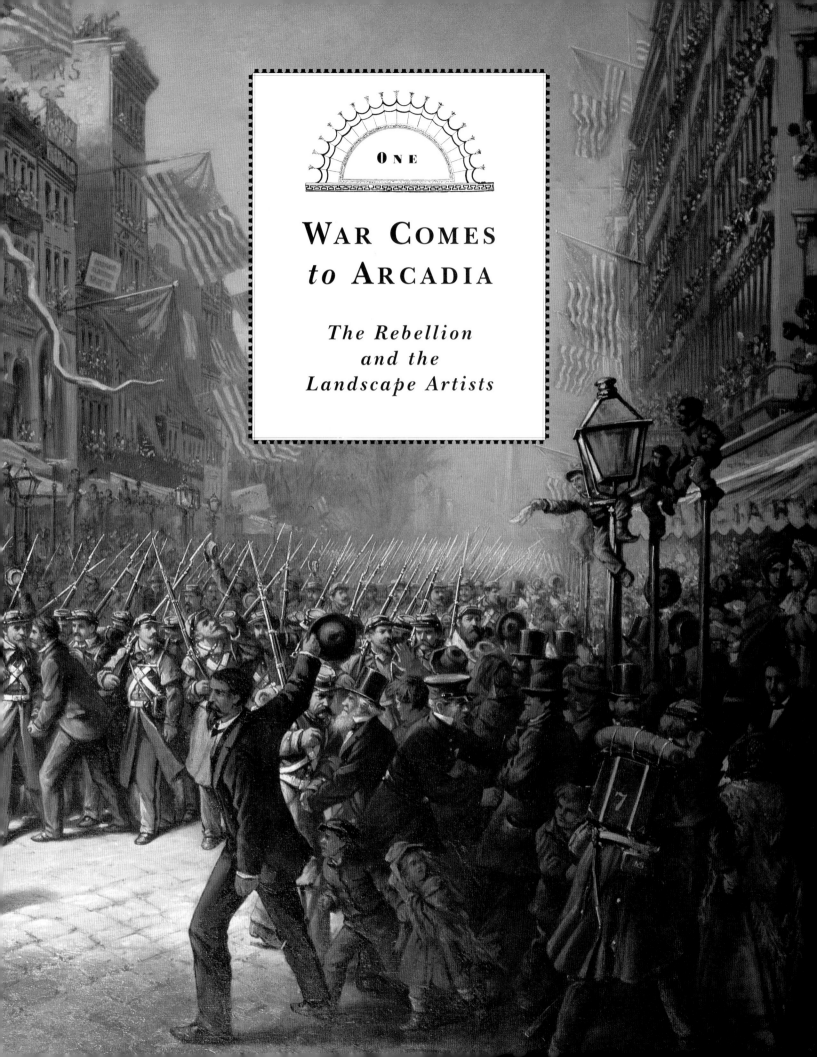

ONE

WAR COMES
to ARCADIA

*The Rebellion
and the
Landscape Artists*

≈ *Preceding Page* ≈

**THE DEPARTURE
OF THE 7TH RGT. TO
THE WAR, APRIL 19TH
1861 (1869)**

Thomas Nast (1840–1902)

*This huge canvas
reminded viewers of Union
determination by showing
the hero of Fort Sumter, Maj.
Robert Anderson, reviewing
the military parade from
atop the Ball, Black & Co.
pediment (left). The balanced
design—note the children
(not present in the original
sketch) seen perched on
lampposts framing both sides
of the painting—also fea-
tured subtle contrasts to the
general air of exuberance;
included among the crowd of
cheering New Yorkers, for
example, are weeping women,
presaging inevitable casualties yet to come. "Nast has
proved one of the most spirited and authentic draughts-
men of the... scenes incident
to the late Civil War," an art
critic declared two years before
this painting was completed.
The painting was exhibited at
the National Academy of
Design in 1870.*

Oil on canvas, 5 feet 6 inches × 8 feet.
Signed, lower left: *Th: Nast.* (The
Seventh Regiment Fund, Inc.)

ews of the firing on Fort Sumter in 1861 caught American artists as ill-prepared for a great war as American soldiers were. "At the commencement of the war," one critic noted, looking back from 1865, "American paintings were

practiced almost exclusively in three departments, landscape, portraiture, and *genre,* the first named being cultivated much more extensively than the other two." None proved entirely satisfactory in capturing the nature of modern war. Despite the prestige of "history paintings"—large canvases on historical subjects—few American artists painted them, at least not ably. In an article on the subject written as late as 1869, one critic could say, "American historical art is still mortifying to us." Before the Civil War, certainly, the youthful United States seemed to many a country without history, and artists often contented themselves with celebrating what their land possessed that Europe could not equal: vigorous, sublime, grand nature.[1]

Landscape—terrain to military men—proved to be only a part of war, and a minimally evocative part when

rendered in paintings. No one recognized that fact better than a landscape painter named Sanford Robinson Gifford, whose opportunity to see military life closely came as a member of New York's elite Seventh Regiment during the early years of the conflict.

A leading member of the "third generation of the Hudson River school" of painting, Gifford by April 1861 was already an established member of the National Academy of Design as well as an enthusiastic volunteer in the Union cause. Though a famous painter, he "entered this service," he insisted at the outset, only to fight and "without any artistic purpose." Gifford's story was apparently typical. As the annual report of the National Academy of Design put it on May 8, 1861, "the Great Rebellion has startled society from its propriety, and war and politics now occupy every

FORT FEDERAL HILL AT SUNSET—BALTIMORE (C. 1862)

Sanford Robinson Gifford (1823–1880)

A Union sentinel's rifle stands upright, parallel to the church spires of Baltimore, in this dramatic depiction of guard duty. As the painter explained, "inaction is very tiresome." Gifford remembered "standing guard and pacing the parapet during rain and burning sun, eating pea-soup and drinking what the commissary calls coffee, sleeping on a bare board and roused at sun rise by the bang of big gun and the restless rattle of ten drums." The artist clearly intended that this portrait, which was widely exhibited, remind civilians of the sacrifices even routine soldier life demanded. "To feel that while he is serving U.S. in this brilliant and splendid way," Gifford wrote, "there are a few good and loving hearts at home, who do not forget him…when they sip their claret, or drink their malt…is worth all the soldier suffers and more." An art critic remembered seeing the original model for this canvas—"cannon and tall sentinel in stark relief against a crimson horizon"—on the wall of Gifford's New York studio, where it served to remind "the artist's friends of the patriotism he repeatedly exhibited…in hastening to the scene of war."

Oil on canvas, 18 × 32 inches. (The Seventh Regiment Fund, Inc.;
photograph courtesy the Metropolitan Museum of Art)

mind. No one thinks of the *Arts*. Even among the Artists, patriotism has superseded painting, and many have laid by the palette and pencil to shoulder the musket." Inevitably, Gifford and other artists came to sense the possibilities for history painting that lay in this great conflict. Stationed in Washington from April 25 to May 2—inside the House Chamber in the Capitol Building, in fact—Gifford quickly gained appreciation of the vast artistic possibilities his enlistment presented, even if he could not yet envision seizing the opportunity himself. Lodged, as he put it, "in the midst of those panels in the Hall of Representatives, which…were designed for national paintings" but still lacked them (today the space is used for Statuary Hall), he wrote home half in jest: "Why could not the artists of the 'Seventh' have had a

[DEPARTURE OF THE
7TH REGIMENT FOR
THE CIVIL WAR]
(1861)

Thomas Nast (1840–1902)

*"Never before were the
people roused to such a pitch
of patriotic enthusiasm…
a universal, heartfelt, deep-
rooted, genuine enthusiasm,"
observed* The New York
Times *of the outpouring
of New Yorkers who massed
along Broadway to bid
farewell to the Seventh
Regiment as it headed downtown to begin its trip to
Washington on April 19,
1861. "The American colors
were present everywhere—on
house tops, on flagstaffs…on
ropes stretched across the
streets . . . . The tears of
kind-hearted women flowed
copiously as a rainstorm."
Nast made this hasty drawing,
previously unpublished, in his
sketchbook as the parade
passed Pine Street.*

Pencil on paper, 4½ × 2¾ inches. (The
John Hay Library, Brown University)

⌐ *Opposite* ⌐

**DEPARTURE OF THE
7TH REGIMENT FOR
THE CIVIL WAR
(1869)**

Thomas Nast (1840–1902)

*From his on-the-scene sketch,
Nast made this oil study on
paper, filling in and perhaps*

premonition of this—it would have been easy to have packed colors and brushes in their knapsacks, and forced some good art on the government at the point of a bayonet." Yet Gifford had already missed an artistic opportunity back home.[2]

On April 19, 1861, the same day the Sixth Massachusetts Infantry was attacked by a mob of Confederate sympathizers as it marched through the streets of Baltimore, Gifford's own Seventh Regiment of the New York National Guard had paraded through the streets of Manhattan to a vastly different public reception. As the unit headed down Broadway toward the docks to begin its trip south to join the belea-guered Massachusetts troops in the defense of Washington, thousands of flag-waving New Yorkers turned out along the route. Thronging sidewalks and crowding into the windows of adjacent buildings, they provided a rousing sendoff for the local sol-diers as they marched off to war. Among the observers was one prescient enough to record this inspiring scene, a twenty-year-old German-born illustrator named Thomas Nast, whose journalistic instincts led him to sketch the event as it unfolded.

A staff artist for the *New York Illustrated News,* Nast chose to portray the regiment as it passed in review before the hero of Fort Sumter (which had fallen only days before), Maj. Robert Anderson, who observed the march from the balcony pediment of a jewelry establishment and was "greeted with prolonged shouts of applause" by both soldiers and spectators. From the rough sketch Nast made that tumultuous April day, he created a small model in oils, and from this a large paint-ing, which for generations has been dis-played in the Seventh Regiment Armory in New York City. Nast's canvas suggested the broad sweep of the march he record-ed in his initial sketch, but his reporter's eye packed the finished scene with myriad vignettes of human interest: a policeman holding back an unruly Irish onlooker, individual soldiers' farewells to fathers, brothers, or sweethearts, and a newsboy hawking papers.[3]

Gifford, an artist with different abili-ties and interests, never managed to focus so closely on individual members of his regiment. His skills led him instead eventually to depict the rather tranquil and pastoral life it would lead in the weeks that followed, a period of national mobilization and training before the first great battle of the war, Bull Run, fought in July. In Gifford's works the individual soldiers tend to vanish into the rural landscape. In fact, war presented a serious problem to most landscape painters. Writing to *The Crayon* in May, the newly promoted Corporal Gifford conceded that "for the figure painter…there are innumerable scenes and episodes full of interest of all sorts" in the field. But he was not a figure painter. And "the fact is," he added, "for the landscape painter the camp and the surrounding country offer but little material."[4]

Further experience changed his mind. For, as another observer of the scene, the writer Theodore Winthrop, recalled in a memoir entitled *A Life in the Open Air*, the unit's picturesque formations and bivouacs seemed to cry out for a talented artist. "As soon as the Seventh halt anywhere, or move anywhere, or camp anywhere," Winthrop marveled, "they resolve themselves into a grand tableau. Their own ranks," he mused, "should supply their own Horace Vernet," a reference to the famous French military painter. Before long, Gifford would find the inspiration to emerge as the Vernet of the Seventh Regiment.[5]

The Seventh was mustered out on June 3, 1861, after seeing action no more perilous than the building of a fort, but by this time the latest edition of *The Crayon* was reporting: "Gifford has ready for reproduction, on a large scale, several studies of scenery and picturesque groupings connected with military events at Washington." Back in his stu-

inventing some details but removing a mounted figure present in the original. Additions include the gentleman in the foreground waving his hat and thus opening the panorama of the parade to the viewer. In the final canvas, Nast removed the gentleman's cane—perhaps an error in judgment, for it removed at the same time the man's excuse for not marching with the regiment himself.

Oil on paper over pencil (mounted on cardboard and wood), 22⅞ × 32⅞ inches. Signed, lower left: *Th: Nast.* (The New-York Historical Society)

A REGIMENT ENTRAINING FOR THE FRONT, DEPARTURE FOR THE SEAT OF WAR FROM JERSEY CITY (c. 1869)

Edward Lamson Henry (1841–1919)

Henry based this canvas on an eyewitness sketch that he titled "A New York Regiment Leaving for the Front to Re-enforce the Army of Gen. Grant ...." The painting was first exhibited at the National Academy of Design in 1869. Henry, who later specialized in railroad scenes, designed the departure depiction as a solemn, highly ordered tableau. The regiment, and even its animals, appear to line up calmly and picturesquely in a static yet somehow touching frieze. By choosing not to allow mounted officers to dominate this line of march, Henry emphasized the shared experience of the common soldier going to war, but he lavished attention on the cars and depot, leaving the soldiers a blur of blue coats and glinting rifles.

Oil on canvas, 10¼ × 15¾ inches (The Seventh Regiment Fund, Inc.)

GENERAL ABNER DOUBLEDAY WATCHING
HIS TROOPS CROSS THE POTOMAC (C. 1864)

David Gilmour Blythe (1815–1865)

Federal forces wade across the shallow Potomac River on June 7, 1863, in pursuit of Lee's army as it moves north en route to Pennsylvania. "Many were the mishaps of such a crossing," John D. Billings wrote in his 1887 memoir, Hardtack and Coffee. *"If the bottom was a treacherous one, and the current rapid, a line of cavalry-men was placed across the river just below the column to pick up such men as should lose their footing." The guard at left holds back civilian onlookers, as Doubleday, depicted as a tiny figure leaning on the cannon at right, surveys the scene. Blythe was not on hand for the 1863 crossing, but two years earlier he had followed the Thirteenth Regiment of Pennsylvania Volunteers, observing them fording the Potomac on July 4, 1861, while Doubleday's units fired their guns in an Independence Day salute; clearly he based his canvas on these events.*

Oil on canvas, 30½ × 40¼ inches. (National Baseball Hall of Fame & Museum, Inc., Cooperstown, N.Y.)

dio, he concentrated on turning these firsthand sketches into oils, Hudson River–style landscapes focusing more eloquently on the foliage and sunlight of the northern Virginia countryside than on his comrades-in-arms. As a fellow artist, John F. Weir, would admit in eulogizing the painter twenty years later, Gifford's art was "poetic and reminiscent…not realistic," showing "nature passed through the alembic of a finely-organized sensibility."[6]

Sunday Morning at Camp Cameron, Near Washington, in May, 1861, Gifford's pan-oramic view of a sabbath service in the field, invoked the spirituality associated with nature in landscape painting and suggested the holiness of the Union cause as well. The artist had observed a similar religious service in 1856 at Les Invalides, the great Paris hospital for war wounded, and had written home in awe to describe the "touching sight" as "veterans presented arms and saluted (the highest military expression of reverence)" at the elevation of the Host. For Gifford the American equivalent of the Invalides service took place, not against a backdrop of historic stone buildings, but rather in a sort of natural amphitheater. In truth, many soldiers disdained religious observance, and around the same time Gifford observed his worship service, a chaplain wrote home to complain that "it seems impossible to draw out the men at all numerously to a morning service." Robert Gould Shaw, later the commander of the famous Fifty-fourth Massachusetts "colored"

regiment, but then a member of New York's Seventh, witnessed just such a sermon, and wrote home to report that "though the men kept very quiet, we could hear very little, which was, perhaps, a disadvantage, and perhaps not." In Gifford's painting the clergyman seems to preach to the American vista beyond the trees as much as to the men of the regiment, many of them seated behind him. The painter secured a patriotic focus with the depiction of a centrally located pulpit draped with an American flag. Purchased for the Union League of New York in 1871 at a cost of $525, the canvas became known colloquially as *Preaching to the Troops.*[7]

Gifford's other canvases also reflected his training as a landscape painter. The works thus revealed little of the individual experiences of soldiers, presenting instead pastoral vistas and grand panoramas suffused with poetically exaggerated light and shadow. Gifford's *Bivouac of the Seventh Regiment at Arlington Heights* was a typical effort, vivifying a "sweet evening" in camp of the type mentioned by author Theodore Winthrop. "It seems always full moon at Camp Cameron," he wrote. "Every tent becomes a little illuminated pyramid. Cooking fires burn bright along the alleys." In the genteel recollections of a belles-lettrist like Winthrop, a full moon may always have shone on the regiment, but other soldiers surely recalled as vividly rainy days and uncomfortable nights

spent sleeping on the damp, hard ground. Such poetic language left little room for war's unpleasant side, and the "alembic" of landscape sensibilities proved similarly inadequate to capture the nature of modern war.[8]

A painting inspired after Gifford's regiment was mustered in for three months' additional service, this time in the Baltimore vicinity, beginning in late May 1862, was entitled *Fort Federal Hill at Sunset—Baltimore, Maryland.* The dramatically lit canvas, streaked with a bold if perhaps imaginary orange twilight, showed one solitary soldier on sentry duty, facing the harbor from Fort McHenry. Yet the soldier remained indistinct, a mere silhouette, and the emphasis lay on the effects of the sunset.

Displayed at the National Academy of Design in 1862, this canvas, not especially evocative of the Civil War to modern eyes, won considerable acclaim, with the *New York Tribune* calling it "impressive and poetical." So deep an impression did it make that one art critic covering the Baltimore Sanitary Fair art exhibition two years later was still citing it as a standard against which other war paintings might be measured:

> *Many of our readers will remember a picture by Mr. Gifford—a gentleman whose reputation stands very high with the general public—called "Baltimore." Mr. Gifford scarcely ever paints a picture in which the light is not exaggerated; there are certain effects which he is very fond of repeating, that are pure inventions on his part, at least as he represents them. But in this particular picture the blaze of light that filled the sky, and threw the bastion of the fort, the columbiad, and the preternaturally tall sentinel into startling relief, was supposed to be the light of sunset,*

SUNDAY MORNING AT CAMP CAMERON, NEAR WASHINGTON, MAY, 1861, OR PREACHING TO THE TROOPS (C. 1861)

Sanford Robinson Gifford
(1823–1880)

"Every Sunday morning," reported artist-correspondent Alfred Waud, "an open air service is held in the camps.... The groups of officers and soldiers, so lately grimed with dust and battle-sweat, and gaunt with fatigue and hunger, refreshed by rest, show few signs of their recent struggles. The sentries, leaning their heads upon their keen sabre-bayonets, join in the hymns—real Ironsides, these. The military band takes the place of the organ." An admirer of Thomas Cole who, like Cole, spent summers painting in the Catskill Mountains, artist Gifford brought a Hudson River School sensibility to this effort.

"How salutary and elevating must be such influences to the soldiers," wrote one observer in 1862, describing a similar religious service in *"a landscape in itself absolutely delicious."*

Oil on canvas, 16½ × 30 inches.
(The Union League Club
of New York)

Sanford Robinson Gifford
(1823–1880)

Soldier-artist Gifford recorded this nocturnal scene in the spring of 1861, as the famous regiment prepared for another uneventful evening on the Virginia Heights. The composition portrayed an encampment a war correspondent described as a "picturesque bivouac." To the journalist, the "fires flaming in the air … the stacks of arms with canteens, haversacks, and red blankets … the groups in gay soldiers' costumes … [made] a memorable picture." This canvas reflected an art critic's acknowledgment of Gifford's "true eye for atmospheric effects" and talent at capturing scenes at once "impressive and winsome." Left unmentioned were Gifford's nonpicturesque vignettes of blacks performing the camp's domestic chores in the foreground.

Oil on canvas, 18 × 30 inches. (The Seventh Regiment Fund, Inc.; photograph courtesy The Metropolitan Museum of Art)

and people accepted it, at Mr. Gifford's hands, with the most undoubting confidence. We never heard any jeers, or ridicule, or quizzing over that. We overheard no schoolgirls wondering what that awful yellow thing was meant for. Nor did we see pretty girls, by the dozen, pull their lovers and brothers up to that canvas and cruelly pelt it with, "Now, did you ever?" and "Well, I never!" til they were tired.

Still, the painting's effect seems more "poetical" than martial, and however heartening its critical reception, Gifford never fully appreciated his opportunities at the front. As late as 1862 he complained to friends, "[I] think often of my … studio—of green fields, and the grand mountains whence, but for these unhappy times, I would now be sitting on a camp stool under a peaceful umbrella." [9]

Gifford served yet another hitch with the infantry regiment in 1863, during which he produced a scene of their campsite near Frederick, Maryland, and then returned to New York to resume the life of a civilian artist. Two years after the war, the influential art critic Henry T. Tuckerman would lavish praise on him:

If we were to select one of our landscape-painters as an example of artistic intelligence—by which we mean the power of knowledge in the use of means, the choice of subjects, and the wise direction of executive skill—we should confidently designate Sanford R. Gifford. His best pictures can be not merely seen but contemplated with entire satisfaction; they indicate a capacity based upon genuine principles … they do not dazzle, they win; they appeal to our calm and thoughtful appreciation; they

minister to our most gentle and gracious sympathies, to our most tranquil and congenial observation. [10]

Yet even to capture the life of a regiment that saw no battles surely required appeals to something other than "calm … appreciation," "gentle and gracious sympathies," and "tranquil … observation." And it would require more than that to paint war.

The northern artists recovered quickly from the initial shock of the war. By late 1861 the National Academy of Design acknowledged that "in time of war or

rebellion, it could not be expected that the Fine Arts should receive much attention; and the knowledge of the many absent at the seat of war, either as soldiers, or in the Art Corps illustrative" would seem to confirm that. Yet "quite the reverse" occurred. Art schools filled up, and by late 1862 the Academy was "happy to chronicle that Art commands attention and high prices...notwithstanding the unfortunate and unsettled condition of the country."[11]

Such was not the case in the underpopulated South, but Gifford's depiction of the Baltimore sunset had its Confederate analogues nevertheless. One of the most adept of these Confederate painters came by his talent and his political views almost as a birthright. Conrad Wise Chapman was the son of the Virginia portrait and landscape artist John Gadsby Chapman. Born in Washington, young Chapman had been reared in Rome, where his father established himself in the 1840s. Nonetheless, a visitor remembered the Chapmans' expatriate lodgings as "a real old Virginia household," and Conrad himself insisted that he "always hailed from Virginia—which would have been

[THE BATTLE OF ANTIETAM: No. 1. LOOKING SOUTH] (c. 1892)

James Hope (1818–1892)

The Seventh Maine marches through the infamous cornfield at Antietam, stepping gingerly over Confederate dead in the Sunken Road as they advance toward the Piper farmhouse in the distance (center). The corpses somehow evoke little sympathy, in part the fault of unskilled foreshortening, uncertain perspective, and lack of proper scale. The city of Sharpsburg, Maryland, can be glimpsed at right center, and the mountains of Maryland and Virginia are visible in the distance, a detail the artist emphasized in a catalog description he wrote himself. The Union troops shown here would soon be bombarded by a deadly cross fire, and two-thirds would fall in less than half a minute in the harvest-tall corn; yet nothing in Hope's landscape provides any sense of that threat.

Oil on canvas, 5 feet 6 inches × 12 feet. (Antietam National Battlefield; from *The Civil War: The Bloodiest Day*;
photograph by Larry Sherer, © 1984 Time-Life Books, Inc.)

⪢ Opposite Top ⪡

[THE BATTLE OF ANTIETAM: No. 2. LOOKING WEST] (c. 1892)

James Hope (1818–1892)

Confederate Col. Stephen D. Lee's artillery fires at Gen. John Sedgwick's troops as they emerge in symmetrical formation from the east woods at right. Stonewall Jackson's artillery can be seen in the background massing around the Dunker Church, a white-washed house of worship belonging to the German Baptist Brethren. Here, some of Antietam's most vicious early fighting was centered. Across these fields, Hope recalled, "The battle raged, the contending forces driving each other back and forth across the ground…with terrific slaughter on both sides." But the insectlike dead shown here improbably close to the artillery detract from otherwise vivid details. Hope also lacked the skill to give the illusion of distance between the cannons and the advancing Union troops.

Oil on canvas, 5 feet 6 inches × 12 feet. (Antietam National Battlefield; from *The Civil War: The Bloodiest Day*;
photograph by Larry Sherer, © 1984 Time-Life Books, Inc.)

[BATTLE OF ANTIETAM: NO. 3. LOOKING NORTH] (1892)

James Hope (1818–1892)

The Mumma farmhouse, burned under orders from D. H. Hill, offers the most vivid sign of destruction in this oddly tranquil view of the action at Antietam looking north. Hope dotted the landscape with Union sharpshooters (left foreground), but was far less suggestive in his portrayal of "McClellan and his escort," as the artist described them, "riding the lines during the battle." The general's headquarters at the Pry House are depicted in the distant center, across Antietam Creek. One veteran who examined these paintings observed that "if I were to criticize, I should say there was not enough dead men on the hills."

Oil on canvas, 5 feet 6 inches × 12 feet. Signed lower left: *Copyright April 17, 1892/All rights reserved. James Hope;*
(Antietam National Battlefield; from *The Civil War: The Bloodiest Day;* photograph by Larry Sherer, © 1984 Time-Life Books, Inc.)

[CONFEDERATES OBSERVING A UNION ENCAMPMENT]
(C. 1862)

William D. Washington
(1833–1870)

Nearly swallowed up by the majestic landscape, cooking smoke billows skyward from a distant Union encampment as a small band of Confederate scouts pauses on the cliffs high above the Gauley River in Virginia. The principal lookout is draped dramatically in red to make him stand vividly apart from the lush green surroundings. This composition was likely designed for symbolic effect: the inherent strength of the Confederacy is suggested by the hulking rock formation at right, its promise embodied by the dense greenery at left.

Oil on canvas, 40 × 48 inches.
(The Museum of the Confederacy, Richmond, Virginia; photograph by Katherine Wetzel)

[CONFEDERATES ESCORTING A SUPPLY TRAIN]
(C. 1862)

William D. Washington
(1833–1870)

In a scene dominated by the rugged landscape of Virginia, soldiers escorting a wagon train take a rest.

Oil on canvas, 40 × 48 inches.
(The Museum of the Confederacy, Richmond, Virginia; photograph by Katherine Wetzel)

William D. Washington
(1833–1870)

Well hidden behind trees and boulders, Confederate sharpshooters, here rather clumsily rendered, open fire on Union troops marching invitingly along a riverbank far below. Writing in frustration to Gen. William Rosecrans in 1863, President Lincoln complained of such operatives: "In no other way does the enemy give us so much trouble, at so little expence [sic] to himself, as by the raids *of rapidly moving small bodies of troops."*

Oil on canvas, 19 × 16 inches.
(The Museum of the Confederacy, Richmond, Virginia; photograph by Katherine Wetzel)

the case had I been born in Italy." Thus it surprised neither friends nor family that when war broke out in 1861, fiercely pro-South "Coony" Chapman, as he was called, defied his father and at age nineteen sold some of his early paintings to pay for passage back home to fight for the South.[12]

Enlisting in the Third Kentucky Infantry later that year, Chapman served through 1863 in the West, seeing action at Shiloh, where he accidentally shot himself in the head, a wound that seems to have incapacitated him only temporarily, although it apparently left him mentally unbalanced for the rest of his life. He continued to draw, as well as to campaign. His fellow soldiers dubbed him "Old Rome" because of his peculiar accent—and marveled at the way he could seize a pencil and paper and pro-

duce lifelike sketches of their campsites and colleagues. In 1863 his father prevailed upon an old family friend, the ex-governor of Virginia and now Confederate general Henry A. Wise (for whom Conrad had been given his middle name), to get the boy transferred to a Virginia regiment. Like many fellow politicians, Wise sought military glory after Fort Sumter but proved a better governor than he did a general; by the time Chapman joined his command he had lost several battles and found himself reassigned to the coastal defenses of South Carolina. Here there were few opportunities for military glory, but apparently plenty of time to sketch.[13]

Assigned to Charleston, Chapman spent the seven months between September 1863 and March 1864 making drawings of the harbor and its extensive fortifications. He routinely defied danger from Federal bombardments to produce his sketches. "Often he sat under a heavy canonade," a fellow soldier noticed. "He minded it no more than if he had been listening to the post band." The drawings produced during this period became the models for a series of thirty-one oil paintings, all painted back home in Rome under his father's supervision. These works, a contemporary correctly predicted, would "forever preserve his name" as a Confederate artist.[14]

One of these Chapman paintings, showing a sentry on duty before a battery at the foot of Charleston's Laurens Street, started from the same subject as Gifford's view of the Union sentry in Baltimore. But the Southern painter employed no exaggerated light or silhouetting, and he dotted the small canvas with fascinating details, from an ironclad seen steaming in the distance to a stockpile of arms in the foreground testifying to the strength of the harbor fortification. Deception in war would inspire more than one artist, and Chapman's view of a so-called Quaker battery—logs painted black at one end to simulate real artillery and then placed within fortifications to fool Union scouts—was perhaps the first such scene. It emphasized the serenity of the battery, with sentries staring distantly out toward seemingly untroubled seas.

Longtime prominent display at the Museum of the Confederacy in Richmond has made Chapman's scenes famous. Less wellknown but impressive Charleston harbor views were painted by another artist, John Ross Key. Key also worked from sketches made on the scene and depicted the second siege of Fort Sumter—not the original 1861 attack that set off the war, but the Union's attempt to recapture the fort

from the Confederacy two years later. This attack left Sumter's seaward walls in ruins, a scene that both Chapman and Key would portray in realistic detail. But Key's major contribution was his portrayal of the event as bird's-eye view, with more emphasis on the topography than on the siege action.

Like Chapman, whom he surely knew, Key, a second lieutenant in the Confederate engineers, was assigned to Charleston Harbor in 1863. According to the Charleston *Courier*, some of the scenes sketched there by Key and others were scheduled for adaptation into popular prints, although only one has been located, a crude lithograph of an attack by Union monitors published by B. Duncan in Columbia, South Carolina, in 1863. In all likelihood, the collapse of the Southern picture publishing industry at around this time—owing to a dearth of en-gravers, lithographers, paper, and ink—doomed the project from further output. Still, Gen. P. G. T. Beauregard, who commanded the Charleston defenses, recognized Key as "a young artist of great promise" and named him to a committee charged with creating a "military history of the siege of Charleston."[15]

That project, too, probably fell victim to wartime shortages and hardships, but once peace was restored, Key headed north to Baltimore—a Union city with Southern sympathies and a more robust art market than the old Confederacy could muster. There he painted and first exhibited his Sumter panorama, along with an exterior view of the fort and an interior depiction of a shell bursting inside its walls. In a front-page article on December 1, 1865, the Baltimore *Gazette* called attention to the paintings' "extreme flatness of surface" and "prevailing coldness of color." A few weeks later, T. C. DeLeon's pro-Southern Baltimore magazine, *The Cosmopolite*,

≈ *Opposite* ≈

BATTERY, LAURENS STREET, CHARLESTON, FEBRUARY 7, 1864 (C. 1864)

Conrad Wise Chapman (1842–1910)

A lone sentry stands guard from a rampart atop the Laurens Street battery in Charleston, silhouetted picturesquely against the harbor as a Confederate ironclad heads toward Castle Pinckney at right. Chapman, who displayed a flair for vivid coloring and a talent for skillful design, depicted the cut doorway opening into the battery's munitions magazine (right) as a square inside a stone triangle within a semicircular mound, a compelling confluence of shapes suggesting man's intrusion into the natural beauty of these surroundings. The small shape in the distance (center) is Fort Sumter.

Oil on board, 11½ × 15½ inches. (The Museum of the Confederacy, Richmond, Virginia; photograph by Katherine Wetzel)

BATTERY SIMKINS, FEBRUARY 25, 1864 (1864)

Conrad Wise Chapman (1842–1910)

Shells explode over James Island in Charleston Harbor as Confederates manning Battery Simkins
exchange fire with Union artillery positioned on Morris Island, barely a mile across the harbor.
Chapman added genuine human drama to this landscape painting in the figure of the soldier at right
who shields his head as a Federal shell explodes in the air.

Oil on board, 9¾ × 13¾ inches. (The Museum of the Confederacy, Richmond, Virginia;
photograph by Katherine Wetzel)

THE ARMY OF THE POTOMAC (1865)

James Hope (1818–1892)

McClellan's army camps at Cumberland Landing along the Pamunkey River in Virginia on May 12, 1862, preparatory to the ill-fated Peninsular campaign. This is the model for Hope's "historical panorama." When it was placed on public exhibition, a catalog advised visitors: "If they would know what a great thing an army is, let them look at this painting." McClellan is visible leading the small group of staff officers on horseback (center foreground), which includes the Prince de Joinville, the Duc de Chartres, and the Comte de Paris, members of a French ruling family now out of power. The artist made the painting three years after the encampment, "from a sketch taken from him on the spot," as he wrote on the back of the canvas. Viewing the final work, the National Intelligencer *called it "one of the grand results of the terrible strife" and a "noble work of art," adding, "It is doubtful whether another military view of equal splendor has ever been witnessed in any country." The canvas was later valued at $25,000. While the towering masts on the ships at right are grossly out of scale, the clutch of curious journalists and onlookers at left, streaming out to see McClellan, provides a nice touch.*

Oil on canvas, 17¾ × 41¾ inches. Signed lower right: *J. Hope/1865*.
(M. and M. Karolik Collection, Museum of Fine Arts, Boston)

THE BOMBARDMENT OF FORT SUMTER (1865)

John Ross Key (1837–1920)

*A complex confluence of land, sea, and sky only barely suggests the event that inspired this painting: the Union bombardment of
Fort Sumter in October 1863, as seen from James Island. Fort Johnson is at the near left, and, just beyond it in the harbor, Confederate ironclads.
Smoke rises in the distance to the left of Sumter from Battery Beauregard and Fort Moultrie, while the smoke from the small strip of land at right
identifies Battery Wagner. Adm. John A. Dahlgren, who commanded the Union squadron during the bombardment, commissioned a smaller
copy of this painting for himself.*

Oil on canvas, 29 × 69 inches. (Greenville County Museum of Art, Greenville, S.C.)

conceded that the paintings were "a little raw, perhaps," but reported that "Mr. Key has carried his *Sumter* pictures to Washington where they have gained the highest praise from press and people."[16]

Washington's *National Intelligencer* admired in particular the "delicate and pleasing…view of the fort from James Island during the bombardment," predicting that the canvas would "command admiration in any picture gallery of modern paintings in the country." One telling adjective in the review, of course, was "modern." Key's landscape style apparently seemed novel and jarring, and several critics refused to warm to it.

His exhibition at New York City's Snedecor Gallery, for example, elicited widespread attention but at best mixed reviews. The *New York Herald* thought "the tone…rather hard and crude," but on March 6, 1866, the *Evening Post* reported that "the exhibition of Mr. Key's three historical pictures illustrating the bombardment of Fort Sumter…continues to attract a large number of spectators, especially among those who were at any time personal actors in the scenes represented."[17]

Eventually the tastemakers came around. By the following year, the art critic Henry T. Tuckerman would

RECONNOITERING IN WOODS AT BIG BETHEL, JUNE 3, 1861

William McIlvaine, Jr. (1813–1867)

Zouaves cautiously search the woods of southeastern Virginia a week before what one Union general remembered as "the disastrous fight at Big Bethel—battle we may scarcely term it." Though they felt their way toward the enemy gingerly, the raw Federal forces practically stumbled onto Confederate earthworks, and the reason seems clear in this rendering of the dense forest they encountered. McIlvaine, a Philadelphia-born landscapist known for his published Sketches of California and Mexico, *was a member of the Fifth New York Regiment of Volunteers.*

Watercolor on paper, 4¾ × 6¾ inches. (The Civil War Library and Museum, Philadelphia)

CAMP LINCOLN, JUNE 21, 1862

William McIlvaine, Jr. (1813–1867)

*"Professor" Thaddeus Lowe's reconaissance balloon floats above a Union encampment in Virginia
during McClellan's Peninsular campaign. As this watercolor suggests, camp life went on undisturbed
despite the arrival at the front of these modern marvels, the largest of which required five seamstresses
and 1,200 yards of silk to build, and cost $1,500. War correspondent George Alfred Townsend saw
the enormous balloon in flight around this time. "Noisily, fitfully," he recalled, "the yellow mass rose
into the sky, the basket rocking like a feather in a zephyr."*

Watercolor on paper, 9 × 13½ inches. (The Civil War Library and Museum, Philadelphia)

WESTOVER, JAMES RIVER (1864)

Edward Lamson Henry
(1841–1919)

The model for Henry's post-war painting, this wash drawing was made from the deck of his transport during Grant's James River campaign. "Old Westover" in Charles City County, one of the most famous plantation houses in the South, had by then been transformed, as Henry noted on his sketch, into "Division Hd Qtrs, Army of the James."

Pencil and wash on paper, 12¼ × 19⅛ inches. Signed, lower right: *E L Henry, Nov. 1864.* (New York State Museum)

acknowledge in an assessment of contemporary "landscape-painters" that Key had shown "much talent in his picture of Fort Sumter." In 1890, T. C. DeLeon, by then a longtime friend of Key's, would devote space in his memoirs to acknowledge that while "young, ambitious, and but little educated in art," Key had brought to his work "venturesome originality in color use," "boldness of subject," and "breadth and fidelity." DeLeon now judged retrospectively that Key's were "perhaps the most strikingly original pictures the war produced." And a full century later, an art historian declared *The Bombardment of Fort Sumter*, long misattributed to Albert Bierstadt, "the finest Confederate historical landscape and arguably the finest southern landscape of the nineteenth century."[18]

That may be, but as a depiction of war, Key's canvas exemplifies one of the two great failings of landscape painting: there are no human beings in it. Gifford's work exemplifies the other principal failing: landscape painting runs the risk of prettifying war. There was no more of warfare about Gifford's encampment scenes than could be found in antebellum pictures of militia picnics on languorous summer afternoons. And there was nothing much more reminiscent of war's intensity in Key's work than in a map. Indeed, in *The Bombardment of Fort Sumter*, war is reduced to topography. More than one phrase from the reviews of Key's painting serve to remind us of the inadequacies of the mid-nineteenth-century critical vocabulary as well as of landscape painting to render the war. Surely the canvases needed to be more than "delicate and pleasing," terms of praise used in the *Intelligencer*'s review. Ultimately Key's painting embodied the inherent constraints of the landscape perspective, which kept military action in the distant background to emphasize light and nature.

Another artist whose training led him to see the war only in broad vistas that underestimated the individual suffering and heroism of military life was Edward Lamson Henry. In mid-1864, the talented twenty-three-year-old Southern-born painter went off to war. Had he grown up in the city of his birth, Charleston, South Carolina, he might conceivably have emerged as a premier artist of the Confederacy. But Henry had been orphaned at an early age and sent to New York City, where he grew up with wealthy relatives. He served in the Union army under Gen. Ulysses S. Grant.[19] "A position was found" for the diminutive painter as a captain's commissary clerk aboard a transport charged with supplying Grant's army on the James River in 1864.[20]

Preparing to head south by railroad with the Seventh Regiment, Henry sketched the eerily tense scene at the Jersey City Depot, where soldiers patiently waited to board cars for

⊰ MINE EYES HAVE SEEN THE GLORY ⊱

Washington. The painting has often been incorrectly identified as a depiction of New York's Seventh leaving for its first period of service in the spring of 1861, three years earlier. But Henry had been in Paris at that time, studying art. The date he placed on his model sketch indicates that his work was rendered no earlier than 1864 and therefore it most likely dates instead to the regiment's March 1864 departure. The artist would later expand his rough sketch into a painting for the Seventh Regiment Armory.[21]

Like most artists, even the celebrated newspaper artist-correspondents, Henry saw the war only from a considerable distance. What he recorded he observed from the deck of the ship on which he served. Moreover, life on a supply ship in the quartermaster's service was hardly designed to inspire vibrant depiction of heroic struggle. His views were therefore panoramic, not intimate. In a crude homemade sketchbook, which he labeled "War Sketches Oct. & Nov. 1864," Henry recorded impressions of shipboard life, river scenery, and occasionally the daily routine of black people. Later he expanded these hasty sketches into wash drawings and used the drawings as models for paintings once the war had ended.

His sketch of the Union troop occupation of the famous Westover mansion on the James River, for example, was later expanded into a painting commissioned by a Philadelphia patron. The idea that Union forces had captured the famous Byrd estate surely appealed to Northerners eager to see the "First Families of Virginia" humbled; Virginia's old-time aristocrats represented in the Yankee mind the epitome of the hated Southern "chivalry."

Henry's best-known scene, a broad view of Union headquarters at City Point, may have had among its admir-

THE OLD WESTOVER MANSION (1869)

Edward Lamson Henry
(1841–1919)

Henry created this canvas on commission from a "Mr. Whitney" of Philadelphia. The painting suggested the vivid contrast between the antebellum elegance of the eighteenth-century Georgian-style mansion and the rude intrusions of modern warfare. Tents, armed soldiers, and a cannon can be seen cluttering the grounds. One of the mansion's dependencies, a library, has been destroyed, and its famous wrought-iron fence has been overturned. Although the soldiers remain secondary to the once-grand mansion and the threatening skies, Henry did add to the painting two signalers not present in the sketch standing on the platform erected on the roof. He wisely eliminated the James River shoreline visible in his initial sketches, and brought the mansion closer to the foreground for the painting. But his overarching interest in architectural details still dominates the composition.

Oil on wood panel, 11¼ × 14⅜ in. Signed, lower right: *E L Henry, 69.* (The Corcoran Gallery of Art, Washington, D.C.; gift of The American Art Association, 1900)

CITY POINT, VIRGINIA, HEADQUARTERS OF GENERAL GRANT (1865–72)

Edward Lamson Henry
(1841–1919)

If the artist's wife can be believed, when Grant first saw this work he reportedly "stood so long looking at it that, dinner being ready, he had to be literally pulled away from it." The general could pick out every detail, "even the seat he sat on before his own quarters." Henry kept a photograph of the painting in his personal album, in which he left a comprehensive list of

ers, according to the artist anyway, General Grant himself. And Henry went to great pains to ensure its accuracy. Although he did most of his work on the model sketches from shipboard, he did once venture to the shoreline to make some drawings from the surrounding riverbank, a move he soon regretted. During the excursion he was intercepted by a sentry who perceived something threatening in the sight of someone making sketches of the Federal supply hub. The guard shouted to the artist, in "no choice language":

"What are you doing? What do you mean taking drawings of this place? If I had my gun, there wouldn't be much left of you, I can tell you." Realizing only then his great danger, he said he never ran so fast in all his life, almost tumbling down the bank, and was

glad enough to get back on the boat completely out of breath, heart beating almost to suffocation, almost dead with fright....

Like other artists, Henry had to make his drawings from a safe distance. His "retreat" was emblematic of the difficulties all artists faced in their efforts to record war close-up in an era of rifled weaponry that was accurate at long range.[23]

Not until 1872 did Henry turn his City Point drawings into a painting, and possibly because Grant liked it, praising it "highly," the artist was invited to the White House, where he told his old commander, now the president, the story of the guard who had accosted him that day on the James. Grant supposedly replied, "Why Mr. Henry, why did you not send directly to me, telling me what you wanted to do? I would have given you permission to go any and every where, and you could have made all the drawings you wanted." According to the artist's wife, Henry had been inspired to adapt his drawings into the large oil painting when, sketching from the deck of his ship, he first "saw a short thick-set man dressed in uniform, standing on the shore, watching him. He saw on his shoulders a band with four stars and instantly knew that it was Grant. Then came to him the thought of the painting." Grant was not a four-star general at the time, however, and like most of these artistic reminiscences, this one exaggerated the painter's proximity to greatness, if there was any truth in it at all. Henry's widow even maintained that President Grant saluted Henry with a most uncharacteristic compliment. "We are the men who make history," Grant allegedly proclaimed, "but you are the men who perpetuate it."[24]

Although the painting's busily detailed depiction of the wharf perhaps invited precise identifications, in fact Henry's painting was essentially an autumn landscape. Maybe that explains Grant's alleged admiration of this painting, for the general was said never to have seen a battle painting he liked. "I never saw a war picture that was pleasant," he admitted. "I tried to enjoy some of those in Versailles, but they were disgusting." Grant quickly added that "there was nothing in our war to be ashamed of, and I believe in cherishing the memories of the war so far as they recall the sacrifices of our people for the Union."[25]

Though the shore depicted by Henry is busily full of activity, the overall scale in Henry's canvas is what naturally strikes viewers who, unlike Grant, had never been on the scene and might now be forced to squint to find a familiar detail. Another of Henry's important Civil War paintings was commissioned by New York's Union League in 1869. By then Henry was one of its members. Under its sponsorship five years earlier, the Twentieth U.S. Colored Infantry had been organized under national authority, somewhat in defiance of New York Governor Horatio Seymour's resistance to organizing black troops under state authority. On March 5, 1864—Henry might have been present at the scene, since he did not leave for the front for at least several more weeks—the new unit paraded proudly down Broadway on their way to active duty in New Orleans. Emotions ran high as the recruits passed

by some of the same streets, now lined with "white and colored ladies" waving handkerchiefs, where blacks had been ferociously attacked by mobs during the city's draft riots the previous summer. A correspondent for the *Christian Recorder* observed the "great day" and reported:

I think that some of the same rabble, who were in the pro-slavery melee of July 13, 1863, were made to shed tears of repentance on beholding the 20th regiment of Colored troops … as they marched through the streets of this great city in glorious array, onward to the defence of their

details such as (left to right): Transport disembarking troops/ horses / Mail dock / Adams Exp. Barge. Embalmed bodies being sent north. Andy Hepburn's barge. Head sutler. Captain's gig. / Grant's Hd Qts / Gen. Ingall's Hd. Qts /15-inch Mortar & 2 Hundred Pound parrots on platform cars. Mouth of Appomatx. / Schooners with stores, forage, & lumber swinging to the current Monitor in the distance, Bermuda Hundreds [the neck of land between the Appomattox and James rivers where Benjamin Butler landed 39,000 troops in May 1864 to start the James River campaign].

Oil on canvas, 29¾ × 61 inches. Signed, lower right: *E L Henry, 1865–1872.* (Addison Gallery of American Art, Phillips Academy, Andover, Massachusetts)

⁐ *L e f t* ⁐

The model for Henry's painting, this sketch was made from the pilot boat of a U.S. transport on the James River, where the artist was serving as a captain's clerk.

(New York State Museum)

PRESENTATION OF COLORS (1869)

Edward Lamson Henry (1841–1919)

On February 15, 1869, New York's Union League commissioned Henry to create a painting depicting the gala sendoff the league's ladies had afforded its first club-sponsored regiment of black troops in 1864. On that day, The New York Times *had marveled at the sight of "solid platoons" of fresh soldiers "everywhere saluted with waving handkerchiefs, with descending flowers, and with the acclimations [sic] and plaudits of countless beholders"—evidence, it contended, of the start of a "prodigious revolution." Henry initially produced this tiny sketch, noting on the reverse: "To be painted by Mr. Henry, 17 × 26 for the Union League Club for 500$. Presentation of colours by the Ladies of NY to the 1st [sic] NY Coloured Reg."*

Pen and ink on paper, 3⅜ × 4⅞ in. (New York State Museum)

PRESENTATION OF THE COLORS TO THE FIRST COLORED REGIMENT OF NEW YORK BY THE LADIES OF THE CITY IN FRONT OF THE OLD UNION LEAGUE CLUB, UNION SQUARE, NEW YORK CITY, IN 1864 (1869)

Edward Lamson Henry (1841–1919)

Citing their "liberality and intelligent patriotism," an impressive roster of political and society wives sponsored this flag-presentation ceremony for the Twentieth U. S. "Colored" Regiment on March 5, 1864. Among those lending their names to the event (see broadside) were Mrs. John Jacob Astor and Mrs. William Earl Dodge. As an expression of their "profound sense of the sacred object and the holy cause, in behalf of which you have enlisted," the women donated the regimental flag, declaring it "the symbol of woman's best wishes and prayers for our common country, and especially for your devotion thereto." Henry might have chosen a more intimate view of this emotional event, but chose instead to strive for grandeur by greatly increasing the painting's scope over that of the sketch and crowning the scene with American flags not visible in the drawing.

Oil on canvas, 17 × 26½ inches. Signed, lower right: *E L Henry 1869.*
(Union League Club of New York)

Courtesy of the New-York Historical Society, New York City

BATTLE OF LOOKOUT MOUNTAIN (c. 1863–64)

James Walker (1819–1889)

Looking all but impregnable, 1,100-foot-high Lookout Mountain in Tennessee looms in the distance on November 24, 1863, as Union general Joseph Hooker, astride his white horse (center), orders an artillery barrage against Confederate positions there. In "The Battle Above the Clouds" that followed, the mountain was engulfed by both the smoke of gunfire and "a heavy bank of fog" that "obscured its whole face"— hardly enticing conditions for a painter. He adapted an oil model into a thirteen-by-thirty-foot battle painting, purportedly on commission from General Hooker. Rather than give special prominence to Hooker, Walker rendered the entire scene as an unnaturally linear tableau dominated by geology, its features arranged like painted stage flats. The soldiers, some merely watching the battle, are arranged in lines as rigidly defined as the landscape backdrop.

Oil on canvas, 14 × 40 inches.
(U.S. Army Center of Military History;
from *The Civil War:
The Fight for Chattanooga.*
photograph by Larry Sherer,
© 1985 Time-Life Books, Inc.)

country, God, and the right, notwithstanding the outrages they suffered a few months past at the hands of the…copperheads.[26]

But before the thousand soldiers headed downtown, the assemblage of brass bands and "influential business men" massed at the Union League on Union Square, where the members' wives presented the soldiers with a regimental flag. It was this moment that the club now wished immortalized, and they offered Henry five hundred dollars to capture it. Unfortunately his impersonal urban vista might as easily have been painted from shipboard a mile away, and the regiment could as well have been a white one.[27]

Assessing Henry and his impact as a Civil War artist is difficult. His commercial and critical success waned with the coming of the twentieth century. "The New Moment intervened," an obituary tried to explain, "and garish impressionism eclipsed the pale-lighted and lavender-shaded canvases [of Henry]." In a memorial address read by the sculptor Herbert Adams at the 1920 annual meeting of the National Academy, Henry's art was praised as "historic," an adjective that spoke as eloquently of his fading reputa-

tion as it did to his colleague's loyal affection. In his depictions of the "politics and pioneering" of nineteenth-century America, Adams conceded in a similar vein, "Mr. Henry stands unrivalled."[28]

Henry's widow faithfully pasted some of the gentler obituary notices in her scrapbook, and among them are two that more perceptively measured Henry's contributions. One referred to him as "the Washington Irving of a painted 'Sketch-Book'" style, "the genial and gracious old-school picture chronicler." And the other, while admitting that his works had drifted "miles out of fashion," recognized Henry's indebtedness to "the style of [Jean Louis] Meissonier," the French military painter.[29]

In truth, some time elapsed after Appomattox before the United States developed from its Civil War any equivalents of the famous French military artists of the second half of the nineteenth century, painters like Meissonier, Alphonse de Neuville, and Edouard Detaille. Hampered by the scarcity of history painters in the North and by the paucity of any sort of painters or patronage in the impoverished wartime and postwar South, American art, though the

war did not seriously impede it, at first took inadequate notice of the great military conflict. Commenting at the end of the war, one observer said, "Scarcely a picture of the large historic type familiar to European galleries has issued from the studio of an American painter; and of the few battle pieces or pictures illustrating the dramatic episodes of the war which have been painted, nearly all were the work of foreign artists residing in the country." Concluded the critic, after visiting one typical 1865 exhibition, "We should gladly have seen more works inspired by the war, which is so profuse of romance, tragedy, and comedy."[30] Such

observations are confirmed by an examination of the lists of pictures displayed in the big art halls of the patriotic sanitary fairs, where Civil War titles constituted only a tiny fraction of the works displayed for the public.

Even those early works praised by Civil War generals themselves seem hardly satisfactory as war paintings today. Battle paintings were the specialty of artist James Walker, for example, and Gen. Joseph Hooker supposedly commissioned him to paint a panoramic depiction of the Battle of Lookout Mountain. But the work he produced presented an impossibly well-ordered mass of soldiers encircling the Union commander as he plans the action with Maj. John Reynolds; it does not even depict the battle.

An English-born, New York–bred artist of limited skill, Walker had a generation earlier found himself trapped in Mexico City during the Mexican War. When he was liberated, he joined American forces as an interpreter. These frightening experiences may have inspired him to attempt portraying the American victory on canvas. But his huge canvas, *Storming of Chapultepec* (c. 1857), although purchased for the U.S. Capitol, revealed all too clearly Walker's difficulty with the human form. While his depiction of the Mexican stronghold was (like that of

UNION ARMY NEAR LOOKOUT MOUNTAIN, TENNESSEE (N.D.)

James Walker (1819–1889)

A train lazily encircles Lookout Mountain in the model for Walker's famous battle canvas, painted on the scene while the memory—but not the evidence—of the hard fighting was still fresh. Later, he would adapt the wisp of smoke escaping from the locomotive into artillery smoke, and thin the clouds encircling the summit to suggest battle smoke. The landscape is again peaceful in the post-battle view: horses and cattle graze while Union soldiers relax atop their new stockade.

Oil on canvas, 20½ × 40¾ inches.
(Courtesy of the American National Bank and Trust Company, Chattanooga, Tennessee)

CANNONADING ON THE POTOMAC (C. 1861)

Alfred Wordsworth Thompson (1840–1896)

Federal troops under Col. Edward D. Baker return Confederate fire from across the Potomac as they attempt to cross the river from Ball's Bluff and Edward's Ferry on October 21, 1861. Thompson was on the scene as the Union thrust ended in disaster, with more than nine hundred casualties, including Baker himself. Painful realities notwithstanding, the painter made the soldiers seem secondary to the pastoral autumn landscape with its corn shocks and muted fall foliage. Thompson did include a vignette found later in many other canvases: a black man giving information to Union officers. The canvas was exhibited at the National Academy of Design in 1870, and was then offered for sale at the 1874 Louisville Industrial Exposition for six hundred dollars.

Oil on canvas, 33⅝ × 70⅛ inches. Signed lower left: *Wordsworth Thompson.* (White House Collection)

Lookout Mountain) realistic and imposing, his foreground portraits of men engaging in hand-to-hand combat was nothing short of ludicrous.

Walker went on to produce panoramic paintings of the Civil War, one of which, his famous picture of the Confederate high tide at Gettysburg, came close to achieving a sense of scale. His other works—several are shown on the pages of this book—suffer the same shortcomings as his Mexican War-era work. Walker is something of a mystery. Although he lived long enough to have joined other Civil War painters in the rush to adapt their works into popular prints to earn both money and public following, he appears to have done little to thus promote himself. Perhaps his modest abilities proved his undoing, since the critic Henry T. Tuckerman, in his influential assessment of current historical painters in 1867, damned him with faint praise for his "accuracy and spirit," while recalling him only as the "Mr. Walker, who made careful studies on the march." When those studies were expanded into large-scale canvases, the spirit remained, but the accuracy vanished.[31]

A now-forgotten, Scottish-born portraitist-turned-landscape painter named James Hope provided another case in point. To the New York *Independent*, Hope had "no rival in Europe in forest and brook scenery," while the Philadelphia *Evening Telegraph* dubbed him the "father of the realistic school of landscape painters in America." When war broke out, Hope joined the Second Vermont Volunteers, rose to the rank of captain (a title he used thereafter, even as a painter), and claimed to have participated in a dozen engagements in the eastern theater, beginning with Bull Run. By 1862, however, he was forty-three years old and serving as a mapmaker, and it was from this vantage point

that he began sketching the army as it camped and fought. At war's end, Hope returned to his New York City studio and began turning his drawings into what he immodestly labeled "huge historical panoramas to preserve for posterity."[32]

Hope's best-known effort from this period in his career depicted the sprawling Army of the Potomac, eighty thousand men strong, deployed together in a huge campsite along the Pamunkey River in Virginia during the ill-fated Peninsula campaign. Gen. Winfield Scott Hancock attested, in a letter to Hope a few years later, that this encampment marked the only time "so many men and so much material [*sic*] of war were congregated on such a small, and yet favorable, place for a perfect view of the whole from a single point of observation sufficiently near to give the details in a painting with such accuracy." From a small model oil, Hope fashioned a four-and-a-half-by-ten-foot canvas, placing it on exhibit in New York. Hancock, an early visitor, pronounced himself "much pleased with it," recalling: "I recollect meeting you when you were making the sketch, and am gratified that your labors have had such a good result."[33]

Another eyewitness to the encampment, wine merchant and literary dabbler Frederick S. Cozzens, wrote a testimonial recalling that "it was a subject of regret at the time that no artist was present to secure a sketch of so intensely interesting a spectacle. In this," he added, "we were all mistaken." Newspaper critics were equally impressed, the *National Intelligencer* praising "the poetic delicacy of sentiment and realistic complexity of detail with which Mr. Hope has rendered every object embraced in the magnificent *coup d'oeil*." And *Watson's Weekly Art Journal* judged "the sunlight, shadow, and atmospheric effects... admirably rendered," the per-

spective "well managed," and the overall result "one of power and ability" that could not "fail of holding a place in the future among the best pictures of the war." Perhaps so, but surely the art world's general inadequacy for dealing with the war can readily be detected in the precious and vaporish language of mid-nineteenth-century art criticism. Did great war paintings really require what the *National Intelligencer*'s critic called "poetic delicacy of sentiment"?[34]

The commanding general of the vast army depicted in Hope's canvas appeared in the scene merely as a tiny figure on the broad landscape. Nevertheless, Gen. George McClellan himself said he was impressed with the painting. Writing to "my dear Captain" on January 21, 1865, General McClellan said:

> *Before leaving the city I must express to you the pleasure experienced by me on beholding your magnificent painting of the Army of the Potomac in camp…. I thought the study I saw at your studio last winter was fine, but*

never dreamed you would produce a work that could so vividly call to mind that wonderful sight. For a moment upon entering the gallery I was spellbound, and could hardly realize that the place and event was [sic] *not actually before me. Every feature of that never to be forgotten scene has been faithfully portrayed, and will be valued in the future as one of the most perfect representations of Army life.*[35]

Perhaps McClellan preferred to remember the encampment, its sea of army tents representing eloquent testimony to his organizational genius, rather than the unsuccessful military campaign that followed.

Hope went on to enjoy considerable success. He painted a series of large panoramic battle-scapes of the action he had witnessed at Antietam, again relegating McClellan to only the barest notice in but one of the oversized panels. One critic lauded the efforts as "among the finest war paintings ever produced."[36]

Hope's paintings of the Army of the

Potomac in 1862 either reduced George McClellan to insignificance or, where Antietam was concerned, eliminated him altogether in favor of the landscape—an Eden now quite literally awash in blood. To George McClellan, the Battle of Antietam, his last and best-known as Union commander, was "a masterpiece of art." But the artists never produced a canvas of the engagement quite worthy of such an appraisal.[37]

The ultimate failure of Hope, Gifford, Henry, Chapman, Key, and other landscape painters, including William D. Washington, Alfred Wordsworth Thompson, and William McLeod, to render the Civil War with telling effect is perhaps best exemplified in the war experience of one of the most famous of these artists, Albert Bierstadt. The German-born Bierstadt was a practitioner of the "Dusseldorf School" of landscape art, which boasted its own gallery in New York City as early as 1849. Dusseldorf-style canvases featured precise drawing, careful composition, and "elaborate finish." Celebrated for producing "great pictures"—huge, panoramic landscapes whose exhibitions attracted large and appreciative crowds—Bierstadt applied to Gen. Winfield Scott in October 1862 for a pass for himself and fellow artist Emanuel Leutze to observe Federal troops "on both sides of the Potomac."[38]

The two painters caught up with the much-pictured Seventh New York soon thereafter, but the encampments they visited apparently did not inspire Bierstadt as he had hoped. (Leutze, perhaps America's premier history painter at the time, was inspired even less; no known artistic record of the visit flowed from his pallette.) Bierstadt produced but one well-known composition, a diminutive oil depicting a small group of Union sharpshooters firing on distant targets far below. He apparently drew his inspiration less from firsthand observation than from a static stereopticon view made the year before by his photographer brother, Edward.[39]

Naturally, the painting more skillfully illuminated its idyllic setting than its inherently disordered and decidedly nonpicturesque subject, guerrilla warfare. The composition suggested what a period critic had joked of another Bierstadt landscape: "The botanist and geologist can find work in his rocks and vegetation." One team of modern scholars has compellingly explained that for Bierstadt, the Civil War represented "blood spilled in Eden," a hideous violation of the precious scenery he clearly preferred portraying. Ultimately he would escape the war rather than capture it in art. Bierstadt appealed to Secretary of War Edwin M. Stanton for a second pass through the lines in 1863, now to head not south but west, accompanying a "regiment...across the country" ordered to protect "the mails and emigrants." The expedition inspired paintings of Rocky Mountain vistas, Indians, and buffalo, but no Civil War scenes.[40]

It is little wonder that painters tended first to deal with the war as landscape. Most were best equipped to render landscape on canvas in the first place, and military campaigning took them out into nature. The juxtaposition of nature's beauty with warfare struck even as tough a campaigner as William T. Sherman, who, in one official battle report, noted, "The scene was enchanting; too beautiful to be disturbed by the harsh clamor of war."[41] Yet landscape artists' attempts to render war's inevitable disturbance of the scene proved inadequate, like the details in Henry's painting of the Westover mansion. Somehow the painting remained more a view of a grand estate than an evocation of the Civil War. Neither heroism nor suffering could be effectively depicted from such distant perspective.

Nor is such a judgment a matter of hindsight, the sort of thing only visible now, seventy-five years after World War I. Critics in the Civil War era could see the problem too, as one observed in 1866:

The tragic or pathetic element, except as developed in the numerous clever designs for the illustrated newspapers, seems to be that with which the artistic mind of the country is unable or unwilling to grapple. In the most exciting periods of the war, when public attention was absorbed with grave events, American artists seemed most occupied in reproducing on the canvas the beautiful scenery of their country; and even the young members of the profession, just coming upon the stage, who might be supposed to be influenced more strongly than their older brethren by the ideas and feelings to which the epoch has given birth, were content to follow in the beaten path marked out by their predecessors.... The time is not yet ripe for the intellectual fruits... of art... of which the great rebellion has sown the seeds.[42]

≈ *Opposite* ≈

GUERRILLA WARFARE (PICKET DUTY IN VIRGINIA) (1862)

Albert Bierstadt (1830–1902)

Federal pickets open fire on guerrillas in the distance from behind a copse at the crest of a Virginia hill in the only well-known Civil War painting by America's great landscape artist. Some years later, Harper's New Monthly Magazine *recalled this effort as "one of the best compositions we have seen from his easel," adding: "This is an excellent piece of work, fresh, original ... and confirms us in the opinion that Mr. Bierstadt is naturally an artist of great ability and large resources."*

Oil on panel, 15½ × 18⅝ inches. Signed, lower left: *ABierstadt 62.* (The Century Association)

BATTLE OF CHICKAMAUGA (c. 1863)

James Walker (1819–1889)

"Turmoil and confusion," in the words of a Union private, engulf the ravaged landscape of Snodgrass Hill at the Battle of Chickamauga on September 20, 1863. In Walker's severely horizontal model for a larger work, Gen. George H. Thomas (on horseback, center, gesturing with his left hand) tries to rally his battered, fleeing troops against another Confederate onslaught. Thomas's resolve staved off defeat and earned him the sobriquet "Rock of Chickamauga." But Walker placed the Union hero in the distant background, focusing his attention instead on the ravaged vista, symbolically cluttered with tombstone-like trees defoliated by gunfire. Despite the unusual choice to show dead horses and human corpses in rigor mortis, Walker's painting lacks a focus for the human action and imposes an unlikely uniformity on the living animals and cavalrymen in the center.

Oil on canvas, 13½ × 40 inches. (U.S. Army Center of Military History; from *The Civil War: The Fight for Chattanooga*; photograph by Larry Sherer, © 1985 Time-Life Books, Inc.)

QUAKER BATTERY (C. 1864)

Conrad Wise Chapman (1842–1910)

A verdant palmetto tree—emblem of the besieged state of South Carolina—dominates this peaceful vista. The tree provides symbolic shade for the confident-looking soldiers relaxing in the trench at right, who no doubt feel a measure of added comfort from the realistic-looking "Quaker guns"— nothing more than large logs painted black at one end to resemble cannons—pointing menacingly into the harbor. Perhaps to suggest the remote possibility of attack, Chapman placed a soldier in a blood red cape at center.

Oil on board, 11½ × 15½ inches. (The Museum of the Confederacy, Richmond, Virginia; photograph by Katherine Wetzel)

Fort Sumter, Interior, Sunrise, December 9, 1863 (1864)

Conrad Wise Chapman (1842–1910)

*By the time Chapman recorded this scene, Fort Sumter had endured months of
Union bombardment, and was so "injured" that it was "hardly possible to do the walls any further
damage." The artist described this and a similar work depicting Sumter: "A scene at sunrise,
it was cool in the early morning, and the negroes before starting to work would warm themselves
at the fires; there was continual work to be done, getting ready sand-bags for breaks in
the fortifications."*

Oil on board, 9¾ × 13¾ inches. (The Museum of the Confederacy, Richmond, Virginia;
photograph by Katherine Wetzel)

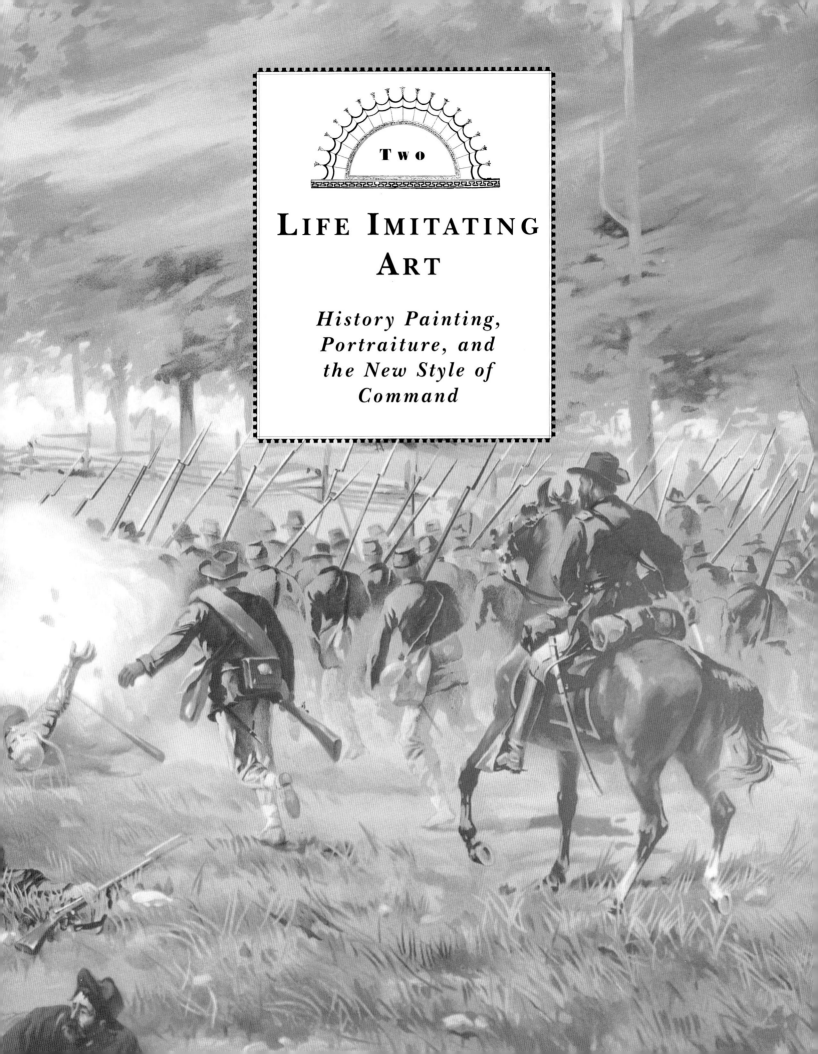

Two

LIFE IMITATING ART

History Painting, Portraiture, and the New Style of Command

**ANTIETAM
(BOSTON, 1887)**

Louis Prang & Co. after
Thure de Thulstrup

By the 1880s, when Prang launched his series of popular prints commemorating the Civil War, George B. McClellan's reputation was so battered that Thulstrup included no likeness of him in the picture of the general's greatest victory. Instead, the artist rendered the dense bank of smoke hiding the enemy with menacing accuracy.

Chromolithograph, 15 × 21½ inches.
Signed lower left: *Thulstrup.*
(The Lincoln Museum)

he Civil War offered American artists their first opportunity for significant historical paintings since John Trumbull had depicted the Battle of Bunker Hill and the signing of the Declaration of Independence seventy-five years earlier. "*Inter arma*

non silent artes," *Harper's Weekly* optimistically reported in late 1863, in its coverage of the cornerstone-laying for the new National Academy of Design in New York. "The fine arts are still eloquent amidst the roar of cannon." But "through the thick smoke of battle," the newspaper admitted, it had found only "the rich and well-proportioned" new building, not the history paintings to line its walls. Sanford Robinson Gifford had sensed artistic opportunities when he camped out amid the bare walls of the new nation's public buildings. But there were problems even for artists keen to paint something other than landscapes. At first, the only Declaration of Independence issued in this war was Confederate, and the South was short of artists who might paint its secession conventions (Enoch Wood Perry in

Louisiana proved the exception) or Jefferson Davis's inauguration in Montgomery, Alabama. The North enjoyed a greater supply of artists but at first lacked stirring moral statements, a political problem for the Lincoln administration, especially among ardent antislavery people. They would have to wait more than a year and a half before President Lincoln issued the Emancipation Proclamation.

Before that, there were many battles but few victories for the North, and even after victories began to occur more frequently and battles grew so large as to become noteworthy by world-historical standards, painters still faced nearly insuperable obstacles. Sheer access to the heroes and the fields where their exploits occurred was impossible, dangerous, or sharply limited as long as the war continued. Matters were further complicated by the visual problem of the new style of command.

General McClellan's camp, with its tents for eighty thousand men on the Virginia Peninsula in 1862, offered the artist a rare example of panoramic military concentration. But it was nothing out of the ordinary in terms of the size of the armies that would fight in the succeeding years of the Civil War. Historians have long struggled to find a term adequate to describe the eventual scale of the war. Allan Nevins called it "the organized war." Emphasizing aspects other than mere size, the British military historian John Keegan has observed: "In a war of amateur armies, transported by railroad, controlled by telegraph, paid by taxes voted by democratic assemblies of which the soldiers were themselves electors, the likelihood was that men who had known the workings of commerce, industry and politics at first hand would be better attuned to the ends and means of the conflict than those who had spent their lives within barrack walls."[1]

Whatever way one chooses to describe the war's scale and complexity, it seems clear that a new form of generalship was called for and eventually emerged from the conflict. The Civil War's great captains may have thought of themselves as Napoleons, but their real role, as Keegan has described it, lay in "unheroic leadership." The obvious example on which Keegan seized to make this point was Ulysses S. Grant, the short, taciturn Union general who loved cigars and spurned military finery in dress. By Grant's day, the time had come when the "commander's place was out of range of fire which, since the introduction of the rifle, swept the field in a density and to a

GEORGE B. MCCLELLAN (1862)

Christian Schussele (1824 or 1826–1879)

The artist intended that this portrait depict "the Young Napoleon" inspiring his troops at Antietam. To reinforce the heroic image, the painter showed the general's horse foaming at the mouth, suggesting fatigue, though McClellan's hair appears neatly combed and his uniform, save for his boots, unsoiled. In reality, as a Boston Journal *correspondent reported, McClellan remained in the rear during most of the battle, at his headquarters in a house behind his army's right wing. "The general was sitting in an arm-chair in front of the house" when the battle began, wrote the reporter, "horses… hitched to the trees and fences." The irony was that McClellan's earlier appearances before his troops, restricted by the nature of modern command mostly to reviews and parades, were known to elicit "one continuous cheer from one end of the line to the other."*

Oil on canvas, 48 × 40 inches. (New Jersey Historical Society)

sketches from wartime, were usually worked up in studios after the war. Most large canvases required months of laborious application of brush and oil. To be sure, some artists, like Winslow Homer, were able to show paintings by 1864 and 1865 based on sketches made in 1861 and 1862, but even Homer supplemented his life experiences by posing models dressed in freshly purchased uniforms on the sunny rooftop of his New York studio. Similarly, in the South, William Ludwell Sheppard epitomized the inherent romanticism of postwar retrospective art by dressing his models far better than the soldiers they were imitating had been equipped in the field. He too worked deliberately. For the most part, Americans during the war derived their vision of it from other, more quickly executed media.

It is little wonder, then, that the "clever designs for the illustrated newspapers" received special commendation at the time for grappling with the Civil War in a visually effective way.[3] The impact of such work has remained great. Newspaper illustrators, popular printmakers, and photographers all made unparalleled contributions to the permanent visual image of the Civil War, and they did so early, when curiosity was highest. Painters offered less, and they offered it later; as a result, the most interesting themes suggested by the war were often dealt with visually first by media that could more aptly be described as businesses rather than arts—complete with all the haste, intellectual indifference, and lack of craft suggested by that invidious comparison.

The evolution of the image of one early war hero, the Union general George B. McClellan, offers vivid examples of the problems the new style of command posed for popular war art and for the generals themselves. In June

range which would have made Wellington's habits of exposure suicidal."[2]

To describe the nature of Civil War generalship alone by its new style of command, with generals far to the rear of the battle lines organizing and dispatching, fails to reckon with the complicated emotions of the generals themselves. Their consciences did not necessarily reconcile them comfortably to this more remote modern organizational role. Moreover, the new style did not always satisfy the press, the public, or artists, most of whom held heroic expectations of their military leaders based on the conventions of past warfare and the representations of it in both words and pictures.

Painters were necessarily the last to respond to the stimulus. The landscape canvases that emerged from the struggle, even when based on eyewitness

1861, the thirty-four-year-old West Point graduate entered western Virginia to take command of a Union army for his first campaign of the Civil War. "Soldiers!" he proclaimed with characteristic bravado. "I have heard that there was danger here. I have come to place myself at your head and to share it with you. I fear now but one thing— that you will not find foemen worthy of your steel."[4] Dreams about leading dangerous bayonet charges, perhaps inspired by the heroic traditions of battle art, seem to have filled the youthful commander's head. He is said to have modeled his proclamations to his troops after Napoleon's.

Yet, like most other high-ranking officers in the American Civil War, McClellan soon adapted himself to a different style of leadership, one more appropriate to the sprawling battlefields, teeming armies, and industrial-revolution weaponry of the mid-nineteenth century than to the cramped canvases of the artist's studio. In fact, McClellan seemed destined to become the very model of a modern major general. Before the war, he had studied engineering, designed advanced military equipment (the widely used McClellan cavalry saddle), observed modern siege warfare in the Crimea, and then became an executive in the most modern economic organization of the era—the only truly "big business"— the railroad industry. When war came in 1861 he returned to military service, and to this day military historians recognize McClellan as a capable organizer of large modern armies of the sort that had spread before the painter James Hope on the Peninsula.

But McClellan may also have been the first such general in American history, and the new style of command not only made politicians anxious, it con-fused newspaper reporters, military pundits, photographers, and artists. It bothered McClellan, too, and from this confusion was born part of the tragedy of his career as a public figure both in American history and in American visual memory.

McClellan, the American people, and the photographers who quickly provided inspiring likenesses of the general, all thought they knew what was needed when war broke out: another Napoleon to lead the Union's armies to victory. The traditional Napoleonic attitude, hand thrust into tunic front, constituted the pose of preference when McClellan sat for photographs in his Union uniform, from the time he assumed command of the Division of the Potomac in Washington after the disastrous Bull Run defeat in July 1861 to the end of his unsuccessful presidential campaign in the autumn of 1864. At least a half-dozen times, and very likely more (for McClellan sat frequently, and previously unknown poses still turn up from time to time), the general put his hand inside his coat and stared confidently into the camera. He even struck the Napoleonic posture, without apparent embarrassment, in group portraits made with his staff members or with his beloved wife, Mary Ellen. McClellan did nothing thereby to discourage the widespread use in the press of his sobriquet, "the young Napoleon."[5]

The publishers of Civil War engravings and lithographs followed their own heroic traditions of battle art, mostly borrowed from European paintings familiar to many Americans in print copies. Such borrowing often resulted in a considerable distortion of events— and of the roles and character of the heroes of the day. Returning again to McClellan's 1862 campaign on the Virginia Peninsula, a protruding finger

~ Opposite ~

MAJ. GEN. GEO. B. MCCLELLAN ON THE BATTLE FIELD OF ANTIETAM (PHILADELPHIA, 1863)

A. B. Walter after Christian Schussele

This engraved adaptation of Schussele's canvas rigidified the portraiture but added several touches to invigorate the original. Mezzotint, with its ability to capture tonalities, showed to better advantage in the dismounted cannon barrel in the right foreground (replacing a fallen soldier in the painting). And the foliage behind the general had to be eliminated in the black-and-white print to avoid presenting a dark mass in the center from which it would be difficult to distinguish the general's figure in dark uniform. The general's foaming horse, shown standing still in the painting, here looks more as if it were being reined in after an exhausting ride. A soldier at right, inexplicably seen turning his back indifferently on the general in the canvas, here not only faces McClellan but doffs his cap in salute.

Steel engraving, 24 × 19 inches. Signed in plate, lower left: *C..Schussele./1863.* (The Lincoln Museum)

His Excellency Jefferson Davis, Painted at the Executive Mansion, Richmond, Virginia, August, 1863

John Roy Robertson (active 1857–1869)

Virtually nothing is known about the Baltimore artist who fashioned this portrait, except that his was the only known likeness of Davis painted from life during the Civil War. Secretary of the Navy Stephen Mallory, for one, found Davis not long thereafter to be more "reserved and drastic" than Robertson's portrait revealed. Mallory concluded that he had "a very haggard, careworn, and plain-drawn look." Not surprisingly, Davis apparently liked this flattering likeness. After the war he took it with him to England, and there presented it to a prominent Confederate sympathizer.

Oil on canvas, 26⅛ × 21¾ inches. Signed right: *Robertson/Richmond/Va/1863*, and on back: *...by John Robertson.*
(The Museum of the Confederacy, Richmond, Virginia; photograph by Katherine Wetzel)

Secession Ordinance, Louisiana Legislature, January 26, 1861 (1861)

Enoch Wood Perry, Jr. (1831–1915)

On January 26, 1861, the Louisiana state convention voted 114–17 to adopt an ordinance of secession. In this oil study for a proposed large painting commemorating the historic event, Perry successfully managed to crowd together an impressive array of political leaders in the majestic legislative chamber, but somehow failed to inject drama into what should have been a scene as momentous as the signing of the Declaration of Independence. Instead he merely grouped the decision-makers almost informally about the hall, clustering the more prominent men in small groups in the foreground, but with few of them appearing to pay attention as the clerk (left) tallies the fateful vote.

Oil on canvas, 14¾ × 30½ inches. Signed lower right: *E. W. Perry, Jr., 61.* (Louisiana State Museum)

≈ Opposite ≈

NAPOLEON À
WATERLOO

P. Jazet after Baron Charles
A. G. H. F. Steuben
(1788–1856)

*Baron Steuben's famous
painting was adapted by
several midcentury
engravers—including
Jazet—and it is clear that
New York lithographers
Currier & Ives borrowed
heavily from one such copy for
their print of McClellan at
Williamsburg.*

Engraving. (Anne S. K. Brown
Military Collection, John Hay Library,
Brown University)

of land east of Richmond delineated by the York River on the north and the James River on the south, one can see in its early depictions in popular media the problems modern leadership posed for heroic expectations.

After approaching by sea, McClellan's Army of the Potomac faced a Confederate army led by Joseph E. Johnston. Johnston's army had at first stood behind fortified works at Yorktown, and McClellan was proud of the siege he laid to those fortifications. He spent most of his time siting batteries and supervising the construction of earthworks and the digging of trenches. Then the Confederate army slipped away unnoticed, abandoning their position to the enemy. There was no need for McClellan to draw his sword for a final Union assault, or for the sorts of heroic attitudes that inspired nineteenth-century artists, though he was pictured that way in popular prints.

McClellan's pursuit of the retreating Confederates led to a bloody rearguard action known as the Battle of Williamsburg, fought on May 5, 1862. The circumstances prefigured those that, in 1864, would lead to Gen. Philip H. Sheridan's famous "ride" to military immortality. In McClellan's case, however, his race to the front on horseback proved disappointing. When the Army of the Potomac caught up with the units of Johnston's army that had headed west toward Richmond via Williamsburg, McClellan himself was still back at Yorktown, fourteen miles to the rear, coordinating the transport of part of his large army by water. Two members of his staff had instructions to report any significant action at Williamsburg, but McClellan until one o'clock "received no information from them leading me to suppose that there was anything occurring of more importance than a simple

affair of a rear-guard."[6] Finally a dispatch indicating that things were not going well reached him, and, after making "the necessary arrangements," the general and twenty-one staff members rode the fourteen miles to the front over roads jammed with soldiers and wagons.

When McClellan reached the battlefield at five o'clock, he "found things in a bad state." But, as he later boasted to his wife:

> *As soon as I came upon the field the men cheered like fiends & I saw at once that I could save the day. I immediately reinforced [Gen. Winfield Scott] Hancock, & arranged to support [Gen. Joseph] Hooker—advanced the whole line across the woods—filled up the gaps & got everything in hand for what might occur. The result was that the enemy saw that he was gone if he remained in his position & scampered during the night.*

He telegraphed Mary Ellen the next morning to announce that "we had gained a battle," and as May 6 wore on, "every hour its importance is proved to be greater." His army suffered 2,239 casualties against Johnston's 1,703.[7]

Northern printmakers at first shared the general's initial high estimate of the battle's significance. The New York firm of Currier & Ives, for example, quickly published a lithograph depicting a final charge against the Confederate lines led by General McClellan himself. In all fairness, it must be said that McClellan never maintained he led such a charge. The printmakers' sources of information on the battle are unknown, but they got some details right—the color of McClellan's horse, for instance: he rode black Daniel Webster that day. The crucial point, one inevitably ignored by

the printmakers who adhered to heroic traditions in battle art, was that McClellan had merely managed the battle once he arrived on the field; he did not fight it himself.

Years later, describing his actions at Williamsburg in some detail, McClellan conceded that the closest he came to the fighting was in the Union center:

> … *I ordered the centre to advance into the woods and gain the more distant edge, driving out any of the enemy who might be there. This was promptly done, and I rode in with them, and into the cleared ground in front, in close view of the enemy's works. There were none of the enemy in the woods, but they held the works in considerable force.*[8]

McClellan completed his reconnaissance, decided the enemy position was too strong to attack, and returned to his headquarters at the Whittaker House. Only in the world of lithographs and engravings did General McClellan look down the very muzzles of rebel rifles.

For all its faults, the lithographed print celebrating the Battle of Williamsburg remains an interesting document. Currier & Ives deposited a print in Washington for copyright as early as June 27, 1862, barely six weeks after the event. Considering that it took some time for news of the battle to reach New York's newspapers, supplying crucial details for the image, one must admire the speed of the New York publisher. But timeliness took its toll on originality. Currier & Ives adapted their design from an engraving of *Napoleon at Waterloo*, after a painting by Baron Charles A. G. H. F. Steuben. Several of the poses were stolen outright from the French print. Prints were a business and not an art, and such haste and dubious practices marred even this, one of the better

Currier & Ives wartime battle prints.

McClellan's enthusiasm about the results of the Battle of Williamsburg did not last long. Despite his Napoleonic image, he did not really fancy heroic and bloody bayonet charges. His wife's lukewarm comments on the siege of Yorktown, which had preceded the Williamsburg rearguard action, stung the young general's (and the young husband's) pride and caused him to appraise the Williamsburg battle coldly:

> *I do not think you overmuch rejoiced at the results I gained. I really thought that you would appreciate a great result gained by pure skill & at little cost more highly than you seem to. It would have been easy for me to have sacrificed 10,000 lives in taking Yorktown, & I presume the world would have thought it more*

brilliant…The battle of Williamsburg was more bloody— had I reached the field three hours earlier I could have gained far greater results & have saved a thousand lives….[9]

Thus, in the words of the victorious commander himself, began the slide in the reputation of the Battle of Williamsburg.

A quarter of a century later the *Official Records* of the Civil War continued the diminution of its reputation, terming Williamsburg a skirmish. McClellan himself described it in his memoirs as an opportunity lost because he had not been soon enough alerted to reach the field and organize a more decisive victory before dark. Retrospectively, printmakers came around to the new view, too. The Kurz & Allison chromolithograph of Williamsburg, issued in 1893 as part of their famous series of thirty-six Civil War battle prints, nowhere included a portrait likeness of McClellan. Instead, the visual honors were now given to General Hancock, who had led the famous charge at the end of the battle.

Nothing occurred in the summer of 1862 to enhance McClellan's reputation. He was ill during the Battle of Fair Oaks, fought on May 31–June 1, 1862, and was sickened in another sense by the suffering evident on the field afterward. McClellan did not like victory at high cost. And if it was inevitable, then he felt, guiltily, he should somehow share the cost or at least the risk of physical pain. After all, his Confederate counterpart, Joseph E. Johnston, had been twice wounded at Fair Oaks (and had to be replaced). McClellan now assured his army, as he had when first entering Virginia a year before, "Soldiers! I will be with you in this battle, and share its dangers with you." The Seven Days' battles, fought at the end of the month, failed to save McClellan's reputation or to alleviate his anxieties about the modern unheroic style of command. "I had no rest," the weary general told his wife afterward, "no peace, except when in front with my men. The duties of my position are such as often to make it necessary for me to remain in the rear—it is an awful thing."[10]

This "awful" dilemma—McClellan's internal struggle with the guilt induced in a brave man by the new organizational demands of generalship—had long since become a matter to be played out before the American public in a form exaggerated and perhaps distorted by partisan politics. As early as February 1, 1862, a New York newspaper printed a cartoon suggesting that McClellan was a man of inaction who preferred to observe the enemy from afar, through a telescope. Such criticism was as yet evenhanded. That is, the war on the Potomac itself was depicted as a phony war, one whose generals on both sides watched while their men engaged in mere snowball fights. The Republicans had not been so gentle with McClellan, a Democrat in politics. Members of Congress and the president had begun to grumble about his inaction as early as December 1861.[11]

The general's battered image suffered irreparable damage at the Battle of Malvern Hill, fought on July 1, 1862. That morning, McClellan sailed away from the field on the gunboat *Galena* to inspect possible fall-back positions at Harrison's Landing. Although he returned to the front in time to approve the placement of his troops before the Confederates attacked, the hostile press left the public with a different impression. Whether McClellan was once again guilty, as his unsympathetic modern biographer suggests, of not marching soon enough to the sound of the guns, remains open to debate. What is inarguable is that the sojourn on shipboard left him open to pictorial scorn. The image-makers never let their viewers forget, and their damning portrayals dogged McClellan for the remainder of his military career in the Civil War, during his unsuccessful campaign for the presidency in 1864, and even in his victorious gubernatorial campaign in New Jersey more than a decade after the war was over. Such open hostility even put McClellan on the defensive, clouding his own recollections of events at Malvern Hill. When Congress's Joint Committee on the Conduct of the War questioned him about it later, McClellan maintained that he could not remember whether he had boarded the ship on the day of the battle.

Opposite

THE BATTLE OF WILLIAMSBURG, VA., MAY 5TH, 1862... (NEW YORK, 1862)

Currier & Ives

A tribute, according to its celebratory caption, to George B. McClellan as "the invincible leader of the Army of the Potomac," this fanciful depiction of the Battle of Williamsburg owed its portrayal of the general in action on the field less to official reports than to the conventions of heroic battle painting. Note the two figures in the foreground nearest McClellan's horse; they are lifted from Steuben's Napoleon à Waterloo.

Lithograph, 9 × 13 inches.
(Library of Congress)

[GENERAL AMBROSE E. BURNSIDE] (1863)

Emanuel Gottlieb Leutze
(1816–1868)

As his troops storm the Antietam Creek bridge, General Burnside, his trademark sidewhiskers luxuriantly fluffed, looks on from a nearby knoll, battle maps at his feet. This painting embodies traditional elements of heroic military portraiture: the general's horse being held by a black aide, careful attention to uniform details like braid, and a reminder of the general's most famous successful battle (there is no reminder of his defeat at Fredericksburg). Visiting Leutze's studio during the war, Nathaniel Hawthorne was impressed that, rebellion notwithstanding, "the artist keeps right on, firm of heart and hand, drawing his outlines with an unwavering pencil, beautifying and idealizing… and thus manifesting that we have an indefensible claim to a more enduring national existence."

Oil on canvas, 11 feet × 7 feet 8 inches. Signed lower right: *E. Leutze. 1863.* (State of Rhode Island and Providence Plantations; from *The Civil War: Rebels Resurgent*, photograph by Henry Groskinsky, © 1985 Time-Life Books, Inc.)

Head Quarters at Harrison's Landing, a lithographed cartoon inspired by the testimony before the Committee on the Conduct of the War, attempted to jog the general's memory. It unfairly depicted him lolling on the deck, sipping champagne through a straw, with his saber drawn in ironic idleness. More than likely the print was issued in 1864, when McClellan was running for president, and it was not the only one of the sort in circulation at the time.

The beleaguered general was removed from command in eastern Virginia in the summer of 1862, only to regain it within weeks when Gen. John Pope lost the Second Battle of Bull Run and Robert E. Lee subsequently invaded Maryland. The ensuing Battle of Antietam, fought on September 17, 1862, carried momentous consequences for the Civil War and all of American history, for by halting Robert E. Lee's invasion of the North there, the victory allowed President Lincoln to announce the Emancipation Proclamation as a policy of strength rather than of desper-

ation. McClellan thought the battle held enormous new promise for his own image, too. "My military reputation is cleared," he exclaimed to Mary Ellen McClellan on September 20. "I have shown that I can fight battles & *win* them." He now felt confident that "one of these days history will… do me justice in deciding that it was not my fault that the campaign of the Peninsula was not successful."[12]

At Antietam, McClellan located his headquarters in a substantial brick house on medium-high ground. On the morning of the battle, his staff viewed the distant initiation of combat from the yard of the house through telescopes mounted on stakes in the ground. About midday, McClellan mounted Daniel Webster and rode with his staff to a knoll behind the Union left. There they were quartered in a hastily fortified wooden outpost and swept the field with a telescope mounted atop a wall of fence rails. Around two o'clock he headed for the front with a few staff officers to lead an assault. But when he arrived, he was dissuaded from attack. By the late-afternoon climax of the battle, McClellan was back at his headquarters, viewing the worsening situation through his "glass."

Understandably, popular lithographs and paintings of the battle typically showed Ambrose E. Burnside's famous assault across a picturesque stone bridge over Antietam Creek. But at least one print, the *Battle of Antietam*, shown at left, lithographed by Max Rosenthal in 1865 in McClellan's hometown, Philadelphia, more generously placed him close to the troops charging into battle with arms at the ready.

For this heroic image Rosenthal based McClellan's pose on that of the central figures in Baron Gros's fifty-year-old painting, *Napoleon on the Battlefield of*

Eylau (see page 52). The heroic tradition in battlefield art, not research or interviews, dictated McClellan's image, down to the curiously effeminate gesture of the right arm. The printmaker was doubtless unaware of the origins of the original Napoleonic painting and therefore misunderstood the meaning of its central pose. The painting stemmed from a competition sponsored by the French government to depict the emperor's recent but bloody triumph in what is now Poland. The administrators of the competition had encouraged the artists to portray Napoleon offering consolation to the victims of battle at its conclusion—hence the delicate gesture of the arm and the uncharacteristically beatific expression on the face of the ruthless French conqueror.

The irony of the situation was surely lost on printmaker Rosenthal, who, like Currier & Ives before him, was rushing to get his product to market. By depicting McClellan at the only moment he was really close to combat at Antietam, the lithographer unwittingly depicted a moment of indecision. In fact, some critics say that McClellan lost his last chance to make the battle a decisive Union victory by failing to press the assault when he rode forward.[13]

Antietam failed to salvage McClellan's military reputation, though the general himself felt it allowed him to "retire from the service…without any stain upon my reputation."[14] Removal as commander of the Army of the Potomac would likely have come even before November had this not been 1862 and the season for off-year congressional elections, when the party out of power historically could be expected to make political gains. The president waited until after election day to dismiss the Democrats' military hero.

For some, McClellan remained a

heroic figure. The Philadelphia painter Christian Schussele, for example, executed, possibly for the general's family, a large oil equestrian portrait of the general, called *McClellan at Antietam*. Completed in 1863 despite the onset of a career-destroying disease that caused the artist's hand to tremble, the painting depicted a campaigner, sunburned

trait was copied by the engraver John Sartain, who altered a few details to make his print copy seem a little more vigorous.[15]

The general's reputation declined further after he lost the presidential election to Lincoln in 1864. When, in the 1880s, a revival of interest in the Civil War led to the publication of not only scores of magazine articles and books, but also various series of popular prints depicting key battles, McClellan's stock rose little. His memoirs were published posthumously (in 1887), but pictorially, McClellan was seldom portrayed heroically in command at Antietam. Kurz & Allison's 1888 chromolithograph of the battle did not even include a portrait likeness of the general, and neither did Louis Prang's 1887 battle print.

But, early in the war, McClellan offered artists ample opportunities. He commanded in the East, in or near Washington, D.C., and therefore was often situated near photographers' studios. Furthermore, he was idled, though still in uniform, for two long years after his dismissal from command in November 1862 (up to the election of 1864), offering still more opportunities for photographers and, perhaps, painters. Active commanders usually remained too busy and too far away to pose in artists' studios, but occasionally other famous Civil War captains stationed near the political and cultural capitals paid visits home that gave the artists a chance.

McClellan was not the only modern major general to inspire artists while the war raged. On the Confederate side, the picturesque Robert E. Lee attracted the interest of whatever portrait painters remained at work in the South, because he was both spectacular looking and spectacularly successful. In the

except where his kepi protected his forehead, wearing dirt-caked boots, and mounted on a foaming horse. The general nevertheless seems too much in repose, perhaps a result of the artist's basing the facial likeness on a photograph. It is otherwise uninfluenced by photography and derived instead from the traditions of European military equestrian portrait painting. The general is framed squarely in the canvas and stands, almost uninvolved, apart from the background, which resembles a sketchy, theatrical backdrop more than the sort of continuum of space that Civil War cameras captured in their outdoor shots. McClellan holds in his right hand, along with his cap, a spyglass, unwittingly an emblem of the era's distant style of command. Like many of his other works, Schussele's McClellan por-

North, Ulysses S. Grant, no match for Lee or even McClellan in martial appearance, eventually far exceeded The Young Napoleon in portraits inspired. That was because Grant won victories. The plain-looking Grant also proved from the first more accessible to artists than the knightly Lee.

On April 23, 1863, Lee wrote home to his wife from camp near Fredericksburg, Virginia, to confess what was for him a rare emotion: apprehension. "I...feel oppressed by what I have to undergo for the first time in my life," he confided. A "Mr. Carole" had "made his appearance" in camp, and Lee was supposed to pose for a portrait by him. "I doubt whether he can accomplish anything," the general insisted. "My portrait I think can give pleasure to no one & should it resemble the original would not be worth having. Get the portraits of the young, the happy, the gay," he advised instead, exhibiting the Victorian modesty all but expected of well-known personages of the time and adding to it a rare touch of despair.[16]

Lee may have successfully deflected Carole's advances, for no sign of his proposed portrait has ever surfaced. But before the war had ended, he had consented to pose for a fellow Virginian named Edward Caledon Bruce, a remarkable man who had carved out a successful career as a portraitist even though he had become totally deaf from scarlet fever at the age of thirteen. More than thirty years after the end of the war, Bruce wrote of his experiences with Lee:

My best known picture is perhaps...Lee, painted in Richmond and begun at Petersburg from life, in...the winter of '64–'65. It was exhibited in the State Capitol in Feb'y. '65, where numbers of

Confederate officers and soldiers saw it, and I was told that their judgment was highly favorable.

Bruce's painting may have originated as a full-length portrait. The artist maintained that it represented "the General standing by a captured gun." But after considerable postwar display in both America and Canada, it was apparently rolled up incorrectly and so stored for more than twenty years. By the time Bruce saw it again, he found it in desperate need of restoration "except in the face and surrounding parts." The artist may well have chosen to save what remained intact of his original: a small detail of Lee's head and shoulders. Bruce's Lee portrait assured his artistic reputation, but the canny observer of Southern society T. C. DeLeon, while conceding that the work "produced much comment in Virginia," was probably right when he suggested that its success may have been attributable to "sympathy with the subject and the condition of the artist, rather than because of intrinsic merit as an art-work."[17]

Some months before "Mr. Carole" first petitioned Robert E. Lee for sittings, an artist named John Antrobus, a former Confederate soldier who now favored the Union, turned up at Ulysses S. Grant's headquarters in Chattanooga, where the commander was preoccupied with deteriorating conditions there. Ten thousand army mules had just "died or totally given out," Grant reported, and "there was not another trip left" in those who survived. "Soldiers were on short rations," Grant added, "and Artillery horses had become so reduced that it would take all belonging to a battery to move one piece." Yet, busy and distracted as he was, Grant found the time to pose for a life-size portrait. On November 17, 1862, the brave general

≈ Opposite ≈

ROBERT E. LEE (c. 1864–65)

Edward Caledon Bruce
(1825–1902)

This portrait of Lee wearing a colonel's uniform remains the only reminder of a lost full-length painting Bruce fashioned from life in Richmond. There, the deaf artist recalled, he "executed in...leisure moments...8 or 10 portraits," Lee's among them. "The details," the painter added, "are all from reality." The original was displayed in the Confederate Capitol in February 1865, but after Bruce appraised the canvas at "one thousand dollars in gold, or its value in Confederate money," Congress proved reluctant to purchase it. Widely exhibited after the war, it disappeared soon after a New York showing in the 1890s.

Oil on canvas, 20¾ × 15½ inches.
Signed right: *E. C. Bruce/pinxt.*
(National Portrait Gallery,
Smithsonian Institution)

[ULYSSES S. GRANT] (1864)

John Antrobus (1837–1907)

*"It is the man himself,"
declared the* Chicago
Tribune *in its review of this
life portrait in 1864, "a full
and complete embodiment of
all his mental and physical
qualities." The picture showed
a grim and anxious Grant,
Missionary Ridge looming
behind him, surveying the
battlefield of Chattanooga,
where Antrobus met and
sketched him. The captured
rebel fieldpiece at his feet is a
traditional device in military
portraiture, but Antrobus
added a modern tool of war,
binoculars, which Grant
grasps rather too daintily for a
soldier. Nonetheless the*
Tribune *declared the work
"no mere … portrait of a great
man," but "a great historical
painting." Viewing it at an
exhibition in Washington, the
journalist Noah Brooks
observed more soberly that the
coloring was "inclined to raw-
ness," but he conceded: "As we
have no great artists in historical painting, this new picture
will pass for a fair specimen."*

Oil on canvas, 8 feet × 5 feet 5 inches.
Signed left: *J. Antrobus/1864.* (Sally
Turner Gallery, Phoenix, Arizona)

cheerfully reported to his Chicago friend, J. Russell Jones: "Mr. Antrobus left here will [*sic*] pleased with his success. I hope you will be equally pleased."[18]

Jones was overjoyed with the result. By January he reported back to the general from Chicago: "The finishing touch has been put to the portrait and if anything in this country beats it, I have yet to see it. Antrobus' Studio is constantly thronged by people desiring to see it, but only the favored few get in." Days later the painting went on public exhibition in the city, with proceeds earmarked for the local soldiers' home, and favorable reviews filled the pages of the press. In Grant's hometown of Galena, Illinois, a journalist proudly reported that the Chicago newspapers had pronounced Antrobus's canvas "a perfect masterpiece, that must give its author a place in the front rank of American painters."[19]

Jones now promised Grant to take the canvas to Washington, this at a time when the general's friends were agitating for him to be promoted to lieutenant general, the rank of George Washington. A few weeks later Antrobus's canvas was shipped to the nation's capital, where it went on display in the Capitol. Lincoln paid his respects to Grant, whom he had not yet met, by going up to the Hill to examine the likeness firsthand. He was reported "highly gratified" by what he saw. The journalist Noah Brooks was also on hand for the Lincoln visit. He knew Lincoln and also knew a bit about art and proved to be a shrewd judge of the painting, taking note of such details as "the general's war horse, held by an orderly," the "dismounted rebel fieldpiece" in the foreground and, in "the distant background, blue and hazy…Missionary Ridge over which

lines of national troops are moving." Brooks felt it was "not a first-class work of art," but what is arresting in his comments followed: "The composition, or arrangement of the painting, is not original, [Gilbert] Stuart's Washington and one or two other semiequestrian portraits of generals being almost identical in design." On that score Brooks was correct. The portrait not only borrowed elements from Washington's image, but also employed the standard devices of military portraiture in western European art. Brooks noticed that "the flesh is too red and white, lacking the bronze vigor of a working warrior, as Grant is." The journalist remained tolerant of the flaws, concluding, "as we have no great artists in historical painting, this new picture will pass for a fair specimen." In quick order, the painting inspired a colorful popular print that kept the Washington-like Grant image before "the public" for the duration of the war.[20]

Willing as Grant may have been to cooperate in this image proliferation, and reluctant as his Confederate counterpart seemed in comparison, there was another factor at work during the war that served to inhibit production of portraits of Lee, or any other Southern hero for that matter. Save for the lame and infirm—like Bruce—most Confederate males, artists included, were mobilized into the military. As T. C. DeLeon put it, "war was the business of life to every man." DeLeon thought it remarkable that "in the short pauses of its active strife," and "amid battles, sieges, and sorrows," the South displayed "both the taste and talent for the prettiest pursuits of peace. And the apparently insurmountable difficulties, through which these were essayed," he maintained, "makes their even partial development more remarkable still." To DeLeon, "the

superior opportunities and larger and better-paying class of patrons." Some of "these errant youths" had come home "when the tug came," DeLeon said, "and some of them found time, even in the stirring days of war, to transfer to canvas some of its most suggestive scenes"—most in or around Richmond, "not only the great army center" but "the center of everything else." But all in all, T. C. DeLeon accurately reported, the overall development of art in the Confederacy remained "scarcely appreciable," adding bluntly, "Art culture—beyond mild atrocities in crayon or water-color…was a myth indeed."[22]

It may be significant that one of those Confederate leaders who somehow enjoyed considerable fame in early portraiture and battle painting engaged, unlike McClellan, in a form of warfare little affected by new developments in mass organization, rapid communication, and speedy transportation. John Singleton Mosby led a small group of cavalrymen organized as partisans. His exploits, though often conducted at night, could thus be rendered accurately by paintings that depicted him close to the enemy and in danger.

Even in the case of a leader like Mosby, there remained problems for the portraitist. The principal stumbling block was the generals' preoccupation with their duties. Sitting for portraits was best done *after* one had become a hero, not while one was actively directing forces in the field. Photographs, of course, offered possibilities, but still left the artist without guidance on color, comparative stature, actual battlefield dress or equipment, not to mention the appearance of the general's horse. The occasional visits made by Civil War commanders to see the highest-ranking officers or civilian government officials behind the lines afforded some oppor-

arts of the Southern Confederacy—looked at in the light of her valor and endurance, shining from her hundred battle-fields—emphasize strongly the inborn nature of her people."[21]

But DeLeon did not delude himself. "In all art matters," he readily admitted, "the South was at least a decade behind her northern sisterhood. Climate, picturesque surroundings and natural warmth of character had awakened artistic sense in many localities," he allowed. "But its development was hardly appreciable from lack of opportunity." Even before the war began, painters with "peculiar aptitude" had "settled in northern cities, where were found both

tunity for artists to arrange sittings that, combined perhaps with photographic models, would make portraits possible.

The legendary Confederate cavalryman Mosby made such a visit to Richmond early in 1865, and, apparently, artists there made every effort to arrange meetings with him. Even when a sitting could be scheduled and even in the case of a rather frequently photographed officer like Mosby, however, problems remained. With Mosby, in fact, a serious problem remained.

How does an artist limn a ghost? That was the question painters must have been asking themselves when they began to create portraits of the legendary "Gray Ghost" of the Confederacy. Operating at times within sight of the U.S. Capitol dome, Mosby and his partisan rangers burned supply wagons and derailed trains, stole military payrolls, captured herds of cattle and horses, seized supplies, and ambushed Union pickets. Whenever Union cavalry patrols caught up with them, the Confederate cavalrymen invariably turned and charged the startled bluecoats with pistols blazing. Though wounded more than once, Mosby was never caught.

Artists enjoyed no better luck accurately capturing his likeness, although he was for a time a popular subject. Photographs leave mixed testimony as to Mosby's appearance. A hatchet-faced hayseed in one, he looked like a neatly uniformed Virginia lawyer-turned-soldier in others. Such confusion about externals matches the internal complexity of the man.

Like many other capable Civil War officers, John Singleton Mosby wrote respectable prose and displayed considerable learning and culture. Writing his wife from the field in Virginia in 1861, when he was still a cavalryman serving a subordinate role in a larger unit, Mosby said, "I want you to send me some books...for reading this winter as we will have but little to do—send Plutarch—Macaulay's History and Essays—Encyclopedia of Anecdotes—Scott's novels—Shakespeare—Byron—Scott's poems—Hazlett's Life of Napoleon...." Though literate, he was also thoroughly cold-blooded, and wrote his wife this chilling letter describing an action in which, dismounted, he had steadied a carbine against a tree and shot a fleeing Union soldier through the head:

> After the fight was over I went & looked at the man I killed— the bullet had passed entirely through his head—Font Beattie [one of Mosby's men] got 26 & 1/4 dollars out of his pocket—also a nice gold pen & holder—(I write this letter with it) he had a letter in his pocket from his sweetheart —signed Clara.

A nineteenth-century man who could write such a letter to his wife (with such a pen) was no ordinary person.[23]

He was really two persons. Part of Mosby longed for respectability—in terms any conventional Virginia gentleman would have understood. Despite the occasional formulaic protestation to the contrary, for example, Mosby showed elaborate concern over his uniforms, instructing his wife about cut, cloth, and decoration. "I want you to send or go up to Lynchburg," he told his beloved Pauline early in 1861, before the war began, "& get me a neat uniform[.] Crenshaw's clothes are the best...all I want is something neat but nothing fine[.]get me a pair of shoulder straps & a blue cap I prefer...." Experience of battle did not alter his outlook on uniforms. Two years later he

≈ Opposite ≈

JOHN SINGLETON MOSBY (c. 1865)

Edward Caledon Bruce (active 1840–1877)

Observing the "Gray Ghost" of the Confederacy for the first time, a recruit admitted that "the shock was something considerable," explaining, "I beheld a small, plainly attired man ... slight but wiry.... The visions of splendor and magnificence that had filled my mind swept away. The absence of visible might, the lack of swagger, the quiet demeanor of the man, all contributed to my astonishment and chagrin. He did not even strut." But Bruce painted the "strutting" Mosby in a traditional portrait, the white brow of the hat-wearing field commander here transformed into the sensitive and intelligent forehead of an aristocrat.

Oil on canvas, 29½ × 24½ inches. (The Museum of the Confederacy, Richmond, Virginia; photograph by Katherine Wetzel)

THOMAS JONATHAN "STONEWALL" JACKSON (1862)

Benjamin Franklin Reinhardt
(1829–1886)

The prewar photographic model on which Reinhardt based this anachronistically clean-shaven portrait was as outdated as the source on which the painter had relied for his Lee. But Reinhardt did not know this from his wartime base in England. In adapting the photograph, Reinhardt sensibly altered the prewar Union uniform to Confederate gray, but failed to capture the general's eccentric and uncomprising personality.

Oil on canvas, 14½ × 11½ inches.
Signed lower left: *B. Reinhardt.*
(The R. W. Norton Art Gallery,
Shreveport, Louisiana)

[Scout Bringing Information to Colonel Mosby] (1868)

Jean-Adolphe Beaucé (1818–1875)

Mosby receives a dawn intelligence report from Lt. John S. Russell, an advance scout, before launching his August 13, 1864, raid on Berryville. This is the first in a series of three canvases depicting this encounter, all painted in 1868 by French artists commissioned by a Confederate veteran. In this opening scene, the scout tells Mosby that a Federal supply train has been spotted on the turnpike between Harpers Ferry and Winchester. Mosby is on horseback at right; the staff officers behind him are Captain S. F. Chapman, "Doctor Sowers, Sergt. Babcock and Sgt. Booker," according to a 1919 description by Chapman.

Oil on canvas, 17¾ × 16¾ inches. (The Museum of the Confederacy, Richmond, Virginia; photograph by Katherine Wetzel)

was giving Pauline instructions on the same subject in considerable detail: "You must put V[irgini]a buttons on the coat you have made for me—I also want a vest of [illegible] to button straight up to the chin—put some yellow braid on the collar." When he traveled to Richmond two years after that, Mosby was wearing even more elaborate uniforms and enjoying the attention shown him by the leadership of the struggling Confederacy. He met with Robert E. Lee, who always impressed Mosby, and was introduced to the Virginia legislature. "I have had every mark of respect & attention shown me in Richmond," the colonel told his wife, "I have spent my time more agreeably than on any previous visit."[24]

Mosby even sat for a portrait by an artist who had fashioned a full-length likeness of the great General Lee him-

self, Edward Caledon Bruce. Mosby gave Bruce at least two sittings and posed during the same Richmond visit for a "French artist," possibly L. M. D. Guillaume, who was, as Mosby told Pauline, "painting several of my men on the same canvass with me—Frank Carter & Ben Palmer among them."[25]

Colonel Mosby reveled in the notoriety and in the signs of respectability because the sort of warfare he waged remained at best marginally respectable. He insisted that he and his men were regularly mustered Confederate soldiers and that he reported to Gen. J. E. B. Stuart and Robert E. Lee, both of whom repeatedly praised Mosby's work. But the fact of the matter was that his men were partisan rangers, given special permission by the Confederate government to keep what personal property they took on the battlefield. The theory behind this seemingly barbarous practice was that rangers, working as independent commands away from the main armies and their lines of supply, could survive only by gaining their sustenance from the field itself. In practice, partisan units had a tendency to attract men more interested in loot than in military glory.

Mosby's men ambushed pickets, and that violated the widely accepted standards of international law. General Order No. 100, a code of law published in 1863 to govern U.S. forces in the Civil War, stated that "outposts, sentinels, or pickets are not to be fired upon, except to drive them in, or when a positive order, special or general, has been issued to that effect." With such views most Confederate leaders were in complete agreement. Secretary of War George Randolph rendered an official opinion in 1862 that read: "It is not admissible in civilized warfare to take life with no other object than the destruction of life. Hence it is inadmissible to shoot sentinels and pickets, because nothing is attained but the destruction of life."[26]

Mosby could not operate by such nice rules. He scrupulously avoided atrocity, but his men did much to gain their reputation among Yankee soldiers as horse thieves and bandits. Such views, though often expressed, were unofficial; Mosby's men were, when captured, conferred prisoner-of-war status along with other regularly enlisted Confederate soldiers who fell into Union hands.

Colonel Mosby was rarely tentative on the battlefield, but he suffered some confusion in his personal role as a Confederate officer of considerable fame—even legendary status. Perhaps nothing suited him better than war. "I like a soldier's life," he told Pauline in the summer of 1861, "far better than I ever dreamed I would—& were it not for the uneasiness & anxiety of mind

which I know it gives to those who are near & dear to me I would be perfectly happy." And yet it was not the camaraderie of camp life, so strangely appealing even to reluctant soldiers in more unpopular wars, that suited Mosby. He commented later in the summer on his "very particular friend in the Company…a young man from Symthe Co. named Beattie…with the exception of one or two or three men I am almost entirely isolated from the rest of the company—camp life has almost entirely destroyed my social feelings & I have never gotten acquainted with any one outside of my company." He apparently liked combat, the riskier the better. Before he took independent command as a ranger, he participated in conventional cavalry actions. "I was in both cavalry charges," he wrote home after a battle fought in the summer of 1862, adding: "they were magnificent."[27]

Mosby liked raids and dangerous scouting actions even better. He developed a distinctive style of ranger warfare, somewhat akin to guerrilla warfare in that the men boarded with local inhabitants between actions and did not thus form continuously organized armies in camp and field. Yet his unit was conventional in that its actions always involved military targets and could in no way be accurately described as acts of terrorism. But the targets tended to be, for want of a better term, inglorious: wagon trains guarded by second-rate soldiers, soldiers literally caught napping in their tents, and small units.

Mosby prided himself on using only revolvers and spurning sabers, boasting in later years that he was "the first cavalry commander who discarded the sabre as useless and consigned it to museums for the preservation of antiquities." Yet when he was photographed in a full-length standing pose, probably in early

≈ Opposite ≈

[MOSBY'S COMMAND ATTACKING A UNION CONVOY NEAR BERRYVILLE] (1868)

Henri Emmanuel Félix Philippoteaux (active 1840–1880)

As the colonel looks on from beneath the Stars and Bars in the background, his rangers launch their sudden attack near Berryville. The victim of one such assault remembered Mosby's men "swooping down like Indians, yelling like fiends." Mosby seized 208 prisoners and one hundred wagons, but not before the Federals made a last stand in the apple orchard and cornfield visible on the hill opposite the road. In this traditional battle painting, Philippoteaux gave Mosby heroic stature by placing him on high ground, in sunlight, dramatically silhouetted against smoke from the Virginians' howitzer.

Oil on canvas, 23¾ × 37½ inches. (The Museum of the Confederacy, Richmond, Virginia; photograph by Katherine Wetzel)

MOSBY RETURNING FROM A RAID WITH PRISONERS (1868)

Charles Edouard
Armand-Dumaresq
(1862–1895)

A rather wooden Colonel Mosby, astride his white charger (right), observes the return from the Berryville raid. The two Confederate officers at left are W. Ben Palmer and A. E. Richards. One Mosby veteran admitted that his colleagues were "as vain a lot of dandies as one would wish to see," but paintings like this one exaggerated their combat attire. Still, the artists of this series strove for accuracy; several subjects to be portrayed were sent rough outline sketches of the postures to be assumed on canvas, and asked to pose for photographs in precisely these positions for use as models.

Oil on canvas, 17⅞ × 26¾ inches. (The Museum of the Confederacy, Richmond, Virginia; photograph by Katherine Wetzel)

1865 for use as a model by one of the painters in Richmond, Mosby wore, along with two revolvers and binoculars, a cavalry saber prominently displayed. When he reported to Lee for conferences, he apparently wore a scarlet-lined cape, plumed hat, and fine uniform. One of his closest associates in the command observed, "I have always believed that he did it for the purpose of impressing the regulars with the importance of his Partisan Rangers." Mosby certainly succeeded in impressing Richmond society. Writing bitterly about what he regarded as Mosby's cowardly exploits, a Union soldier commented scornfully that the Gray Ghost was still "the gallant chevalier of Southern maidens." Perhaps it was more than coincidence that four painters with Gallic names, Guillaume, Beaucé, Philippoteaux, and Armand-Dumaresq, painted his likeness during or immediately after the war.[28]

By posing in such garb for artists and photographers, Mosby also impressed upon them the legitimacy of his style of warfare. Thus the painter Edward Caledon Bruce eventually produced a portrait likeness that resembled a rather long-faced aristocrat. The sunburned face contrasted in the painting with the white forehead (protected on campaign by Mosby's hat) in such a way as to emphasize the noble brow at the expense of the weathered cheeks and nose. What the portrait missed or avoided altogether in Mosby's character was his indifference to human suffering. L. M. D. Guillaume managed little better. His equestrian portrait of Colonel Mosby, with several of his closest lieutenants pictured in portrait likenesses in the background, suggests nothing of Mosby's unconventionality as a commander. The traditional pose of leadership, pointing toward the enemy, made

Mosby's portrait largely indistinguishable from Guillaume's other equestrian portraits of Confederate leaders. (The French artist was mainly a portrait painter; his horses seem barely acceptable as stiff props for images of heroic military leadership.) Both Bruce and Guillaume were played false by the circumstance that Mosby sat for them during one of the brief periods in the Civil War when he wore a beard. Most of the time he was clean-shaven.

Three more ambitious paintings stemmed from an 1867 commission by Confederate veteran Joseph L. McAleer. He sought "in Europe...three of the most eminent battle scene painters living" to produce models for chromolithographs. The prints were never produced and the canvases remain unfinished in spots, but McAleer found his artists: Frenchmen named Jean Adolphe Beaucé, Félix Emmanuel Philippoteaux, and Charles Edouard Armand-Dumaresq. All were experienced military painters who had executed works commissioned by the French government. They likely knew nothing of the Confederacy, but could work from photographs, published accounts of Mosby's exploits, and anecdotes supplied by McAleer. The three canvases focused on the Berryville Raid of August 13, 1864, when Mosby captured a large Union wagon train holding five days' rations for 2,250 men.

Ultimately, the paintings provided fuel for the fires of cavalier myth, adding little to

the dashing view of Mosby already established in story and picture, except in Armand-Dumaresq's depiction of the Rangers' return from the raid. The painter highlighted an element of light-heartedness present in Mosby's self-consciously colorful exploits, by depicting two Confederates playing captured violins on horseback while disgruntled Union prisoners file by.[29]

Any artist who wished to capture Mosby's likeness assumed a difficult task, complicated by the fact that the great cavalryman enjoyed legendary status in the very midst of his career. Herman Melville, a Northerner, composed a poem about him, of nearly epic length. "The Scout toward Aldie" (Aldie is a town in Loudoun County, Virginia, located in an area widely known as "Mosby's Confederacy") was the longest poem in Melville's *Battle-Pieces,* the book of poetry written, for the most part, soon after the fall of Richmond in 1865.

Although his fame was immediate and fascination with him crossed sectional lines to include Northern poets as well as Southern portraitists, Mosby faced pictorial oblivion in states of the old Confederacy after he became a Republican in the 1870s. He began to recover his hold on the imagination

**JEFFERSON DAVIS REVIEWING A LOUISIANA REGIMENT
AT RICHMOND, VA. (C. 1862–65)**

Louis Mathieu Didier Guillaume (1816–1892)

*An early Davis biographer maintained that to troops in the field during the
war, the president's "name and bearing were the symbols of victory." Guillaume not
only conveyed this impression successfully, but also visually countered the abiding
image of the president as a military man—some period prints clothed him in
Confederate army uniforms—by dressing him here in a black suit and stovepipe
hat of the type more closely associated with Davis's counterpart in Washington,
Abraham Lincoln.*

Oil on canvas, 36 × 29 inches. Signed lower left: *L. M. D. Guillaume.*
(R. W. Norton Art Gallery, Shreveport, Louisiana)

only in the twentieth century, when another French painter, Charles Hoffbauer, chose to depict Mosby in celebration of the Confederacy in "Battle Abbey," now a part of the Virginia Historical Society in Richmond. Hoffbauer's moonlit scene at last captured an element of Mosby's image heretofore missing, the part that could be seen only in the dark of night, when Mosby most often marched and initiated his raids. The dark side of this complex man, who had been forced to leave the University of Virginia before the war because he shot a local bully with a pistol and served time in jail, eluded all the painters, just as the man himself eluded the U.S. cavalrymen who pursued him. Military glory and the work of partisan rangers were not exactly compatible.

The French-born Virginia artist, Louis Mathieu Didier Guillaume, was apparently well situated to capture the likenesses of the other Confederate heroes like Mosby who occasionally visited Richmond. "Didier" to friends and patrons, Guillaume attracted a wide circle of admirers in prewar Charlottesville and Richmond, where he moved from New York in the 1850s. One patron described him glowingly as "an eleve of the ecole des Beaux Arts," adding: "I know of no one man in the U.S. as good." Part of Guillaume's appeal to Richmond's aristocrats was surely the artist's flamboyant Continental manner. Letters to prospective customers began, "Monsieur," not "Dear Sir," and his bills were sent not for the price of a portrait, but "*pour prix d'un portrait.*" When war broke out he adroitly shifted his focus from civilian to military subjects. He quickly won orders to paint portraits of newly commissioned Confederate officers for the wives, sweethearts, and mothers left behind. But he never ventured outside the Confederate capital to observe, much less sketch, the realities of combat itself, scenes that might have inspired a touch of realism in his lively but romanticized canvases.[30]

As the war dragged on, Guillaume, like others in the city, suffered economic hardships. He was compelled to sell artists' supplies as well as portraits.[31] But soon after the war, Guillaume recovered both artistically and commercially with a profitable and ambitious series of individual equestrian portraits of President Jefferson Davis and five leading Confederate generals: Lee, Jackson, Johnston, Beauregard, and Mosby. In 1866 he signed a lucrative contract for their engraved adaptation with Michael Knoedler, the American agent for the prestigious French printmaking firm of Goupil et cie. Knoedler advanced Guillaume two thousand dollars for the right to produce "in the best possible manner" mezzotints of the entire series (minus Johnston), guaranteeing a 20-percent royalty on each impression sold, after expenses. As a further sign of respect for the painter's work, the agent agreed to insure each three-and-a-half-by-three-foot painting for the considerable sum of three thousand dollars.[32]

As it happened, the original works of art nearly failed to survive the Reconstruction. Scheduled for display later in 1866, "these battle pictures were so perfect that…General [Alfred H.] Terry [then serving as assistant commissioner of the Freedmen's Bureau there] would not permit them to be exhibited in Richmond at a ladies' fair for the benefit of Confederate soldiers," as a newspaper account reported some twenty-five years afterward. "Professor Guillaume, fearing that they might be injured in some way, sent them to Washington City."[33]

STONEWALL JACKSON AT THE BATTLE OF WINCHESTER, VA.
(c. 1862–65)

Louis Mathieu Didier Guillaume (1816–1892)

Glimpsing Stonewall Jackson "in his musty suit" astride his unimpressive old horse, Little Sorrel, Lee's aide Armistead K. Long judged him "very poorly mounted…anything but a striking figure." But battle action seemed to transform him. Galloping with his troops, as Guillaume depicted him here before Winchester, Jackson suddenly looked to Long "truly heroic and appeared a man made by nature to lead armies to victory." Guillaume's portraiture marked a distinct improvement over Reinhardt's early effort, aided by the availability of newer, bearded photographic models.

Oil on canvas, 42 × 34¼ inches. Signed lower left: *L. M. D. Guillaume.*
(R. W. Norton Art Gallery, Shreveport, Louisiana)

GEN. ROBERT E. LEE AT THE BATTLE
OF CHANCELLORSVILLE, VA. (C. 1863–65)

Louis Mathieu Didier Guillaume (1816–1892)

A biographical sketch of Lee, published the year after his triumph at Chancellorsville, maintained that he "rides like a knight of the old crusading days," but in this rather awkward equestrian scene, Guillaume inexplicably made the general seem uncomfortable in the saddle, while portraying his reliably calm horse, Traveller, as a foaming white charger. "Mr. Guillaum [sic] worked carefully and industriously at his Richmond studio," an observer noted after the war, "producing portraits of Lee, Jackson and others; which, having exaggerated mannerisms of the French school, still promised no little merit."

Oil on canvas, 41¾ × 34 inches. Signed lower right: *L. M. D. Guillaume.*
(R. W. Norton Art Gallery, Shreveport, Louisiana)

Nor were all the paintings ultimately published as popular prints by Goupil, as the 1866 contract stipulated. In November 1867, two of the promised pieces, mezzotints of Lee and Jackson engraved by Dubois Tesslin, were registered at the Cabinet des Estampes of the Bibliothèque Nationale in Paris; that same year they were first offered in Knoedler catalogs for five dollars apiece. But there is no surviving registry for any other engraving from the proposed series, and no copies have surfaced here in the United States. [34]

Commercial setbacks notwithstanding, Guillaume's heroic paintings gained admirers in the old Confederacy. For example, a University of Virginia professor named Basil Gildersleeve fondly remembered in his memoirs "a battle scene painted by a friend of mine, a French artist, who had watched our life with an artist's eye." Gildersleeve would recall the picture in which "General Lee was the main figure" as superior even to Peter Rothermel's celebrated paintings of the Battle of Gettysburg:

> *One of the figures in the foreground was a dead Confederate boy, lying in the angle of a wooden fence. His uniform was worn and ragged, mud-stained as well as blood-stained; the cap which had fallen from his head was a tatter, and the torn shoes were ready to drop from his stiffening feet; but in a buttonhole of his tunic was stuck the inevitable tooth brush which continued even to the end of the war to be a distinguishing mark of gentle nurture,—the souvenir that the Confederates often received from fair sympathizers in border towns.* [35]

Gildersleeve had recognized in Guillaume's work one of its most distinguishing features: a canny eye for accessory detail. It mattered little that the professor had confused in his mind two separate subordinate characters in the Lee canvas—there is a dead soldier in the background, but the man with the toothbrush is a wounded soldier appearing in the foreground, dramatically saluting Lee with a wave of his hat as the general rides by. Gildersleeve and others of the day saw in all such figures—in the dead bodies littering the Jackson canvas, or the speeding cavalry racing by in the distance under Mosby—genuine and stirring incidents of war.

Yet it is difficult for the modern observer to overlook the awkwardness with which Guillaume placed each of his fabled subjects on horseback, or the poor depictions of the animals themselves. Jackson, who was the least impressive horseman of the group, was nevertheless painted more dramatically than the others, and his steed looked little like the general's own "Little Sorrel." Guillaume succeeded in evoking what Jackson's earliest biographer, John Esten Cooke, dismissively described as the "popular idea of a great general...an individual who prances by upon a mettled charger." The artist could hardly afford to show an adoring public that the martyred Jackson was a silly-looking rider who typically galloped along "with his knees drawn up by the short stirrups." It likely escaped notice, too, that Guillaume's Jackson also bore a resemblance to an equestrian lithograph of Jackson by another Frenchman, J. C. Giles, which had been published in Philadelphia in 1866—perhaps before Guillaume commenced his Knoedler commission. One cannot help but suspect that Guillaume consulted the published print before embarking on his own, only slightly different, mirror-image representation.[36]

COL. JOHN SINGLETON MOSBY (C. 1863–65)

Louis Mathieu Didier Guillaume (1816–1892)

John Singleton Mosby's exploits, as the Richmond journalist John Esten Cooke put it, "would furnish material for a volume which would resemble rather a romance than a true statement of actual occurrences." Cooke described Mosby as "muscular, supple and vigorous," a far cry from the unprepossessing figure new recruits seemed astonished to behold. One such volunteer admitted, on first glimpsing Mosby: "I could scarcely believe that the slight figure before me could be that of the man who had won such military fame by his daring." Mosby's men were known for charging with pistols, and his officers likewise affected surprisingly elaborate uniforms—details Guillaume rendered accurately here.

Oil on canvas, 42 × 34 inches. Signed lower right: *L. M. D. Guillaume.*
(R. W. Norton Art Gallery, Shreveport, Louisiana)

BRIG. GEN. P. G. T. BEAUREGARD AT CHARLESTON, S.C.
(c. 1863–65)

Louis Mathieu Didier Guillaume (1816–1892)

Beauregard was the Confederacy's first military hero, but nothing he did after the summer of 1861 could equal his celebrated triumphs at Fort Sumter and Bull Run, and he faded in the popular imagination. "Beauregard is not handsome," sniffed Mary Chesnut, although she added, "I have only seen his counterfeit presentment—photographs which are called, wittily, 'Justice without mercy.'" Showing more mercy than justice, artist Guillaume here gave Beauregard all the panache that inspired Louis Wigfall to summarize him as "a soldier and a gentleman." Barely visible in the distance is Fort Sumter, the scene of the general's early conquest.

Oil on canvas, 41¾ × 34 inches. Signed lower left: *L. M. D. Guillaume.*
(R. W. Norton Art Gallery, Shreveport, Louisiana)

Mosby, of course, was a legendary horseman, and to the degree that he could be made to appear naturally poised on a steed resembling a hobby-horse, his was perhaps the best of Guillaume's equestrians, at least reflecting in its dynamic portraiture the artist's opportunity for life-sittings with the guerrilla leader. There is less conviction in the awkward view of Jefferson Davis in black mufti and stovepipe hat, depicted reviewing a regiment near Richmond.

No one believed more completely in the heroic ideal than Jefferson Davis (political leaders still remembered the rulers of old, and longed to emulate them; even Lincoln directed one small military campaign at Norfolk, and Queen Victoria once vowed to lead her troops in the Crimea). Largely through his own well-publicized foray to the field on the day of the Battle of Bull Run in 1861, Davis had encouraged the notion that he was an active, militarily oriented leader. And he was indeed an inspiring horseman; the diarist Mary Boykin Chesnut, observing him once on his "beautiful grey horse," insisted: "Even his worst enemy will allow that he is a consummate rider, graceful and easy in the saddle." As late as 1863, Davis confided to his wife his conviction that "if I could take one wing and Lee the other, I think between us we could wrest a victory from these people," and in later years he told his daughter that, if he had his life to live over again, he "would be a cavalry officer and break squares." A number of period prints added luster to this image by depicting Davis in uniform. In fact, he had earned a military reputation on the field of battle long ago, during the Mexican War, and the Confederacy, like the North, firmly maintained civilian control of the military. Guillaume captured him not in the military glory he preferred, but, more appropriately, as a wholly civilian leader.[37]

As for Guillaume's Lee, this most elegant of all Confederate generals was made to look uncharacteristically rigid and ill-at-ease in his portrait. What was more, he was shown astride a foaming mount that bore little resemblance to his famous horse, Traveller, who Lee's aide A. L. Long insisted always remained "as calm as his master under fire." Recalled another eyewitness who observed Lee astride Traveller: "Every movement of the erect and graceful figure of the most stately cavalier in the Southern army revealed his elevated character."[38]

The paintings are all but unknown today, having remained in private hands until recently. The best known of Guillaume's works was his huge canvas of the surrender at Appomattox, which his friend Gildersleeve believed "bore evidence of minute study of every detail of that historic event." The piece has been long displayed at the Appomattox Court House National Historical Park and frequently reproduced in books and magazines, earning it a reputation as one of the best known, though surely not the best, of all the depictions of Robert E. Lee's surrender.[39]

When the finished painting was first offered for sale in 1875, the gallery advertising it advanced the story that Guillaume had been present at the surrender and had sketched the scene from life inside the McLean House parlor itself. No evidence has been found to corroborate this allegation; indeed, the painting, whose details contradict the recollections of participants in the historic surrender, itself suggests otherwise. But that did not inhibit early appreciation for the tableau. "No painting has ever been put down upon canvas that represents so much," the 1875

GEN. JOSEPH E. JOHNSTON AT THE BATTLE OF BULL RUN (C. 1862–65)

Louis Mathieu Didier Guillaume (1816–1892)

The aging, balding Johnston lacked the physical stature or pugnacious reputation to inspire equestrian portraiture, but Guillaume included him in his series anyway. The French print-publishing firm that contracted to adapt the pictures conspicuously omitted Johnston; perhaps that is why Guillaume left the figures at right unfinished. Long forgotten was the early image of Johnston as a "gamecock, the most courageous of all 'the fowls of the air,'" as one war correspondent described him.

Oil on canvas, 42 × 34 inches. Signed lower right: *L. M. D. Guillaume.*
(R. W. Norton Art Gallery, Shreveport, Louisiana)

THE GENESIS OF A HISTORY PAINTING

In February 1864, the New York portrait artist Francis Bicknell Carpenter "landed" in Washington, as he put it, to commence work on a painting depicting President Lincoln's first reading of his draft Emancipation Proclamation to his cabinet on July 22, 1862. Subsidized by a wealthy New York lawyer and armed with a letter of introduction from Illinois congressman Owen Lovejoy—obtained through "shrewd ... wire-pulling," according to a period report on his project—Carpenter introduced himself to Lincoln at a White House reception. An "electric thrill" ran through his "whole being," he would recall, as Lincoln enthusiastically agreed to cooperate. "We will turn you in loose [sic] here," he told the artist, "and give you a good chance to work out your idea." For the next six months, Carpenter was virtually "an occupant of the White House," he recollected. By day the artist sketched, commissioned photographs of Lincoln and his ministers, made model oil portraits, and drew detailed studies of accessories. By night he worked on his large canvas, set up in the state dining room, often working until dawn, "unable to break the spell which bound me to it."

catalog insisted, "and it ought to interest every American, and all lovers of liberty and good government." Added the promotional flyer: "General Grant says of the depiction of the room that it is perfect, and that the portraits are good. General Sheridan says of it, that it is magnificent." In short, "it is considered the most important Historical Painting in the United States."[40]

Superlatives notwithstanding, the canvas remained unsold for many years thereafter, perhaps because its price was too high. A Michigan newspaper reported nine years later, in 1884, that "the artist for a long time refused to take less than $20,000 for it." But the paper also echoed the view that "certainly the importance of the event entitles it to become an historic masterpiece." To buttress the burgeoning legend of the artist's presence at Appomattox, the newspaper reprinted this comment about the "perfect reproduction," written by the widow of Gen. George Armstrong Custer (he *was* present at the surrender): "I cannot but think that whoever painted the picture must have taken a sketch from the room the day of the capitulation."[41]

On close examination, Guillaume's work reveals a number of telltale factual errors that point decisively to the debt it owed other sources. The painter seated both General Grant and Lee at the same table for the surrender, when in fact they had sat separately throughout the brief meeting. Guillaume also outfitted Grant in a four-star uniform, indicating a rank the general did not display until after the war. At Appomattox, Grant had worn what he described himself as a "rough traveling suit, the uniform of a private with the stripes of a Lieutenant-General." It seems more than likely that L. M. D. Guillaume fashioned his Appomattox painting from

both photographic models and from the popular print copyrighted in 1867 by Wilmer McLean, owner of the surrender site.[42]

Despite obvious limitations in both vision and technique, L. M. D. Guillaume helped define the image of the Confederate hero as cavalier—sitting nobly on a foaming steed whether or not he had earned such a martial pedestal by reputation. In terms of pure skill, however, Guillaume was a portraitist first, who clearly had difficulty liberating himself from the studio in which he produced his "battlefield" art.

Perhaps the most famous of the history paintings begun while the war still raged depicted another scene off the battlefield. Upon reflection, that makes sense, for it was all but impossible to study the details necessary for an accomplished history painting of a battle until the war was over. Most successful captains remained too busy to pose or reminisce until peace was restored.

The war's great political events were another matter. The statesmen, though not accessible to everyone, at least were not behind enemy lines, nor did they usually operate within range of the enemy's weapons. Moreover, even when they were hard at work, the politicians generally sat still and labored indoors. A painter could get his sittings without much interfering with their duties and without exposing either his own person to enemy fire or his easel and brushes to the elements.

The New York portrait artist Francis Bicknell Carpenter apparently realized all this. More important, he realized that the Emancipation Proclamation was the greatest political event of the war, perhaps of the entire age. And he set out to make the history painting to commemorate it.

When Carpenter arrived at the White

House to begin his work, Lincoln jokingly challenged him: "Do you think, Mr. C———, that you can make a handsome picture of *me*?" The result, a small oil study that Carpenter later sold to the Union League Club of New York for $2,600, was subsequently engraved for a popular print the president's widow pronounced "the most perfect likeness of my beloved husband, that I have ever seen, the resemblance is so accurate, that it will require far more calmness, than I can now command, to have it continually placed before me."[43]

For six months in early 1864, Carpenter worked inside the White House—functioning almost as a latter-day court artist—to create a huge history painting celebrating Lincoln's first reading of his Emancipation Proclamation to his cabinet. Carpenter enjoyed access to the president's "shop" and the full cooperation of the cabinet secretaries. The painter kept meticulous written and sketch records of his progress. Much of this record remains unpublished, but he also wrote a best-selling memoir of his experiences, which sold for two dollars and went into several editions. The vast and illuminating Carpenter archive provides an unsurpassed record of the creation of a Civil War–era history painting.

The painting proved to be essentially an effort at group portraiture, and therefore photographs figured in important ways in the enterprise. Carpenter arranged to have a photograph of President Lincoln taken by Brady Gallery camera operator Anthony Berger inside the White House cabinet room on April 26, 1864. The result proved dim and grainy, because the chamber was not as well lighted as a studio. But Carpenter wanted the pose only to fix Lincoln's position in his canvas, not for facial details, for which he had commissioned

other photographs in Brady's studio some weeks earlier, in February (a sitting that produced the most famous Lincoln photographs made).

After interviews, Carpenter sketched the group and later himself sat for a photograph in precisely the pose in which he would paint Secretary of State William H. Seward. The lucky painter was working daily in the White House at the time, and could photograph as well as study firsthand the other details, from wallpaper and light fixtures to maps and books.

Carpenter, who, like Seward, came from New York, would feature the secretary of state more prominently than any other cabinet member in the painting, even though Seward eventually told the artist with brutal frankness that the incident he was depicting was not the "central and crowning act of the Administration" but one "wholly subordinate to other and much greater events," including "the firing on Sumter" when "the first measures were organized for the restoration of the national authority." Moreover, Seward had actually blocked issuance of the proclamation at the meeting Carpenter chose to paint. Carpenter had painted Salmon P. Chase before, as a U.S. senator, a portrait lithographed in Boston by Francis D'Avignon. Now he placed the ambitious secretary of the Treasury in a

FROM A
PHOTOGRAPH...

Carpenter had this picture of President Lincoln taken by Brady Gallery camera operator Anthony Berger inside the White House cabinet room on April 26, 1864. The artist had his subject pose at the head of the cabinet table, in much the same pose in which he would paint him. This is probably where Lincoln sat to sign the Emancipation Proclamation the previous January.

⋄Right and

Opposite⋄

And Sketches...

These pages from Carpenter's scrapbook shed light on his careful preparation and planning. As shown (near right), he preserved (top) a rough outline of the group he would later paint on canvas; pasted a photograph of himself (middle) assuming precisely the pose in which he would paint Secretary of State Seward; and inserted an early photograph that shows how the final canvas probably looked before it was altered by the artist. On the scrapbook page at right, Carpenter preserved his final sketch, which included a key to all his carefully recorded accessories.

(Here and previous page: Carpenter descendants; photograph by Nelson Bakerman)

position clearly subordinate to that of his cabinet rival, Seward. Several years later, when Carpenter was soliciting endorsements from those depicted in the painting, Chase wrote one of the most curt, conceding only: "I do not see that improvement is possible." Secretary of the Navy Gideon Welles not only posed for Carpenter but went with him to "Brady's rooms" to have a photograph taken for the artist's use. A month later, he confided in his diary, "The President and Cabinet have given him several life sittings, and the picture is well under weigh." Carpenter also painted studies of Postmaster General Montgomery Blair and Attorney General Edward Bates, but not of Secretary of the Interior Caleb B. Smith, who died a month before the painter arrived in Washington to begin the project.[44]

To unite the individual portraits and the correctly observed room details, Carpenter, of course, needed an artist's vision. To hear him describe it, in certain texts, is to imagine that he would have produced one of those allegorical paintings, full of imaginary but symbolic details, that have become repellent to modern sensibilities. To Carpenter, secession was "the 'beast,'" slavery was "the 'dragon,'" and the proclamation the "immaculate conception of Constitutional Liberty." The artist thus intended to portray Lincoln ascending to a "glory almost divine" by giving "freedom to a race."[45]

In the end Carpenter produced a work that by no means matched his overwrought language. It showed only a group of well-dressed men sitting around a long table, but to modern eyes, accustomed to the candid images of snapshot photography, the group seems stiffly posed and barely interactive, as though eight statues had been carefully arranged in a meeting room. The painting still falls short of what would pass for "realism" today, and yet Carpenter specifically termed his approach in the painting realistic.

What he meant was that he eschewed the symbolic school of painting and sculpture that was still influential in his younger days as an artist: neoclassicism. This provided a symbolic visual vocabulary that, though it stopped short of dragons and angels, nevertheless might well clothe a nineteenth-century politi-

cian in a Roman toga. At its most palatable, to popular taste, neoclassicism would pose statesmen with classical buildings or columns in the background, suggestive of the neoclassical models of Roman republicanism. By spurning these classical allusions, Carpenter could paint what to him constituted a "*true historical picture*," not like "most...merely the fancy pieces of their authors." Portraits, according to the British critic John Ruskin, whom he admired, were the only historical picture.[46]

The result nevertheless had plenty of artifice about it, the various administration figures being arranged, left to right, on a spectrum of intensity of anti-slavery sentiment. "There was a curious mingling of fact and allegory in my own mind," the painter said accurately, yet in his attempt to spurn "false glitter," his effort failed to suggest exaltation. In Carpenter's mind it depicted historic political consensus, with cabinet "radicals" (Stanton and Chase) positioned at left, conservatives (Smith, Seward, Welles, Blair, and Bates) at right, and Lincoln "between the two groups...the uniting point of both." But to the mod-

⚹ *Overleaf* ⚹

...TO PAINTED STUDIES

[STUDIES FOR "FIRST READING OF THE EMANCIPATION PROCLAMATION"] (1864)

Francis Bicknell Carpenter
(1830–1900)

To "give that prominence to the different individuals which belonged to them respectively in the Administration," Carpenter labored over both their portraits and placement in the final canvas. His goal for each likeness was to capture "the conflicting emotions of satisfaction, doubt, and distrust with which such an announcement would be received by men of varied characteristics." To The New York Times, *the artist succeeded admirably. "Every one of these likenesses," they proclaimed, "are striking pictures."*

(The Union League Club of New York; photographs by Don Perdue)

[ABRAHAM LINCOLN]

Carpenter determined to portray the president "bowed down with the weight of care and responsibility." Lincoln's eldest son, Robert, at one time judged it "the best likeness" he ever saw of his father, though in later life he preferred another, and Mrs. Lincoln was so impressed with it she sent the artist a gift of one of her husband's walking sticks. According to Samuel Sinclair, a New York publisher who helped arrange Carpenter's White House visit, Lincoln himself said of this painting, "I feel that there is more of me in this portrait than in any representation which has ever been made."

Oil on canvas, oval: height 33¾ inches × 27 inches. Signed, lower left: *From life by/F. B. Carpenter/1864.*

[WILLIAM H. SEWARD]

To Carpenter, Secretary of State Seward, rather than Lincoln, was "the great expounder of the principles of the Republican party" and would naturally enjoy "the attention of all" at the cabinet meeting he was painting. Seward, perhaps not surprisingly, lauded the final effort for its "portraits of rare fidelity to nature." According to the 1867 book issued to promote the best-selling engraving of the Emancipation Proclamation painting, Seward's face was drawn to express "steady sense and calm thought, as the Secretary advises to wait for military success before the issuing of the Proclamation."

Oil on canvas, 35 × 28 inches.

[SALMON P. CHASE]

Carpenter believed his portrait of the secretary of the treasury depicted him "actively supporting the new policy," but Chase complained that the Emancipation Proclamation canvas made even Lincoln "subsidiary to Seward while every one else either listens or stares into vacancy."

Oil on canvas. 35 × 28 inches.

[EDWIN M. STANTON]

During the war, the Boston
Commonwealth *observed of the stern sec-*
retary of war: "His features are rather
round and full, his hair very dark, though
thin, and his appearance sallow. Those
peculiarities, combined with his intense
and penetrating dark brown eyes, and his
heavy beard sprinkled freely with gray, give
somewhat of an Oriental air to his general
appearance." Perhaps pleased with the
way Carpenter portrayed him, Stanton
thought the final Emancipation
Proclamation painting "worthy of nation-
al attention, as a fitting commemoration
of Mr. Lincoln's great deed."

Oil on canvas, 35½ × 28 inches.

[MONTGOMERY BLAIR]

Lincoln remembered that when
he first read his proclamation to his
cabinet, the postmaster general "deprecated
the policy, on the ground that it
would cost the Administration the fall elec-
tions." Chase wrote tartly in his
diary that Blair also expressed
"apprehensions" about the proclamation's
potential impact on the border states
and the army, and went so far as to
insist that his brief "against the policy"
be filed with the proclamation. Such
an appraisal exaggerated Blair's
opposition, but Carpenter determined
to make Blair "less conspicuous" than
his fellow ministers in the final
canvas, relegated to "the background
of the picture."

Oil on canvas, 35 × 28 inches.

[GIDEON WELLES]

According to one period description
of the bizarre-looking secretary of the
navy, "the grave, reflective features, long
beard, and wig of Secretary Welles" were
"familiar to most persons, so extensively
has his portrait been placed before the
public, either in earnest or in jest." By the
time Carpenter encountered him, the press
had aptly nicknamed him "Father
Neptune." Carpenter painted a seventh
sketch (not shown here) of Attorney
General Edward Bates.

Oil on canvas, 35½ × 28 inches.

...TO FINAL PAINTING

FIRST READING OF THE
EMANCIPATION
PROCLAMATION OF
PRESIDENT LINCOLN
(1864)

Francis Bicknell Carpenter
(1830–1900)

*As Lincoln and his cabinet
ministers look on, Secretary of
State Seward (center, hand on
table) suggests that the*

ern observer the painting appears to lack inspiration, and even in its day the critic Henry T. Tuckerman noted that the canvas lacked "vitality."[47]

Its limitations notwithstanding, Carpenter's painting proved an enormous success; it clearly touched a popular nerve. Exhibited throughout the North, it earned Carpenter a hefty royalty of fifty dollars per week. He received another two-thousand-dollar advance for granting New York publishers Derby & Miller rights to issue an engraving. But Carpenter remained dissatisfied with his canvas, and he pro-

ceeded to work with its engraver, Alexander Hay Ritchie, on repeated alterations. By the time the heavily retouched painting was purchased for the government in 1878, it looked rather different from Ritchie's engraving of the original, which had become a best-seller at ten dollars per copy. The portrait of Lincoln in particular, cited for its "strange blending of firmness and anxiety" when first painted, had now been overlayered into an expressionless mask. Earlier, the *New York Tribune* had proclaimed the canvas "next to Trumbull's Picture of the 'Dec-

laration of Independence'... the best work of this class that has been painted in America."[48]

The Civil War actually never produced a single image as enduring as Trumbull's of the Revolution, though such success might have been predicted for the other great history painting dealing with a political subject inspired by the war. This work came from the easel of one of the country's best painters, a man who had long since created evocative genre scenes from the Mississippi River valley and the best depictions of electoral politics ever to come from an American artist's studio. If passionate feeling could make a great painting, then George Caleb Bingham's *Order Number 11* would rank with the best. But Bingham ultimately failed when he dealt with war.

An active elected official as well as a painter, Bingham, despite his vigorous pro-Union sentiments, came to resent bitterly the controversial actions of Federal forces in Missouri. When Gen. Thomas Ewing issued General Order No. 11 in August 1863 as a response to guerrilla activity on the Missouri border, Union troops forced the evacuation of four counties, creating as many as twenty thousand refugees. Bingham was outraged and swore to portray the

"*brutality* and *ferocity* toward the defenseless." But he did not begin working on a painting to mark the infamous order until after the war was over, and he did not finish until 1869. A contemporary handbill advertised a viewing of the painting with the overwrought and yet somehow inert language of political outrage of the period:

> *The principal group in the foreground of the picture, chiefly consists of a venerable patriarch and his family, who have just been ejected from their dwelling, which is about to be committed to the flames. A daughter clings to the defiant form of the old man, imploring him to temper his language so as not to incur the vengeance of the brutal assassin, who, in the act of drawing a pistol, threatens him in front. Another daughter is on her knees before this wretch, vainly endeavoring to awaken some emotion of humanity in his callous breast. A married son lies weltering in his blood, his young wife bending in agony over his lifeless body. His murderer is seen in the scowling ruffian near by with a discharged pistol in his hand. The aged mother has fallen in a swoon, and is supported in the arms of a faithful negro woman. A negro man retires weeping from the scene, accompanied by a negro lad, whose face bears the unmistakable marks of fright and horror.*
> *Immediately in the rear of the outraged family the mirmidons of Kansas, aided by their criminal allies in Federal uniform, are busily engaged in the work of pillage.*

The painting looks as the handbill described it, and its melodramatic yet

Proclamation be postponed until it can be backed up by military success. Eschewing "imaginary curtain or column, gorgeous furniture or allegorical statue," Carpenter conceived the re-creation as a "realistic" scene that would express "the spirit...of its own age." He believed the cabinet room's "republican simplicity...with its thronging associations," would "more than counterbalance the lack of splendor and the artistic mania for effect." But to modern eyes, the self-proclaimed "strictly historical picture" seems a coldly static, expressionless tableau. Nonetheless, in its own day it was a critical and popular favorite. To the New York Evening Post, *it was nothing less than "a success which time will go on ripening to the latest day that Americans honor the nobility of their ancestors." First displayed publicly inside the White House, "thronged with visitors" for the occasion, in Carpenter's words, the canvas was subsequently exhibited throughout the North, transported on a collapsible frame with built-in rollers to prevent creasing. On display in Pittsburgh the day news of Lincoln's death reached the city, the painting caused public interest to rise "to such a pitch that, once at least, the doors of the exhibition room had actually to be closed."*

(U.S. Capitol)

ORDER No. 11, MARTIAL LAW (1869–70)

George Caleb Bingham
(1811–1879)

Outraged by Union general Thomas Ewing's order essentially depopulating four Missouri counties wracked by guerrilla warfare, Bingham vowed: "I will make you infamous with pen and brush as far as I am able." His melodramatic painting portrayed a family pleading for mercy after Federal soldiers have killed or injured two of its members. The saintly visages of the civilians, and the hideous sneers of the soldiers, seem clichés in comparison to the portraiture in Bingham's early works. Bingham employed devices favored by Confederate artists to make his point: an inspiring-looking patriarch, pious women praying for deliverance, even devoted slaves, some in tears. Bingham copyrighted a photograph of the original painting in 1868, and a steel engraving was made later. But when the original first went on display, a newspaper accused Bingham of "prostituting an art which should be dedicated to the noblest purposes."

Oil on canvas, 55½ × 78½ inches.
(Cincinnati Art Museum,
Cincinnati, Ohio; The Edwin and
Virginia Irwin Memorial)

static qualities seem accentuated by the mezzotint engraving based on it, executed by the able John Sartain and published in 1872. Bingham never was called upon to comment on its merits as a painting, but he did have to defend the politics of the work. In doing so, he stressed his own record of loyalty to the Union and disclaimed any desire to defend slavery. But what was the spectator to make of the black woman at left holding the woman who fainted at the scene of murder under Federal auspices? Did she not represent a slave loyal to her enslavers? Whatever the divisive political content, the painting, intent upon having its protagonists shriek their political protests on the one side and darkly indulge tyranny on the other, came to resemble a group of statues clustered for a drawing class.[49]

Ultimately the painting, or its print adaptation at least, failed. Not many in the North wished to be reminded of the political complexities of the Lincoln administration's victory in the war. And

Civil War into scenes of glory, but Missouri's inglorious civil warfare was not the stuff of art either. What warfare could do to the home, though Americans were given a chilling foretaste in Civil War Missouri, would rarely attract painters' attention. American artists proved better equipped to sentimentalize home than to dramatize war's ability to burn it to the ground.

The popular illustrated newspapers, not surprisingly, maintained that they had covered every aspect of the war with unqualified success. In one endorsement of its own war record, published only a few months after peace was restored, *Harper's Weekly* lavished praise on its corps of battlefield illustrators:

> *We may be pardoned for a special pride in our artists who have gone through all the long and stirring campaigns of the war, commemorating its most interesting incidents and noted men…scarcely less imperiled than the soldiers. They have made the weary marches and dangerous voyages. They have shared the soldiers' fare; they have ridden and waded, and climbed and floundered, always trusting in lead pencils and keeping their paper dry. When the battle began they were there. They drew the enemy's fire as well as our own. The fierce shock, the heaving tumult, the smoky sway of battle from side to side, the line, the assault, the victory—they were a part of all and their faithful fingers, depicting the scene, have made us a part also.*[50]

perhaps not many Southerners could afford such an expensive steel engraving. Whatever the cause, a print dealer as recently as 1990 was still able to unearth several copies in mint condition, stacked and surely unsold since their publication a century and a quarter earlier.

History painting, even in the otherwise capable hands of George Caleb Bingham, could degenerate into histrionics. To be sure, painters would take too much poetic license in turning the

Yet the more astute readers of the weekly might have remembered that a few weeks earlier, the newspaper's art critic had bitterly lamented the scarcity of Civil War art at the most prestigious

LINCOLN CRUSHING THE DRAGON OF REBELLION (1862)

David Gilmour Blythe
(1815–1865)

Lincoln raises his famous railsplitter's maul to slay the fierce dragon of rebellion, in this typical painting by Blythe, a political cartoon in oils, with grotesque symbolic figures, sketchy detail, and broad brushstrokes. Conceived as a visual attack on New York City's Democratic political machine, referred to here as "Tamony Hall" (the "o" boasting a caricature of New York's Democratic governor, Horatio Seymour), the painting depicts Lincoln's heroic efforts being constrained by both the opposition "Democracy" and the fetters of the "Constitution," aided and abetted by a stock caricature of a New York Irishman, complete with whiskey bottle nearby. Behind them, a scaffold for traitors sits conspicuously unused even as a Northern city burns in the background.

Oil on canvas, 18 × 22 inches. Signed lower left: *Blythe.* (Bequest of Maxim C. Karolik for the Karolik Collection of American Paintings, Museum of Fine Arts, Boston)

public exhibition of the year, complaining that even one of the war paintings of Thomas Nast—himself a veteran artist-correspondent for the illustrated weeklies—had been disrespectfully displayed in a "sunken panel…[an] unfortunate niche" where "it can not be seen."[51]

The truth was that, while some of the early newspaper artists would eventually contribute acclaimed paintings of their wartime experiences—Nast, Homer, and Edwin Forbes come primarily to mind—while the war raged, and even immediately afterward, their output was minuscule, due perhaps to a confluence of conditions that included confusion over the changing styles of command and warfare, the impact of war on sanctified home and hearth, the initial indifference of the American audience, and the lack as yet of robust patronage. What William J. Hoppin, a leading member of the New-York Historical Society, concluded as late as 1864 was that the art of war had yet to make an impression, notwithstanding the weekly press:

> *It is true that the illustrated newspapers are full of sketches, purporting to be pictures of important scenes; but the testimony of parties engaged shows that these representatives are, when not taken from photographs, not always reliable. The desire of producing striking effects sometimes overcomes all other considerations, and the truth is now and then sacrificed to the demand for dramatic action or pleasing play of light and shadow. Many of these designs are of little value.… Some of them are positively lying and fabulous.*[52]

The author of this criticism complained that Civil War artists had "inadequately expressed the heroism, patriot-

ic devotion, the noble charities of the North." But while insisting that "scarcely anything has been produced of an enduring character illustrating the war," Hoppin made an "exception of Leutze's clear portrait of [Union general Ambrose E.] Burnside." Yet as readers of this book, many of them encountering this painting for the first time, realize, Leutze's work in this case did not endure. The great American history painter failed to produce a *Washington Crossing the Delaware* for the Civil War. He died in 1868. Art aside, Leutze had bet on the wrong horse: Burnside was no George Washington. Artist-correspondents, printmakers, and photographers worked fast and captured the heroes of the headlines. Painters worked more slowly and intently. Their works required time and long consideration. Where the Civil War was concerned, only later did art learn to imitate life. But it would require the retrospective appeal of wartime glory and the growing affection for the common soldier to inspire it.

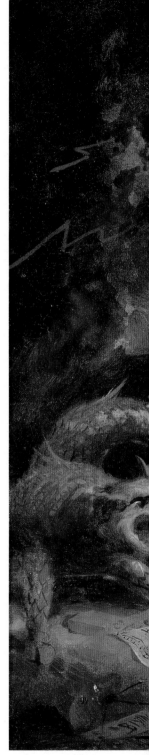

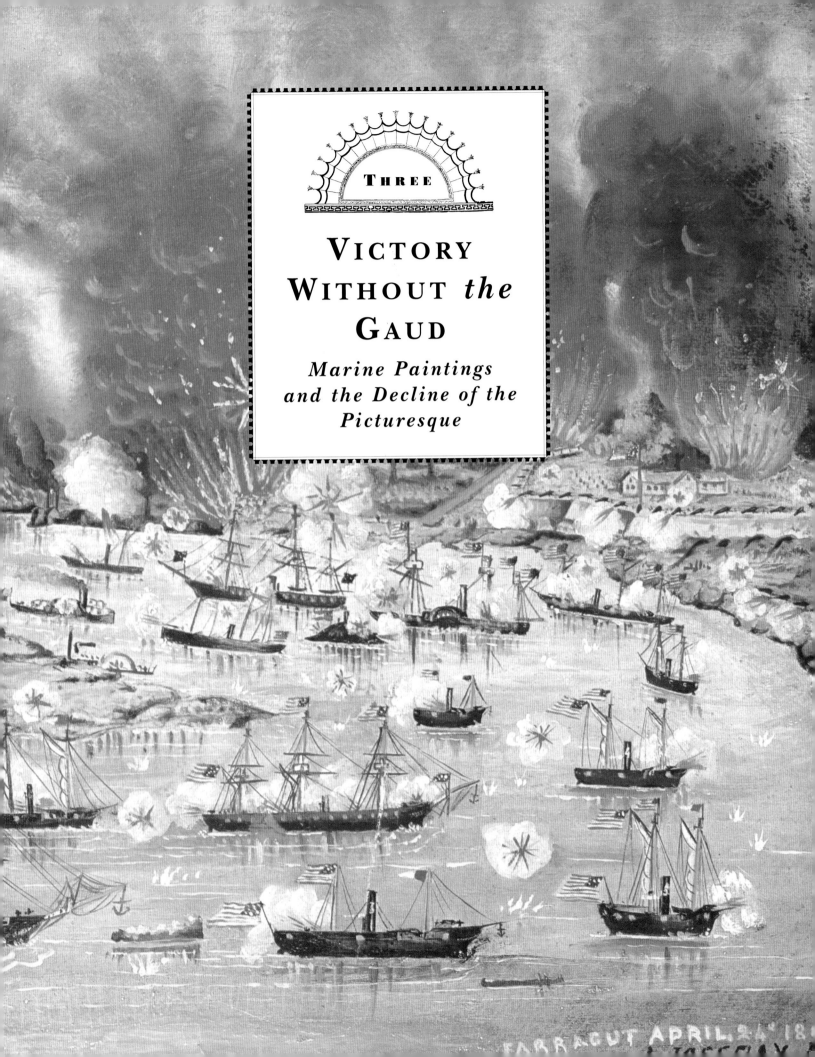

THREE

VICTORY
WITHOUT *the*
GAUD

*Marine Paintings
and the Decline of the
Picturesque*

≈ *Preceding Page* ≈

FARRAGUT APRIL 24TH 1862 (N.D.)

J. Joffray
(nineteenth century)

More than forty Union vessels stormed past two Mississippi River forts at New Orleans on April 24, 1862. And all seemed visible on this moonless night as the torrent of fire and counterfire, one witness recalled, "turned night into day." Explained the observer: "Combine all that you have heard of thunder, add to it all that you have ever seen of lightning, and you have, perhaps, a conception of the scene." Joffray, however, exaggerated the illumination, transforming the 2:00 A.M. sky to a noonlike blue. And he erroneously depicted Farragut's orderly, single-file procession as a congested gridlock of naval traffic.

Oil on canvas, 27¼ × 34 inches. Signed lower right: *J. Joffray, Pinxt.* (Chicago Historical Society)

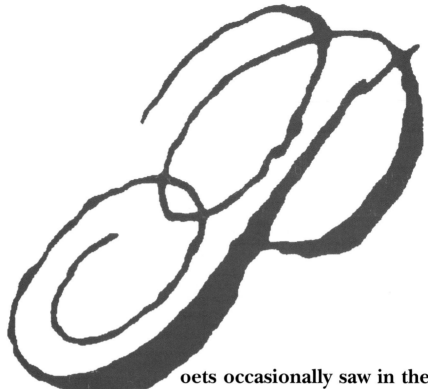

oets occasionally saw in the Civil War what other observers, even artists, overlooked. Herman Melville, who after all knew something about the sea, took "A Utilitarian View of the Monitor's Fight" in one of the poems in his *Battle-Pieces* collection. He not only depicted accurately the meaning of the battle between the Union ironclad *Monitor* and the Confederate ironclad *Merrimac* on March 9, 1862, off Hampton Roads, Virginia, but also reached beyond that landmark of naval technology to create a symbol for the whole Civil War.

Hail to victory without the gaud
    Of glory; zeal that needs no fans
Of banners; plain mechanic power
Plied cogently in War now placed—
    Where War belongs—
Among the trades and artisans.

Yet this was battle, and intense—
    Beyond the strife of fleets heroic

Deadlier, closer, calm 'mid storm;
No passion; all went on by crank,
    Pivot, and screw,
and calculations of caloric.

Needless to dwell; the story's known.
    The ringing of those plates on plates
Still ringeth round the world—
    The clangor of that blacksmith's fray.
    The anvil-din
    Resounds this message from the Fates:

War shall yet be, and to the end;
    But war-paint shows the streaks of
    weather;
War yet shall be, but warriors
Are now but operatives; War's made
    Less grand than Peace,

And a singe runs through lace and feather.

Yet Melville's vision of the triumph of the industrial revolution over military glory—a forerunner in its way of the nightmare vision in Mark Twain's *A Connecticut Yankee in King Arthur's Court*—was rarely shared by the artists of his generation or the next.

Marine painters had perhaps the best opportunity to recognize the growing impact of the machine age on war. Naval warfare had long exemplified the ultimate in the technology of violence. Even the old wooden sailing warships of Admiral Nelson's day delivered their explosive payloads with efficiency that

NAVAL SCENE, CIVIL WAR—C. S. SHIP VIRGINIA AND U.S.S. CONGRESS [SIC] AT HAMPTON ROADS (N.D.)

Artist unknown, Signed: H H

On March 8, 1862, a massive, floating, iron-plated mound steamed ominously into the harbor of Hampton Roads, off Newport News, Virginia. Within hours the clumsy but seemingly impregnable armored vessel had rammed and sunk the stately USS Cumberland; *shelled the USS* Congress *into a burning ruin; and chased the USS* Minnesota *aground. This unattributed canvas of the first day's action at Hampton Roads has long been identified as the Confederate iron-clad's March 8 attack on the* Congress, *but it much more closely suggests the ramming of the* Cumberland *the same day, during which the* Merrimac *was temporarily embedded in her target, nearly sinking along with her. The* Congress *and the* Minnesota *can be glimpsed maneuvering in the background. Not until the Japanese attack on Pearl Harbor, seventy-nine years later, would the U.S. Navy endure such devastating losses on a single day.*

Oil on canvas, 12 × 17 inches. (West Point Museum, U.S. Military Academy)

Farragut's Fleet (n.d.)

Mauritz Frederik Hendrik de Haas (1832–1895)

Amid a thunder of fire so deafening it seemed to an eyewitness "one long, wild, protracted crash,"
Farragut's fleet slips through a makeshift blockade of moored hulks at 2:00 A.M. on April 24, 1862,
and runs the gauntlet past Forts Jackson and St. Philip, up the Mississippi toward New Orleans.
Farragut's flagship Hartford *can be seen in this virtuoso painting coming under attack by the*
Confederate ram Manassas, *while the tugboat* Mosher *lists dangerously to port (right), one of eight*
Southern ships lost that morning. "The white smoke rolled and heaved in vast volumes along the shud-
dering waters," the eyewitness continued, in "one of the wildest scenes in the history of the war."
Farragut was moved to recall that it was "as if all the artillery of heaven were playing upon the earth."
Night fighting was unusual, and exaggerated the terrifying flashes of gunfire, but it attracted skilled
painters who prided themselves on their ability to master these difficult subjects.

Oil on canvas, 59 × 105¾ inches. Signed lower left: *M F de Haas, NA.* (The Historic New Orleans Collection)

[C.S.S. Manassas Pushing a Fire Barge into the U.S.S. Hartford in New Orleans Harbor] (n.d.)

Xanthus R. Smith (1839–1929)

Of all the "hell of terrors" awaiting them along the Mississippi River as Farragut's fleet
raced past Forts Morgan and St. Philip before dawn on April 24, 1862, the most hellish of all, one
observer recalled, came when "a fire-raft, pushed steadily forward by the ram Manassas, *loomed*
through the smoke like a phantom from the unseen world." The fire barge engulfed the Union's wooden
flagship in a conflagration that sent its crew into a frenzied "death struggle with the flames, heat
and smoke," an officer on a nearby vessel testified. Farragut's men eventually doused the fire, and
the flagship resumed its inexorable progress toward New Orleans.

Oil on paper, 5¼ × 9¾ inches. (Courtesy Robert M. Hicklin, Jr., Inc., Spartanburg, South Carolina)

**LAST OF
THE WOODEN NAVY
(WASHINGTON, 1907)**

A. B. Graham Co.,
after W. B. Mathews

*W. B. Mathews's portrayal
enjoyed the aptest title of any
of the depictions of the*
Monitor *and the* Merrimac,
*making explicit what other
painters clearly had in mind
in their works as well.*

Photogravure (Special Collections,
University of Georgia Libraries)

could only be envied by army men. Cannons were so heavy, and ships so much better than horses at moving them, that the fleet at Trafalgar mustered six times the number of cannons that Napoleon's army had at Waterloo, and the naval guns generally threw heavier projectiles. Halving the number of naval guns because they had to be fired in broadsides from one side of the ship or the other still leaves the advantage overwhelmingly with naval firepower, three to one.[1]

To counter such efficiency in firepower, naval technology had by the time of the Civil War incorporated armor plating to provide greater protection against shot and shell. It was almost as though the writer Ambrose Bierce's "Ingenious Patriot," a fictional character who kept inventing successively better military equipment, were steadily at work in the Navy Departments of the Civil War antagonists, alternately devising irresistible weaponry and impregnable walls behind which sailors could work. Though naval artillery could demolish masonry fortifications, the

technology of impenetrability at sea was in the ascendant, with the result that the rate of naval casualties continued lower than that of land forces. The relative lack of danger of naval battles seems to have been little noticed, since they took place in an environment frighteningly inhospitable to man.[2]

Poets and painters could not help but notice the technology. Yet painters who depicted the advent of ironclads at Hampton Roads—and more than fifty such pictures are listed in the Smithsonian's Inventory of American Art—generally proved unable to invest the historic encounter with more than obvious significance. W. B. Matthews captured the surface meaning in 1906 in a painting, given broad exposure in a print adaptation, called *Last of the Wooden Navy.* His painting of the action at Hampton Roads the day before the *Monitor* arrived showed the *Merrimac,* a smoking, metallic floating fortress with sloping sides, steaming toward the viewer of the canvas while stately old sailing vessels recede into the background. (After it was refitted with an iron hull, the *Merrimac*'s official name was changed to the *Virginia*, but its old name stuck.) Matthews aptly imbued the whole image with a twilight nostalgia.

In addition to armor, Civil War navies applied another technological marvel directly to battle: steam power. On land, armies might ride swift steam trains to depots in the theater of war, but steam power could not yet be employed in battle (or farming, as Abraham Lincoln had noted, unhappily, on the eve of the war). Steam power was limited in its effects, however, because the weight of the armor slowed down the ships.

In a depiction of combat between a new armored vessel and an old sailing ship, an unidentified artist, who signed the canvas only "HH," showed the sun near the horizon over a seascape while the *Merrimac* rams the starboard side of the USS *Cumberland*, a not-very-useful relic of the age of sail. In the background, small Confederate gunboats engage the *Congress*, another sailing ship from the prewar navy, lying at anchor. Later, devastating gunnery from the *Merrimac* set her on fire. Of these two antiquated Union blockaders the acer-

bic but fair-minded naval historian James Russell Soley noted: "Nothing shows more clearly the persistence of old traditions than the presence of these helpless vessels in so dangerous a neighborhood." These sailing ships were "of no value for modern warfare," and the *Merrimac* quickly showed it. The low sun in the painting, however, was more symbolic than historically accurate, for the *Merrimac* engaged the *Cumberland* at two in the afternoon and finished with her in less than an hour! Painters could depict nostalgic glory, but it was not their role to show the imbecility of relying on antiquated sailing vessels. The sunset haze of past glory clinging to the old wooden sailing ships is better dispelled in the withering text of Soley and other sober analysts of modern warfare at sea than by looking at the works of the painters. Some 250 U.S. sailors died at Hampton Roads that day, most of them victims of "fruitless sacrifice."

On the following day the *Monitor* steamed to the rescue. The accomplished naval painter Xanthus Russell Smith, who served during the war on the old wooden screw frigate USS

ENGAGEMENT BETWEEN THE U. S. ERICSON BATTERY MONITOR AND CONFEDERATE STATES RAM VIRGINIA OR MERRIMAC IN HAMPTON ROADS, VIRGINIA, MORNING OF MARCH 9, 1862 (1869)

Xanthus R. Smith
(1839–1929)

In the first battle between ironclads in naval history, the Monitor *and the* Merrimac *traded withering gunfire for nearly four hours—"mercilessly but ineffectively," according to a witness to the engagement. Shells were powerless to penetrate the thickly armored hull of either vessel. In his panoramic depiction of their battle, Smith bathed both vessels in smoke—grim black for the Confederate ship, and billowing white for the Union's, an overtly symbolic device by a painter who had served two years in the Union navy.*

Oil on canvas, 30 × 66 inches. Signed on back: *Painted by Xanthus Smith, 1869.* (The Art Collection of The Union League of Philadelphia)

LANDING AT FORT FISHER (1865)

Flora Bond (Fanny) Palmer (c. 1812–1876)

*Fort Fisher, in North Carolina, proved a stubbornly elusive Union target until January 1865, when
General Grant and Admiral Porter mapped a coordinated land-and-sea assault. On January 15,
Porter sent forty-four Union ships into battle, and almost all of them are shown here bombarding the
Confederate stronghold with devastating fire that destroyed several cannon and neutralized the fort's
protective mines. English-born artist Palmer enjoyed a long career as an artist for the New York lithographers Currier & Ives, for whom she prepared this watercolor as a model. It was adapted in 1865
into a large-folio print entitled* Victorious Attack on Fort Fisher.

Pencil with watercolor wash on paper, 12 × 27½ inches. (U.S. Marine Corps Museums Art Collection, Washington, D.C.)

ENGAGEMENT BETWEEN THE CUMBERLAND AND THE MERRIMAC (N.D.)

Charles Sidney Raleigh (1830–1925)

The Merrimac's *awesome, brutally swift destruction of the USS* Cumberland *is legendary: the ironclad simply rammed the wooden ship, inflicting a gaping hole in her side that promptly sent her to the bottom. But Raleigh offered a mere suggestion of the destruction to follow by showing the* Cumberland *listing gracefully to one side as the* Merrimac *strikes her hull. There is no explaining the gunfire coming from the ironclad directly toward the viewer; most likely, there was not crew enough aboard to man guns on both sides of the vessel.*

Oil on canvas, 51½ × 86 inches. (Courtesy Robert M. Hicklin, Jr., Inc., Spartanburg, South Carolina)

Melodramatically distressed female passengers drop their books in mid-sentence and cluster around a broad-backed sailor who observes the approach of the dreaded raider Alabama. *Such illustrations contributed mightily to the growing mystique of the infamous "pirate" ship. In truth, women had little to fear from the* Alabama's *crew, who behaved with the respectfulness, if not the gallantry, typical of Victorian-era soldiers.*

Woodcut engraving, 13¾ × 9¼ in.
(The Lincoln Museum)

Wabash, later depicted the battle that ensued between the *Monitor* and the *Merrimac*. He painted the two ironclads in shadow in the foreground, with a ship of the wooden blockading squadron highlighted in the distance. The effect, intensified by the crisp line of white paint across the wooden ship's battery, was to show the older ship to bright advantage. Smith seemed reluctant to acknowledge in oils the point made by Mathews, that is, that the hideous ironclad vessels represented the wave of the future in shipbuilding technology.[3]

The Chicago lithographers Kurz & Allison seemed to know better, making the battle at Hampton Roads the only naval engagement featured in their series of thirty-six popular Civil War prints published near the end of the century. Yet the publishers ultimately gave the ironclads only grudging respect. The two ships were drawn very small on the far horizon, and the Confederate ship was ludicrously misdescribed. The whole scene was structured as a traditional land battle picture, with general officers on shore in the left foreground surveying the military vista before them (along with the print's viewer, who shares the generals' vantage point). The most interesting action in the chromolithograph is the rescue of the sailors who are swimming ashore from the burning *Minnesota*, a screw frigate that ran aground the previous day. Though her funnel is invisible, the ship in the print must necessarily represent the *Minnesota*, for the *Congress* (the only other wooden ship there) had blown up at one o'clock on the morning of the battle. The wooden vessel appears larger and more lovingly drawn than the squat ironclads in the distance, but it is far from accurately detailed. The firm of Kurz & Allison, making its fame with gaudy chromolithographs

depicting correctly uniformed Union and Confederate soldiers clashing in traditional scenes of glory, apparently did not put their hearts into this attempt to show what "plain mechanic power" had done to the picturesque qualities of warfare at sea.

No artist in any medium achieved Herman Melville's profound understanding of the symbolic significance of the engagement. Surely the literary critic Edmund Wilson underestimates the poet's powers when he dismisses most of Melville's *Battle-Pieces* with the curt remark: "The celebration of current battles by poets who have not taken part in them has produced some of the emptiest verse that exists."[4]

One other circumstance dictated the failure of artists to give Civil War naval combat realistic or insightful appraisal: artists usually relied heavily on camera studies as models to augment sittings and sketches, but the navy proved inhospitable to photography. As Union Adm. David D. Porter noted after the war: "Naval ships did not travel with reporters, photographers or sketchers, there was no room for these on board ship, and if perchance some stray reporter should get on board, the discomfort of a man of war, the exacting discipline, and the freer life in camp sent him back to shore, where in most cases he only remembered his association with the Navy as a trip without any satisfaction, and with no desire to do justice to the work of the naval service." The story in the army, according to Porter, was quite a bit different: "The photographer, while he traveled with the army, would spend his days in photographing every noted scene, reprints of which were scattered broadcast over the Union, keeping the movements of our armies as clearly before the millions of people in the North as if the battles had been reflected in a mirror."[5]

The artists could not or at least did not hold up a mirror to modern naval warfare, but they came eventually to interpret many of the great naval actions of the war with brush and pen. The marine painter who dealt most comprehensively with new naval technolgies was Julian O. Davidson. In dozens of illustrations executed for the four-volume *Battles and Leaders of the Civil War*, published in 1888, in paintings commissioned for printmaker Louis Prang's chromolithographs of the war, and doubtless in other works, Davidson depicted scores of different vessels with close attention to detail. A Marylander, born in 1853, too late to serve in the Civil War, Davidson went to sea at age eighteen. Afterward he studied art with the marine painter Mauritz F. H. DeHaas (who himself portrayed the Civil War's Battle of New Orleans) and began exhibiting his works in the New York area as early as 1872.

Many of Davidson's works display mastery of a great variety of technical details of ship furnishings. He must have prided himself on this, for he often used an elevated perspective for painting naval actions. This gave him a panoramic view of many different ships and shore fortifications at once, a *tour de force* of historical research that occasionally had the unfortunate effect of making the spectator think of a great basin with many finely detailed ship models floating in it. Even *Monitors Riding Out a Gale*, with its emphasis on rough water, retains something of this massed-model effect, as the spectator is allowed to see three well-delineated vessels in a six-by-eight-inch space, along with silhouettes of five others.

But such is a minor criticism of a naval illustrator of talent and energy who could make believable images of

ironclad monitors, wooden screw ships, and side-wheelers from any angle. A familiar example is his illustration of the surrender of the Confederate ram *Tennessee* at Mobile Bay for *Battles and Leaders*. The line drawing contains images of nine carefully rendered vessels, steaming in different directions and all viewed from a high vantage point. He also executed illustrations of ships being rammed, thus creating the opportunity of showing them thrust partly out of the water on some rather interesting, unusual,

UNITED STATES MONITORS RIDING OUT A GALE
DURING THE BLOCKADE OFF CHARLESTON, S.C. (N.D.)

Julian Oliver Davidson (1853–1894)

Union monitors are tossed like toys by heaving seas off Charleston in this vivid scene. These Federal warships first appeared in Charleston Harbor in April 1863, when they opened a bombardment on Fort Sumter. The initial attack failed, however, and a new fleet of monitors returned in July to begin a prolonged siege. Davidson, known for meticulous research and careful attention to detail, grew increasingly interested in the technical demands of depicting water in motion—a fascination clearly evidenced by his careful work here.

Gouache on paper, 5½ × 13⅜ inches. Signed lower right: *J.O. Davidson.*
(The New-York Historical Society)

J. O. DAVIDSON.

THE MONITOR AND THE MERRIMAC AT SHORT RANGE BY AN EYE WITNESS (N.D.)

Artist unknown

In rolling seas, painted in unnaturally parallel ridges by the unidentified artist, the Monitor *and the* Merrimac *fight head to head, guns blazing, but flags still waving untattered. In truth, neither ship was particularly seaworthy, and, indeed, the* Monitor *sank in a gale in December. This oil painting was owned by Franklin D. Roosevelt, who collected naval pictures.*

Oil on canvas, 13¼ × 20 inches. (The Franklin D. Roosevelt Library,

and even exciting angles and planes.

Davidson enjoyed a stroke of fortune when Louis Prang's Boston-based chromolithography firm decided to publish a series of Civil War battle prints, for, unlike their landlocked competitors in Chicago, Kurz & Allison, these Massachusetts publishers worked in an ocean port that may have inspired their attention to the war at sea. Prang included six naval actions in his series, and Davidson painted the originals for all of them.

Whether by choice or direction from his publisher-patron, Davidson executed one each of the various types of naval illustrations. *The Battle of New Orleans* was a night scene painted more or less from a shipboard participant's eye level. *Mobile Bay* showed a bird's-eye view duel between a fleet and a fort. He depicted a gun crew on deck in the *Alabama and Kearsarge* picture, and a Union naval landing party's approach from the viewpoint of the defending Confederates in Fort Fisher. *Port Hudson* was another night scene, and the *Monitor* and *Merrimac* battle was viewed at very close range.

Davidson offered subjects rarely depicted elsewhere, like the huge 150-pounder Armstrong cannon (with its barrel of concentric metal rings to withstand the huge powder charge) and the masonry fort at Mobile Bay. His rendering of the *Monitor* and *Merrimac* was as effective as any, giving them center stage without any serious visual competition from attendant sailing vessels and shrouding the battle in smoke and steam. He put the *Monitor* in white smoke and the *Merrimac* in black, a device used by other naval artists who portrayed this engagement from the Union point of view.

Although the battle between the *Monitor* and the *Merrimac* presaged the future of naval warfare and merited more attention than any other naval phenomenon of the Civil War, later illustrated books often slighted that contest in their choice of pictures to focus instead on a more traditional Civil War battle fought on the high seas in Europe two years later between two wooden ships, the *Kearsarge* and the *Alabama*. There are many paintings from which to choose. According to the Inventory of American Paintings, depictions of the *Kearsarge* and *Alabama* are second only in number to paintings of the *Monitor* and *Merrimac*. By focusing on this backward-looking battle, traditional marine painting attempted to survive the Civil War's dramatic technological changes in naval warfare. No ship inspired better artists than did the Confederate commerce raider, *Alabama*. Winslow Homer succumbed to its allure, as did the great French painter Edouard Manet. An Irish marine painter named Edwin Hayes and an English one, James Wheldon of Hull, also chose the *Alabama* as a subject. So did others, including Xanthus Smith and J. O. Davidson.

How does one account for the prominence of this memorable but rather archaic-looking sea battle in the visual imagination of the nineteenth century? The lure of this stately engagement between three-masted wooden ships surely exceeded both its impact on the Civil War and its importance in the history of naval warfare. Most observers had immediately realized, when the *Monitor* engaged the *Merrimac*, that the future of naval shipbuilding would be forever changed. But the revolutionary quality of the Hampton Roads battle never obliterated the affectionate memory of the ironclads' feeble old wooden sisters in the fleet. The battle between the *Alabama* and the *Kearsarge* off the

Opposite

ALABAMA AND KEARSARGE (1864)

Edouard Manet
(French, 1831–1883)

The great French painter Manet, who might have been present at Cherbourg to witness the epic sea battle between the Alabama *and* Kearsarge, *portrayed the encounter from the perspective of the little French vessel in the foreground, racing toward the combatants to rescue survivors as the Confederate raider begins listing to the stern. If he was present, Manet obviously could not have observed the details of the* Alabama's *rigging; he had to rely on the same view from illustrated newspapers used by other painters. The prominence of the French flag makes this French painting stand out from other depictions of the event, as does the startling color of the sea and the sky. Writing about this canvas on July 4, 1864, a critic for* Le Gaulois *called the work "a miracle of observation and execution."*

Oil on canvas, 54⅜ × 51¼ inches.
(Philadelphia Museum of Art, The John G. Johnson collection)

BATTLE OF MOBILE BAY (1890)

Xanthus R. Smith (1839–1929)

While some artists saw in the Battle of Mobile Bay a rousing example of personal heroism by Admiral Farragut, Smith, working near century's end, was inspired instead to highlight the confrontation there between modern ironclads. Here he depicts a Federal monitor sliding past the CSS Tennessee, while Union sailors crowd the decks of adjacent ships as if witnessing firsthand the dawning of a new navy. In the end, however, Farragut's older wooden vessels bested the fearsome Confederate ram. The ghostly appearance of the ship at the right of the Tennessee gave a hint of what the future held for wooden ships.

Oil on canvas, 40 × 66 inches. Signed lower left: *Xanthus Smith, 1890.* (U.S. Naval Academy, Annapolis)

DAVID GLASGOW FARRAGUT (1891)

Ulysses Dow Tenney (1826–?)

Commissioned by the Portsmouth, New Hampshire, Grand Army of the Republic to produce this portrait for a new local school that would bear Farragut's name, Tenney ruined the effect of the stern portraiture by inserting comically short arms. When the painting was unveiled, the orator for the occasion correctly recognized that the portrait of the admiral highlighted not "the blue and gold that adorned his form, but ... the man within ... the spirit of good patriotism that was his crowning glory."

Oil on canvas, 54 × 36 inches. Signed left: *U. D. Tenney/1891.* (Portsmouth Athenaeum: Photograph by Andrew Edgar)

BATTLE OF MOBILE BAY (BOSTON, 1886)

L[ouis]. Prang & Co., after Julian Oliver Davidson

*Farragut's awesome armada of warships and ironclads steams into Mobile Bay
on August 5, 1864, exchanging fierce fire with Fort Morgan (left), as the Confederate ram*
Tennessee *(left foreground) races toward the battle. Davidson's elaborate, smoke-suffused panorama
trained a bird's-eye perspective on the crowded encounter, thus adding scope and sweep to a scene that
rival artists who focused solely on the fleet did not provide. In doing so, Davidson gave at least equal
prominence to the thick-walled Confederate fort, whose men can be glimpsed manning the guns
pounding the Union vessels from the waterline. The Federal monitor* Tecumseh *is seen about to sink
(right) from the tremendous explosion of a mine on its port side, away from the Confederate fort.*

Chromolithograph, 15 × 22 inches. Signed lower right: *J. O. Davidson/1886.* (The Lincoln Museum)

ENGAGEMENT BETWEEN THE PIRATE ALABAMA AND THE U.S.S. KEARSARGE OFF CHERBOURG, JUNE 19, 1864, (1874–75)

Xanthus R. Smith
(1839–1929)

In a majestic painting that owed a heavy, if unacknowledged, debt to the wartime illustration in Harper's Weekly, *the stricken Confederate raider* Alabama *slips into the sea stern-first as the triumphant USS* Kearsarge *stands off in the distance, her flag flying high. An officer on board the Union*

coast of Cherbourg, France, kept those memories alive.

Leaving aside the broad question of the future of shipbuilding technology, one can say as well that within the Civil War itself the battle between the *Monitor* and the *Merrimac* was a far more decisive contest that assured, against its greatest Confederate threat, the continuation and ultimate success of the Union naval blockade. Indeed, Union naval strategy can be said to have chosen the blockade over protection of the merchant marine. This made the *Alabama*'s destructive impact on the U.S. merchant fleet a rather easy accomplishment. Admittedly, the *Alabama* enjoyed an illustrious career and also shaped American maritime history for decades to come, but her impact on naval warfare was not great. The British, America's major rivals for international commerce, nevertheless quickly recog-

nized her importance in shaping the world's carrying trade. As early as January 20, 1864, Milner Gibson, president of Great Britain's Board of Trade, gave a speech noting that Confederate commerce raiders, and mainly the *Alabama*, had destroyed or driven for protection under the Union Jack half of all U.S. ships engaged in English trade.[6] The effect on commerce with Latin America and in the Pacific was at least as disastrous for American shipping. The U.S. merchant marine literally never recovered from these blows. Yet somehow the paintings of the *Alabama*'s last battle say nothing of commerce or trade statistics. And the exaggerated fame of the *Alabama* is well illustrated by the "Alabama claims," a prolonged dispute over reparations payments to be made by Great Britain for damage done to United States commerce by ships like the *Alabama* that were built in British docks in violation of international law. After international arbitration, Great Britain paid $15,500,000 in gold for damage done by the *Alabama* and ten other ships. The little-known Confederate commerce raider *Shenandoah* caused nearly as much harm, but the *Alabama* held the limelight and lent her name to the more general damage proceedings.

Thus the *Alabama* stirred popular imagination and fear in her own day. Universally called a "pirate" ship by the Northern press (though not so treated in fact by the U.S. government), the *Alabama* projected a frightening but swashbuckling image that inspired Winslow Homer's illustration for *Harper's Weekly*, with its melodramatically distressed female passengers huddled together on a Union merchant ship contemplating imminent attack. The sinking of the *Alabama*, on June 19, 1864, naturally made headlines throughout the world (although the news took weeks to reach America).

The published account of the *Alabama*'s demise written by her commander, Raphael Semmes, himself a dashing character with a flamboyantly waxed mustache, offers the key to understanding the fame of the event and its conservative appeal to marine painters during and after the Civil War. Semmes pointed out that the *Kearsarge* held a slight superiority in armament, size of crew, and "stanchness of construction." Still, the Confederate commander added, "the disparity was not so great, but that I might hope to beat my enemy in a fair fight. But he did not show me a fair fight, for, as it afterward turned out, his ship was iron-clad. It was the same thing, as if two men were to go out to fight or duel, and one of them, unknown to the other, were to put a shirt of mail under his outer garment."

As if two men were to go out to fight a duel! The question of fairness will be examined shortly, but the most important aspect of Semmes's account is his general characterization of the battle as a duel. That explains much about the nature of the fight between the two ships, and even more about its appeal to poets and painters.[7]

Semmes admitted that "the days of chivalry" were "past" and that Captain John A. Winslow, who commanded the *Kearsarge*, could not reasonably have been expected to warn his Confederate rival beforehand that he had covered vital areas on the sides of the *Kearsarge* in protective sheet chain covered over with deal boards, thin strips of sawed yellow pine. Had such a warning caused Semmes to refuse combat, Secretary of the Navy Gideon Welles would, as Semmes himself acknowledged, have cut Winslow's "head off to a certainty." Winslow, far from boasting of his Yankee cunning in using the chains, in fact scarcely mentioned the ploy and then only in a supplemental report demanded by the secretary of the navy. "The *Kearsarge* had only 120 tons [of

ship recalled of the Alabama's death throes: "Her bow rose high in the air, as if preparatory for a suicidal plunge, and then, in a moment, the greatest curse to which any commerce had ever been subjected was engulfed in the uncompassionate waves of the ocean." But as a sailor from the sunken ship remembered, employing the clichéd romantic language of the sea, the Alabama was "graceful even in her death." This painting was exhibited to much praise at the Centennial Exposition of 1876 in Philadelphia. Smith retouched it at age sixty-six in 1905, and was present the following year as the guest of honor when it was unveiled at its new, permanent home at the city's Union League Club.

Oil on canvas, 56¼ × 96 inches. (The Art Collection of The Union League of Philadelphia)

**THE U.S. SLOOP OF WAR "KEARSARGE"...
SINKING THE PIRATE "ALABAMA"**

Currier & Ives (Museum of the City of New York)

coal] in," he said, "but as an offset to this, her sheet chains were stowed outside—stopped up and down as an additional preventive and protection to her more empty bunkers."[8] He said nothing at all about the "deal boards that hid the chains."

What a picture of naval combat Semmes offers! His description of the battle's origins is especially remarkable. After the *Alabama* ended a long cruise by sailing into the French port of Cherbourg, the *Kearsarge* stationed herself outside the port. In a short time Semmes addressed a "note to…our agent [in the port], requesting him to inform Captain Winslow, through the United States Consul, that if he would wait until I could receive some coal on board—my supply having been nearly exhausted, by my late cruising—I would come out and give him battle. This mes-

sage was duly conveyed, and the challenge was understood to have been accepted."[9]

How could Admiral Semmes say that chivalry was dead? Here two national adversaries in a war have contacted each other through seconds on neutral soil and agreed to duel, once adequate preparations for combat have been completed. Indeed, Captain Winslow reported that Semmes's note asked "that the *Kearsarge* would not depart, as he intended to fight her and would not delay her but a day or two." When the *Alabama* steamed out for the contest, Frenchmen gathered on the heights above town, at the second-story windows of houses facing the sea, and on the harbor fortifications to observe the prearranged spectacle. Even some Confederates were appalled that their most effective raider had risked all in one-on-one combat. "[Adm.] Semmes, of whom we have been so proud," diarist Mary Chesnut exclaimed, "he is a fool after all—risked the Alabama in a sort of duel of ships!…Forgive who may! I cannot."[10]

The scene inspired Thomas Buchanan Read, who wrote precisely the sort of hollow patriotic verse that Edmund Wilson later denounced, to recall, in "The Eagle and the Vulture":

The Cherbourg Cliffs were all
*   alive*
With lookers-on, like a swarming hive;
While compelled to do what he dared not
*   shirk,*
The pirate went to his desperate work;
And Europe's tyrants looked on in glee,
As they thought of our Kearsarge sunk in
*   the sea.*

But our little bark smiled back at them
A smile of contempt, with that Union
*   gem,*
The American banner, far-floating and
*   free,*
Proclaiming her champions were out on
*   the sea;*
Were out on the sea, and abroad in the
*   land,*
Determined to win under God's com-
*   mand.*[11]

Most Civil War naval battles, even the ones not involving ironclads, bore little resemblance to this tournament-style duel between two vessels in the open sea. Union attacks on Confederate harbors like New Orleans, Charleston, and Mobile involved large numbers of ships and threatened civilian lives in ship-to-shore bombardments. But the stately quality of the wooden ships, prowling alone on the open seas, always suggested something of the chivalry of Semmes's nautical world. The battle

between the *Monitor* and *Merrimac* was essentially a two-vessel duel as well, for the wooden ships nearby could have little effect on their battle, but it lacked any of the other chivalric connotations Semmes gave the fight between the *Kearsarge* and the *Alabama*.

No one captured that quality more skillfully than Xanthus Smith, the son of a Philadelphia artist, who had, throughout his own service in the war, kept "busy with his sketch-book and pencils at all times that permitted." After the war, during which Smith served with Adm. Samuel du Pont in Charleston, he returned to Philadelphia and launched a long and successful career as a marine painter. His immense painting of the *Alabama* engagement might appear to have little about it that could be differentiated from other pictures of the same subject, and it must be confessed that marine paintings generally seem dauntingly similar at first glance. But a closer look at works depicting this battle reveals the differing sentiments of the marine artists of the American Civil War.

In Smith's painting, the *Alabama* sinks in the foreground while the *Kearsarge*, shown in profile in the background, observes from a respectful distance. The Union ship's profile, however, is notable for the absence of the three lifeboats customarily suspended by davits above each side of her hull. Presumably these boats have been launched and are the ones seen carrying to safety the surviving sailors from the Confederate ship. Barely visible at the *Kearsarge*'s stern is the English yacht *Deerhound*, heading in the direction of the *Alabama* to pick up the rest of the floundering crewmen, some of whom are seen clinging to wreckage in the center foreground (the *Deerhound* saved Semmes himself).

The *Alabama*'s broken mainmast,

≈ *Opposite* ≈

DESTRUCTION OF THE CONFEDERATE STEAMER ALABAMA BY THE U.S. IRONCLAD KEARSARGE (1864)

Edwin Hayes (1820–1904)

As suggested by both its perspective and its title (with the invidious reference to the Union ship as an ironclad), this painting presented the sinking of the Alabama *from the Confederate point of view. The British yacht* Deerhound *can be seen steaming toward the survivors of the rapidly sinking* Alabama, *whose decks are, in an eyewitness's words, "covered with the dead and the wounded…the ship…careening heavily to the starboard from the effects of the shot-holes on her waterline."*

Oil on canvas, 20 × 30¼ inches.
(The Chicago Historical Society)

≈ Opposite ≈

**ALABAMA AND
KEARSARGE
(BOSTON, 1887)**

L[ouis]. Prang & Co., after
Julian Oliver Davidson
(1853–1894)

*Among the innumerable peri-
od depictions of the famous
naval encounter off
Cherbourg, this one was
unusual in portraying the
fray from the deck of the
Union vessel. Sailors are
shown close up and in various stages of action: directing
fire, hauling lines, and cheering on the attack on the
Confederate raider. The blood-
spattered deck, meanwhile, tes-
tifies to the sacrifice the*
Alabama's *conquest required.
Like many other artists who
depicted the battle, Davidson
relied on the* Harper's
Weekly *woodcut of the sinking* Alabama *as the model for
the ship as viewed from the
deck of the* Kearsarge.

Chromolithograph, 15 × 22
inches. Signed, lower left: *J. O.
Davidson.* (The Lincoln Museum)

incidentally, was an accurate detail available in Captain Winslow's report.
Accuracy in marine paintings typically
posed highly technical problems stem-
ming from bewildering rigging patterns
and mysterious jargon. Smith was a
sailor but, of course, was not present at
Cherbourg in 1864, and he very likely
derived his image of the sinking
Alabama (as did J. O. Davidson) from
the illustration of the event in the July
23, 1864, issue of *Harper's Weekly*.

Whatever the source, the result was
declared accurate when Smith's canvas
was finally presented to Philadelphia's
Union League in 1906. At ceremonies
attended by the sixty-seven-year-old
painter, the club's art association
announced that "a participant in the
scene depicted" had given it "careful
scrutiny" and verified its accuracy.[12]

The Union League's observer was surely a veteran of the Federal side, for others
saw a different contest from the one
Smith painted. The Irish painter Edwin
Hayes, by comparison, depicted the same
event but with a dissimilar visual message.
The major elements are the same as in
Smith's later canvas: the *Alabama* sinks in
the foreground while the *Kearsarge* waits
in the background, and the *Deerhound*
steams around the Union ship's stern on
its mission of rescue. But in Hayes's painting the lifeboats of the Union vessel are
still conspicuously hanging from their
mounts. In fact, Hayes puts the focus
more on the struggling Confederate
sailors in the foreground, an emphasis
heightened by the poor souls shown div-
ing into the ocean at horizon level in the
very center of the canvas.

Smith's may be called the Union view:
Captain Winslow dispatched his
lifeboats as promptly as he dared, to save
the Confederate sailors from drowning.
Hayes, on the other hand, presents the
Confederate view, well articulated by

Raphael Semmes: through cowardice,
incompetence, or malice the Union
commander left the Confederate sailors
to their fate—until the English yacht
and a couple of nearby French boats
went to the work of mercy. For his part,
Captain Winslow at first tacitly admitted
some delay, reporting that

> *toward the close of the action between
> the* Alabama *and this vessel all
> available sail was made on the for-
> mer for the purpose of again reach-
> ing Cherbourg. When the object was
> apparent the* Kearsarge *was steered
> across the bow of the* Alabama *for a
> raking fire, but before reaching this
> point the* Alabama *struck.
> Uncertain whether Captain Semmes
> was not using some ruse, the*
> Kearsarge *was stopped. It was seen
> shortly after that the* Alabama *was
> lowering her boats, and an officer
> came alongside in one of them to say
> that they had surrendered and were
> fast sinking, and begging that boats
> would be dispatched immediately for
> saving of life. The two boats not dis-
> abled were at once lowered....*[13]

Thus Winslow admitted to some
delay, caused by fear of a piratical trick.
Semmes said flatly, "There was no
appearance of any boat coming to me
from the enemy until after the ship
went down."[14] The pro-Confederate
painter Hayes went so far as to call his
work *Destruction of the Confederate Steamer
"Alabama" by the U.S. Ironclad "Kearsarge."*
The *Kearsarge* was no "ironclad," but
Semmes had made a point of the
unfairness of Winslow's laying chains
over the sides of his wooden vessel and
concealing them.

> *At the end of the engagement it was
> discovered by those of our officers who*

went alongside the enemy's ship with the wounded that her midship section on both sides was thoroughly iron-coated, this having been done with chains constructed for the purpose, placed perpendicularly from the rail to the water's edge, the whole covered over by a thin outer planking, which gave no indication of the armor beneath. The planking had been ripped off in every direction by our shot and shell, the chain broken and indented in many places, and forced partly into the ship's side. She was most effectually guarded, however, in this section from penetration.... I did not know until the action was over that she was ironclad.[15]

Only a Confederate, or a Confed-erate sympathizer, would call the *Kearsarge* an "ironclad." And only a Yankee would call the *Alabama*, as Smith did in the title of his painting, a "Pirate."

Smith and Hayes thus offered their patrons visual partisan propaganda along with their seascapes. These paintings cannot properly be used together to "illustrate" the sinking of the *Alabama*, though they have been, for example, in the *American Heritage Picture History of The Civil War*. They illustrate only the diametrically opposed points of view of the two individual painters and require some critical assessment to be fully understood. The circumstances that led Smith to depict the battle off Cherbourg make clear the viewpoint of the resulting canvas. The Union League of Philadelphia commissioned Smith to

(The Lincoln Museum)

FLAG OF FORT SUMTER, OCTOBER 20, 1863 (1864)

Conrad Wise Chapman (1842–1910)

*Union ships choke Charleston harbor in a formidable blockade, as seen from the vantage point
of a lone Confederate sentry standing beneath the tattered flag of Fort Sumter. Conceived as a
landscape painting, part of a series of harbor studies Chapman created for Gen. P. G. T. Beauregard,
the view also took honest measure of Federal maritime might. By the time Chapman made this scene,
the constant bombardment by the Union fleet had reduced the Sumter parapet wall almost to rubble.
His painting nevertheless suggests eternal endurance and defiance, as the Confederates continue to
fly their banner from a makeshift flagpole.*

Oil on board, 9¾ × 13¾ inches. (The Museum of the Confederacy, Richmond, Virginia;
photograph by Katherine Wetzel)

SUBMARINE TORPEDO BOAT H. L. HUNLEY, DECEMBER 6, 1863 (1864)

Conrad Wise Chapman (1842–1910)

The so-called submersible Hunley *prefigured one of the greatest nightmares of World War I: submarine warfare. Its operation, however, was almost primitive: it took a crew of eight to propel it by hand with a crank, and it could achieve speeds of no more than four miles per hour. Here the tiny vessel sits in drydock on a Charleston wharf, guarded by two informally dressed soldiers, one of whom (right) is a self-portrait of artist Chapman. The sailboat at left provides a counterpoint to the hideously efficient machine-age vessel, depicted virtually with the details of a technical drawing. The* Hunley *sank with all hands lost in an action on February 17, 1864, when she torpedoed the* USS Housatonic *in Charleston harbor.*

Oil on board, 9⅞ × 13⅞ inches. (The Museum of the Confederacy, Richmond, Virginia; photograph by Katherine Wetzel)

paint the scene, and the club had already awarded Captain Winslow a silver medal and published his account of the battle.[16]

Though they enlisted on opposite emotional sides in their painting, the artists Hayes and Smith shared, on a different level, a common outlook: they both romanticized naval warfare and glossed over the pivoting and clanking meanness captured in Melville's poetic vision of naval engagements in the machine age.

Even ignoring the advent of the hideous-looking ironclad vessels, one can see that Civil War naval combat, if thoughtfully considered, seems hardly adaptable to the conventions of heroic war painting. For one thing, individuals counted for less on sea than on land. Machines counted for more, for if a ship sank, all heroic individual human effort became useless. Among the humans at sea, success obviously depended on teamwork: coal stokers, pilots, and gun crews all had to work at once to move a vessel into position and fire projectiles at the mostly unseen enemy, sailors and marines like themselves, cowering behind oaken walls. The days of closing with the enemy's ship, grappling her sides, boarding, and fighting with cutlass and dirk were over. Skilled gunnery, with high-powered artillery aimed in pitching seas, held the real key to success. Even a commander

as chivalry-minded as Raphael Semmes recognized that his defeat by the *Kearsarge* stemmed mainly from two artillery problems. First, as a commerce raider, the *Alabama* enjoyed few opportunities to practice gunnery on the unarmed merchant prey that surrendered to her without a fight. Second, because she did not often fire her guns, the *Alabama*'s ammunition was old and damp and frequently failed to detonate (this included a potentially fatal shot that lodged in the *Kearsarge* in a spot unprotected by her "chain mail," but did not explode).

Nevertheless, marine painters sometimes managed to invoke an atmosphere of individual courage by featuring elegant wooden ships dueling, almost as individuals themselves, in rolling seas. This vision had grown dimmer with the advent of the ironclads, their crews completely invisible and banging away at each other through slits in curved or slanting walls of, as one technical naval writer described them, "5½ inches of yellow pine, laid horizontally…4 inches of oak laid up and down…and…armor, 6 inches thick, in thin plates of 2 inches each…. Within, the yellow pine frames were sheathed with 2¼ inches of oak." Those happened to be the specifications of the Confederate ironclad ram *Tennessee*, a vessel that proved to be the most important floating obstacle to the Federal capture of Mobile later in the same summer in which the *Alabama* sank.[17]

It was the genius of William Heysham Overend's painting of the *Hartford*, seen as that ship brushed against the sides of the *Tennessee* in the Battle of Mobile Bay on August 5, 1864, that it gave to naval combat a close-up focus similar to that more often given to land battles. What the viewer sees is a group of individuals struggling mightily on deck in combat against the darkly menacing smoky gun-port and 45-degree-slanted iron sides of the Confederate ship. In the near background, Rear Adm. David G. Farragut leans out bravely into the combat zone, daringly lashed to the port main rigging of his flagship. Farragut was sixty-three years old at the time and hardly in the best of health, as years of sailing in southern waters had left him with several chronic disabilities (Overend made the rear admiral perhaps a little too youthful in appearance, though Farragut did try to maintain his vigor with regular exercise). Farragut's heroic action inspired other artists, and popular prints as well, but it failed to gain quite the fame it deserved.

Nevertheless, the battle at Mobile Bay may well be the most storied large-scale naval engagement of the Civil War. As the Union fleet steamed through a narrow channel left open for Confederate blockade runners to depart, it was battered by fire from Fort Morgan. The lead ship, one of four ironclad monitors, struck a sea mine, which was called a torpedo in that era, and sank immediately, with only twenty-one saved of her crew of more than one hundred men. When another vessel balked at the sight of floating mines, Farragut is said to have shouted, "Damn the torpedoes! Full speed ahead." Accounts differ in regard to his specific words, but the *Hartford* did steam into the bay and, avoiding the *Tennessee* through superior speed, pulled up a good distance away for her crew's breakfast. It was about eight-thirty in the morning and the ship had been fighting since about seven o'clock. In twenty minutes, just as the sweating sailors sat down to their well-deserved meal, the *Tennessee* was seen steering toward the *Hartford.* Sweeping the mess aside, the men sprang to action, and the *Hartford* attempted to ram the *Tennessee.* She avoided the Union vessel and the two ships brushed against each other on their port sides. That was the moment Overend chose to capture in his canvas.

The dramatic encounter left the *Hartford*'s anchor bent double between the two ships' sides. At first, seven nine-inch guns charged with maximum powder load and firing solid shot did not harm the *Tennessee,* though they fired from only ten feet away. Shortly thereafter the *Tennessee* was finally disabled by the *Hartford* and other Union ships. As she surrendered, an officer waved a white flag from the roof of the armored casemate. A Union ship, seeing the gesture too late to halt, rammed the *Tennessee* again, a glancing blow apparently, and as she did so, the captain of the U.S. ship shouted to the Confederate with the flag, "Hallo, Johnston, old fellow! How are you? This is the United States Steamer *Ossipee.* I'll send a boat alongside for you. LeRoy, don't you know me?" And with that eerie reminder of the gallantry of dueling individuals in warfare, the battle ended, and in a short time Mobile fell to the Yankees.[18]

With competing events as dramatic as Mobile Bay and as revolutionary as the *Monitor* and the *Merrimac,* why should a quite different and distant event—the sinking of the *Alabama*—loom so large in the art of the Civil War? It was perhaps because the victory of the *Kearsarge* enjoyed two memorable qualities transcending its strategic value. For one thing, this naval victory played a subtle role in Republican political victory in 1864. Celebrating these recent Union triumphs in the presidential election year proved to be a way of promoting Lincoln's leadership without any overtly partisan message. Gideon Welles hinted at this in his famous diary when he com-

[ADMIRAL DAVID DIXON PORTER] (C. 1877)

Carl J. Becker (nineteenth century)

Porter spent most of the early war in the shadow of other Union admirals. Only reluctantly admitting that he had "capabilities," Secretary of the Navy Gideon Welles was still insisting as late as March 1863 that Porter was "by no means" even "an Admiral Foote." But Porter emerged a hero in his own right at Vicksburg and Fort Fisher, and proved particularly adept at cooperating with the army on joint land-sea assaults. Navigating the tree-lined bayous near Vicksburg one day, Porter, typically suppressing instincts for interservice rivalry, jokingly wrote to Sherman, "Hurry up, for Heaven's sake. I never knew how helpless an ironclad could be steaming around through the woods without an army to back her." Yet this formidable military portrait revealed nothing of the effacement crucial to this naval hero's success.

Oil on canvas, 72 × 48 inches. (United States Naval Academy Museum, Annapolis)

THE USS WABASH LEAVING NEW YORK FOR THE SEAT OF WAR, 1861 (N.D.)

Edward Moran
(1829–1901)

The handsome screw frigate Wabash, *flagship of Admiral du Pont, prepares to take on Union volunteers in the choppy waters of New York Bay in 1861. Troops thus transported would never have recalled the* Wabash *as romantically. One who endured such a passage to war recalled "the contents of hundreds of disordered stomachs cast in every direction and dripping through the berths upon the occupants of the berths below." The odors, he remembered, were "indescribable." This skilled marine painting offered no reminders of such unpleasantness, emphasizing instead patriotism and natural grandeur.*

Oil on canvas, 40 × 60 inches. (U.S. Naval Academy Museum, Annapolis)

mented on another Union success in 1864, Sheridan's Shenandoah Valley campaign, by saying that the general's "victory...had a party-political influence. It is not gratifying to the opponents of the Administration. Some who want to rejoice in it felt it difficult to do so, because they are conscious that it strengthens the Administration, to which they are opposed."[19] Union military victories in the autumn of 1864, most notably the capture of Atlanta, by all admissions provided the key to Lincoln's political success.

On the very eve of election day, the night of November 7, 1864, the *Kearsarge* returned to Boston harbor, and the celebrations of the naval victory that followed, of course, could not have been calculated for political effect. But when the secretary of the navy had told the president and the rest of the cabinet about the victory off Cherbourg early in July, it had become "a matter of general congratulation and rejoicing."[20] And there followed "great rejoicing throughout the country."[21] With little else to rejoice about before September, this naval victory probably received more than its fair share of public attention in the North.

The sinking of the *Alabama* had another thrilling quality, long since forgotten by twentieth-century Americans: it was, as Gideon Welles put it at the time, "universally and justly conceded a triumph over England as well as the Rebels."[22] About this, Welles was surely correct. Currier & Ives, for example, published two different lithographs of the battle between the *Alabama* and *Kearsarge*, and both carried this subtitle:

The "Alabama" was built in a British ship-yard, by British workmen, with British oak, armed with British guns, manned with British sailors, trained

in the British navy, and was sunk in the British channel in 80 minutes, by the Yankee sloop of war "Kearsarge" Capt. John A. Winslow.

The protracted dispute with Great Britain over the *Alabama* claims for years after the war likewise helped keep alive the memory of the *Kearsarge*'s extraordinary feat and emphasized the degree to which it had constituted a victory over the European power.

These factors made the "duel" between

the *Alabama* and the *Kearsarge* perhaps disproportionately famous, but they did not determine the way it would be depicted in art. What guaranteed its fame among artists was its antique appearance and the fact that it involved only two vessels. Artists preferred to focus on decisive moments of individual courage, like the one shown in an illustration in *Battles and Leaders* (and in paintings as well) of individual cavalrymen locked in a death struggle. The naval equivalent of such rare moments in land warfare was the victory of the *Kearsarge*, achieved not by a fleet, as were Farragut's important triumphs at New Orleans and Mobile Bay, but by one ship, battling under what might fairly be described as the terms and conditions of an old-fashioned duel. So pervasive was this anachronistic ideal of warfare that Farragut himself said of Winslow's victory, "I had sooner have fought that fight than any ever fought upon the ocean!"[23] (Farragut fought his own famous actions in bays and harbors rather than on the ocean, and his statement may have been cannily worded.)

CONFEDERATE BLOCKADE RUNNERS IN HARBOR, CIVIL WAR (1881)

William Torgerson
(nineteenth century)

Blockade runners, small, sleek, and painted white to blend in with the horizon, are poised to take on supplies from larger European cargo ships in the thronged harbor off St. George, Bermuda. This crowded vista, reminiscent of traditional harbor scenes celebrating commercial prowess, documented what would come to be regarded as Bermuda's golden age. The Civil War blockade brought the island unparalleled prosperity as a transfer point. Visiting St. George early in the war, a Confederate observed "eight or ten blockade-runners lying in the harbor," as this scene recalls.

Oil on canvas, 34 × 52 inches. Signed: *Wm. Torgerson, 1881.* (West Point Museum, U.S. Military Academy)

The picturesque imperative that boosted the popularity of the *Alabama* and *Kearsarge* as a subject for marine painting lay in the engagement's involvement of wooden ships on the open sea. The bolts and rivets of the *Merrimac*, like the machine-shop perfections of Columbiads and Armstrong cannons, Parrott rifles and Whitworth guns, rarely engaged the imaginations of Civil War painters. True, the battle off Hampton Roads could not be ignored, but only Conrad Wise Chapman and J. O. Davidson painted such subjects as coastal artillery or the bolted iron sides of the innovative submarine vessel *Hunley* with meticulous fascination. The triumph of military technology was rarely a theme of Civil War paintings.

All the same, technology could not easily be ignored in naval paintings, which dealt with the branch of warfare most affected by technical innovation. And time, to some degree, rectified matters of historical reputation for the ironclad ships. *Fin de siècle* navalism, prompted by the great naval theoretician Alfred Thayer Mahan (who also wrote an excellent history of Civil War naval action), saw the United States join in great shipbuilding contests with the European powers and Japan. Surely this gave a boost to naval painting just as the 1880s revival of interest in the Civil War did. Mahan's book appeared in 1890. And it even helped marine painters who nostalgically preferred the old wooden ships. Armored ships were all the rage in the world's navy yards, but a general emphasis on naval tradition proved a boon as well to those painters who looked at the sea nostalgically.[24]

Edward Moran, for example, one of three painting brothers (he specialized in seascapes; Peter, animals; Thomas, landscapes), executed a series of thir-

teen large canvases of maritime events in American history. The group included some very old wooden sailing ships and culminated in a painting of the triumphant return of the American ships from the Spanish-American War. His one Civil War scene was the sinking of the *Cumberland* by the *Merrimac*, and its thematic role seems obvious: the appearance of the Confederate ironclad off Hampton Roads caused the disappearance of the wooden sailing navy and foretold the coming of armored naval vessels, powered by steam, that brought victory and imperialism to the United States at the end of the nineteenth century.

Thus the foreshadowing role of the *Merrimac* and the *Monitor* remained inescapably evident, and the fight off Cherbourg eventually dimmed in memory as the ironclads seemed ever more relevant to twentieth-century warfare.

But in art the reputations had been established. Historians might revise the war in books, but painters did not return to Civil War themes for decades and decades in the twentieth century. In the reproductions of old paintings used to illustrate new books on the Civil War, the *Kearsarge* has sailed on and on, and the sinking of the *Alabama*, as much as those of the *Cumberland* and *Congress*, marks the symbolic last stand of the wooden navy, both in art and on the seas.

AN AUGUST MORNING WITH FARRAGUT: THE BATTLE OF MOBILE BAY, AUGUST 5, 1864 (1883)

William Heysham Overend (1851–1898)

Adm. David Glasgow Farragut leans dramatically out into the fray as the fearsome Confederate ironclad Tennessee *brushes menacingly against the side of his flagship. In this rare depiction not of the exterior of a vessel, but of the crew aboard it, Overend captured the intense concentration of the sailors. Whereas Farragut was heroically depicted, Overend gave him a role in the painting subordinate to the gripping work of the nameless seamen. In fact, he was lashed to the futlock rigging of the* Hartford *in a widely reported act of courage, inexplicably omitted here.*

Oil on canvas, 6 feet 5½ inches × 10 feet. (Wadsworth Atheneum, Hartford, Connecticut; gift of the citizens of Hartford)

FOUR

GLORY

*Poetic License
in History Paintings
and Portraits*

≈ *Preceding Page* ≈

THE HORNET'S NEST
(1895)

Thomas Corwin Lindsay
(1839–1907)

*For six hours on April 6,
1862, courageous Union
troops held their ground
against ferocious Confederate
attacks opposite the Peach
Orchard at Shiloh. Although
they were eventually
overrun and crushed, their
spirited defense gave the
Union time to reinforce Shiloh
and likely turned a defeat
into victory. Because bullets
swarmed into the field like
hornets, Confederates dubbed
the stand "The Hornet's
Nest." Lindsay focused this
visual record on Capt.
Andrew Hickenlooper
(astride his horse), a fellow
Cincinnatian, but showed
little interest in portraying
the equipment necessary for
firing cannon.*

Oil on canvas, 35½ × 54½ inches.
Signed lower right: *T C Lindsay/1895*.
(The Cincinnati Historical Society;
gift of Mrs. Eugene R. Farny, 1980)

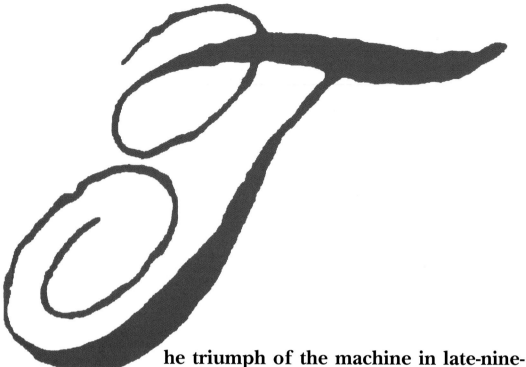

he triumph of the machine in late-nine-teenth-century America did not bring with it a dark realization of what the industrial revolution had wrought in the recent Civil War. Instead a renaissance of interest in the Civil War brought a glorious luster to the remem-bered exploits of the 1860s. Along with this new enthusiasm for the subject came artistic perspectives different from those of the landscapists and marine painters. But it took time for glory rather than rancor to dominate reflections on the war: these developments did not occur until about twenty years after Appomattox.

The 1880s witnessed a surge in interest in the Civil War—no one can say exactly why. Who knows how much time must pass before memories of war change from raw irritants to vaguely pleasing recollections of glory? Early on, Americans shunned the subject of their recent war. Fewer Civil War novels appeared in the decade of the 1870s than in any other subsequent period in American history. Popular magazines at first avoided a subject thought to be divisive and possibly offensive or painful to some readers. *Scribner's Monthly*, founded in 1870, did not publish any Civil War articles before the country's centennial year. Afterward, a few were accepted, thirteen between 1876 and 1880. The magazine's competitors exhibited similar tastes: *Harper's Monthly* accepted but two Civil War articles between 1869 and 1873, and the *North American Review* carried only one from 1869 to 1876. Magazines now carried illustrations, of course, but their pages as yet offered little to stimulate visual interest in the Civil War or to develop further the skills of military illustrators.[1]

The 1880s proved to be the water-

THE HEROES OF MANASSAS (C. 1863–65)

W. B. Cox (1829–1873)

Jefferson Davis's appearance at Bull Run surprised few of his Richmond admirers. Cheered government clerk John B. Jones, "I… believe he will gain great glory in this first mighty conflict." In fact, as Gen. Joseph E. Johnston reported, Davis "arrived upon the field after the last armed enemy had left it." But the president did little to correct reports that he had actually led a wing of the army. Neither did sympathetic artists. This equestrian war council not only portrayed the commander-in-chief on the field with authentic Bull Run heroes P. G. T. Beauregard, Stonewall Jackson, and Joe Johnston; the artist inserted a live shell with a burning fuse in close enough proximity to blow up the entire Confederate high command.

Oil on canvas, 20 × 26½ inches. (West Point Museum, U.S. Military Academy; photograph courtesy *American Heritage*)

shed decade. The United States government opened the new era with the publication in 1880 of the initial volumes of *The War of the Rebellion: A Compilation of the Official Records of the Union and Confederate Armies*, a series eventually comprising 128 books and including an additional thirty-one-volume series of naval records. These, except for the naval volumes (published later), carried no illustrations save in an atlas appendix, and those consisted mostly of technical drawings and photographs. In 1881, Scribner's began publishing a series of books entitled *Campaigns of the Civil War*, each by a distinguished military writer. Fifteen volumes in all appeared by the end of 1883, including

three called *The Navy in the Civil War*. All were bound in blue cloth stamped with military motifs, but none carried illustrations inside. Late in 1886, *Century Magazine* (formerly *Scribner's*) began serialization of the mammoth history of the Lincoln administration written by the president's former private secretaries, John G. Nicolay and John Hay. The series was unillustrated.

The turning point for art was the decision of the editors of *Century* in 1883 to publish in their magazine a con-tinuing series of articles on Civil War battles written by participants, mainly famous generals from both sides, and illustrated with new line drawings and copies of photographs. The editors shrewdly chose to suppress the political issue of race in favor of pure military history. Editor-in-chief Richard Watson Gilder told a series researcher, "'*Battles*' is the main thing. 'Events' might seem as if we were going into, say, the condition & action of the freedmen—The Emancipation Proclamation—& other

events not connected with the battles." The articles, which began to appear in November 1884, ran through 1887 and nearly doubled the magazine's circulation in the first year alone. The pieces were gathered, supplemented, and then published as the famous four-volume set, *Battles and Leaders of the Civil War*, in 1888. It sold 75,000 copies.[2]

Illustrations proved crucial to the success of the series, so much so that in 1894 a one-volume *Century War Book*, subtitled the "People's Pictorial Edition" of *Battles and Leaders*, also appeared. By the middle of the 1890s, however, the impulse given to Civil War art had already borne considerable fruit at all levels of employment of pen, pencil, and brush, with veterans' organizations increasing in size, stimulating interest, and offering patronage.

It is significant that the renaissance in battle art came from private patronage or from the artists themselves who, unlike the painters of old, produced many of their wares "on speculation"—without a buyer or already-contracted patron. In fact, perhaps the most notable quality of Civil War art is that almost none of it was "official." Lincoln's tiny government never dreamed of patronage of military artists while soldiers shivered in shoddy blankets. Likewise, the Confederacy's patronage—like Beauregard's of Chapman—seems not to have been a matter of official government policy, but of the commanding officer's whim

in finding an appointment for a soldier who happened to know how to draw or paint. Mid-nineteenth-century governments had virtually no notion of propaganda and what little they had focused exclusively on words rather than pictures. What is remarkable is that many painters produced Civil War art quickly.

Makers of popular prints rose to the occasion, too, initiating series of Civil War battle prints in distinctive styles. Heretofore, lithographers and engravers had produced portraits and an occasional battle scene, but there had been no series of battle depictions since the rather crude ones quickly turned out during the war by Currier & Ives and other popular printmakers as news items more than "collectible" sets. Boston's Louis Prang and Chicago's Kurz & Allison changed all that in the 1880s, producing popular prints that dominate dust jackets and advertisements for Civil War books to this day. Perhaps feeling the same impulse that *Century*'s editors had felt, the chromolithographers also focused on battle scenes. The date of the initial chromos is so early—1885—that, allowing the time necessary for commissioning original paintings to be copied on stones, it seems unlikely that the articles in *Century*, which began only in late 1884, spurred their appearance. All of these serial Civil War productions were instead more than likely stimulated by the same mysterious phenomenon ushered in by the simultaneous cooling of war animosities and the warming of curiosity about the great conflict.

The result was a flowering of retrospective Civil War glory. The veterans themselves had quickly learned that people at home did not want to hear about war's gruesome realities any more than the old soldiers wanted to admit to some of them—for example, fear.

BEHIND THE UNION LINE (c. 1886–87)

Thure de Thulstrup (1848–1930)

Seeing Gen. John A. Logan "powder-stained…his long, black hair floating in the breeze" at Kenesaw, one soldier thought he "looked like a mighty conqueror of medieval days." Here, astride the black mount at left, he orders his troops to charge up Kenesaw Mountain, as Union artillery lends support by pounding away at Confederate positions on the heights. In the foreground, the fragility of these heroic fighting men is acknowledged in the vignette of the early casualty of the fighting being carried to the rear. Thulstrup may have been at his best when painting groups of staff officers, observing battle and identified by their pennant, near a mounted general—as in the group at left. He managed to focus interest on both the fighting men and their general.

Watercolor and gouache on paper, 15 × 21 inches. Signed lower left: *Thulstrup*. (The Seventh Regiment Fund, Inc.)

FIGHT FOR THE STANDARD (c. 1865)

Artist unknown

A Union cavalryman plunges his saber into the heart of a Confederate color bearer in this dramatic portrayal of a life-and-death battlefield confrontation over a regimental flag. During the war, such banners were regarded as almost sacred, and their bearers achieved the status of cavaliers (and of prime targets for enemy marksmen). Writing of "Rebel color-bearers at Shiloh," Herman Melville immortalized the men who faced death, "glorying in their show," noting that "their battle-flags about them blow, and fold them as in flame divine." But this painting, widely reproduced, in fact falsified Civil War history in several ways: few men suffered wounds from edged weapons; cavalrymen rarely fought each other on horseback; and ultimately the war was not decided by duels between individuals on horseback fighting like knights or musketeers.

Oil on canvas, 26⅜ × 21½ inches. (Wadsworth Atheneum, Hartford: Ella Gallup Sumner and Mary Catlon Sumner Collection)

BVT. MAJ. GEN. ROBERT ANDERSON (1892)

Alban Jasper Conant (1821–1914)

The man who surrendered Fort Sumter to the Confederacy in April 1861 was quickly transformed into a Union hero, defeat notwithstanding. Only a few days later, appearing in New York City to salute the Sixty-ninth Regiment as it marched off to war, Anderson was greeted with "prolonged shouts of applause" by the troops and equally vociferous cheering from the crowds of civilians. The huge cannon here, the sort used only in fortifications and not on the field, suggested the locus of his most important action.

Oil on canvas, 62⅜ × 45¼ inches. (West Point Museum, U.S. Military Academy)

DEATH OF ELLSWORTH (c. 1862)

Alonzo Chappel (1828–1887)

The dashing young Zouave colonel Elmer Ephraim Ellsworth became the first elaborately mourned Union martyr of the war when innkeeper James Jackson (right) shot him dead after he ripped down the Confederate flag flying over his hotel in Alexandria, just across the river from Washington. Ellsworth "dropped forward with the heavy, horrible, headlong weight which always comes with sudden death," said a New York Tribune *correspondent who accompanied the publicity-conscious colonel and described the event Chappel here immortalized in oil. Here the artist shows him frozen picturesquely against a wall. Seconds later, Corporal Francis E. Brownell, shown here trying to deflect Jackson's attack, killed Ellsworth's slayer. (In the painting, Brownell's posed figure appears to be based on a photograph.) The prolific painter Alonzo Chappel became principally a book illustrator and apparently painted this scene, like many others, for Johnson, Fry & Company, who engraved a copy of it in 1862.*

Oil on canvas, 24½ × 20 inches.
(Chicago Historical Society)

Opposite

**BATTLE OF KENESAW
MOUNTAIN (1889)**

Thure de Thulstrup
(1848–1930)

*As General Sherman looks
on, oblivious to enemy fire,
Confederate artillery from the
cloudy heights of Kenesaw
Mountain near Marietta,
Georgia, rains down on
Federal troops as they mass
for their assault on June 27,
1864. Thulstrup presented
a full panoply of Union
might in this panoramic
scene: caissons moving to the
front (left), lines of foot
soldiers poised to charge
(center), and color bearers
and musicians (right). But
the focus remained on the
immovable Sherman, on
whose face Thulstrup inexplicably painted whiskers far
thicker than the beard he wore
at the time.*

Oil on canvas, 43 × 65 inches. Signed
lower right: *Thulstrup/copyright 1889.*
(Kenesaw Mountain National
Battlefield Park)

Likewise, as the historian Gerald Linderman had suggested, many among the rest of the American people, who had not seen warfare firsthand and thus had less reason to sober their attitudes about war than the old soldiers had, came to desire celebrations of individual courage along with sanitized depictions of battlefield actions.[3]

Chromolithography satisfied the demands of a mass audience, but even such popular media brought patronage to painters and illustrators, who in some instances provided the model works of art to be copied on the printmakers' stones and plates. And the prints themselves sometimes provided useful views of Civil War battles. For example, the truth about the Battle of Kenesaw Mountain, Georgia, fought in 1864 by Gen. William T. Sherman against Gen. Joseph E. Johnston, was told simply but well by a cheap chromo. In Kurz & Allison's chromolithograph, Gen. Charles Harker, receiving a mortal wound, leads Union soldiers while Gen. Daniel McCook (of the celebrated "Fighting McCooks"), already mortally wounded, is carried to the rear. The Confederate infantry, impregnably entrenched (but improbably uniformed in matching spruce clothing and splendidly equipped), sweeps the attackers with devastating rifle and cannon fire.

General Sherman should have known better than to attempt such an attack. He admitted as much in his *Memoirs*:

> *…the enemy's position was so
> very strong, and everywhere it was
> covered by intrenchments, that we
> found it as dangerous to assault
> as a permanent fort. We in like
> manner covered our lines of battle
> by similar works….*

> *The enemy and ourselves used*

the same form of rifle-trench, varied according to the nature of the ground, viz.: the trees and bushes were cut away for a hundred yards or more in front, serving as an abatis or entanglement; the parapets varied from four to six feet high, the dirt taken from a ditch outside and from a covered way inside, and this parapet was surmounted by a "head-log," composed of the trunk of a tree from twelve to twenty inches at the butt, lying along the interior crest of the parapet and resting in notches cut in other trunks which extended back, forming an inclined plane, in case the head-log should be knocked inward by a cannon-shot.*

Entrenchments were a distinguishing feature of Civil War battles by 1864, and especially of those fought by the cautious Confederate Gen. Joseph E. Johnston, who tried to block Sherman's approach to Atlanta. "During this campaign," Sherman recalled, "hundreds if not thousands of miles of similar intrenchments were built by both armies, and, as a rule, whichever party attacked got the worst of it."[4]

Generals rarely find good excuses for defeat. In his official report on the battle, written in September 1864, Sherman said,

> *I had no alternative…but to
> assault his lines or turn his position.
> Either course had its difficulties
> and dangers, and I perceived that
> the enemy and our own officers had
> settled down into a conviction that
> I would not assault fortified lines.
> All looked to me to outflank. An
> army to be efficient must not settle
> down to a single mode of offense,
> but must be prepared to execute any
> plan which promises success.*

When he wrote his memoirs a decade later, Sherman changed his story, maintaining that his lines were so thinned by attempting to stretch them around Johnston that they could stretch no more and he was compelled to attack the defenses atop Kenesaw Mountain. Whatever the reason, Sherman attacked on June 27, 1864. Kurz & Allison, who always listed the number of casualties in the battles depicted in their prints (an odd statistical counterweight to their otherwise sanitized depictions of warfare), put them at three thousand for Sherman and six hundred for Johnston. These are nearer the figures Sherman used in his *Memoirs* than Johnston's. In fact, modern authorities put them at about two thousand to four hundred fifty. Kurz & Allison obviously relied mostly on Union sources. And they did

some research: their depiction of General Harker, for example, was more or less a portrait likeness (he wore the sort of muttonchop sidewhiskers shown in their print).[5]

The battle was also depicted by military artist Thure de Thulstrup. Many of Thulstrup's paintings that survive in public collections today also came as a result of printmakers' entrepreneurship. One of his two depictions of the Battle of Kenesaw Mountain provided the basis for a chromolithograph issued in 1887 by Boston's Louis Prang. Thulstrup's work showed more polish than the stiff Kurz & Allison views, which were as stylized as Epinal prints, the primitive woodcuts mass-produced in Epinal, France. But Thulstrup surveyed the scene from a point so far to the rear as to lose the simple force of

THE BATTLE OF GETTYSBURG: REPULSE OF LONGSTREET'S ASSAULT, JULY 3, 1863 (1863–68)

James Walker (1819–1889)

Union forces hold the Angle at Gettysburg against the fierce onslaught of Pickett's Charge in this swarming, richly detailed panorama depicting what journalist Charles Carleton Coffin called "a turning point of history and of human destiny." While the battle rages, the fatally wounded Confederate general Lewis A. Armistead can be seen (foreground, right center), presenting his personal possessions to Union soldiers, and asking that they be turned over to his old friend, Union general Winfield Scott Hancock—himself wounded in the same action. When Union commander George G. Meade (who can be seen at right center, holding field glasses) first saw this canvas, he declared it "wonderfully accurate in its delineation of the landscape and position of troops." And, seeing it in uncompleted form in 1868, Confederate general James Longstreet said, "This picture...is a remarkably fair and complete representation of that eventful scene." Longstreet supposedly added:

"There's where I came to grief." This immense composition was *"historically arranged"* by Col. John
Badger Bachelder, appointed by Congress as the official historian of the battle. He spent months
sketching the topography, interviewing Confederate prisoners, and touring the field with survivors.
Bachelder and Walker first surveyed the scene while *"the debris of that great battle lay scattered
for miles around"* and while *"many of the dead lay yet unburied."* Before paint was applied to canvas,
Bachelder also issued an open invitation to Union officers to return to the scene to recall their
movements during the battle. Some one thousand veterans came back—including forty-six generals—
and pointed out *"all the details of this great turning point of the Rebellion, each explaining the
movements of their several commands."* Walker spent *"weeks at Gettysburg,"* Bachelder testified
in a booklet he issued to accompany publication of engraved copies of the painting in 1870,
"transcribing the portraiture of field to canvas." Concluded the man who engineered the widely
exhibited result, *"This great representative battle scene has not its equal in America, for correctness
of design or accuracy of execution."*

Oil on canvas, 7 feet 6 inches × 20 feet. (The collection of Jay P. Altmayer)

the Kurz & Allison scene. In Thulstrup's canvas, massed Union troops proceed to assault Kenesaw Mountain, its crest smoking with gunpowder. A cannon in the right foreground, its barrel considerably elevated, is aimed by artillerymen who are entrenched (and one sees evidence of the earlier work of axes on the trees used in such field fortifications). At left, Gen. John A. Logan directs the attack. In a larger canvas depicting the same battle, painted the same year, Thulstrup retained a similar compositional scheme, moved the portrait figures to the right, replaced the gunners aiming the cannon with an artillery team riding to the front, and made General Sherman and his staff, rather than Logan and his aides, the impor-

tant figures. The Sherman painting is the less accurate of the two, for the commanding general reported that he stationed himself not on the field of battle itself, but on high ground to which telegraph wires had been laid.[6]

Thulstrup was a Swedish-born soldier of fortune who turned to art and illustration in midlife. A graduate of Sweden's national military academy, he had joined the French Foreign Legion and fought in Algeria; Thulstrup knew what nineteenth-century warfare looked like and opted to render a feeling for the impressive range of the weapons and the considerable mass of the armies. He did not, however, like the landscapist Hope, opt for scale at the expense of depicting the soldiers with detailed accuracy. His artistic constructions were often based on horizontal lines (rather than the "faster" diagonals favored by many military action painters), giving his work a somewhat static quality. Thus, the Kenesaw composition consists of three sections delineated by the parallel ranks of Union infantry, the parallel line of breastworks and the center of Logan's staff, and the sinuous line following the entrenched crest of the mountain objective. And yet the full scope of a modern battle inevitably lay beyond the size of any canvas: Sherman estimated that Johnston's lines stretched out for ten miles or more, and his own, in the perpetual attempt to envelop and flank, stretched even longer.

Thulstrup launched his American art career after the Civil War as a *Harper's Weekly* illustrator "under the aegis of Thomas Nast," according to his obituary seventy years later. He remained affiliated with *Harper's* for twenty years in all, painted portraits of Grant and Sumner for adaptation into lithographs, and then turned his attention to what *The New York Times* would acknowledge at his death were his "famous battle scenes...some of the most familiar scenes of American life now extant."[7]

The series was commissioned by the giant Boston print publisher L. Prang & Co., which paid Thulstrup to execute twelve portrayals of wartime land battles. Surviving records are sketchy, but apparently Thulstrup received $250, $457.75, and $400 for three of these paintings, the last-named sum for his Battle of Shiloh depiction. Prang's goal was to reproduce them "for the enjoyment of the masses and the spread of art-education as well as art-appreciation." In the words of a period catalog, "the illustrated press, the patriotic portraiture, and the episodic pictures of the war had fostered the popular taste for pictorialism. The American nation now wanted pictures. It should have them." Prang's Civil War "aquarelle facsimile pictures," as he called them, were intended to enter "into the homes of the rich and the homes of the poor...the school-room, the drawing-room, making summer sweeter and lighting up the snows of winter." Thulstrup's original model paintings, however, useless to the printmaker after the stones were drawn, were later ordered sold to raise cash for the strapped Boston lithography house. The catalog advertised them this way: "The spectator identifies himself with the persons watching the battle from afar.... Mr. Thulstrup has produced a series of honestly painted and vital compositions, in which every detail has been thoughtfully studied out." The spectator's vantage point was distant, all right, but not so far away as to reduce the pictures to landscapes. Some, in fact, were able to focus on individual heroes—and these proved especially popular: prints of Sheridan at Winchester, Hancock at Gettysburg, and "the good American military types" at Atlanta.[8] The full scope of the tragedy in the Battle of Kenesaw Mountain likewise eluded the artist, who could not equal the poet's rendering of its meaning. Herman Melville, in verse that resurrected glory from its machine-age demise, wrote:

> *They said that Fame her clarion*
> *   dropped*
> *Because great deeds were done no*
> *   more—*
> *That even Duty knew no shining ends,*
> *And Glory—'twas a fallen star!*
> *   But battle can heroes and bards*
> *   restore.*
> *   Nay, look at Kenesaw:*
> *Perils the mailed ones never knew*

≈ *Opposite* ≈

SHERMAN AT THE SIEGE OF ATLANTA

Thure de Thulstrup
(1848–1930)

An artillery officer reports his progress to Gen. William T. Sherman, calm and ramrod-straight astride his horse, while the general's aide uses field glasses to survey the early results of the Union bombardment of Atlanta. Thulstrup emphasized Sherman's almost serene demeanor, but Sherman himself admitted in communications to Washington, "I am too impatient for a siege." He was by all accounts restless, nervous, and energetic.

Watercolor on paper, 15 × 21 inches. Signed lower left: *Thulstrup 87.* (The Seventh Regiment Fund, Inc.)

BATTLE OF KENESAW MOUNTAIN

[Louis] Kurz & [Alexander] Allison

(Chicago, 1891)

Chromolithograph, 22 × 28 inches. (The Lincoln Museum)

GENERAL STUART AND HIS STAFF (1863)

John Adams Elder (1833–1895)

Though at least one of his men appears here to be dressed in tatters, Gen. "Jeb" Stuart is, as always, magnificently tailored in this romantic view of the cavalier hero at mid-war. To one Virginia politician of the day, Stuart "with his plumed hat... looked like an equestrian statue... it was really a grand spectacle to see these gallant horsemen coming toward us." And the Prussian aristocrat–turned–Confederate volunteer Heros Von Borcke observed that Stuart "delighted in the neighing of the charger." Astride his impressive mount, Stuart "did not fail to attract the notice and admiration of all who saw him ride along."

Oil on canvas, 32¾ × 39¼ inches. (R. W. Norton Art Gallery, Shreveport, Louisiana)

[STONEWALL JACKSON]
(1869)

William Garl Browne
(1823–1894)

*"His eyes fairly blazed,"
recalled a fellow general of
Stonewall Jackson, and this
postwar portrait captures that
characteristic. In reality,
Jackson was rarely so handsomely dressed; one Northern
war correspondent found
him "in general appear-
ance…in no respect to be distinguished from the mongrel,
barefooted crew who followed
his fortunes." Jackson's wife
liked the photograph on which
Browne modeled this portrait,
because, she said, it showed
"the beaming sunlight of his
home-look."*

Oil on canvas, 46 × 35 inches. Signed
on reverse: *Wm. Garl Browne Pin't.
1869.* (Stonewall Jackson House,
Historic Lexington Foundation,
Lexington, Virginia)

*Are lightly braved by the ragged coats
  of blue,
And gentler hearts are bared to deadlier
  war.*[9]

Sherman's *Memoirs* had appeared in 1874, among the earliest (and the greatest) of the recollections of the great Civil War generals, and Thulstrup therefore had available, when he accepted the assignment from Prang, an account that would locate the commanding general on the day of the battle. Instead, the painter focused on Logan. There were several possible reasons: Logan was closer to the action and his vantage point made the vivid depiction of troops feasible given the modest scale of the canvas; Sherman figured in another

Prang print (the excellent scene at the siege of Atlanta) and the firm probably desired variety; or perhaps it was because Logan, unlike Sherman, had enjoyed a brilliant political career after the war. As the unsuccessful vice-presidential candidate on 1884's Democratic ticket, Logan had reminded the nation of his (genuinely distinguished) Civil War career. He was so much on Americans' minds that the cyclorama depicting the Battle of Atlanta, on which work began in 1885, featured Logan so prominently as to give rise to the myth that he had commissioned the painting himself with $42,000 to boost his political career.[10]

Thulstrup was fortunate to have any portraits of Sherman from which to work. The general loathed the press and made no effort to accommodate reporters during the war, and that lack of interest in what would be called "public relations" today, along with the fact that Sherman's most successful campaigns came late in the war, meant that few visual representations of Sherman's victories were attempted before war's end. He told his brother, Senator John Sherman, on December 30, 1863:

I have been importuned from many quarters for my likeness, autographs, and biography. I have managed to fend off all parties and hope to do so till the end of the war. I don't want to rise or be notorious, for the reason that a mere slip or accident may let me fall, and I don't care about falling so far as most of the temporary heroes of the war. The real men of the war will be determined by the closing scenes, and then the army will determine the questions. Newspaper puffs and self-written biographies will then be ridiculous caricatures. Already has time marked this progress and indicated this conclusion.

If parties apply to you for materials in my behalf, give the most brief and general items, and leave the results to the close of the war or of my career.

On the brink of greatness in the spring of 1864, Sherman wrote his brother again, saying, "I am bored for photographs, etc. I send you the only one I have, which you can have duplicated, and let the operator sell to the curious." The general could be quite cynical about pictures and picture-makers. Once, according to an artist-correspondent, Sherman watched a *Harper's*

Weekly artist sketching his army's advance into South Carolina and suggested, with his customary modern-sounding cynicism and his ingrained race prejudice, that *Harper's* artists could create one huge image to represent the entire state: "One big pine tree, one log cabin, and one nigger."[11]

The fall of Atlanta assured Sherman's fame (and President Lincoln's reelection), and the subsequent March to the Sea, capture of Savannah, Carolina campaigns, and surrender of Joseph E. Johnston outside Durham, North Carolina, only made the hero more famous. With fame secure, the general could afford to pose for artists. The results, for example Chester Harding's handsome postwar oil portrait, do not necessarily match the image that the tough-talking, nervous, and combative general presented on campaign.

Sherman could always be a difficult subject. When the Norwegian-born painter Ole Peter Hansen Balling, for example, arrived at City Point, Virginia, in September 1864, armed with an important commission, an impressive pass through the lines from Lincoln, and a distinguished war record of his own, even these credentials were not enough to win Sherman's cooperation without a struggle. Balling had served as a lieutenant colonel with the New York volunteers before a wound compelled his resignation from the army. He had resumed his career as an artist, and then was commissioned by a wealthy New Yorker to produce a life-sized equestrian painting of Grant and his generals, which its sponsor proposed to exhibit nationwide to raise money for the Sanitary Commission.[12]

Grant offered his full cooperation, but Sherman, once the artist caught up with him in Washington at war's end, proved another matter. When Balling

Opposite

GRANT AT MISSIONARY RIDGE (C. 1886–87)

Thure de Thulstrup
(1848–1930)

Perched atop Orchard Knob to the right of the signal flag, Gens. Gordon Granger (left) and George H. Thomas (right) flank the diminutive Ulysses S. Grant at an impromptu battlefield conference, as Grant looks through his field glasses to observe Union troops in the distance charging the base of the Confederate line at Chattanooga's Missionary Ridge on November 25, 1863. In his memoirs, Grant admitted that "I watched eagerly to see the effect" of the assault, and was proud that "rebel and Union troops went over the first line of works almost at the same time." The sense of observing battle from a considerable distance is well rendered here, as is the respectful distance the spectator feels from Grant and Thomas, with staff officers intervening in the foreground.

Oil on canvas, 15 × 22 inches. Signed lower left: *Thulstrup*.
(The Seventh Regiment Fund, Inc.)

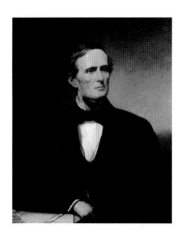

[JEFFERSON DAVIS]
(N. D.)

Benjamin Franklin Reinhardt
(1829–1885)

"Jefferson Davis," declared a British official after studying one of his portraits, "bears out one's idea of what an able administrator and a calm statesman should look like."

But most such portraits, including this one, carefully disguised Davis's true appearance, which the journalist Murat Halstead said combined "the face of a corpse, the form of a skeleton." This painting, possibly made from life during the war—it bears no resemblance to the few wartime photographic models upon which other artists relied—emphasized the Confederate leader's aristocratic bearing and exaggerated his robustness by broadening his shoulders and arms. It did, however, present an accurate glimpse of Davis's hands, which Halstead recalled as "thin, bloodless, bony."

Oil on canvas, 14½ × 11¼ inches.
(Courtesy R. W. Norton Art Gallery,
Shreveport, Louisiana)

SURRENDER OF A CONFEDERATE SOLDIER (1873)

Julian Scott (1846–1901)

A lone Confederate soldier waves a white flag of surrender, as his wife, child, and slave wait in the shadows behind him. The circumstances that might have led to such a moment seem improbable: a wounded soldier, reunited not only with his family but with his servant, is separated from his regiment, yet in full uniform. More than likely, Scott intended that the scene be symbolic, not realistic; the suffering family and loyal slave were staples of Lost Cause mythology, and may have been featured in muted tones in the background here only to suggest the trooper's thoughts of home as he gives himself up. He used an almost identical figure in his depiction of the death of General Kearny.

Oil on canvas, 20 × 15 inches. (The Collection of Jay P. Altmayer)

⋇ MINE EYES HAVE SEEN THE GLORY ⋇

THE DEATH OF GENERAL KEARNY (N.D.)

Julian Scott (1846–1901)

Wandering unsuspectingly into a Confederate position at Chantilly, Virginia, on September 1, 1862, the one-armed Union general Philip Kearny was spotted, shot, and killed. Out of respect for this Mexican War veteran and soldier of fortune who had fought on three continents, the enemy placed him on a stretcher and held aloft a white flag of truce so his body could be reclaimed by Federal forces. "Poor Kearny," Confederate general A. P. Hill lamented when he saw the body of his onetime friend. "He deserved a better death than that." Scott captured the moment when Kearny's body was being covered, and added a poignant detail in the general's blood-spattered effects lying in the mud in the foreground. But inevitably the composition focused on the noble Confederate officer signaling to the Union, his expression reflecting both the satisfaction of the kill and the respect due a fellow soldier in death. Scott, who lived in New Jersey, probably produced this work on commission to honor his fellow New Jerseyite, for whom a city in his home state was soon named. Scott's homely little scene suggested none of the intense focus by all participants on the dead general, none of the theatrical poses or carefully arranged still-life accoutrements of war that marked Benjamin West's famous Death of General Wolfe.

Oil on canvas, 25 × 30 inches. (The Union League Club of New York)

Ole Peter Hansen Balling
(1823–1906)

*General Grant fixes blue
eyes on the viewer in a painting
intended to represent
him as he looked during the
siege of Vicksburg in 1863.
"This is the only Painting that
exists of him of the period that
may be described as the turning
point of his own destiny,"
declared a pamphlet issued years
later to promote a print adaptation. "Balling was in no sense
employed in a mercenary venture," the publishers hastened to
add. "His heart was in it."
Indulging in hyperbolic promotional efforts typical for commercial adaptations, the printmaker called Balling "undoubtedly
the greatest artist in this country
at the time of the Civil War,"
and declared this work "one of
the most truthful and priceless
memorials of Gen. U. S.
Grant."*

Oil on canvas, 48¼ × 38¼ inches.
(National Portrait Gallery)

first approached him, the general told him bluntly "to go to a hot place," he recalled in a memoir published in a G.A.R. organ. His next plea for sittings was rebuffed with a curt "I have not time." Sherman did not surrender until Balling persuaded the general's sister-in-law to trap the reluctant subject on a visit to the home of his brother, Senator John Sherman. "I suppose I am cornered now," the general said, and reluctantly gave the painter his sitting. Witnesses to the scene "all laughed," Balling remembered, "as they knew me and my purpose"—and, more to the point, knew how Sherman hated to pose. Now the group "assured the general that the operation of sitting for me was not a painful one."

> *The general asked how I wanted him
> and I told him simply to sit down
> and finish telling the party present of
> his trip through the south, which I
> probably had interrupted. So he did,
> and in less than an hour I succeeded
> in making the sketch which is pre-
> sented in my painting.*[13]

By comparison, Grant demonstrated remarkable courtesy, especially for a man so acutely aware of his own uninspiring demeanor. Years earlier, as a West Point cadet, glimpsing the grand Winfield Scott for the first time, the young Grant had admitted that he "could never resemble him in appearance," even as he revealingly envisioned himself one day occupying "his place on review." One explanation for his cooperativeness as a sitter may lie in Grant's genuine enthusiasm for art, a taste that may have originated during those days at the military academy, when he showed artistic promise of his own in drawing class. Now Grant allowed Balling to sketch him repeatedly, took

him to inspect his horses so that the artist could choose the most appropriate steed for his painting, and admonished him to be certain to include Winfield Scott Hancock in the group, because, he explained, he is "my handsomest general."[14]

After breakfast at headquarters one morning, Balling remembered:

> *...the whole staff was on horseback,
> in their best trim for, as I learned
> afterwards, the officers had been told
> that I was to make a great painting
> of Grant and his staff. The general
> went on horseback just as he went
> about every day, with his big slouch
> hat and unbuttoned coat, and with-
> out his sword. I was all observation
> and used all the collodion my brain
> possessed.*

Balling's photographic metaphor was more apt than he realized. For despite his five weeks of work drawing both officers and horses "after nature," the painter turned to photographs as models for most of his likenesses. More to the point, Grant appeared in the painting not realistically slouch-hatted as Balling had seen him, but bare-headed, and attired in uncharacteristic parade dress complete with an elegant sword.[15]

Balling finished a design sketch for his work by mid-autumn of 1864, but it took him more than a year to transform it into a completed canvas, a delay caused by his commitment to the kind of research that somehow failed to manifest itself in his final work. First he traveled to Appomattox in search of General Philip H. Sheridan, sketching him there the day Lincoln was assassinated. He also journeyed to the Grant family's temporary residence in Wilmington to make a "careful drawing" of an elaborate engraved dress sword awarded the general at a New York charity fair. And before Balling was done he succumbed to the "strong...influence" of Grant's colleagues to delete the controversial Gen. Benjamin F. Butler from his composition and replace him with Gen. Alfred H. Terry. To do so, Balling insisted on going to Richmond to sketch Terry and his horse from the flesh.[16]

Balling's slow pace proved his undoing. By the time he had completed his ten-by-twenty-foot "masterpiece"—his own estimation of the work—his patron had died and the national tour he had promised was abandoned. The art critic Henry T. Tuckerman did say in 1867 that the painting had elicited "much praise," and some of that praise may have come from Grant himself, who inspected the work on November 21, 1865, and is said to have declared it an "excellent composition." But after a brief public showing in New York in 1866, *The Heroes of the Republic*, as the painting was first known, was stored away and forgotten. Its principal fame came as a result of an 1867 lithographed adaptation by Ferdinand Mayer & Sons.[17]

But having been privileged to observe Grant on occasion "sitting alone in the sunshine smoking his cigar" with an expression that conveyed "cheerfulness and ease of mind," Balling now determined to paint a more intimate Grant portrait. Adding a battle map and field glasses at his subject's side, he identified the new picture as a depiction of Grant at the time of his capture of Vicksburg, a full year before the painter met and sketched him. Balling justified the artistic license by explaining that the work represented the general "as I remember him sitting before the camp-fire before his tent at City Point Headquarters...where he

inspired me by telling me of...the work around Vicksburg." But when a New York publisher named Herman Linde issued an etching of the Balling painting more than thirty years later, in 1899, he promoted it inaccurately as a life portrait of Grant painted at Vicksburg in 1863. And so it has been featured as an illustration since.[18]

"Balling's work was accomplished to the accompaniment of the bursting shells of the memorable siege of Vicksburg," Linde's promotional brochure declared, adding, "and the paint of it was hardly dry when Grant

THE BATTLE OF ANTIETAM (1893)

Julian Scott (1846–1901)

This fragment or partial copy of an original painting of the storming of the Burnside Bridge at Antietam is all that remains of Scott's original canvas, which depicted Shepard's Rifles crossing the bridge at the climax of the 1862 battle. Colonel Shepard paid Scott one thousand dollars for the canvas, and presented it to the Seventh Regiment Armory in New York. It has since disappeared. Years later this fragment surfaced in the art collection at West Point, mistakenly identified as a depiction of the Battle of the Wilderness, so little did the truncated canvas look like the famous scene at Antietam. The figure who dominates the scene is inexplicably not the Colonel Shepard who commissioned the work, but Col. Robert Potter of the 51st New York, who was also at Antietam. The photograph of Potter at left was found among artist Scott's effects after his death.

Oil on canvas, 34 × 46 inches. Signed lower right: *Julian Scott.* (West Point Museum, U.S. Military Academy)

(Leon Kramer, Kramer
Gallery, Inc., St. Paul,
Minnesota)

[GEN. AMBROSE POWELL HILL] (1898)

William Ludwell Sheppard (1833–1912)

A. P. Hill, promoted to lieutenant general after Stonewall Jackson's death, disappointed those who held high expectations for his success, Lee included. Thin and sickly, he took prolonged medical leave late in the war, his ailment attributable either to psychological problems or the lingering effects of an early bout with venereal disease. When he returned to action, he was promptly killed—just a week before the end of the war. Fellow general E. P. Alexander, who remembered him as a "handsome young lieut." competing with George McClellan for the hand of the Union commander's future wife, lauded him as an "ideal soldier." Depicting Hill as rather robust in this flattering postwar portrait, the painting reveals nothing of Hill's slight stature, though the general's sword nearly dwarfs him.

Oil on canvas, 56 × 38 inches. Signed lower left: *W. L. Sheppard/1898.* (Virginia Historical Society)

GEORGE GORDON MEADE (1869)

Daniel Ridgeway Knight (1840–1924)

His war-horse ready for action, General Meade nonetheless directs the Battle of Gettysburg from afar, the field glasses in his hand his only unsheathed weapon. Such portraits, designed to be heroic, testified to the gap separating the traditions of battle-field art and the requirements of modern command. Admittedly, the gray-haired Meade offered a difficult subject. Seeing him for the first time right after Gettysburg, a Washington journalist found him "a little past his prime," and Carl Schurz, who observed him at Gettysburg, insisted, "There was nothing in his appearance or his bearing…that might have made the hearts of the soldiers warm up to him." Nevertheless, the Philadelphia GAR lodge asked to borrow this canvas in 1880 and exhibited it at the Academy of Music to raise funds for a Meade monument. "Members in full uniform formed on stage," a post official reported proudly, "above the centre of which the painting was suspended."

Oil on canvas, 7 feet 6 inches × 6 feet. Signed lower right: *D. R. Knight/1869.*
(The art collection of the Union League Club of Philadelphia)

⊰ *Glory* ⊱

141

Ole Peter Hansen Balling
(1823–1906)

To accommodate him in accomplishing this ambitious painting, the artist boasted, U. S. Grant galloped back and forth astride one of his mounts, Egypt, a scene "never to be forgotten," in Balling's words. Altogether, the monumental canvas depicted twenty-seven "heroes of the republic"—the name by which the painting became known. From left to right, the generals were Thomas C. Devlin, George Armstrong Custer, Hugh Judson Kilpatrick, William H. Emory, Philip H. Sheridan, James B. McPherson, George Crook, Wesley Merritt, George H. Thomas, Gouverneur Warren, George G. Meade, John G. Parke, William T. Sherman, John A. Logan, Grant, Ambrose E. Burnside, Joseph Hooker, Winfield Scott Hancock, John A. Rawlins, Edward O. C. Ord, Francis P. Blair, Alfred H. Terry, Henry W. Slocum, Jefferson C. Davis, O. O. Howard, John M. Schofield, and Joseph A. Mower.

Oil on canvas, artist's 23¼ × 36½-inch copy of his 12 × 6-foot original. (National Portrait Gallery; gift of Mrs. Harry Newton Blue in memory of her husband)

entered the town as victor on the Fourth of July." The portrait had suddenly been transformed into "the only Painting that exists of him of the period that may be described as the turning point of his own destiny, and that of the Nation"—when, of course, it was nothing of the kind. And Balling himself was touted as "the greatest artist in this country at the time of the Civil War." In the words of Linde's advertisement, he was "the Rembrandt of this historical period, and, therefore, his portrait of the great general will live throughout the history of our nation as one of the most truthful and priceless memorials of General U.S. Grant."[19]

But Balling was no Rembrandt, and Linde's extravagant claims for the Grant portrait ("valued by competent experts at $50,000. And why should it not reach the valuation of $100,000, and why not more?") likely fell on deaf ears, judging from the scarcity of surviving etched copies of the "Vicksburg" portrait. Sadly lost in the hyperbolic hard sell was the fact that, as the brochure put it in a moment of calm judgment, Balling's Grant boasted a truly "winning countenance. There is great firmness in that aspect," the brochure noted, "and yet a judicial mildness." But its promoters had promised too much, and in the end commerce conspired to consign Ole Balling's Grant to an undeserved oblivion.[20]

There was glory to be mined from defeat as well, and the Confederate experience inspired art no less celebratory of the so-called Lost Cause than could be found in the northern artists' depictions of the victorious one. Few native painters captured the essence of southern heroism as effectively as John Adams Elder, a Virginia-born artist who had studied in New York under Daniel Huntington. Elder returned to his native Fredericksburg in time to flee

before the Union bombardment of December 1862, and like many refugees from the battle he found his way to Richmond, where he became a draftsman at the Confederate War Department and later took an assignment in the field.[21]

Proximity to the Confederate capital offered Elder inspiration and opportunity. He went on to paint Robert E. Lee from photographs, for example, some-

how managing to bring out "the *germ* of truth in the sitter's character," as his teacher Huntington had advised him a decade before. Elder was said to have been present at Petersburg on July 30, 1864, the day the Union exploded a frighteningly destructive underground mine before a broad sweep of Confederate entrenchments, inflicting horrible destruction and mass maiming and death. What surely seemed to most observers the most brutal incursion yet of machine-age war was interpreted by Elder instead as the pinnacle of personal valor. He chose not to focus on the mine as a feat of engineering or a blight on the Virginia landscape, but the battle that ensued, in which Confederate forces somehow beat back Union troops who charged forward to seize the moment of their disarray. Personal heroism triumphed over the industrial

GENERAL GRANT AT FORT DONELSON (N.D)

Paul Philippoteaux (1846–1923)

Surrounded behind his lines by horribly wounded men being treated by both white medical officers and black orderlies, a somber Ulysses S. Grant stares resolutely at Fort Donelson, looming on the hill in the center of this picture, as his artillery bombards and his troops storm the fortification. Philoppoteaux, best known for his vast Gettysburg cyclorama, here painted a far more intimate view of war, suggesting the loneliness of command.

Oil on canvas, 18¾ × 25½ inches. Signed lower right: *PPhiloppoteaux.* (Chicago Historical Society)

GEORGE HENRY THOMAS
"THE ROCK OF CHICKAMAUGA" (1871)

Caroline L. Ormes Ransom (1838–1910)

At Atlanta in 1864, Gen. George H. Thomas seemed to one admiring Union officer the image of "a noble Roman, calm, soldierly, dignified…no trace of excitement about that grand old soldier who had ruled at Chickamauga." Ransom, who painted this similarly dignified portrait six years after the war, may have studied him from life—and thus made the "grand old soldier" look even older. A founder of the Daughters of the American Revolution, Ransom was a well-known Washington-based portrait painter who executed several portraits, including another of Thomas, for the U.S. Capitol.

Oil on canvas, 31 × 26 inches. Signed left: *C. L. Ransom/1871.* (U.S. Army Infantry Center, Fort Benning, Georgia)

BATTLE OF WILSON'S CREEK (DEATH OF GENERAL LYON) (N.D.)

Artist unknown

His men reach up to aid Brig. Gen. Nathaniel Lyon as he is shot on Bloody Hill while leading an impetuous counterattack at the Battle of Wilson's Creek, Missouri, on August 10, 1861. This naïve painting likely brought the opposing forces far closer together than they had been on the field, but it skillfully juxtaposed the death of the seasoned West Pointer with that of the young drummer boy, already lying dead below him.

Oil on canvas, 23 × 30½ inches. (Missouri Historical Society)

A ragged-looking black resident offers information to General Philip H. Sheridan and his staff (including George Armstrong Custer) at Dinwiddie Court House, Virginia, on March 29, 1865. That day, Sheridan's forces seized the town. Taylor, who covered Sheridan's campaign for Leslie's *"regardless of flying bullet and shell," had gone home by the time this event took place. He rarely saw bullets or shells flying anyway, because artists kept to the rear to avoid danger. Even his eyewitness sketches were later reworked. Sheridan reported the roads and fields as very muddy that day, but he and his staff appear spic-and-span in Taylor's watercolor.*

Watercolor on paper, 12⅝ × 20½ inches. Signed lower right: *James E. Taylor/N.Y.* (From the Tharpe Collection of American Military History)

age at the Crater, and Elder's friend Raleigh T. Daniel, also a Civil War artist, acknowledged that his colleague's specialty lay in "stirring scenes of action, as he exemplified in 'The Battle of The Crater.'" As the Richmond journalist T. C. DeLeon put it, Elder's canvases may have been "less careful in finish" than those of his Richmond competitor, William D. Washington, but "were nothing inferior as close character-studies of soldier life. Their excellence was ever emphasized by their prompt sale." The "ghastly, but most effective picture of the 'Crater Fight' at Petersburg," DeLeon added, "made the young artist's reputation." So famous did the painting quickly become, in fact, that the philanthropist William Wilson Corcoran, founder of the Washington, D.C., art museum that bears his name, rushed down to Richmond to attempt to purchase it, only to find that it had already been bought by Gen. William Mahone, who had been promoted to major general for leading the Confederate counterattack at the Crater. Corcoran went on to commission Elder to paint a number of portraits of Confederate leaders, including generals Lee and "Stonewall" Jackson.[22]

Not all Southern artists were so quickly rewarded for their retrospective portrayals of Lost Cause glory. In 1870 another artist, Everett B. D. Julio, was finding it necessary to solicit newspaper notices in New Orleans in a final and, as it turned out, fruitless effort to find a purchaser for a monumental painting of the last meeting of Lee and Jackson before Chancellorsville. The February 20, 1870, edition of the New Orleans *Bee* carried the report:

The undersigned, having heard that Mr. E. B. D. Julio has the intention of painting pictures which will recall souvenirs and exploits of the soldiers of the South, and realizing that this will incur heavy expenses, wish to help in the subscriptions for the purchase of the portrait of Generals Lee and Jackson.[23]

While the Julio canvas would inspire print adaptations in 1872, 1879, and again in 1906, and eventually reign as a great icon of the Lost Cause, its fame was slow in arriving. Julio, born in 1843 on St. Helena, the island of Napoleon's exile, came to America in 1860 and first resided in Boston. Settling eventually in St. Louis, he there produced his *Last Meeting* canvas by 1869, a mammoth painting that portrayed both military giants heroically, but wisely gave clear precedence in gesture and appearance to Lee, who is shown commanding Jackson while the ill-fated lieutenant listens attentively. Lee's gesture, it might be noted, was reminiscent, perhaps intentionally, of General Washington's in Rembrandt Peale's equestrian *Washington Before Yorktown* print, copies of which were undoubtedly available to Julio in the 1860s.[24]

Given this focus on Lee, it is not surprising that Julio tried at first to give his completed painting to the old general during his term as president of Washington College in Lexington. Lee rejected the offer with a firm but encouraging letter, although he did pronounce the work "spirited" and expressed his hope that Julio received "credit and advantage" for his labors. Understandably the disappointed painter preferred to recall that "that noble man...would not listen to the idea of my giving away my labor. It was his kind expression that induced me to look forward to a glorious future, as I felt, perhaps through proper study, I could proclaim myself the historical

painter of the South, towards which goal I am now struggling."[25]

But the goal proved as elusive as the simpler one of finding a buyer for his great work. The picture had been encased in a stupendous gilded and carved standing frame, and exhibited from Memphis to New Orleans in 1870, with Jefferson Davis himself among its viewers. Davis would concur with the *Picayune*'s assessment of the canvas as capturing "a memorable circumstance in the history of war." But such reviews failed to interest the New Orleans community in purchasing the painting for permanent public display. Lotteries, subscription attempts, "ladies of New Orleans" fund-raising schemes, even private sale attempts all failed. The humiliating ordeal proved "a terrible drag," in Julio's own words, "and the

slow process...has forced me to look to other means of obtaining money." These included a complicated deal with the New York engraver Frederick D. Halpin to publish the first print adaptation of *The Last Meeting of Lee and Jackson*, in return for some sort of lottery to place the original with a permanent owner. When it was over, Halpin had a money-making engraving in his catalogs, but Julio still had the original painting in his possession, unsold.[26]

Not until the painter had won a commission from the president of Louisiana State University to execute a smaller copy of the canvas did Julio earn enough money to travel to Europe for the advanced art study he felt crucial to achieving his goal of becoming the great historical painter of the old Confederacy. He never fulfilled his

JACKSON ENTERING WINCHESTER (C.1862–65)

William D. Washington (1834–1870)

After routing a superior Federal force at Winchester on May 25, 1862, "Stonewall" Jackson made a triumphant entrance into the city. One eyewitness observed "old men and women, ladies and children, high and low, rich and poor" lining the streets to greet him, many "weeping or wringing their hands over the bodies of those who had fallen before their eyes…others shouting for joy at the entrance of the victorious Stonewall Brigade." That is the event Washington successfully portrayed here. Jackson considered his welcome at Winchester "one of the most stirring scenes of my life." To his wife he wrote, "I do not remember having ever seen such rejoicing." Appropriately, Washington portrayed him almost as an equestrian statue in a public square.

Oil on canvas, 60⅛ × 48⅛ inches. (The Valentine Museum, Richmond, Virginia; from The Civil War: *Decoying the Yanks;* photograph by Larry Sherer, © 1984 Time Life Books, Inc.)

STUDY FOR HALT OF THE STONEWALL BRIGADE (C. 1862)

David English Henderson (1832–1887)

This sketch was produced the year after Jackson's brigade earned him the nickname "Stonewall" for holding their ground at the First Battle of Bull Run. Henderson apparently made the rough study from life somewhere in the Shenandoah Valley, and the tall figure with the kepi at center may well be Jackson himself.

Ink on paper, 9 × 12¼ inches. (Greenville County Museum of Art, Greenville, South Carolina)

HALT OF THE STONEWALL BRIGADE (1865)

David English Henderson (1832–1887)

In adapting his hasty sketch into this idealized painting, Henderson placed Jackson and his staff astride their mounts, thus separating them in status from their men by literally elevating them. The troops still rest, drink water, and wash in the foreground, as they had in the ink drawing, but now battle flags are in evidence, providing patriotic and martial formality to the naturalism of the life sketch. But by 1862 a member of the Stonewall Brigade wrote that "the romance of the thing is entirely worn off."

Oil on canvas, 26 × 38 inches. (Greenville County Museum of Art, Greenville, South Carolina)

thus been "forced, like other local artists, to descend from his pedestal and paint portraits...for a living. He lost heart and with it the sublime energy which creates masterpieces." But the rival paper, the *Picayune*, likely came closer to the truth when it pointed out that for all his ambition, E. B. D. Julio lacked "that magic touch and delicacy of portrayal which belong only to the great masters of the brush." Julio had found a great theme, but ultimately proved unequal to the task of conveying the fateful meaning present in this scene of two generals conversing on horseback, one of them only days away from his untimely and—for the Confederacy—catastrophic death.[27]

If there was a difference between Northern and Southern paintings of Civil War glory, it may be that the victors were more willing to show death than the vanquished. James Walker, for example, reserved a prominent vignette in his colossal canvas of Pickett's Charge for the poignant death of Confederate Gen. Lewis Armistead, but no similar work would come from Southern painters. Julian Scott, best known for painting common soldiers, created two superb canvases of Northern generals struck down in action: John Sedgwick and Philip Kearny. Southerners, on the other hand, failed to provide death scenes for J. E. B. Stuart, Turner Ashby, Albert Sidney Johnston, or Stonewall Jackson.

Scott's depiction of Sedgwick's last moments was somewhat reminiscent of Benjamin West's 1770 painting, *The Death of General Wolfe*, in which Wolfe, like Sedgwick, dies with his most trusted aides surrounding him. To create his tribute to Philip Kearny, however, Scott was constrained by a different set of circumstances: Kearny was killed behind enemy lines, and his body returned by Confederates under a flag of truce.

dream. Returning to New Orleans, he got by in life as a part-time painter and part-time artists' agent, and died tragically of consumption at thirty-six, his masterpiece still not purchased. Passed along to creditors after Julio's death, it was still being advertised in the *Confederate Veteran* as late as 1909, for sale for only eighteen hundred dollars.

The New Orleans *Times* may have helped explain the indifference Julio experienced in his adopted city by explaining that his painting had been brought there "in advance of the age in which New Orleans now lives." Julio had

Kearny's body was surrounded not by friends but by foes. To accomplish this more difficult portrayal, Scott appears to have used as his model an earlier painting he had made of a Confederate waving a flag of surrender at a roadside. What originated as an unremarkable depiction of a common soldier thus evolved into a scene of a general's martyrdom in combat.

Southern artists answered no similar muse. Both revenge and resurrection required a more positive emphasis. Focusing on death—or, as Union artist Edwin Forbes did, on deserters, stragglers, and camp thieves—would have made the Confederacy's Lost Cause seem like good riddance. Realistic appraisals of military life were likely to come from artists on the side of the victors, not the vanquished.

While the Northern lithographers Currier & Ives would show the South's greatest martyr, Stonewall Jackson, in a reverential deathbed print, no Southern painter is known to have produced a similar scene, perhaps in part because of the ignominy of Jackson's having been shot down by his own men, who mistook him for the enemy. A morbid focus on death, even heroic death, seemed what the South wanted to escape in the aftermath of defeat. A brief, gloomy period may have followed immediately after the war, but soon Confederate memorials metamorphosized from funereal to glorious.[28] Artistic tributes to the living Jackson of course abounded. But these featured the modest-acting and modest-looking general posing in uncharacteristic grandeur (as in William Garl Browne's flattering portrait), camping with his brigade in the woods (David English Henderson's canvas), or triumphantly entering Winchester, Virginia, on horseback (as depicted by William D. Washington).

Washington, who did portray battle death in his memorable painting, *The Burial of Latane*, a home-front canvas to be discussed later in this book, won enough acclaim for this work to prompt the writer T. C. DeLeon to suggest that had not the Confederate currency collapsed during the war, his fees "might have made him a Meisonnier in pocket, as well as in local fame." But on Washington's canvasses, Jackson would forever remain a conquering hero, not a dying one.[29]

By contrast, Northern audiences were offered more heroic death scenes, and most numerous among them were depictions of the death of the commander-in-chief. Abraham Lincoln's dying moments inspired more pictures than even his triumphant arrival in Richmond after the fall of the Confederate capital in April 1865 (of which there were at least three depictions: by Winslow Homer, Thomas Nast, and Dennis Malone Carter). For all their glory, martyred Confederate heroes like Jackson, by contrast, came, saw, and died. They did not conquer. And their deaths would go unrecorded in Civil War art.

Forever blameless in defeat, Lee inspired more portraits than perhaps any military leader of the war, at least among those who fought for the Confederacy. This was remarkable, given Lee's notorious reluctance to sit for painters. Ironically, just a few short weeks after refusing E. B. D. Julio's offer of *The Last Meeting of Lee and Jackson*, Lee welcomed the Swiss artist Frank Buscher to his Lexington home, where he posed for him alongside the memorabilia of his campaigns—although he refused to don his old uniform for the sittings, declaring, "I am a soldier no longer." Such protestations merely increased the artist's regard for his sub-

≈ *Opposite* ≈

ROBERT E. LEE (C. 1866)

John Adams Elder
(1833–1895)

To Mary Boykin Chesnut, the well-connected Richmond diarist who met many of the Confederacy's great military heroes, the "splendid looking" Robert E. Lee was the ultimate cavalier, exuding both "blood and breeding." He was "of the Bayard, the Philip Sidney order of Soldiers," Mrs. Chesnut wrote admiringly. Lee was hardly vain, however, and discouraged portrait painters from recording his likeness, reluctantly agreeing to sit for only a few after he became famous. The general's wife, Mary, believed that if Lee had sat more often, his portraits would have shown "his genial expression" instead of "a weary one," as in this painting. Of the existing likenesses, Mary Lee said, "none are perfect though each has some merit. The sublime repose as well as the strength and harmony of Gen. Lee's features & countenance it seems very difficult to portray, for no one has succeeded perfectly."

Oil on canvas, 48 × 35 inches. Signed left: *J A Elder/Va.* (Washington and Lee University, Lexington, Virginia; from *The Civil War: Lee Takes Command*; photograph by Larry Sherer, © Time-Life Books, Inc.)

≈ Opposite ≈

THE LAST MEETING OF LEE AND JACKSON (1864)

Everett B. D. Julio
(1843–1879)

One of the enduring icons of the Lost Cause, this monumental painting of the generals' final meeting, known at first as The Heroes of Chancellorsville, *failed to earn for Julio the credit he craved as the foremost history painter of the Confederate experience. Julio had the canvas encased in this colossal, specially designed walnut frame emblazoned with details from the Lee family coat of arms. Unable subsequently to find a buyer, Julio could never "derive a just compensation" for the work, as a Memphis newspaper put it. He wound up "starving for money," even as critics praised the painting, one citing it as "the beginning, we hope, of a series that shall perpetuate the deeds and prowess of the gallant and chivalrous soldiers of the South." Only after Julio's death at age thirty-six was the canvas sold to satisfy his debts.*

Oil on canvas, 12 feet 10¾ inches × 9 feet 7 inches. Signed lower left; *Julio./St. Louis Mo. 1864.* (Courtesy Robert M. Hicklin, Jr., Inc., Spartanburg, South Carolina)

ject, and Buscher determined to add Lee's likeness to a small gallery of portraits he was commissioned to paint for the Swiss Federal Parliament, to signify "the friendly relations between Switzerland and its great sister-republic in North America."[30]

"He is a great personality," Buscher wrote home exuberantly of his famous subject, "and the hatred of the South has abated. Thus he ought soon to be sitting in the country's Senate: he is altogether the ideal of American democracy." His patrons disagreed, however; they wanted a portrait of General Grant, not Lee. Buscher was adamant. Lee, he insisted, was by far "the greater character," adding: "of all my American portraits, the one of Lee is the perfect picture to hang in the democractic Swiss parliament." His patrons' final answer was to decline to pay his fee. Buscher produced his portrait anyway.[31] The appeal of great individuals sometimes transcended patronage—or the lack of it.

No event of the Civil War captured popular imagination more thoroughly than Sheridan's Ride, an incident at the Battle of Cedar Creek, fought in the Shenandoah Valley of Virginia on October 19, 1864 (and none was more quickly erased from popular memory in the twentieth century). To read the secretary of war's report from 1865 is to understand, in part, the importance of the event. "At the moment when a great disaster was impending Sheridan appeared upon the field, the battle was restored, and a brilliant victory achieved." Even President Lincoln specifically commended the "splendid work of October 19, 1864." The battle was of considerable size: the Union incurred 5,665 casualties and the Confederacy 2,910. And it was truly decisive: the Confederates forever left

the Shenandoah Valley, the scene of many humiliating Northern defeats earlier in the war.[32]

In his initial reports from the field, General Sheridan did not describe his ride, saying only, "I hastened from Winchester, where I was on my return from Washington, and joined the army between Middletown and Newtown…. I here took the affair in hand and quickly united the corps…."[33] He gave a fuller but still rather modest description of the event in his memoirs, published in 1888, the year he died. Sheridan recalled that he was returning from a conference in the capital with Secretary of War Edwin M. Stanton and Gen. Henry W. Halleck, traveling rather slowly with a fat engineer and a skinny one, neither of whom had done much horseback riding. Awakened in Winchester on the morning of October 19 by news of artillery firing at Cedar Creek, Sheridan dismissed it as a reconnaissance and tried to go back to sleep.[34] But he could not. The firing continued, and Sheridan decided to investigate.

We mounted our horses between half-past 8 and 9, and as we were proceeding up the street which leads directly through Winchester… I noticed that there were many women at the windows and doors of the houses, who kept shaking their skirts at us and who were otherwise markedly insolent in their demeanor, but supposing this conduct to be instigated by their well-known and perhaps natural prejudices, I ascribed to it no unusual significance. On reaching the edge of town I halted a moment, and there heard quite distinctly the sound of artillery firing in an unceasing roar. Concluding from this that a battle was in progress, I now felt confident that the women along the street had received intelligence from the battle-field by the "grapevine telegraph," and were in raptures over some good news, while I was utterly ignorant of the actual situation.[35]

The sounds grew louder, and Sheridan now concluded that his army was falling back toward him. At Mill Creek he was joined by an escort of three hundred cavalrymen (arranged for before he departed for Washington). Cresting a hill, they were shocked to see "the appalling spectacle of a panic-stricken army—hundreds of slightly wounded men, throngs of others unhurt but utterly demoralized, and baggage-wagons by the score, all pressing to the rear in hopeless confusion."[36]

Proceeding at a walk, Sheridan considered what he should do:

My first thought was to stop the army in the suburbs of Winchester as it came back, form a new line, and fight there; but as the situation was more maturely considered a better conception prevailed. I was sure the troops had confidence in me, for heretofore we had been successful; and as at other times they had seen me present at the slightest sign of trouble or distress, I felt that I ought to try now to

restore their broken ranks, or, failing in that, to share their fate because of what they had done hitherto.[37]

Once again, one can glimpse the guilt of the remote Civil War commander, here bringing about what proved to

be a stunning reversal of fortune. Because his men had bravely followed his commands hitherto, he felt obliged to share their fate in a defeat brought on by his absence in Washington when the Confederates counterattacked.

Then Sheridan heard that his headquarters had been captured and all was lost. With two aides-de-camp, named Forsythe and O'Keefe, and twenty of the cavalry escort, the general started for the front on his black horse Rienzi. Galloping along a road thronged with refugee soldiers halted to cook coffee, Sheridan inspired them to abandon their fires and return to the front. Throwing their hats in the air, they shouldered their muskets and followed him with cheers. "To acknowledge this exhibition of feeling I took off my hat, and with Forsyth and O'Keefe rode some distance in advance of my escort, while every mounted officer who saw me galloped out on either side of the pike to tell the men at a distance that I had come back."[38]

The effect proved sudden and electric; the whole army changed front. Meanwhile, General Sheridan made his first halt north of Newtown, where a rare humorous incident occurred.

...I met a chaplain digging his heels into the sides of his jaded horse, and making for the rear with all possible speed. I drew up for an instant, and inquired of him how matters were going at the front. He replied, "Everything is lost; but all will be right when you get there"; yet notwithstanding this expression of confidence in me, the parson at once resumed his breathless pace to the rear.

Sheridan could not pass through the thronged streets of the town and had to go around it. Eventually he reached "the only troops in the presence of and resisting the enemy,"[39] holding a line of fence rails on a reverse slope about three miles north of the original Cedar Creek line. "Jumping my horse over the line of rails," Sheridan recalled, "I rode to the crest of the elevation, and there taking off my hat, the men rose up from behind their barricade with cheers of recognition."[40] Color-bearers and officers, among them a future president of the United States, Rutherford B. Hayes, rallied more men.

Sheridan then crossed a narrow valley to the opposite crest in the rear and established his headquarters. As his staff joined him, he planned the counterattack and gave orders to redistribute his command. This absorbed much time, and Sheridan decided to return to high ground to observe the enemy.

Arrived there, I could plainly see him getting ready for attack, and Major Forsyth now suggested that it would be well to ride along the line of battle before the enemy assailed us, for although the troops had learned of my return, but few of them had seen me. Following his suggestion I started in behind the men, but when a few paces had been taken I crossed

to the front and, hat in hand, passed along the entire length of the infantry line; and it is from this circumstance that many of the officers and men who then received me with such heartiness have since supposed that that was my first appearance on the field. But at least two hours had elapsed since I reached the ground....

The Union armies swept the Confederates from the field and regained their old lines. Sheridan was promoted to major general in the regular army.

And to glory. As the historian Gerald F. Linderman has noted, Sheridan's Ride epitomized the Civil War's view of courage as an active and individual virtue that could affect a nation's fortunes on the field of battle. Sheridan's single act synthesized as no other the military ideals of the period. And it was understandably celebrated throughout the North for years to come. Since the poet-painter Thomas Buchanan Read alone executed seventeen copies of his equestrian portrait called *Sheridan's Ride*, it is surely one of the three Civil War events most often represented on canvas (along with the Battle of Gettysburg and the fight between the *Monitor* and the *Merrimac*). Read, whose once considerable reputation both as painter and poet has vanished even more completely than the fame of Sheridan's Ride, also composed a poem of the same title. It became so well known that schoolchildren in the North were required to memorize it.

Surely no wartime event ever found a more suitable chronicler than Sheridan's Ride enjoyed in Read, the Pennsylvania-born painter whose fame once nearly rivaled that of Sheridan himself. Modern analysis of his output does not easily

≈ *Opposite* ≈

THE DEATH OF GENERAL SEDGWICK, SPOTSYLVANIA, MAY 9, 1864 (1877)

Julian Scott (1846–1901)

Maj. Charles Whittier gently swabs blood from the head of the mortally wounded Gen. John Sedgwick, shot by a Confederate sniper as he directed the placement of artillery preparatory to the Battle of Spotsylvania in May 1864. Scott's eloquent death scene, rendered in mournfully bleak colors and without theatrical gestures in its figures, included one officer checking Sedgwick for a heartbeat and another calling desperately for help. The curious young drummer boy watching the scene may be something of a retrospective self-portrait; Scott had been a camp musician himself. The bloodstained stretcher at left seems the sort of detail only a veteran might know about, and provides for modern spectators a gruesome reminder of the nature of military medicine before the germ theory of disease.

Oil on canvas, 6 × 8 feet. (Courtesy Drake House Museum, Plainfield, New Jersey; from *The Civil War: The Killing Ground;* photograph by Henry Groskinsky, © 1986 Time-Life Books, Inc.)

THE PEACEMAKERS (1868)

George Peter Alexander Healy
(1813–1894)

As a rainbow representing peace bursts forth symbolically outside the after-cabin window, Gen. William T. Sherman,
Gen. Ulysses S. Grant, and Adm. David D. Porter confer with President Lincoln on board the sidewheeler River Queen, docked at Union headquarters at City Point, Virginia, on March 28, 1865. The so-called peace conference depicted here actually focused first on war strategy,
with Lincoln expressing his hope for a speedy end to the fighting. Sherman, perhaps to justify the liberal—and subsequently countermanded—
peace terms he went on to offer to Gen. Joseph Johnston's Confederate army the following month, would later recall that Lincoln had
insisted aboard the River Queen that he favored a peace with "'charity for all, malice toward none,'" echoing his second inaugural address.
Lincoln's own view of Reconstruction was undoubtedly more complex, and included tentative steps toward Negro suffrage, as his final
public address revealed. But since Sherman was Healy's "dear friend," in the general's words, Healy's interpretation of the shipboard conference
mirrored Sherman's; it would portray great warriors, the artist explained, generously exploring "the possibilities of peace." To help Healy
fashion the group portrait, Sherman sat for the painter and persuaded Grant to pose as well, even though the latter protested, "I have sat so often
for portraits that I had determined not to sit again." While posing, Grant regaled the artist with stories of horses. Sherman later got
Admiral Porter to supply diagrams and descriptions of the River Queen cabin, and wrote a long letter to Healy recalling the meeting and
describing Lincoln's "haggard" and "careworn" appearance in repose. Determined to portray the scene accurately, the artist rejected his
daughter's humorous suggestion that he enhance the unembellished scene by adding "a table or something." Much in debt to Sherman,
Healy depicted the general himself leading the shipboard discussions—and Lincoln merely listening. Healy completed the canvas
in Rome. The original was destroyed by fire in 1892, but the artist had produced several copies.

Oil on canvas, 47¾ × 66 inches. (The White House Collection)

LINCOLN'S DRIVE THROUGH RICHMOND (1866)

Dennis Malone Carter (1818 or 1820–1881)

As a throng of well-wishers surrounds his carriage, President Lincoln—painted here as the conquering hero—drives through the ravaged Confederate capital on April 4, 1865. "Everywhere he rode," the Boston Journal *reported, "men who through many years have prayed for deliverance" now greeted their liberator with "jubilant cries…unspeakable joy, and the tossing of caps." Carter attempted to rewrite history, however, by showing white citizens joining in the enthusiastic reception. As another journalist on the scene observed, the Confederates there turned away from Lincoln's party "as if it was a disgusting sight." The officer sharing the president's carriage is Adm. David Dixon Porter.*

Oil on canvas, 35 × 68 inches. (Chicago Historical Society)

explain his high reputation in the 1860s, but for the few years he lived after the Civil War, he was a genuine celebrity on two continents. "His pictures are poems," gushed one contemporary, "his poems are pictures." Added an Italian admirer, after studying a bust Read had sculpted of his favorite subject—Sheridan, of course: "A poet—a painter—a sculptor! Ah, gentlemen, I find we have a Michaelangelo in *Signor* Read!"[41]

A professional turning point for Read, who was already both an experienced painter and a popular poet, occurred on July 4, 1861, at an Independence Day dinner for American expatriates at the ambassador's residence in Rome. There his poem *The Defenders* was read aloud, and the encouraging response to it surprised and gratified him. Thereafter, Read determined to use poetry to fan the flames of patriotic fervor in war-torn America. By November he was back home in Cincinnati.[42]

From then on, his verse not only became more robust, it seemed almost to cry out for public recitation. In the entertainment-bereft popular culture of the day, dramatic readings were a staple of theatrical repertoire. Thomas Read developed a close friendship with the popular elocutionist James E. Murdoch, who specialized in such performances. Murdoch was soon embarked on a national tour of recitals to raise money for war relief, the highlight of which was an impassioned reading from Read's sixty-seven-page-long epic, *The Wagoner of the Alleghanies, a Poem of the Days of Seventy-six.* The poet witnessed firsthand the response his work inspired when read aloud, for he accompanied Murdoch on the circuit after granting him exclusive rights to perform the piece. Nor was the poem's popularity limited to culture-starved patrons in the boondocks. General Sheridan commended him in his memoirs. And on Christmas Eve of 1862, Mary Lincoln borrowed a copy from the Library of Congress, and presumably read it in the White House.[43]

The Civil War now became Read's chief subject, and he learned to react quickly to events with celebratory verse—functioning almost as a Currier & Ives of poetry, so quick was he with the pleasing, stirring portrayal of newsworthy happenings. For example, when Union Gen. Robert Latimer McCook of the "Fighting McCooks" was killed by Confederate guerrillas on August 6, 1862, while being transported by ambulance near Decherd, Tennessee, Read responded in only "a few days," Murdoch remembered admiringly, with a sentimental but indignant poem called "The Oath." Drawing inspiration from the ghost's oath in *Hamlet*, the poem exhorted inflamed Northerners to swear vengeance on the Confederacy "by the blood of our murdered McCook."

The poem quickly became popular in the North—so much so that when James Murdoch traveled to Washington to perform before Congress and in the White House, Abraham Lincoln himself requested that he recite it, referring to it colloquially, as undoubtedly many Americans did, as "The Swear." The "victim" celebrated in the poem was actually killed while driving the now-famous ambulance, not while lying prostrate in it, and before dying, McCook never suggested that his shooting was anything but a legitimate act of war. Nevertheless, the North was whipped into such a sustained frenzy over the event—for which Read's poem was in no small way responsible—that after the war, a nationwide search was undertaken to find McCook's "killer," and he was located, tried, and sentenced

= Opposite =

SHERIDAN'S RIDE (1869–71)

Thomas Buchanan Read
(1822–1872)

Barely five feet in height, and mounted on his "medium size" stallion Rienzi, General Philip Henry Sheridan nonetheless impressed his troops as "a good looking Soldier" who "rides well." On October 19, 1864, "Little Phil" astonished even his admirers by embarking on a breathtaking ride from Winchester to the front. Recalled one eyewitness, "On he rode, his famous war-horse covered with foam and dirt, cheered at every stop by men in whom new courage was now kindled." Originally painted on commission from the Union League Club of Philadelphia, this work—one of several subsequent copies by the artist—was owned by General Sheridan himself, whose daughters donated it to the U.S. Military Academy. Learning that it would be displayed in the First Classmen's Club Room where many cadets could see it, Sheridan's daughter Mary wrote, "How grateful we are that the 'Sheridan's Ride' has been hung in such an appropriate place at West Point."

Oil on canvas, 5 × 7 feet. (West Point Museum, United States Military Academy)

GEN. PHIL SHERIDAN

(CHICAGO, 1891)

Shober & Carqueville

Chromolithograph, 15 × 21 inches.
(Library of Congress)

to hang before President Andrew Johnson intervened and spared him. To Murdoch, understandably, "The Oath" was "a master-stroke of artistic effect and poetic inspiration."[44]

In 1863, his reputation as a Civil War Homer soaring, Read joined the Army of the Cumberland, serving for a time on Gen. Lew Wallace's staff. Later attached to the command of Gen. William Rosecrans, Read wrote and performed verses for Rosecrans's staff officers. After attending one such reading, Gen. John Beatty complained in his diary that while Read's pieces might well sound "capital…in a parlor," they came across as "too ethereal, vapory, and fanciful for most of us leather-heads." What Read may have learned from such experience was to make his work even more stirring, or at least to leave the public recitation of it to others.[45]

The inspiration for Read's most famous achievement came right off the pages of an illustrated newspaper. On October 31, 1864, Read was conversing at home with his friend Murdoch when his brother-in-law burst into the room clutching a copy of the latest edition of *Harper's Weekly*. Appearing on its front page was an engraving after Thomas Nast depicting Sheridan's Ride from Winchester. Exclaimed Read's brother-in-law: "There is a poem in that picture. Do it now!" Murdoch concurred enthusiastically, and with good reason. That very night he was scheduled to perform a program of recitations. He not only echoed the suggestion that his friend write about Sheridan, he urged him to do so in time for that same evening's appearance.

"Do you suppose I can write a poem to order," Read replied indignantly, "just as you would…order a coat?" But he, too, became captivated by the challenge, and before long retired to his room, armed only with a pot of black tea, leaving instructions not to be disturbed "even if the house takes fire."[46]

When Read emerged some hours later, he had finished a multi-stanza poem, and that same night, James Murdoch recited it from the stage of Pike's Opera House. The Cincinnati *Enquirer* reported that by the midpoint of the maiden performance, the audience "could no longer contain itself," erupting into "rapturous applause." The final "glowing verses," the report went on, were greeted with "peal after peal of enthusiasm." Thereafter, eulogized *The New York Times* after Read's death, "his fame as a poet became worldwide, an event secured by his celebrated poem Sheridan's Ride…thrown off in a happy moment of inspiration."[47]

The dramatic story of the poem's origins comes from family recollections, never a very trustworthy source. It is difficult to see inspiration in the dingy woodcut from *Harper's*, with nothing heroic about the pose or scene. Suffice it to say Read composed the poem quickly.

And it enjoyed unqualified success. Only a week after its first recitation in Cincinnati, "Sheridan's Ride" was published in the *New York Tribune*, with the famous poet and travel writer Bayard Taylor fulsomely introducing it as a "magnificent lyric." By 1865, Read had also published it in a volume of his own poetry. And with the passing years the fame of "Sheridan's Ride" grew: it became a staple at Civil War reunions, campfires, school graduation exercises, and amateur theatricals.[48] A part of the poem follows:

> Up from the South at break of day,
> Bringing to Winchester fresh dismay,
> The affrighted air with a shudder bore,
> Like a herald in haste, to the
>   Chieftain's door,
> The terrible grumble, and rumble, and
>   roar,
> Telling the battle was on once more,
>   And Sheridan twenty miles away.
>
> …But there is a road from Winchester
>   town,
> A good, broad highway leading down;
> And there, through the flush of the
>   morning light,
> A steed as black as the steeds of night
> Was seen to pass, as with eagle flight;
> As if he knew the terrible need,
> He stretched away with his utmost
>   speed;
> Hills rose and fell; but his heart was
>   gay,
>   With Sheridan fifteen miles away.
>
> Still sprung from those swift hoofs,
>   thundering South,

≈ *Opposite* ≈

SHERIDAN'S RIDE (BOSTON, 1885)

L[ouis]. Prang & Co., after Thure de Thulstrup

Thulstrup inexplicably added a major detail to the iconography of Sheridan's fabled ride—and subtracted another. He, like other artists, did not portray Sheridan with the beard he wore that day. And Thulstrup added the overwrought touch of a dramatically wind-whipped battle flag (Sheridan waved only his hat). One soldier on the scene that day recalled that the mere sight of the general was enough to thrill the troops, who leaped to their feet, "swung their caps around their heads and broke into cheers as he passed beyond them."

Chromolithograph, 15 × 22 inches. Signed lower left: *Thulstrup*. (The Lincoln Museum)

The dust, like smoke from the cannon's mouth;
Or the trail of a comet, sweeping
faster and faster,
Foreboding to traitors the doom of
disaster,
The heart of the steed and the heart
of the master
Were beating like prisoners assaulting
their walls,
Impatient to be where the battlefield
calls;
Every nerve of the charger was strained
to full play,
 With Sheridan only ten miles away.

…The first that the general saw were the
groups
Of stragglers, and then the retreating
troops;

What was done? What to do? A glance
told him both,
Then, striking his spurs, with a terrible
oath,
He dashed down the line 'mid a storm of
huzzas,
And the wave of retreat checked its course
there, because
The sight of the master compelled it to
pause,
With foam and with dust the black
charger was gray;
By the flash of his eye, and the red nos-
tril's play,
He seemed to the whole great army to say,
"I have brought you Sheridan all the way
 From Winchester down to save the
 day!"

Hurrah! Hurrah for Sheridan!

Hurrah! Hurrah for horse and man!
And when their statues are placed on
high,
Under the dome of the Union sky,
The American Soldier's Temple of Fame;
There with the glorious General's name,
Be it said in letters both bold and bright:
"Here is the steed that saved the day,
By carrying Sheridan into the fight,
From Winchester, twenty miles away!"

So great was the poem's popularity that Sheridan's Ride itself was seldom mentioned without allusion to the poem that helped ensure its renown. Often forgotten is the fact that an indisputably greater writer than Read, Herman Melville, had produced a rival poetic tribute to the event, "Sheridan at Cedar Creek," but with far different results. Featured in *Battle-Pieces*, Melville's poem, like Read's, told the tale more or less from the standpoint of Sheridan's horse, Rienzi. But there the similarity ended. Literary hindsight may be inadequate to explain why Melville's version never approached Read's in popularity. Being first with the poetic response surely helped Read (Melville's work, too, was widely published—but probably no earlier than its *Harper's New Monthly Magazine* appearance in April 1866). And Read's rhythmic, accessible style surely made a difference as well. Melville's work was poetically more complex, and expressed a more sophisticated sentiment in the end:

There is glory for the brave
Who lead, and nobly save,
But no knowledge in the grave
Where the nameless followers sleep.[49]

Read was the people's choice. By 1868, Herman Meville's *Battle-Pieces* had sold but 468 copies. Its author decided to abandon literature altogether, while Read's literary career flourished.[50]

Read eventually applied his other skill, that of painter, to his most popular subject. Again, he did not originate the idea himself. The impetus came instead in the form of a "request by several gentlemen of the Union League of Philadelphia," mainly the club's leading art enthusiast, James L. Claghorn. Claghorn would later get Read to produce an additional copy for his own private collection. And more copies would follow later.[51]

But first, as soon as the war ended, Read journeyed to Sheridan's peacetime headquarters in New Orleans, where the general was now commanding the military division of the Gulf, to sketch him from life. Then he took his studies to Italy and there finished his first Sheridan's Ride painting between 1869 and 1871, boasting to one friend of the result: "It 'takes the shine' out of anything I have ever done on canvas." To Murdoch, Read had now earned "the honors of both poetry and painting in a high degree." *Sheridan's Ride* copies soon flowed from the artist's brush, one painted at the request of Sheridan's own family and later donated by his daughters to West Point.[52]

The fame of Read's painting never approached that of his stirring verse, though it was widely acclaimed. His portrait of Sheridan, saber outstretched, eyes glowing with determination, proved a graceful enough figure, but Rienzi in mid-gallop seemed hopelessly awkward, and the very concept behind the composition—the idea that the ride inspired the troops—was barely suggested by the shadowy presence of some dust-shrouded soldiers on horseback in the distant background. Besides, Sheridan did not draw his saber; he waved his hat. Overall, the spare design of rider and horse is closer to a portrait than a panorama of a

Opposite

THE FIGHTING McCOOKS (1862–71)

Charles T. Webber
(1825–1911)

Fourteen members of Ohio's McCook family served the Union during the Civil War. Seven were the sons of one man, Maj. Daniel McCook, who dominates this family portrait, posing proudly with his rifle. The senior McCook, who enlisted at age sixty-three, was killed in action, as were his sons Daniel, Jr. (reclining at center), Charles Morris (seated with Dan, Jr.), and Robert Latimer (standing behind his father). Another son, Gen. Alexander McDowell McCook (facing his father, a red cape across his lap), saw much action but survived the war. Understandably, this heroic family became known as "the Fighting McCooks." This fictitious family gathering was portrayed in the style of aristocratic family portraits with the tools of their trade about the family members and a vista to what would be their estate in a more peaceful scene.

Oil on canvas, 56¼ × 80¼ inches. Signed on scroll, lower left: *C. T. Webber/1862–1871.* (The Ohio Historical Society)

great event. Apparently Read came to agree with his rival, Melville, who, in a famous lecture on "Statues in Rome," endorsed the ancients' reverence for horses "as majestic" second only to man: "To the Greeks nature had no brute. Everything was a being with a soul, and the horse idealized the second order of animals just as man did the first."[53]

Sheridan's fame was to fade, but not as quickly as Read's. The painter-poet lived for only a few months after painting *Sheridan's Ride,* mostly in Italy. "Abroad he was highly esteemed as one of the leading American poets," an observer explained. In Naples, he met Sheridan for the last time during the general's European tour. But in "feeble health" as a result of a carriage accident in Rome in 1871, Read sailed for home,

* MINE EYES HAVE SEEN THE GLORY *

falling gravely ill on the sea voyage.[54]

In May 1872, only days after his arrival in New York City, he died of pleuropneumonia in his hotel room. His obituary appeared the next morning on the front page of *The New York Times*, but by the turn of the century, a leading critic would declare that from all Read's books only "two or three poems" had survived the test of time. It was, the critic concluded, "a slender legacy."[55]

That assessment ignored Read's artistic-patriotic legacy. Stirring as Sheridan's Ride was, visual imagination, heightened from the smudgy depiction of a lonely rider on *Harper's* pages to Read's vision of a dashing swordsman, often strove to make it more exciting. Thulstrup, who painted his own version of the scene at least twice, for one depiction seized on the moment Sheridan's horse leaped the rail fence line, but in both pictures chose to depict the general waving a red-and-white cavalry guidon in his right hand. Sheridan said only that he waved his hat, and did so only after he jumped the fence and crested the hill. In reality, it surely required both hands on the reins to jump his horse over the fence. The longevity of the event's fame was such that one confused printmaker depicted Sheridan's horse leaping the rails, but showed the general himself as he looked in postwar photographs: fat, with a much thicker moustache, and wearing a lieutenant general's uniform. Shober & Carqueville's print was copyrighted in 1891 and mistakenly based the general's likeness on the one found in the frontispiece of the second volume of his memoirs, showing Sheridan as he appeared many years after the war.

The fame of Sheridan's Ride, it goes almost without saying, represented an entirely Northern emotional phenomenon. Gen. Jubal A. Early, the Con-federate general at Cedar Creek, did not mention in his battle report the electric effect of Sheridan's return, if he even knew about it. Instead Early attributed his defeat to disorganization brought about by his troops' plundering when they initially captured the Union camps. His remaining field officers, now that the able ones were mostly dead or wounded, proved so inept they could not prevent it. Finally, a panic seized the disorganized Confederate army—a panic that Early described as "an insane idea of being flanked" and "a terror of the enemy's cavalry."[56] In explaining the disaster to Robert E. Lee, Early also revealed the usual guilt complex of the Civil War commander about personal physical courage:

> It is mortifying to me, general, to have to make these explanations of my reverses. They are due to no want of effort on my part, though it may be that I have not the capacity or judgment to prevent them. I have labored faithfully to gain success, and I have not failed to expose my person and to set an example to my men.[57]

Little wonder the artists of the era preferred to depict actions in which individual courage seemed to matter.

Matter as it did for nineteenth-century men, individual courage came to seem irrelevant to twentieth-century warfare, where victory was measured by fire power and economic might. Sheridan's lonely ride would have been a physical impossibility on modern battlefields. Rienzi would have stumbled into shell craters, and General Sheridan would surely have been killed at long range. When war came to call more for endurance than individual risk and initiative, Sheridan and Rienzi were quickly forgotten. Except in art.[58]

≈ *Opposite* ≈

GENERAL WILLIAM T. SHERMAN (1865–66)

Chester Harding (1792–1866)

Sherman, who customarily eschewed trappings of rank, was portrayed in this heroic postwar portrait arrayed not only in full uniform, but with a beribboned medal decorating his lape. "His eyes had a half-wild expression," a journalist wrote of the general, quickly adding that the look was "probably the result of excessive smoking." To the journalist he looked "rather like an anxious man of business than an ideal soldier." He also looked far older than he was; in his mid-forties he was frequently taken for sixty. The Union League of New York purchased this portrait from the family of the artist in 1871. Harding, who was near the end of his life when he painted this portrait, inexplicably drew the "S" in the "U.S." insignia on Sherman's hat backward.

Oil on canvas, 40 × 34 inches.
(The Union League Club of New York)

SURRENDER OF GENERAL LEE TO GENERAL GRANT, APRIL 9, 1865 (C. 1866)

Louis Mathieu Didier Guillaume (1816–1892)

Although some early descriptions of this painting contended that Guillaume was present to witness and record Lee's surrender, evidence in the picture itself suggests that he constructed it from secondhand reports, and not all of them accurate. The two generals, for example, did not sit at the same table during their meeting, nor did Grant wear a four-star uniform until 1866. The artist did subtly suggest, through Lee's ramrod posture, taut expression, and sad eyes, his well-cloaked feelings during the event. Grant thought Lee's face remained "impassible" throughout; sad though he may have been, Grant concluded that Lee was "too manly to show it."

Oil on canvas, 5 × 6 feet. Signed lower left: *L.M.D. Guillaume.* (Appomattox Court House National Historical Park)

LINCOLN BORNE BY LOVING HANDS (1865)

Carl Bersch (nineteenth century)

Interrupted in mid-parade, a blur of soldiers looks on in horror as the mortally wounded Abraham Lincoln, victim of an assassin, is carefully borne from Ford's Theatre on the night of April 14, 1865. This is the only eyewitness view of the extraordinary scene. Artist Bersch happened to be sitting on the balcony of his residence directly across the street, sketching the torchlit procession of victorious Union soldiers, when he noticed the sudden commotion from the direction of the theater door. As the stunned painter watched, a "hushed committee" carried the president's inert form across the street toward the Petersen boardinghouse next door, where Lincoln would die nine hours later. According to his granddaughter, Bersch immediately "incorporated this solemn and reverent cortege into his sketch," and then "started work on the painting." Having been employed briefly as an artist at Brady's Gallery, he may earlier have observed Lincoln from the flesh, simplifying his task.

Oil on canvas, 40 × 60 inches. (U.S. Department of the Interior, National Park Service, Ford's Theater National Historic Site, Washington, D.C.; photograph by Ed Owen)

THE LAST HOURS OF LINCOLN (1868)

Alonzo Chappel (1820–1887)

*Forty-six visitors crowd around Lincoln's deathbed in this fanciful recreation by
Chappel, an attempt to portray together all the visitors who attended the dying president during the
long night of April 14, 1865. In reality, the tiny boardinghouse bedroom in which Lincoln
died could barely accommodate a handful of people at once. Using his precisely posed photographic
models, he managed to include Robert T. Lincoln (center, holding handkerchief); Edwin M. Stanton
(conferring with Union officer, right); Hugh McCullough, William Dennison, and Montgomery
Blair (all crowding around Vice-President Johnson, who is seated at left). The design for the composition was credited to John B. Bachelder, who performed similar duties for Walker's colossal Gettysburg
canvas. The result, according to the Washington* Sunday Herald, *was "a great picture." The critic
was particularly impressed by "the cold hues of death…warmed to the eye by the red rays of a
candle … the flickering flare causing a Rembrandt-like effect," details he praised as "very felicitously
managed." Added the writer, "Portraits so minutely like I have never seen."*

Oil on canvas, 52 × 89½ inches. (Chicago Historical Society)

Mathew Brady studio

These privately commissioned Brady model photographs of the figures to be featured in Chappel's painting were all preserved in a sales book for engraved copies of the painting. The prints were offered to subscribers at prices ranging from fifteen dollars for "plain" copies to one hundred dollars for artist's proofs. Among the initial subscribers, according to the sales book, were General Grant (one-hundred-dollar proof) and Speaker of the House Schuyler Colfax (sixty-dollar india proof). Pictured in these poses, all of which required their sitters to re-create mournful expressions, heads reverentially bowed, were Lincoln's son Robert T. Lincoln (upper left); Secretary of the Treasury Hugh McCullough (lower left); and Secretary of War Edwin M. Stanton (lower right). The pose of Vice-President Andrew Johnson (next to Robert's) was apparently rejected for the painting in favor of a profile.

(Chicago Historical Society)

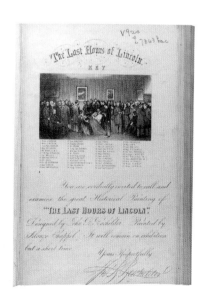

INVITATION TO AN EXHIBITION
OF THE LAST HOURS OF LINCOLN, WITH A KEY
TO THE PAINTING

(Chicago Historical Society)

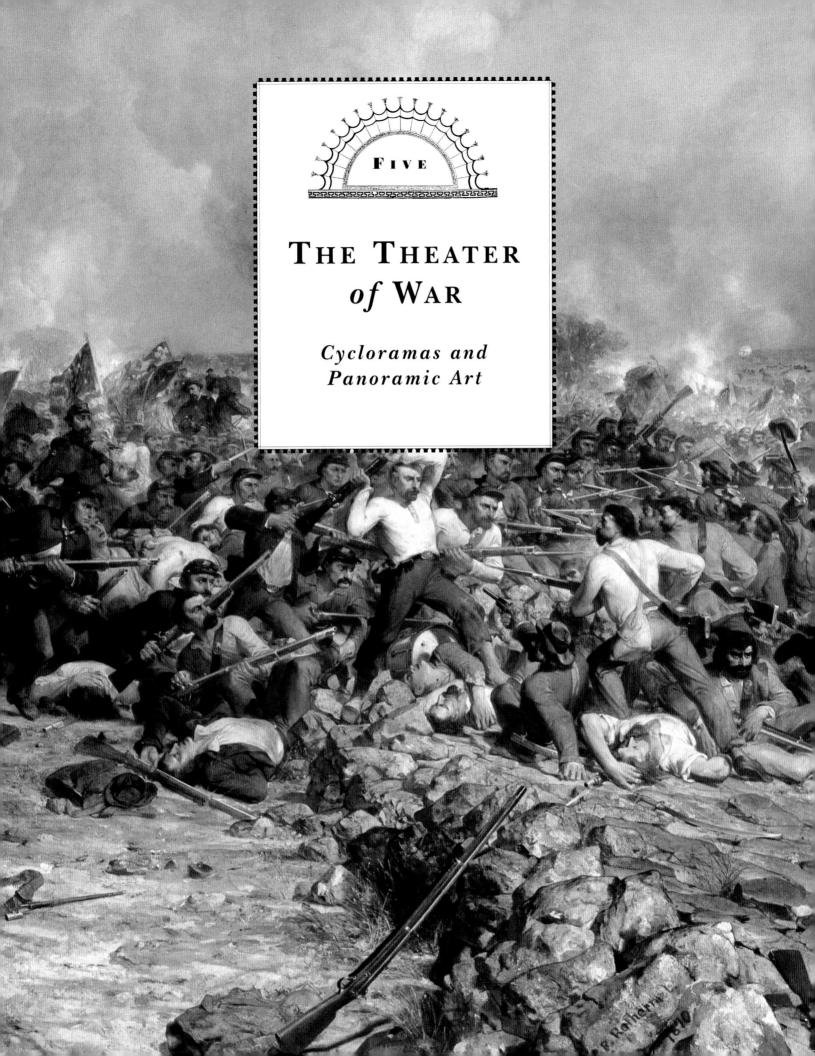

FIVE

THE THEATER
of WAR

Cycloramas and Panoramic Art

Preceding Page

THE BATTLE OF GETTYSBURG: PICKETT'S CHARGE (1870)

Peter F. Rothermel

(1817–1895)

Rothermel's colossal canvas of Pickett's Charge included Union commander George G. Meade (on horseback, far left) in the action, when in fact he did not appear on the field until the assault had been repulsed. Having been commissioned to portray the event by the State of Pennsylvania, Rothermel may have felt obliged to depict Meade, a respected native son. But he made the central figure of the composition an ordinary Pennsylvania soldier shown stripped down to his unrealistically gleaming white undershirt to make him stand out in the fury of the fighting (even more apparent in the 1885 mezzotint by the engraver John Sartain). Many of the dark-bearded men in the painting look quite alike (Rothermel apparently did not use models to pose for the common soldiers), and there does not appear to be a single blond in Pickett's Charge.

Oil on canvas, 16 feet 9 inches × 32 feet. (The State Museum of Pennsylvania)

ndividual courage was important to myth, but most people realized that modern war had another side: the spectacular mobilization of great numbers of men. Historians and painters alike have struggled to capture the extraordinary scale of America's great Civil War.

No ordinary canvas could cope. A comprehensive perspective within the confines of a modest canvas rendered an essentially topographical sense, boasting all the human drama of a map. A possible solution lay in adopting canvases of grand, even grandiose dimensions, some of them beyond the powers of any single painter to fill in a reasonable amount of time. This chapter will deal with the grandest projects of Civil War painting: cycloramas, circular paintings with multiple "vanishing points," meant to surround and even smother the viewer; large sequential paintings meant to show the development of a military campaign over time; and other very large canvases that comprehended vast panoramic views of the great struggle.

As an 1891 exhibition catalog put it: "To the artist, eager to depict the romantic and picturesque in warfare," the Civil War's sprawling, panoramic battles "displayed the scenery which thrills the emotions." The catalog was referring specifically to a new cyclorama that was opening in Atlanta that year called *Battle Above the Clouds,* a depiction of the fight for Lookout Mountain that would feature as much grandeur as the fabled mountain itself: a fifty-by-four-hundred-foot circular painting weighing seven tons. Created in Berlin by Eugene Bracht, Karl Roechling, and George Koch, and assembled by "a stock company organized for the purpose,"

the massive painting was assessed a ten-thousand-dollar customs duty when it arrived in America, a levy promptly publicized by the painting's promoters. They called it "the greatest battle painting in the world."[1]

Such tales of monumental size, prodigious bulk, and artistic tenacity successfully gripped the imagination of a public in the midst of a major revival of Civil War interest and apparently eager to revisit the great scenes of the struggle through the time-honored and still-impressive technology of the cyclorama. In the days before motion pictures revolutionized American tastes, these huge "circular panoramas," introduced in Europe toward the end of the eighteenth centu-

THE DEATH OF GENERAL REYNOLDS (1870)

Peter F. Rothermel (1817–1895)

At the peak of the first day's fighting at Gettysburg, stretcher-bearers rush from the field the body of Union general John Reynolds, shot dead by a sharpshooter, as Confederate forces under Gen. Henry Heth (background) overrun McPherson's Farm. Subjected to "an infernal fire" from the Confederates, the Iron Brigade, seen charging onto the scene from both right and left, held their ground, and "the rebel line swayed and bent." Rothermel studied the ground, knew it well, and painted it with painstaking care, but the many figures demanded by the subject taxed him to the point of painting them in sketchily; most seem very flat.

Oil on canvas, 36 × 66 ¼ inches. (The State Museum of Pennsylvania)

CYCLORAMA OF THE BATTLE OF ATLANTA (1885–86)

William Wehner and the American Panorama Company

On an immense canvas on which a team of a dozen artists worked simultaneously from various levels of a movable scaffold (bottom right), the American Panorama Company immortalized the Battle of Atlanta, fought on July 22, 1864. This scrupulously researched painting captures the moment at which Maj. Gen. John A. Logan, brilliantly filling a void left by the death of Gen. James B. McPherson, rallied Union forces to regain control of a position near a half-built brick plantation house outside the city. Sherman used only one of his three armies that day, not wanting to make the Army of the Tennessee jealous. Nevertheless, he could write after surveying the scene of this "bloody conflict," "Terrible was the slaughter done to our enemy." More than 8,000 Confederates and 3,700 Union soldiers were killed or wounded in the fighting.

Oil on canvas, 42 × 358 feet. (City of Atlanta, from *The Civil War: Battles for Atlanta*; photographs by Henry Groskinsky, © 1985 Time-Life Books, Inc.)

ry, dazzlingly combined art and spectacle, reproducing war with stunning scale in specially constructed buildings that offered the aesthetic imperative of an art gallery together with the breathtaking experience of theater. As much as ten times larger than today's cinema screens, nineteenth-century cycloramas provided Civil War spectacle for the urban masses. The large paintings were wrapped around the interior walls of specially constructed circular buildings so that a spectator standing in the center could see nothing but the picture surrounding him. A glass-covered slit hidden by a false ceiling at the top of the cylindrical building admitted light from above so viewers would cast no shadows on the picture. Everything but the cyclorama was painted gray, and the visitor, led through a darkened corridor to the center of the viewing room, was awed by the bright canvas before him.[2]

Cycloramas were more than, as one recent critic has described them, "a means by which information was pictorially conveyed to the public in an age before illustrated newspapers and widespread literacy." Indeed, they thrived in the late nineteenth century, when literacy was very high and illustrated newspapers had been functioning for decades. The great cities of Europe—London, Brussels, Paris, Edinburgh, St. Petersburg, Berlin—had enjoyed them for years. Audiences flocked to cyclorama buildings to view these gigantic paintings-in-the-round, and the exhibitions grew so popular they were typically dismantled, moved, and reassembled in other cities on national tours whose frenzied atmosphere and exuberant welcomes likely rivaled the arrivals and departures of the traveling circus. People visit some of the surviving cycloramas to this day.[3]

The same city that welcomed the Lookout Mountain cyclorama in 1891

provided the subject and eventually the permanent home of what is now called the Atlanta Cyclorama, the project of William Wehner's American Panorama Studio in Milwaukee. *The Battle of Atlanta* employed three landscape painters, six figure painters, and two animal painters, who in less than two years together filled a canvas measuring a mind-boggling 358 by 42 feet. Little wonder the resulting work is hardly an artistic masterpiece. However, its artists did at least strive for historical accuracy. Theodore Davis, a *Harper's Weekly* artist who had accompanied Sherman on campaign, returned to the old battlefields and showed the Milwaukee crew

ATLANTA CYCLORAMA #1

Dead men and horses felled in Confederate general Benjamin F. Cheatham's successful breakthrough litter the tracks along a battle-scarred cut of the Georgia Railroad (left), as Illinois troops advance toward the unfinished brick plantation house (left center) from whose upper windows Confederates unleash steady rounds of gunfire. To the right of the house, desperate Federal troops kill their own battery horses to prevent the enemy from carrying away captured guns. Meanwhile, more Union troops counterattack (right center) from the opposite side to regain their lost earthworks, and yet another wave of charging Federals follows Lt. Edward Jonas (on horseback, glancing behind him). Visible faintly in the background behind the railroad tracks is the Atlanta skyline. Among the vignettes in this section of the cyclorama are the tree draped with a white flag to the right of the Troup Hurt House, identifying a temporarily abandoned Union signal station; and the fright-ened Confederate courier (near the American flag, extreme left), trapped between the lines, and crouching on his horse as he races to safety.

(Photo courtesy of Milwaukee Co. Historical Society)

the site from a specially constructed platform forty feet high. The artists displayed the cyclorama for the first time in Minneapolis in 1886.[4]

The scene is depicted from the point of view of the Union lines, and it seems probable that it was not intended originally for permanent exhibition at a Southern site. After its initial showing in Minneapolis, the cyclorama did not make it to Atlanta until 1892. Luckily for its promoters, the artists had depicted Sherman very small in the distance, so Atlantans would not have to study a heroic portrait of Georgia's nemesis. Even so, the cyclorama by no means enjoyed steady financial success and eventually sold for one thousand dollars

at a sheriff's sale in 1893 and was donated to the city of Atlanta. In the Great Depression, three-dimensional figures and landscape of dubious artistic merit were added to the foreground as WPA relief projects for unemployed craftsmen. As much as these crude fiberglass-and-plastic mannequins (recently installed to replace the wood-and-clay models of the 1930s) mar the picture, the overall effect may well remain what the original promoters had in mind back in the nineteenth century. An early brochure advertising the Gettysburg cyclorama, a product of the same period but of different (and more skilled) artists, mentioned similar foreground detritus in its early exhibitions.

Seen in full, the Atlanta Cyclorama (of which only a portion is usually reproduced in modern publications) must be said to celebrate Gen. John A. Logan, seen rallying Union forces, waving his hat as he gallops along their lines. The image was similar to the one that appeared on the cover of the early biography by George F. Dawson, the *Life and Services of Gen. John A. Logan*, published in 1887, the year after the general's death. Sherman had praised Logan for stepping into the breach, but he afterward refused to give the command of the Army of the Tennessee to this politician-turned-general. It is well known that William T. Sherman never liked politicians very much.

The more famous of the surviving cycloramas, Paul Philippoteaux's Gettysburg cyclorama, provided an excellent example of the art made possible by the cooling of sectional animosities in the 1880s. It opened for viewing in Boston late in 1884, and the nickel souvenir brochure sold at the site carried a telltale image on its cover: a Union soldier shaking the hand of a Confederate soldier. With his right foot treading on a saber on the ground, the Yankee places his left hand on the Confederate's shoulder in a gesture of reconciliation at least as old as Velasquez's painting of the surrender of Breda.

Despite their wild scenes of battlefield turmoil, both of these circular depictions of hard fighting were ultimately monuments to sectional reconciliation. Their careers as public attractions prove it, for both got their start in the North but were traveled southward without resistance. It surely helped matters that the painter—or rather the supervisor—of the Gettysburg work hailed neither from North nor South, but from France. There, after the country's disastrous defeat in the war with Prussia of 1870–71, Philippoteaux and his father, Félix, like the more famous military artists Edouard Detaille and Alphonse de Neuville, painted a cyclorama—the first for the father-and-son team—of an incident from the recent war. These works depicted French defeat on the very heels of the war and served less to reconcile than to inflame, keeping alive a sentiment of revenge that would smolder into the twentieth century.

The younger Philippoteaux seems to have become a specialist in cyclorama painting, executing three that were displayed in St. Petersburg, Russia; two for Brussels, Belgium; and one for London, celebrating British imperialist adventure. Philippoteaux was born in 1846, and started cyclorama work only after 1871. He must have worked fast, for he had

Crying "McPherson and revenge, boys," as he races toward a plank bridge, Union general John A. "Black Jack" Logan, hat in hand and mounted on a foaming black charger (left), leads his staff across the corpse-littered field and toward the decisive fighting around the Troup Hurt House. The general managed to rally Union forces to re-form broken lines around the building. Logan, one of his soldiers testified, was "a human hurricane on horseback." Just above him, an ambulance wagon transports badly wounded Gen. Manning F. Force, whose closely tethered riderless horse follows. High above and to the left of Logan, the equestrian figure silhouetted within a puff of artillery smoke (to the left of the Augustus Hurt House in the distant background) is Gen. William T. Sherman, calmly surveying the battlefield.

Beneath the American flag in the foreground (left center), Union general Joseph Andrew Jackson Lightburn leads his brigade across a wheatfield before the badly damaged Beer's Tannery, around which are clustered a cavalcade of Federal hospital wagons. "Generals, colonels, captains, lieutenants, sergeants, corporals, and privates were piled indiscriminately everywhere," a Confederate soldier testified. "Blood had gathered in pools." It was, he said, the very "picture of carnage and death." Mounted on a gray horse in the foreground (right center), Union colonel James Martin looks back to urge on reinforcements as his troops race for the woods at right to regain earthworks lost earlier to the Confederates. Meanwhile, farther to the right, Georgians charge furiously down from the slope to take on Union soldiers in hand-to-hand fighting.

completed nine of them by the end of 1884. In truth, they were not the work of one artist but of several; even so, the work had to be hasty, for the Gettysburg painting filled ten thousand square feet of canvas (roughly 375 feet long and 25 feet high) and required over four tons of paint.

Apparently Philippoteaux came to the United States to research his work around 1882, visited Gettysburg and sketched the environs, hired a local photographer to take panoramic camera studies from atop a wooden tower, studied maps in Washington, and corresponded with Generals Winfield Scott Hancock, a hero of the battle, and Abner Doubleday, who had just completed a book called *Chancellorsville and Gettysburg*. The actual painting was executed in Paris, with Philippoteaux supervising five artists. If he made an effort toward sectional balance in soliciting testimony, it is unknown, and the resulting painting of Pickett's Charge is made from the Union lines looking out toward the Confederate lines. After executing the work in France, Philippoteaux unveiled his first Gettysburg cyclorama in Chicago in 1883 to acclaim great enough to cause other entrepreneurs to pay him for a second version. (Two others, now lost, were produced for Philadelphia and Brooklyn.)

After a preview for the Boston press on December 21, 1884, the second cyclorama opened in a specially built structure with "the stolidity of a medieval castle." Tens of thousands of visitors thronged to view the picture between 1884 and 1892, paying twenty-five to fifty cents each for admission. It received enthusiastic reviews that suggest something of the appeal these works held for people in an era before cinema:

> *When one reaches the platform from which the cyclorama is shown,*

the effect upon him is simply astounding. He suddenly finds himself upon a high hill and everywhere within the range of his vision, on the hills, in the valleys, in the woods, on the open fields in ditches and behind stone walls, and in shot-shattered shanties he beholds the soldiers of the blue and gray engaged in the awful struggle for the supremacy. No words can adequately describe the wonderful effects of this life-like portrayal of this great battle.

The experience that the cyclorama afforded awestruck visitors can be understood from comments by the

Boston *Daily Transcript* on December 30, 1884. Visiting the "extraordinary affair" for the first time, the critic reported:

> It is as though the laws of this world were suspended.... Some portions of the foreground appear to change their positions as the spectator changes his.... In short, one feels quite help-less and wondering in the midst of this new and extraordinary nature. It would seem as though all these queer impressions might be at once met and settled by the simple consid-eration of the fact that it was only a picture. But that is just it; it is impos-sible to accept the thing as a picture. Not because it is absolutely natural, but because there is nothing by which to gauge the thing, one has no idea whether the canvas is ten feet distant or a thousand. And so, all means of rational judgement being removed, the spectator must remain, dazed and helpless, feeling much like the little girl in "Alice in Wonderland," when told that she was but a thing in the dream of the sleeping king.

The reporter from the *Sunday Herald* continued: "Old soldiers who saw the cyclorama yesterday pronounced it as accurate as if photographed on the field." The critic even found in the painting a patriotic message that was surely not attributable to Philippoteaux:

The atmosphere is simply marvellous in its fidelity to nature, and, looking upward, it is difficult to realize that it is not the real sky that meets the eye. It is also a thoroughly American sky, and could belong to no other clime. In the ranks of the contending armies, it will be noticed that not only are the portraits of the leading officers true to life, but that the artist has taken into account the fact that our armies were composed of naturalized citizens, as well as native-born men, and here and there a face distinctively Irish will be seen, with near it the form and unmistakable carriage of the Frenchman, the German, or the Italian.

Cycloramas were recognized as "popular" art in their own day, though Boston's critics went out of their way to commend the artistic skill evident in the Gettysburg painting and to indicate that

Boston's artists (and not only children and veterans) visited the attraction. The critics generally praised the rendering of the landscape, and indeed cycloramas might be thought of, to the degree that they constitute art rather than spectacle, as landscape paintings that solved the problem of depicting modern war: with a canvas large enough, a group of artists could comprehend both topography and genuine human struggle in their work. As the Boston *Transcript* expressed it in February 1885, "One section suggests the beautiful in Nature, another the horror of war."

Of horror there was but a pale presentation, as the *Transcript*'s art critic had noted at the time of the first unveiling:

The general conception and treatment of the painting are commendable in the extreme, for it is restrained, moderate, and in really good taste, and therefore the expectation of possible

horror and disgust with which many enter the building is quickly changed to a grave consideration of the nobler characteristics of a great battle. Had the painter been absolutely literal in his execution of the subject, painting all the ghastly and sickening details of the fight—details which of course were, and which would have been received and gloated over by a most lamentably large number of the people of any city—had he done this, painting all the carnage and horror that he could have done with perfect truthfulness, then would the work have been without higher value than police news. But with a moderation worthy of all praise, he has avoided absolutely all this sort of thing, with the result that the painting is truly valuable, not only as a means of amusement, but as a most instructive lesson with regard to the great battle.[5]

Scale did not necessarily alter the historic content of a painting. These painters offered what the reviewer characterized as "the nobler characteristics of...battle." And this was deemed preferable to "perfect truthfulness."

Even the grand proportions of a cyclorama necessarily compressed the scale of a Civil War battle. Although Philippoteaux apparently depicted Confederate Gen. George Pickett, commander of the famous charge that climaxed the Battle of Gettysburg, near some farmhouses on the Emmittsburg Road, he was actually stationed farther back in the more protected position dictated by the modern style of command, a style as unsuitable to cyclorama painters as any others. Nor could the cycloramist afford to ignore drama for the sake of a too-scrupulous historic accuracy. Philippoteaux portrayed the spectacular explosion of a caisson behind Union

lines as reinforcements arrived to halt the Confederates. Indeed, eleven Union caissons were destroyed that day, as Abner Doubleday testified, but in the artillery duel preceding the arrival of the remnants of Pickett's seventeen thousand men at the Union lines. And unheroic details were best left out of the picture altogether. Philippoteaux chose not to show at all the line of wounded Federal soldiers posted at the rear of the Seventy-second Pennsylvania, with orders to drive back or shoot all Union deserters fleeing the action instead of charging the attacking Confederates.[6]

Sanitized and telescoped though it was, Philippoteaux's vision of the great battle apparently proved popular. He went on to produce three other Gettysburg cycloramas for other cities. Two were later destroyed, but the Boston canvas reached Gettysburg itself in 1913, for the fiftieth anniversary of the battle, and it can still be seen there today.

The continuing lure of the Gettysburg and Atlanta cycloramas owes much to their appeal as physical feats and at least a little, perhaps, to their success in solving the problem of war painting. They achieve scale without sacrificing humanity. But they did not provide a practical or permanent solution to the vexing problem of how best to portray the late war. They required specially built round fireproof buildings and impressive engineering to wield their hefty tonnage for display. And they required the work of teams of anonymous artists: landscapists painted terrain, figure painters depicted soldiers, and others produced the horse images. The results offered spectacle to the viewing public, but could not easily present an individual artistic vision.

Inevitably—with the notable exceptions of the enduring tourist attractions in Atlanta and Gettysburg—Civil War

≈Opposite≈

CHARGE OF THE PENNSYLVANIA RESERVES AT PLUM RUN (1870)

Peter F. Rothermel (1817–1895)

With the Round Tops looming large in the smoke-enshrouded background, a Pennsylvania division under Gen. Samuel Crawford (on horseback, saber raised), fights its way toward Longstreet's Corps in the Plum Run Valley on July 2. Although Rothermel here proved unimaginative as a portraitist—too many of the Confederates in the foreground look alike, and some of the Union soldiers' faces are featureless—he did painstakingly introduce such arresting details as the blood-spattered rifle that has just been dropped by the injured soldier on the rocks at right.

Oil on canvas, 35½ × 60 inches.
(The State Museum of Pennsylvania)

**BATTLE OF
SHILOH—APRIL
6TH, 1862
(CHICAGO, 1885)**

Cosack & Company

"Copied by special permission from the panorama painting on exhibit in Chicago," this colorful commercial adaptation of the Shiloh cyclorama celebrated neither the fighting men of the Hornet's Nest, nor even General Grant (right). Rather, this was a shameless promotion for the McCormick Harvester, going so far as to add to the scene (left) a bullet-scarred shed containing a McCormick device labeled in easy-to-read lettering. As the caption of the print shamelessly declared: "The 'McCormick' Machines come victoriously out of every contest and without a scratch." Like prints of the same period showing Custer's Last Stand, this one offered gore and grotesque corpses.

Chromolithograph, 23 × 34⅝ inches. (Chicago Historical Society)

·BATTLE OF SHILOH · APRIL 6TH 1862·
THE 'McCORMICK' MACHINES COME VICTORIOUSLY OUT OF EVERY CONTEST AND WITHOUT A SCRATCH
PRESENTED WITH COMPLIMENTS OF McCORMICK HARVESTING MACHINE COMPANY

cyclorama paintings became the victims of both changing technologies and, for all their heft, fragile construction. Some examples went up in smoke, while others were either relegated to protracted storage or vanished without a trace, testifying to a growing indifference ushered in by the arrival of the motion picture early in the twentieth century as well as declining interest in depictions of historical carnage. After D. W. Griffith redefined battlefield spectacle with *The Birth of a Nation,* the 158-minute movie epic that took the nation by storm in 1915, the comparatively static cyclorama would never seem quite the same. Cycloramas depicting Second Bull Run, Vicksburg, Missionary Ridge, and the battle between the *Monitor* and the *Merrimac* all disappeared.

Among the notable casualties of this change in popular appeal was the once-successful *Battle of Shiloh* panorama, exhibited for a time in the late 1880s or early 1890s. Billed as a pictorial tribute to "Gen. Grant's greatest battle," the dis-

play featured eight large panels, some focusing on battlefield commanders like Grant or Don Carlos Buell, and others paying tribute to the common soldier in the midst of hellish action like the Hornet's Nest, a scene Junius Henri Browne of the *New York Tribune* described thus:

> *There was no pause in the battle. The roar of the strife was ever heard. The artillery bellowed and thundered, and the dreadful echoes went sweeping down the river, and the paths were filled with the dying and the dead. The sound was deafening, the tumult indescribable. No life was worth a farthing.... Death was in the air, and bloomed like a poison-plant on every foot of soil.[7]*

Unfortunately, nothing of the original Shiloh panorama survives to allow for a modern appraisal, except for a period chromolithograph of one section of the painting (a print skewed in its focus by its blatant advertising message), and a series of black-and-white glass plate negatives taken at the time by a Wisconsin photographer. They suggest a welter of furious action, but neither relic convinces us that the lost Shiloh panorama captured the "death in the air" so evident to *Tribune* correspondent Browne "on every foot of soil." The focus was clearly on glory.

The difference between "cycloramas" like Atlanta's and "panoramas" like Shiloh's probably rests solely in the way they were displayed, but even in the absence of the large circular buildings erected especially to showcase the former, panoramic pictures enjoyed similarly enthusiastic patronage, sometimes in unlikely places, sacrificing nothing to scale or realism. When, for example, an artist known only as "Church" unveiled a series of panoramic depictions of such Civil War events as the bombardment of Fort Sumter, troops marching down Broadway, and the Battles of Fredericksburg and Gettysburg, their exhibition caused a sensation in faraway London. Noted the *Art Journal:* "This panorama has...an interest far beyond all similar pictorial exhibitions, inasmuch as this fearful war, independently of all the considerations, comes more nearly home to us than any other foreign war recorded in history." Clearly, the failure of some of these acclaimed pieces to survive must be attributable to factors other than want of audience or appreciation. And to be sure, some boasted a highly partisan or political point of view; others suffered from artistic incompetence or perhaps poor management.[8]

So-called moving panoramas, pulled across a stage from spindle to spindle so that a military campaign unfolded in a series of sequential vignettes, had enjoyed their first domestic popularity

during the Mexican War. The key to their lack of fame as enduring art lies in part in their theatrical origins: many panorama painters apparently began their careers as scene painters, and indeed the few surviving works have the quality of stage scenery. That would explain as well the poor quality of some of the human figures, for stage scenery usually required simple renderings of buildings, rooms, and landscapes only. But at one time, Civil War panoramas were popular enough to inspire the manufacture of miniature versions as toys—like the late-nineteenth century "Myrioptioon," featuring tiny lithographed Civil War scenes that could be rolled and unrolled before a paper proscenium, and came complete with small admission tickets.[9]

A case in point was the *Army of the Cumberland* panorama, apparently commissioned by Gen. William S. Rosecrans in an effort to vindicate the record of his controversial command at the Battle of Chickamauga in 1863, where he yielded high ground to the enemy and might have lost the day had not Gen. George H. Thomas heroically come to the rescue. Grant subsequently relieved Rosecrans of his command, and the demoted general may have intended the panorama to help rescue his reputation. If so, he would be disappointed, and its failure may well be due to the fact that its painter was up to the task emotionally but not artistically.

The *Army of the Cumberland* panorama was the work of a sole artist, William DeLaney Travis, who had developed a deep affection and respect for Rosecrans when he covered the campaigns of his army as a staff artist for both the *New York Illustrated News* and *Harper's Weekly.*

To illustrate these campaigns in heroic scope, Travis produced thirty-two dif-

≈ *Overleaf* ≈

BATTLE OF SHILOH PANORAMA (1885)

Theophile Poilpot
(nineteenth century)

Poilpot's Shiloh cyclorama might be described as the ultimate history painting. It was created by a team of twelve artists who are said to have faithfully modeled all the likenesses of the soldiers on some two thousand carte de visite *photographs of the survivors of the 1862 battle! Be that as it may, William Trego, for example, created more persuasive effects by using local residents to pose, thus portraying convincing Union cavalrymen as rural types, some with jug ears and crossed eyes. The Shiloh cyclorama vanished during a subsequent national tour, but not before it was recorded on glass-plate negatives by a Wisconsin photographer, Henry H. Bennett, two of whose pictures of the lost Shiloh cyclorama appear on the following pages.*

Oil on canvas, 50 feet × approx. 400 feet. (Photographs courtesy H. H. Bennett Studio Foundation, Wisconsin Dells, Wisconsin)

SHILOH PANORAMA #1

General Grant (gesturing, on horseback) gives an order to Gen. James B. McPherson as fighting rages on all sides. The artist may have exaggerated the commander's proximity to the fighting, but not by much. Grant remembered riding up with McPherson to inspect the fighting when "suddenly a battery with musketry opened upon us from the edge of the woods.... The shells and balls whistled about our ears very fast for about a minute.... A ball...struck the metal scabbard of my sword, just below the hilt, and broke it nearly off." With characteristic honesty, Grant also reported that it took no longer than a minute "to get out of range and out of sight." In the "sudden start" to escape the gunfire, a major on his staff lost his hat. "He did not stop to pick it up," Grant reported laconically.

ferent panels, each nine feet high by sixteen feet wide, for a staggering total of 528 feet. To facilitate their display, he created all the scenes on coarse cotton to ensure their flexibility, then stitched them together and mounted them on a giant roller. A special machine was used to crank the roller by hand so that it wound slowly onto an empty spool as an audience watched the procession of larger-than-life vignettes—in a primitive precursor of the reel-to-reel motion picture. Thus the picture showed the battle's development over time rather than a cyclorama's sweeping vista of a whole battlefield at one moment. Travis and his brother apparently handled all of the equipment themselves, taking the panorama on a tour of the states of the Old Northwest, perhaps as early as the war years themselves. Not surprisingly, Rosecrans pronounced the result one of the art world's "great conceptions of struggles on the battlefield," but Travis's early critical and popular success, if any, was not long-lasting. The vogue for panoramic battlefield depictions had not fully flowered, a problem compounded by the fact that Travis's primitive artistic style was hardly suited to paintings that required depth, range, and perspective. Travis's descendants nonetheless preserved the composition intact, donating it in 1962 to the Smithsonian Institution—which has yet to place it on permanent display.[10]

The subject of the *Army of the Cumberland* panorama also lacked universality of appeal: the "High Water Mark of the Confederacy" at Gettysburg and the fall of the great city of Atlanta were turning points of the war; the same could not be said for Rosecrans's adventures in Tennessee. Nor were the exploits of "Andrews' Raiders" enduringly well known, however exciting, which may help explain the obscurity of yet another panorama, devoted to a detailed depiction of their swashbuckling clandestine mission in 1862.

James J. Andrews was a spy under the command of Brig. Gen. Don Carlos Buell, and in 1862 he was given his most challenging assignment: to penetrate enemy territory, find and seize a train, and run it up and down the line on the East Tennessee and Georgia State railroads, burning tracks and bridges in order to cut transportation connections between Atlanta and Chattanooga. Andrews commandeered a locomotive from under the noses of Confederates at Big Shanty, Georgia (while passengers and crew ate a leisurely breakfast inside the station), and lurched off, with the Southerners in hot pursuit. But Andrews could not fulfill his mission as planned. Heavy rains had earlier flooded the area, and most bridges on the line remained so damp they would not catch fire. But the raid, with his small party of twenty-four, managed to cut telegraph lines and create no small amount of havoc for eighteen days before the train ran out of fuel and the soldiers escaped into the woods, finally being captured by the Confederates. In June, Andrews and his fellow captives were executed as spies. But a colleague named William Knight, of the Ohio Infantry, survived the "Great Locomotive Chase" and, after the war, embarked on a lecture tour in which he thrilled audiences with dramatic tales of the fabled raid, illustrating his talk with a multipanel cyclorama. In one surviving scene, the raiders are seen huddled in the fuel car of the captured locomotive, the *General*, steaming along with a Confederate train following closely behind. Once again, a primitive, one-dimensional style, not compatible with the demands of cyclorama exhibitions for urban

SHILOH PANORAMA #2

Confederate troops, sabers and rifles raised, charge forward toward the Hornet's Nest. The New York Tribune *reported: "Men with knitted brows and flushed cheeks fought madly over ridges, along ravines, and up steep ascents, with blood and perspiration streaming down their faces.... Everywhere was mad excitement; everywhere was horror." Bennett apparently photographed this section of the panel after it had been decorated with additional three-dimensional features: the flag at left, the bushes in the foreground, and the thin tree at direct center, were all placed at the base of the cyclorama to add "reality" to the scene.*

4th of July. Behind the breastworks on the right flank of the Union army... (1863)

Edwin Forbes (1839–1895)

Forbes made this sketch the day after the fighting ended at Gettysburg. It showed the battered remains of the foliage atop Culp's Hill, and the Union breastworks fashioned from cordwood and piled between the rocks.

Pencil on paper, 9⅜ × 13¼ inches. (Library of Congress)

⌐ *Opposite* ⌐

Scene behind the breastworks on Culps Hill morning of July 3rd 1862 [sic]. 10 A. M. Union forces repulsing the attack of Johnston's [sic] Div. (n.d.)

Edwin Forbes (1839–1895)

Cleverly adapting his on-the-spot sketch, Forbes fashioned a vivid portrayal of Union sharpshooters manning the breastworks and firing against General Johnson's attack. It is difficult to imagine why the artist retained the central figure of the trooper leaning against the tree (left center), unless the viewer is supposed to assume that he has been wounded. The Union defense that morning was an overwhelming success, as artillery fire rained down the slopes on the Confederate attackers. "We had no means of replying," a junior officer in the brigade explained, "as our guns could not be dragged up that steep and rugged ascent...[and] a galling fire was poured into our ranks."

Oil on canvas, 13⅞ × 29¾ inches. Signed lower left: *Edwin Forbes.* (Library of Congress)

audiences, may have kept this otherwise charming presentation from enjoying broad and long-lasting appeal.[11] The appeal of Andrews's exploit should nevertheless be clear to modern Americans; the subject inspired two famous motion pictures: Buster Keaton's *The General*, a comedy made in 1926, and *The Great Locomotive Chase*, a Disney film of 1956.

But even where the most universal of battlefield experiences was involved, and an artist chosen for the task armed with credentials equal to the challenge, some panoramic depictions appear to have provided too much of a good thing. Again, timing appeared to be important.

In 1866 the Pennsylvania legislature appropriated $25,000 to commission the Philadelphia history painter Peter Frederick Rothermel to produce for the state capitol in Harrisburg a canvas of the great battle that had raged only a few miles away at Gettysburg. Rothermel threw himself into the task, but after more than three years of research that included repeated visits to the scene and voluminous correspondence with veterans who had survived the battle, the painter concluded that he could not compress his vision into a single canvas, as requested. Instead he produced a series of paintings, among them a massive, sixteen-by-thirty-one-foot view of Pickett's Charge, which boasted the distinction of showing the action at various fronts from an unusually low vantage point. Rothermel's perspective produced what a modern critic has called "emotionally charged" portraiture.[12]

Completed in 1870, the Pickett's Charge canvas was first exhibited for a twenty-five-cent admission at the Academy of Music in Philadelphia that December, with Gen. George Gordon Meade, the Union commander at Gettysburg, in attendance. There, a veteran of the action exclaimed: "This is not a picture only—it is an epic—a national struggle, a national record." Similar approbation followed the painting and its companion tableaux as they were taken on a national tour to Boston, Pittsburgh, and Chicago, where

SKETCH OF THE POSITION OF THE 2ND
AND 3RD DIV. OF THE FIRST CORPS (JULY 3, 1863)... (1863)

Edwin Forbes (1839–1895)

"This sketch was made on the fifth of July after the retreat of General Lee's forces," Forbes wrote. He produced seven drawings in all that day, after complaining to Frank Leslie that "my horse is lame." Here he re-created the charge of Longstreet's corps on the Union lines on Friday afternoon, July 3.

Pencil on paper, 9⅜ × 13¼ inches. (Library of Congress)

⸺ *Opposite* ⸺

PICKETTS CHARGE ON THE UNION CENTRE AT THE GROVE
OF TREES ABOUT 3 P.M. VIEW LOOKING TOWARD THE FRONT (N.D.)

Edwin Forbes (1839–1895)

In an ingenious adaptation of his July 5 sketch, Forbes imposed on his background design a depiction of a small but dramatic section of Pickett's Charge. The full force of the assault can be seen in the distance. In Pickett's own words, such an attack had "never previously been enacted—an army forming in line of battle in full view…charging across a space nearly a mile in length, pride and glory soon to be crushed by an overwhelming heartbreak." To Pickett, the ensuing "awful rain of shot and shell was a sob—a gasp."

Oil on canvas, 13¾ × 29¹⁵⁄₁₆ inches. Signed lower left: *Edwin Forbes*. (Library of Congress)

the canvas was slightly damaged during the 1871 fire. The Philadelphia print-maker John Sartain went on to produce a faithful engraved adaptation of one of the scenes in 1872. Then, after a return exhibition at Philadelphia's Fairmount Park, the paintings were given a place of honor in the "Art Annex" of the city's Centennial Exposition of 1876. Their display there prompted a quite different response from Basil Gildersleeve, a writer with decidedly unreconstructed Southern sympathies. "Pictorial representations of Yankees and rebels in all their respective fiendishness are still cherished here and there," acknowledged Gildersleeve. But the observer was particularly offended by the Rothermel paintings because "the face of every dying Union soldier is lighted up with a celestial smile, while guilt and despair are stamped on the wan countenances of the moribund rebels." Added the observer: "I hope that I may be pardoned for the malicious pleasure I felt when I was informed of the high price

that the State of Pennsylvania had paid for that work of art. The dominant feeling was amusement, not indignation." To Gildersleeve, American audiences by 1876 had "got beyond the Rothermel stage." More likely, they had not quite reached it. The age of the blue-gray reconciliation movement had not yet arrived and could not, at least until the next year, when Reconstruction ended. (The principal Rothermel work proved too large for the state capitol anyway; it was never displayed there.)[13]

To date there has been little research on battle panoramas and cycloramas, and it is not clear how many existed, let alone what made successes or failures of them. Besides the ones seen or discussed in this book, others appeared from New England to the West. Charles Hardy Andrus created a 150-foot-long *Grand Panorama of the Late War* (now at the Vermont Historical Society). His *Sheridan's Ride* panorama of 1889 has vanished. And Union infantryman Thomas Clarkson Gordon's *Battle Scenes*

Above

VIEW FROM THE SUMMIT OF LITTLE ROUND TOP AT 7:30 P.M. THE PENN. RESERVES DRIVING BACK A PORTION OF LONGSTREETS CORPS BEYOND THE DEVILS DEN RIDGE (N. D.)

Edwin Forbes (1839–1895)

Adapting details from his drawings, Forbes here showed Union batteries firing on a scattered line of retreating Confederates, using the boulders at the crest of the hill as natural breastworks. By viewing the field from atop the safe summit of Little Round Top, Forbes missed the more dramatic scenes unfolding below, where "the deadly din of battle," according to Confederate general John B. Gordon, roared unceasingly. "The rattle of rifles, the crash of shells, the shouts of the living and groans of the dying convert that dark woodland into a harrowing pandemonium."

Oil on canvas, 13⅞ × 29¹⁵⁄₁₆ inches. Signed lower left: Edwin Forbes. (Library of Congress)

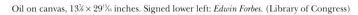

CHARGE OF EWELLS CORPS ON THE CEMETARY GATE AND CAPTURE OF RICKETTS BATTERY. 8 P M JULY 2ND 1862 [SIC]. GENL. O. HOWARD COM. (N. D.)

Edwin Forbes (1839–1895)

The Louisiana Tigers' attack on the east slope of Cemetery Hill is presented from behind the gatehouse to Evergreen Cemetery.
At left, a horse-drawn artillery battery flees the scene to prevent its guns from falling into enemy hands. The twilight assault overran Capt. R.
Bruce Ricketts's batteries (middle distance) but reinforcements plunged into the fray and overwhelmed the Confederate attackers.

Oil on canvas, 13¹⁵⁄₁₆ × 29⅝ inches. Signed lower left: *Edwin Forbes.* (Library of Congress)

≈ *Opposite Bottom* ≈

ATTACK OF JOHNSTONS DIV C. S. A. ON THE BREASTWORKS ON CULPS HILL DEFENDED BY WADSWORTHS DIV 1ST CORPS AND A PART OF THE 12TH CORPS GEN SLOCUM. HALF PAST SEVEN P.M. JULY 2ND (N. D.)

Edwin Forbes (1839–1895)

Using the boulders at the base of Culp's Hill for cover, Confederates charge toward the heights near the end of the second day's fighting. They are
met with an enfilade of Union fire and fall back, leaving piles of dead and wounded behind them. "The sight was ghastly," Forbes remembered.
"Everything bore the mark of death and destruction…the whole slope was massed with dead horses…the earth was torn and plowed by the terrible
artillery and…fire, anywhere that a light shelter offered, the dead lay in dozens…. It was difficult to tread without stepping on them."

Oil on canvas, 13⅞ × 29⅝ inches. Signed lower left: *Edwin Forbes.* (Library of Congress)

≈ Opposite ≈

[PANEL FROM THE
ANDREWS' RAIDERS
PANORAMA] (C. 1870)

William Knight
(nineteenth century)

*Cows flee from the captured
train hurtling toward Atlanta
in this primitive but compelling scene from soldier-
artist Knight's panorama of
Andrews' Raiders. In the
background, Confederate
troops pursue the Union force,
but are about to be stopped by
a loose car that has been set
afire inside the wooden railroad bridge. In truth, heavy
rains had so dampened the
wood of the bridges that the
raiders on this 1862 mission
were unable to set the fires
they had planned.*

Oil on canvas.
(Ohio Historical Society)

of the Rebellion is now stored at the Henry Ford Museum in Dearborn, Michigan. There were surely others, but, except for the Gettysburg and Atlanta cycloramas, all ultimately failed.

Perhaps the most unlikely failure was the work of the well-known artist-correspondent for *Frank Leslie's Illustrated Newspaper*, Edwin Forbes. Soon after the war, he produced a series of twelve tableaux of the Gettysburg experience—based on on-the-spot sketches he had made shortly after the battle ended—and the look and scale of these little oils strongly suggests they were designed as models for larger works. Yet by the time Forbes exhibited his "Historical Art Collection of Battles, Incidents, Characters, and Marches of the Union Armies" in 1876, he had done no more than assemble the small studies into a modest portfolio within the show. To General Sherman, who, it should be remembered, had not been at Gettysburg, Forbes's work was capable of recalling "to the survivors the memory of many scenes which are fading in the past." The general purchased a set of Forbes's famous *Life Studies of the Great Army* for the War Department.[14]

But by 1884, when a bill was introduced in Congress to purchase Forbes's entire output, there was already another Gettysburg cyclorama being displayed. The bill was voted down. Financier J. P. Morgan came to the rescue by purchasing the collection for $25,000 in 1901, and a mere footnote to the story recalled that the trove included "twelve oil paintings of the Gettysburg campaign." Edwin Forbes's beautiful works were confined ever since to the bowels of the Library of Congress.[15]

Yet even the much-viewed cycloramas disappeared in time, save for the two notable examples of Atlanta and Gettysburg. Most others, like the afore-mentioned Lookout Mountain cyclorama, vanished. A blatantly exploitative notice appearing in that section of the Lookout Mountain cyclorama catalog reserved for commercial announcements neatly suggested the transitory appeal of these once-popular artistic blunderbusses. "Everyone is delighted with the *Cyclorama*," went the advertisement. "But a Joy Forever is Beautiful Laundry Work."[16] These were popular works, not usually good enough to be preserved in art museums, and when the fickle public lost interest in the Civil War, they were doomed to storage or destruction. Before long, the sun had set ingloriously on the brief age of the Civil War cyclorama.

Even the most famous of all cycloramas, Philippoteaux's circular painting of Gettysburg, very nearly did not survive. After a brief display in Philadelphia in 1891, it was shipped back to Boston and stored away in a large crate behind its old exhibit hall. The crate was periodically vandalized, and failed as well to protect its priceless cargo from the elements. Not until 1910 did a Newark, New Jersey, merchant named Albert J. Hahne come to the rescue, purchasing the remains of the Gettysburg cyclorama and placing them on display in sections in the rotunda of his department store. Taken on a brief tour in this condition, it was seen in Baltimore by LaSalle Corbell Pickett, widow of the general whose ill-fated charge formed the basis of the composition. "Profoundly moved," Mrs. Pickett delivered a lecture on the charge to an audience enthralled both by her recollections and the canvas of "the scenes she was describing," majestically decorating "all four sides of the great armory" where she appeared.[17]

Not long thereafter, its merchant-owner was able to build a permanent exhibition hall for the Philippoteaux cyclorama in Gettysburg itself. For the first time in twenty years, the scenes were reassembled and displayed in a cyclorama building as originally intended. The cyclorama opened in time for the fiftieth anniversary of the Battle of Gettysburg, and survivors of the momentous struggle gathered to view the masterpiece of this lost art. A few years later, another distinguished visitor arrived to inspect the work: Paul Philippoteaux. In case any doubts remained as to the origin of the panoramic painting, the aging artist pointed to the likeness of a Union officer leaning against a tree; this, he explained, was a self-portrait—an artist's "signature" on this mammoth relic of the high water mark of popular Civil War art.

As a medium for full visual appraisal of the war, cycloramas always held the potential to contain more controversial subject matter than could ordinary small canvases, as the critic from the Boston *Daily Transcript* realized upon

viewing the Gettysburg Cyclorama. To the degree that they competed more with P. T. Barnum–style attractions than with galleries, they might benefit from emphasis on the sensational or grisly features of war. Thus they offered rich opportunities for any artist whose goal was to warn spectators against the miseries of modern combat. The more common impulse was to glorify war or at least lend it a twilight nostalgia under the

rubric of comradeship in arms. Some, though, professed other goals.

One such painter was James Hope, the landscapist who produced works that achieved almost panoramic scale and purpose and chose as their subject one of the bitterest losses of the war. Surely no wartime sacrifice seemed greater or more ideally suited to teach the bitter lessons of modern warfare than the carnage that filled the Bloody Lane at the

ARMY OF THE CUMBERLAND
(c. 1864–65)

William DeLaney Travis (1838–1916)

One of the veterans of Gen. William S. Rosecrans's Army of the Cumberland who viewed this mammoth panorama during its midwestern tour, during or just after the war, lauded its "rare beauty," an assessment that seems in retrospect overzealous. Consisting of thirty-two panels, the panorama was unrolled for public viewing between two huge hand-cranked spools, theater-style, but theatricality could not disguise its hopelessly naïve style. Travis, who had followed the army as a staff artist for two illustrated news weeklies, maintained that he had sketched all the events "while the scenes were being enacted." The following panels provide a sample of his prodigious output.

Oil on cotton, 9 × 512 feet. (National Museum of American History, Smithsonian Institution)

An officer bids farewell to his family near the portico of his splendid mansion, while just across the road a fellow soldier departs from a rustic log cabin. Travis probably juxtaposed these domestic vignettes to suggest the solidarity of rich and poor in the Union cause. But he succeeded only in suggesting a bizarre neighborhood of improbable economic extremes.

Federal troops charge forward from a burning barn (right) toward Confederate forces in butternut uniforms under Gen. Bushrod Johnson in this dramatic moment from the Battle of Perryville, Kentucky, on October 8, 1862. The short range that artist Travis imposed on the opposing forces here is improbable, and the Confederate officer slumping to the ground is poorly drawn.

Battle of Antietam in 1862. To one horrified Union eyewitness, it was beyond question "the most terrible slaughter seen during the war." Viewing the piles of corpses of Confederate soldiers, who had been mowed down in a sunken road by a deadly Union cross fire, he saw bodies stacked there "three deep for half a mile, and there was only one man who breathed in all that distance."[18]

Those vivid words of description were written by a veteran who went on to turn his nightmare observations into a harrowing canvas, specifically designed for public exhibition. Capt. James Hope, who had served in the Army of the Potomac, was determined to display the painting so "coming generations of possible soldiers...should learn how terrible a thing war is." And more than one generation might well have received such instruction standing before the impressive oil painting, had not public indifference, inadequate artistic skill, changing tastes, and finally the forces of nature all conspired to cut short his noble dream.[19]

A skillful nature painter, Hope seems to have executed the work as a giant landscape, with regiments, corpses, and batteries imposed on it afterward. This caused problems of proportion, scale, and perspective well beyond Hope's abilities, as was figure-painting in general: there is not a convincing human form in the work, though the landscape is littered with them. Hope produced a series of panoramic depictions of the Battle of Antietam, and all suffered the same shortcomings.

Despite his modest abilities as an artist, Hope was a canny promoter of his work. He had once petitioned Gen. Robert E. Lee himself for support in mounting an exhibition of paintings, in the "hope you can find a way for their preservation in some (yet unbuilt) National Art Gallery."

And his work inspired Union general Winfield Scott Hancock to endorse "some public grant or fund available for the purchase of works of this character. They are of high historical interest, and should belong to the nation." But Hope found no takers among government funders. He would manufacture "historical interest" on his own and, for a time, profit handsomely from it.[20]

At first, Hope placed his works on display at his Fifth Avenue studio in New York City, but, finding the space there far too cramped for his giant canvases, he relocated to Watkins Glen, a spa and resort community in the Finger Lakes region of upstate New York, and there built his own "Hope's Glen Art Gallery" near the area's most fashionable hotel. The artist began charging admission for a look at both "superb transcriptions of Nature's Beautiful and Majestic Masterpieces," as he described his landscape work, and of his "great battle scenes of the war." He printed a thick catalog, and filled it with personal endorsements from generals such as Hancock and McClellan, as well as critical accolades from the nation's press.[21]

Along with his other battle art, Hope's evocative Bloody Lane canvas became a particular highlight of the permanent exhibition, with the artist adding special interest by framing the eight-and-a-half-by-fifteen-foot vista in what he described as "weather-stained, bullet-riddled oak from the battlefield itself, bound together with the battle's emblems."[22]

"These are paintings," Hope's hyperbolic catalog declared, "before which great patriots like Lincoln, and great soldiers like Grant, Hancock, McClellan, and [Nelson] Miles have stopped, absorbed; forgetting time, place and circumstance, they were again on the field so perfectly portrayed. Then—recalled to the present by some nearby move-

Thomas Clarkson Gordon
(nineteenth century)

At the peak of the national mania for Civil War cycloramas and panoramas, even unschooled painters could attract audiences to their large-sized pictures of battles and their commanders. Gordon, who served in the Union army after 1864, afterward worked as a hardwood finisher at a furniture factory in Spiceland, Indiana. There, in its varnishing room, he painted a fifteen-panel panorama that depicted such incidents as the Battle of Shiloh and the destruction of the Macon Railroad—some of the scenes undoubtedly based on newspaper woodcuts. In this example, Gordon portrayed the bombardment of Fort Sumter in 1861, showing shells setting fires inside the Federal garrison.

Panorama, oil on unbleached sheeting, each panel approximately 6 × 13 feet. (The Edison Institute, Henry Ford Museum & Greenfield Village, Dearborn, Michigan)

ment—they have turned from these masterly records of historic deeds with tear-dimmed eyes." The report was surely exaggerated; there is no evidence, for example, that Lincoln ever viewed any of Hope's canvases, though McClellan and Hancock did. But there can be little doubt that the exhibit evoked emotional and perhaps even tearful responses.[23]

For years, while interest in Civil War art and landscape painting prevailed, people came to Watkins Glen. But the vogue for such galleries faded with the coming of the new century, the growing public museum movement, the change in artistic styles from the naturalistic to the impressionistic, and then the decline of Watkins Glen itself as a tourist site.

Hope died in 1892, and his descendants neglected the art gallery to concentrate on a restaurant and souvenir stand that they opened nearby. Then a calamitous flood surged into the region, and what was left of James Hope's art gallery was immersed in four feet of water. Some of the canvases were badly but not irrevocably damaged, but when an enterprising local enthusiast named Larry Freeman persuaded Hope's

descendants to admit him for an inspection in the 1950s, he found the Bloody Lane painting buried under mounds of mud, long beyond restoration. An art critic whom Freeman brought in to view the mess declared the paintings "The Hopeless Hopes."[24]

Freeman nevertheless managed to preserve some of Hope's other Antietam panoramas, and today they are on public display at the visitors' center of the Antietam National Battlefield. A small model oil for the lost Bloody Lane canvas was subsequently discovered elsewhere; today it is in a private collection. But the huge painting of the war's greatest sacrifice—the canvas that had once attracted impassioned audiences to a private gallery—was forever lost. Time and indifference, nudged along by a natural disaster, doomed James Hope's *Bloody Lane.*

Panoramas, cycloramas, and giant scrolled artworks had one feature in common whose appeal rapidly faded with the advent of new technologies: spectacle. The true heirs of these paintings are found today in cinema houses, not art museums.

AFTER THE BATTLE, THE BLOODY LANE—
BATTLE OF ANTIETAM, MARYLAND, 1862 (1889)

James Hope (1818–1892)

The sunken road at Antietam offered perhaps the most "ghastly spectacle"of the entire Civil War, in
the words of a war correspondent who came upon this grisly scene only moments after Union forces
swept through, leaving the enemy piled where they fell under furious fire. "Confederates," reported
Coffin, "had gone down as the grass falls below the scythe." A battle veteran who viewed the now-
destroyed painting that Hope adapted from this surviving model commented, "'Round the point, just
beyond the foreground of this painting, for three rods, they lay five and six deep." Thereafter, the
sunken road was known as "Bloody Lane." It would have required a figure painter, rather than a
landscape artist like Hope, to do justice to the scene, if any painter could.

Oil on canvas 19 × 36 inches. Signed lower left: *Copyright secured Aug. 28, 1889/All rights reserved by Capt. J. Hope.*
(From the Tharpe Collection of American Military Art)

CYCLORAMA OF THE BATTLE OF GETTYSBURG (1884)

Paul Philippoteaux (1846–c. 1913)

*Seen here in three broad sections, this most famous of all Civil War cyclorama paintings
took critics and the public alike by storm when it was unveiled in Boston, displayed majestically along
the inside wall of a huge, specially built circular building. Originally more than four hundred
feet long, it depicted the climactic moments of Pickett's Charge on July 3, 1863: the Confederate attack
across the Angle on Cemetery Ridge, where the surge was greeted, one of Pickett's officers recalled,
with "cannon and muskets... raining death upon us." It became known as "the high tide of the
Confederacy." As the Boston* Herald *declared when the painting was first shown in that city: "It tells,
and in the most vivid manner possible, the whole story of that dreadful afternoon.... Thrilling
incidents of this memorable fight, are graphically depicted, and with historical accuracy." To another
critic of the day, the cyclorama was nothing less than "truly colossal... a marvel of artistic
learning and sentiment... a great piece of work." Most of the surviving cyclorama can be seen
in the following three panels.*

Oil on canvas, 25 × 375 feet. (Gettysburg National Military Park, National Park Service; from
The Civil War: Gettysburg; photograph by Henry Groskinsky, © 1985 Time-Life Books, Inc.)

GETTYSBURG #1

*With Big Round Top and Little Round Top looming in the distance, and below
them the scene of the second day's fighting at the Devil's Den, Union general Winfield Scott Hancock,
astride his stately black charger (left center, middle) rallies Federal artillery and infantry toward
the copse of trees to fill the gaps in the Union line created by Confederate general Lewis Armistead's
breakthrough near the Angle. To a Union survivor of Gettysburg, "Hancock the Magnificent"
there became "one of the most inspiring figures that ever roused and led men on any battlefield." Gen.
Abner Doubleday is in the cluster of men in the left background. In the vignette above the felled
tree at right, General Armistead, seen with his men around captured Union guns, suddenly falls
backward from his mount behind the three flags, mortally wounded by Union fire. This "heroic Rebel,"
as a Northern eyewitness called him, was "determined to conquer or die." Philippoteaux
erred here; Armistead was on foot when he took the fatal shot.*

GETTYSBURG #2

With the smoke from Confederate artillery rising picturesquely from atop Seminary Ridge in the background, Pickett's Charge reaches a bloody crescendo at the infamous Angle, the intersection of the stone-and-rail fence at center and the perpendicular stone wall running beneath the large tree, farther in the background. Union forces rush forward to meet the charge originating from the right, all but ignoring the caisson that rears up and explodes at left, scattering bodies in its wake. A Confederate force lunges forward to cross the stone wall, while at the far right, another Confederate force dashes across a wheatfield, as Federal reinforcements rush in to meet the attack. "On they come," a horrified Union soldier recalled. "Our men are shot with rebel muskets touching their breasts." But in the end the line held, and the Confederate attack wavered and failed. The Union soldier lounging almost nonchalantly against a tree at the far right foreground, sword drawn, is a self-portrait of Philippoteaux.

GETTYSBURG #3

*In the comparative quiet of a ravaged farmhouse—artistic license by Philippoteaux,
since no such dwelling existed here during the battle—surgeons work furiously on the wounded in a
field hospital thrown together under a splintered shed, as orderlies carry fresh victims across the
corpse-strewn landscape. "There are ghastly heaps of dead men," a New York Times correspondent
reported. "Seconds are centuries; minutes, ages.... The ground is thick with dead, and the
wounded are like the withered leaves of autumn." Some of the injured can be seen grouped around the
circumference of European-looking haystacks (though some historians contend the German-American
farmers of the region indeed so shaped them), while to the far right a New York artillery battery
races toward the fray. In the left center of the scene, Capt. William Arnold's Rhode Island battery
unleashes a withering round of fire against an assault by Confederate general James J. Pettigrew. The
water well in the right foreground was intentionally drawn with but two sections of its tripod,
and lacking a rope leading to the bucket. As originally displayed, a real wood support and actual rope
were inserted into the foreground to provide a three-dimensional effect. As the Boston Globe
marveled: "On the ground at your feet lie broken cannon, guns, bayonets, and so finely is the work
done that a person cannot tell where the artist ends and the painting begins."*

REPULSE OF THE LOUISIANA TIGERS (1870)

Peter F. Rothermel (1817-1895)

As the Louisiana Tigers charge Cemetery Hill at twilight on the second day at Gettysburg—their battle flags have just appeared on the horizon above the high ground (center)—they are whipsawed by furious artillery fire from the Fifth Maine Battery (foreground), as well as a countercharge by the Union II Corps (left). Rothermel portrayed the vortex of the action as a veritable furnace. The "deadly avalanche of shell and canister" finally sent the Confederate charge reeling back.

Oil on canvas, 35½ × 60 inches. (The State Museum of Pennsylvania)

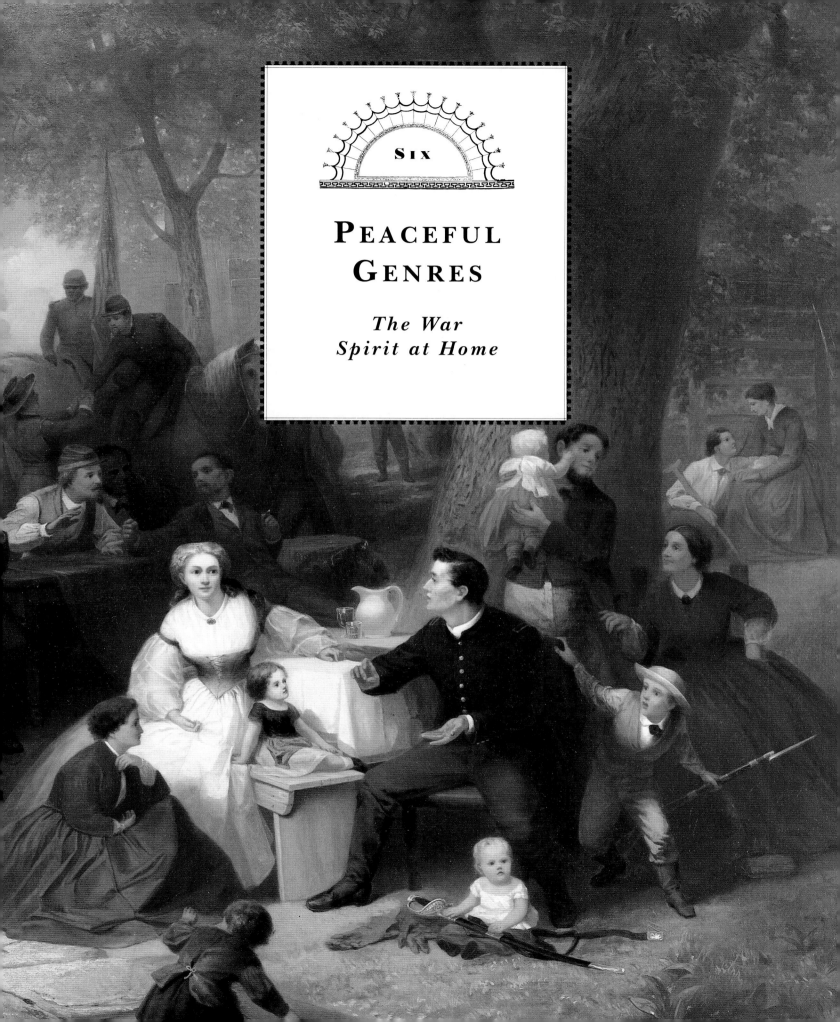

Six

PEACEFUL GENRES

The War Spirit at Home

Preceding Page

HARVEST HOME: WHEN THE WAR WAS OVER (1867)

Joseph W. John (1833–1877)

This exuberant scene of regeneration—its depictions of marriage and children suggesting the peacetime renewal of land, home, and family—was first exhibited at the Pennsylvania Academy of the Fine Arts, where the artist worked as a curator. It was also photographed by Frederick Gutekunst of Philadelphia, who apparently sold copies for family albums, accompanied by a descriptive card that explained the inspiration for the painting: "When the war was over, and our brave defenders had returned to their homes, there was a general reunion of friends and relatives to honor the return of peace with feast and song beneath the shade of a loyal homestead of Eastern Pennsylvania." The text alerted readers to such symbolic details as the bride, the widow in mourning, the returning Union officer addressing assembled family and friends, and the children "mimicking battle with their father's cast-off swords and guns."

Oil on canvas, 54 × 78½ inches.
Signed and dated: *J. John, 1867.*
(Union League of Philadelphia)

ne of the best and most enduringly popular novels set during the American Civil War and published near the time of the event hardly ever refers directly to the great conflict. No specific battle or general is mentioned, though the characters' lives are profoundly affected by the circumstance of war. When Christmas comes to the home in which the story unfolds, one of the children, who has artistic proclivities, is given a present not of a general's portrait or a lithographed battle scene, but instead a picture of the Virgin Mary and infant Jesus. Although the women knit socks for the soldiers, the war is not otherwise discussed except in passing reference to the circumstance that takes the children's father away from home. A young male tutor, clearly of military age, who boards next door, rather casually decides that he will enlist once his pupil's studies are complete. The young pupil himself makes his wedding plans, as does his fiancée, entirely without reference to military duty. And no one talks about the headlines or the latest news from the front.

Although *Little Women* is not always thought of immediately when the subject of Civil War fiction arises, it nevertheless was a Civil War novel, written by a woman who had experienced nursing the wounded firsthand and had written on the subject ("Nelly's Hospital") for the children's illustrated magazine *Our Young Folks* in 1865. Louisa May Alcott's *Little Women*, or rather its first part, was published three years later, in 1868, and as Christmas comes in the story, the March girls merely acknowledge obliquely: "We haven't got father, and

shall not have him for a long time."

Otherwise, the war hardly figures in the dialogue of Meg, Jo, Beth, Amy, and their mother, or even of their male friends Laurie and his tutor. Although the family suffers considerably straitened economic circumstances, this is not the fault of war scarcities or rationing. Somehow, the father lost his money before the war began. Political or patriotic feeling informs the important dialogue or plot of the story not at all: the young girls go on a picnic, dance, put on amateur theatricals, worry about their physical appearance and their spiritual virtue, and perform chores in traditionally domestic scenes. Although the novel takes place in

DEPARTURE FROM FREDERICKSBURG BEFORE THE BOMBARDMENT (1865)

David English Henderson (1832–1887)

When it appeared inevitable that a great battle would occur in Fredericksburg, Virginia, Federal forces urged civilians to leave the city quickly to avoid danger. "The evacuation of the place by the distressed women and helpless men was a painful sight," recalled Gen. James Longstreet. "Many were almost destitute and had nowhere to go, but, yielding to the cruel necessities of war, they collected their portable effects and turned their backs on the town. Many were forced to seek shelter in the woods and brave the icy November nights to escape the approaching assault." Refugees like those described by Longstreet huddle bravely around a fire in this night scene painted by Henderson, who served as a mapmaker on the staffs of Jackson, Lee, and Johnston.

Oil on canvas, 25⅜ × 30⅜ inches. (Gettysburg National Military Park)

abolition-minded New England, no one ever mentions the antislavery movement. The name of the president of the United States never once appears.

Such insular domesticity may well have characterized much of the Northern home front in the Civil War. Its effect on the daily lives of civilians, at least those living far from the battle lines, seems slight by comparison with the trauma that twentieth-century warfare can bring home—with its airborne bombing raids and fast-moving armored columns; its deliberate government planning and direction of domestic economic production for the war effort; and its government-concocted propaganda in the mass media and in art. When Rhode Island soldier John H. Rhodes returned to Providence while the war still raged, he "scarcely noticed…the depletion in population made by the thousands sent to the front." He saw "little which indicated the existence of a gigantic Civil War."[1]

By comparison, citizens who lived in the paths of the armies, mostly Southerners, were not insulated. They sometimes suffered hardships similar to those of the soldiers, like the women and children of Fredericksburg, Virginia, who were forced to flee Union bombardment in December 1862. Recalled a Confederate officer who witnessed the evacuation:

I never saw a more pitiful procession than they made trudging through the deep snow as the hour drew near. I saw little children trudging along with their doll babies, holding their feet up carefully above the snow, and women so old and feeble that they could carry nothing and could hardly hobble themselves. There were women carrying a baby in one arm and its bottle, clothes and covering in the other. Some had a Bible and a toothbrush in one hand, a picked chicken and a bag of flour in the other. Most of them had to cross a creek swollen with winter rains and deadly cold with ice and snow.... Where they were going we could not tell, and I doubt if they could.[2]

The artist David English Henderson would depict such refugees at their eventual destination, the safety of the Virginia woods outside the besieged city. But the painter portrayed the gathering almost idyllically: not even a dusting of snow appears in the scene, trees appear to be in bloom, and the women gather rather snugly around a campfire, a soldier nearby.

The Baltimore artist Adalbert Johann Volck fared better with his etching *Cave Life in Vicksburg*, saluting the endurance of the civilians forced to live there within excavations "in the earth" in their quest for shelter from the relentless forty-day-long Union bombardment of 1863. "One evening I heard the most heart-rending screams and moans," Mary Ann Loughborough reported in her journal, *My Cave Life In Vicksburg*. "I was told that a mother had taken a child into a cave about a hundred yards from us and laid it on its bed. A mortar shell entered the earth about it, crushing in the upper part of the little sleeping head." Not even the vitriolic Volck, however, could bring himself to re-create such scenes. Instead he portrayed a pious woman kneeling in her cave to pray for deliverance; it is an affecting scene, with its depictions of rather pathetic domestic utensils. But Volck's focus on Southern deprivation proved something of an exception.

America's artists were as well equipped to depict details of life on the home front as they were ill equipped to capture the nature of the battle front. Genre painters in particular must have enjoyed pursuing their careers in an era that made a cult of home and family; not only did such homes inspire their compositions, but the wealthier ones could also provide repositories for the finished works themselves. Genre painters did produce many evocative, if somewhat sentimental, images of the home front during the war, but these, unlike the battle pictures, are virtually unknown today. When sentimentalism fell from favor with the twentieth-century reaction against Victorian taste, these pictures were doomed to oblivion, and Civil War hobbyists and military historians, fixed in their focus mainly on land warfare between 1861 and 1865, have done little to keep these paintings and prints before us in book illustrations or art exhibits. The modern revival of interest in the painting of Civil War scenes, much in evidence today in hobbyists' magazines and in galleries and bookstores near Civil War sites, has not been comprehensive in its scope; there are few modern equivalents of the old genre scenes featuring children and women and aged parents and slaves and servants gathered in a parlor with meticulously observed decorations and furnishings. Today's painters, like the Civil War hobbyists, seem preoccupied by land warfare.

Things were different in the nineteenth century, but the degree to which the genre paintings are genuinely representative of the effect of the war at home is difficult to assess—because of

≈ *Opposite* ≈

THE RETURN TO FREDERICKSBURG AFTER THE BATTLE (1865)

David English Henderson (1832–1887)

Confederate general Lafayette McLaws found it "impossible fitly to describe the effects" of the Federal assault on the town of Fredericksburg. "The roar of the cannon, the bursting shells, the falling of walls and chimneys, and the flying bricks and other material dislodged from the houses by the iron balls and shells," he testified, created a wasteland horrifying enough "to appall the stoutest hearts." Henderson's painting of one family's return to its shattered dwelling was evidently painted as a companion piece to his refugee painting.

Oil on canvas, 23¾ × 30 inches. (Gettysburg National Military Park)

WRITING TO FATHER
(1863)

Eastman Johnson
(1824–1906)

There is a universality in this tender scene of a sun-light-bathed youngster writing to his soldier-father at the front. For the specially made uniform he wears appears in the canvas to be gray, while the kepi on the nearby chair is of an unmistakable Union blue. News from home invariably cheered the fighting men of both sides, but also increased their homesickness. Wrote a Union soldier: "You can have no idea what a blessing letters from home are to the men in camp. They make us better men, better soldiers."

Oil on canvas, 12 × 9 ¼ inches.
Signed lower right: *E. Johnson./—63.*
(Museum of Fine Arts, Boston;
bequest of Maxim Karolik)

EQUIPMENT 61 (N.D.)

William Ludwell Sheppard
(1833–1912)

A latter-day Betsy Ross figure—note the recently sewn flag draped over the chair in the foreground—adjusts the freshly made headgear on an enlistee's new Confederate uniform. The scene is idealized, from the unrealistically handsome outfit to the Stars and Bars, which were not even featured as the insignia on Confederate flags in 1861, the year this scene is supposed to have occurred. In a far franker vein, the journalist Charles C. Coffin observed that Confederate soldiers wore so many different colors and styles of dress that "one would have thought that ... the odds and ends of humanity and of dry goods, had been brought together."

Watercolor on paper, 11¼ × 8 inches. (Museum of the Confederacy, Richmond, Virginia; photograph by Katherine Wetzel)

KNITTING FOR THE SOLDIERS (1861)

Eastman Johnson
(1824–1906)

A young girl, her own impoverished circumstances notwithstanding, knits socks for Union soldiers, her diligence representing devotion to the war effort among home-front women of all ages. It was not unusual for soldiers to run out of supplies and write home for replacements. "Arrived in camp out of rations and out of clothing," went one such plea from a member of Sherman's army as it marched through the Carolinas. "The soles of my shoes were gone. Had no socks." A period art critic, calling Johnson "a painter of the fireside," particularly praised his portraits of children: "All the tenderness, all the sympathy of the man is expressed."

Oil on board, 9⅜ × 11⅜ inches. Signed lower left: *E. Johnson/1861.* (New-York Historical Society)

Opposite

**CAVE LIFE
IN VICKSBURG
DURING THE SIEGE
(BALTIMORE
c. 1863–64)**

Adalbert Johann Volck
(1828–1912)

*During the war, Volck, a
Bavarian-born Baltimore den-
tist and Southern sympathizer,
secretly etched a number of
provocative scenes—some sav-
agely lampooning Northern
leaders, others sentimentaliz-
ing the Confederate experience.
This stark example shows a
pious Vicksburg matron at
prayer in her makeshift home
inside a cave during the
Union siege, where many residents lived to escape the bombardment. "Terror stricken" in
such a shelter, Mississippi
diarist Mary Ann
Loughborough remembered
similarly crouching in her cave
"while shell after shell followed
each other in quick succession.
I endeavored by constant
prayer," she added, "to prepare
myself for the sudden death I
was sure awaited me." These
Vicksburg cave-dwellers were,
from Volck's point of view, the
Southern analogue to Lilly
Martin Spencer's comfortable,
well-dressed, and secure
Northern family celebrating the
end of the Vicksburg siege.*

Etching, 6⅝ × 4⅛ inches.
(The Lincoln Museum)

the relatively primitive state of scholar-
ship about the home front. As late as
1990 a historian could, with good reason, write an essay that asked the question "Have Social Historians Lost the
Civil War?" The fact is, as he stated it:
"Despite the popularity of military history, little effort has been made to study
the demographic and socioeconomic
impact of war on society." Unpacking
the academic language, one must agree
that it is difficult to conjure up clear
images or succinct statements that
would characterize the nature of the
war experience for women and children, for laborers and farmhands, for
college professors and students, for cler-
gymen and actors—even for painters
and sculptors.[3]

The present work cannot solve this
general problem, but perhaps it will
help to make a case for examination of
paintings and popular prints as an inte-
gral part of the studies that will some-
day answer our questions about the
social history of the Civil War. Genre
painting, after all, was supposed to
depict "everyday life," and the effective-
ness or the truthfulness of its product
merits comment by historians.

One domestic image, created by a
painter of modest talent, has proven so
durable and was so obviously "successful" in its print adaptations that it could
not be ignored and has already
emerged as a subject of analysis among
historians more interested in the social
history of the Civil War than in its military history. This is William D.
Washington's *The Burial of Latane*. Its
reputation, too, has benefited in recent
years from the painting's prominent display at the Museum of the Confederacy
in Richmond. But the testimony of
Southerners today to the pervasiveness
of prints based on the painting, hanging on the walls of their childhood

homes, suggests that *The Burial of Latane*
genuinely embodied vital myths of the
Lost Cause. Respect for Washington's
creation seems to grow and grow. What
historians have heretofore discovered in
it—"one of the best-known Confederate
renditions of [the] reassuring narrative
of unswerving black loyalty" to their
masters in the war—is certainly present
in the painting. But so are other things
as well.[4]

Like other powerful Civil War visual
images, *The Burial of Latane* was based
on a real event, the death of the sole
Confederate cavalryman to lose his life
in Gen. J. E. B. Stuart's brilliant ride
around the Army of the Potomac in
1862. And like some other important
paintings of the war, Washington's was
first filtered through a poet's vision, in
this case John R. Thompson's popular
1862 poem, "The Burial of Latane." In
this case, the resulting visual image,
though powerful, appealed especially
and almost exclusively to Southerners.
It was as true of the poem as the painting and its engraved adaptation. The
initial publishing history of the poem is
particularly instructive. It appeared as
early as the summer of 1862 in the
Southern Literary Messenger, of which the
poet Thompson had been an editor,
and in small broadside form elsewhere
in the Confederacy afterward.[5]

Proof of the picture's almost exclusively Southern appeal lies in the early
compilations of Civil War poetry. The
U.S. government during the Civil War
did not seriously attempt, as modern
governments do in wartime, to control
the thoughts of its people. Numerous
books were published in the North
while the war raged that contained sympathetic portrayals of Southerners and
the Southern cause. Frank Moore, who,
during the war, anthologized the poetry
produced on Civil War themes, includ-

ed, as a companion volume to *Songs of the Soldiers* and *Personal and Political Ballads of the War* in his "Red, White, and Blue Series" of cheap octavo books, a fascinating compilation entitled *Rebel Rhymes and Rhapsodies*. The books appeared in 1864. After the reader turned past the title page of *Rebel Rhymes* with its little symbolic woodcut showing a rattlesnake (along with an alligator and a pelican) at the foot of a palmetto tree, he found this simple explanatory note, dated March 1864:

> *In the preparation of this volume, it has been the purpose of the Editor to present as full a selection of the Songs and Ballads of the Southern people as will illustrate the spirit which actuates them in their Rebellion against the Government and Laws of the United States. Most of the pieces have been published in the magazines and periodical literature of the South, while many are copies of ballad-sheets and songs circulated in the Rebel armies, and which have come into the possession of the forces of the Union in their various marches and advances during the present conflict.*

It is a remarkable comment on the lack of totality in the war's impact that such a book, put together by a respected author and published by a firm as well established as Putnam's, could appear in New York in the midst of the war. The poems, no matter how scathingly anti-Northern their content,

IN THE HOSPITAL, 1861 (C. 1861)

William Ludwell Sheppard (1833–1912)

Making the rounds one day among "fever wards and dying men"
in Chimborazo Hospital in Richmond, pioneer nursing matron Phoebe Yates
Pember heard an emaciated, unwashed patient implore her, "Kin
you writ me a letter?" She obligingly took dictation, for which she was
rewarded with a repulsive marriage proposal. In creating a romanticized
version of such scenes, artist Sheppard bathed this unrealistic hospital room
in reassuring light, dressed his lovely nursing volunteer in springtime pas-
tels, and added a vase of fresh flowers. The wounded soldier at rear appears
well attended indeed: by two army physicians and a nurse. Such portrayals
contributed to the evolving myth of the heroines of Dixie, but ignored the
grim realities of life for hospitalized soldiers.

Watercolor on paper 11¼ × 8 inches. Signed lower left: *W. L. Sheppard* (Museum of the
Confederacy, RIchmond, Virginia; photograph by Katherine Wetzel)

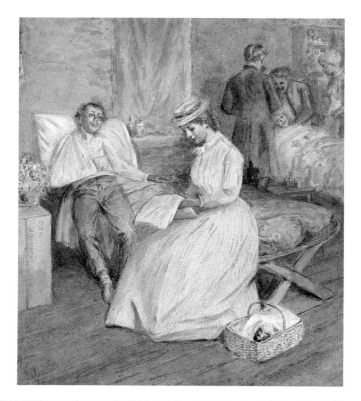

WOMEN'S SANITARY CORPS (c. 1861–65)

Anna Mays
(nineteenth century)

Two battlefield nurses enter a Union hospital tent to minister to wounded soldiers, in this appealing primitive tribute to the volunteers of the Sanitary Commission. Under the direction of the intrepid Dorothea Dix, such women operated tirelessly to "disburse special supplies bestowed by individuals or associations for the comfort of ... soldiers." Mays portrayed their arrival here almost theatrically, throwing tent flaps open, like a stage curtain, to herald their entrance as angels of mercy.

Oil on canvas, 18 × 21 inches.
(Courtesy Edward R. Hageman)

⇒ Opposite Bottom ⇐

THE FIELD HOSPITAL, OR THE LETTER HOME (1867)

Eastman Johnson (1824–1906)

A volunteer from the U.S. Sanitary Commission, the tools of her trade lying on the ground nearby, patiently takes dictation from a helpless wounded soldier. Louisa May Alcott, who served as a Civil War nurse, recalled first ministering to soldiers' wounds, then working "to minister to their minds by writing letters to the anxious souls at home." In this scene, possibly suggested by an 1863 Homer lithograph, The Letter for Home, *artist Johnson painted the principal subjects in soothing shade, while the sun shines on tents and an able-bodied soldier in the distance, a reminder that the war was still raging. The wounded soldier, dressed in white and covered with a white blanket, is portrayed almost angelically, while the bold streak of red across his coverlet may have served to remind viewers of the bloody results of war.*

Oil on board, 23 × 27½ inches. Signed lower left: *E. Johnson/1867.* (M. and M. Karolik Collection, Museum of Fine Arts, Boston)

THE BURIAL OF LATANE (1864)

William D. Washington
(1834–1870)

In a painting that inspired a best-selling engraved adaptation, Confederate captain William D. Latane is buried by pious plantation matrons. The evocative scene, however static its composition, ingeniously provided comforting images to war-weary Southerners: the nobility of women left in charge of the home front; the eternal loyalty of the slave population; the assurance that every lonely casualty of war would be so tenderly treated; and the belief that the Southern landscape, however ravaged by war, would remain an Edenlike paradise. For these reasons the canvas created a "furor" at its first exhibition in Richmond in 1864, with "throngs of visitors" crowding to see it, and a critic praising it as a "most touching and impressive scene."

Oil on canvas, 36 × 46 inches.
(Judge John E. DeHardit Collection;
From *The Civil War: Lee Takes Command;* photograph by Larry Sherer, © 1984 Time-Life Books, Inc.)

appear without any editorial apparatus explaining or denouncing them.[6]

Yet it is also interesting to note that Moore, though he published another of Thompson's poems, failed to include "The Burial of Latane." The same oversight can be found in two postwar anthologies of verse. Neither Richard Grant White's *Poetry Lyrical, Narrative, and Satirical of the Civil War* nor Moore's later compilation contains "The Burial of Latane." Only *Bugle Echoes*, an anthology edited by Francis F. Browne in 1886, does. It seems to have been, for whatever reason, a poem mainly for Southerners. Yet its political content was hardly noxious. The most anti-Northern stanza in it merely accused the Yankees of refusing to allow a clergyman through the lines to preach the burial service over the Confederate cavalryman's body:

> No man of God might say the burial rite
> Above the "rebel"—thus declared the foe
> That blanched before him in the deadly fight,
> But woman's voice, in accents soft and low,
> Trembling with pity, touched with pathos, read
> Over his hallowed dust the ritual for the dead....

Otherwise, the poem described the lonely death of a soldier away from home, his body prepared for burial by strangers, and his soul commended to God by a woman doing service as clergy. The theme seems nearly universal for war, and it is surprising that the poem was not included in prominent anthologies of war poetry.[7]

The painting was perhaps even more Southern in outlook than the poem, which stated: "The aged matron and the faithful slave / Approached with rever-

ent feet the hero's lowly grave." That was the only mention of slavery in the verse, but Washington included a panoply of slave types in his canvas, complete with differing socioeconomic roles. The best figure in the painting is that of a male slave leaning on a shovel with which he has obviously dug the soldier's grave, his battered straw hat lying on the ground; a female slave in a kerchief is also well depicted. By contrast, the white women—perhaps because Washington modeled them after prominent Richmond women who posed as models and whom he may have felt compelled to flatter—are poorly delineated. The matron who presides over the service by no means appears "aged," and some of the others resemble silhouetted cameos more than real people.

It is true that Washington's painting, as the historian Drew Gilpin Faust put it,

> *speaks specifically to the peculiar circumstances and realities of the Confederate situation, for it directly reflects prevailing notions of southern nationalism and the place of slavery within the Confederacy.... White women and children are favored by God's light; blacks are cast slightly into shadows. Working together, the races are still kept carefully apart, with the slaves segregated on the left side of the painting.... The message was above all one of common Christian sacrifice in face of northern cruelty, with blacks and women uniting the homefront in support of the nation's divine mission.*[8]

Certainly that is adequate to describe the political significance of *The Burial of Latane,* but it somehow misses the painting's deepest appeal, which was more than political. In fact, the painting for a

long time did not appeal to Southern hearts as strongly as its postwar print adaptations did. After the painting's initial exhibition in Richmond late in 1864, it was not seen again in public until the 1960s. True, its early exhibitions in wartime Richmond, as T. C. DeLeon reported, "attracted wide attention and favorable verdict from good critics." Some observers maintained that when pails were set up beneath the canvas, visitors routinely threw in money and even jewelry to purchase materials for the care of the war wounded.[9] But afterward, even though the painting disappeared from public view, popular engravings based on it spread throughout the South.

Where these pictures were displayed offers the key to their appeal: in the home. *The Burial of Latane* is less a history painting than a domestic image, even a genre painting, a scene of everyday life in the Confederacy—or what Southerners wanted to remember as the Confederacy. The picture does not broadcast a loud political message. In truth, it is not a history painting in the

sense that Carpenter's Emancipation image was, because William D. Washington's are not portrait likenesses of the real participants, but of stand-ins. And these Richmond belles stand, not for the historical moment of this plantation burial, but for all Confederate women everywhere and at all times. The painting's emotional route to viewers' hearts lay through sentimentalism as much as patriotism.

Sentimentalism, which arose in the United States in part to cushion the fears aroused by deaths of children in an era of high infant mortality and lingering Calvinist belief in original sin, gained a renewed prominence in the Civil War, soothing the new anxieties provoked by the deaths of young men far from home, church, and familiar influences. Many of the common soldiers were young enough not to have made a religious commitment before leaving home for the war, where the temptations of camp life were notoriously capable of undoing God's work. Between the two sides, religion seems to have figured larger in the lives of Confederate soldiers than of their Union counterparts; the Confederate camps were swept by great evangelical revivals in 1863 and 1864. Religious anxiety surely ran high among Southern mothers and wives as well, and *The Burial of Latane* offered the solace of imagined Christian burials for loved ones killed far from home.[10]

Moreover, *The Burial of Latane* can only be described as a loser's image. Here lay its peculiarly Southern appeal.

The wartime painting called to mind staggering Confederate losses—eventually 250,000 dead—and the deprivations of life in the Confederacy (in this case, no preacher for the funeral and a woman left at home to run the plantation). After the war, when the image really enjoyed its broadest popularity, *The Burial of Latane* became a gloomily sentimental reminder of sacrifice to the old order. But it was also something more, and this quality made it an exception to Southern distaste for anything less than heroic in war art. *The Burial of Latane* affirmed the endurance of home and family in the midst of catastrophic political and military circumstances. And its print adaptations were likely aimed at women. One cannot imagine such a print hanging in an old soldiers' home. There, scenes of past glory reigned. The North did not experience proportionate loss, such great physical deprivation, or ultimate defeat. And the North did not clutch to its bosom any similarly maudlin image.

Finally, William D. Washington deserves credit for an achievement never before noted: there appears to be no other Civil War–era painting like his in theme and focus. For all its faults of execution, it remained an evocative image, uniting religion, women, children, and domestic social tranquillity with the war effort.

Though there are many other well-executed domestic images from the Civil War—some of them more skilled in execution than Washington's—none, with the possible exception of the political painting of Francis B. Carpenter, has ever equaled *The Burial of Latane* in its ability to linger in American memory and in American parlors in popular print adaptations.

To understand why most of the other home-front images lost whatever appeal they boasted at the time of their creation, one need only look at the triter aspects of Washington's painting. The rolling of the pious eyes upward in the face of the plantation mistress-turned-clergywoman and the golden-haired innocence of the pudgy-faced, precious child to her right, were sure to displease Americans who, in the twentieth century, joined in cultural revolt against Victorian taste.

Lilly Martin Spencer's pro-Union painting, *The War Spirit at Home—Celebrating the Victory at Vicksburg*, included some of these improbably precious images, for example, the baby in her mother's lap resting on an arm gracefully outstretched but hardly adequate to prevent a real-life writhing infant from rolling onto the floor. The other children depicted, including the young girl wearing in celebration an incongruous military kepi with her strangely lascivious off-the-shoulder dress, perform a band march such as never occurred, apparently, to Meg, Jo, Beth, and Amy. Spencer, one of the leading female artists of her day, was one of several who sentimentalized the war. (When her *War Spirit* painting was first displayed at

≈ Opposite ≈

THE WAR SPIRIT AT HOME — CELEBRATING THE VICTORY AT VICKSBURG (1866)

Lilly Martin Spencer
(1822–1902)

As she balances her suckling infant so she can read The New York Times's *report of the "Great Victory" at Vicksburg— news that reached a grateful North on Independence Day of 1863—a Northern mother's older children erupt into a mock-heroic celebration of the Federal triumph as a domestic looks on with curiosity. Artist Spencer, who specialized in painting children, was also a practicing feminist; her own husband worked for her. "Let Men…know," a period journal declared, "that with the skill of her hands and the power of her head, she sustains a family." Appropriately, Mrs. Spencer modeled the youngsters in this scene on her own children, and made the strong mother figure a self-portrait.*

Oil on canvas, 30 × 32¼ inches. Signed: *L. M. Spencer 1866.* (The Newark Museum; purchase 1944, Wallace M. Scudder Bequest Fund)

≈ Left ≈

THE DOMESTIC BLOCKADE

Currier & Ives

Lithograph.
(The Lincoln Museum)

INTERIOR OF GEORGE HAYWARD'S PORTER HOUSE, 187 SIXTH AVENUE, N.Y.C. (1863)

Edmund D. Hawthorn
(active 1863–1876)

Soldiers gather in improbably formal groups and poses in the fashionable barroom of George Hayward's elegant porter house on the corner of Sixth Avenue and Thirteenth Street in Manhattan. Such home-front drinking establishments offered a welcome respite from the hardships of war, but it is doubtful that even Hayward's featured quite the ordered solemnity and impeccable decor depicted here. The paintings shown lining the walls, however, are not an exaggeration. When the contents of the house were sold at auction in 1878, the catalog boasted two Hogarths, a Gilbert Stuart painting of George Washington, and such incongruous religious scenes as Birth of the Savior *and* Crucifixion. *Hawthorn's scene was first exhibited at the National Academy in 1864.*

Oil on canvas, 36 × 47 inches.
Signed lower right: *E. D.
Hawthorn/1863.* (New-York
Historical Society)

Campbell's framing shop in Newark for two months in 1866, a newspaper praised the work as the "most delicate in sentiment of the many illustrations we have seen.")[11]

That such infections of the home by war spirit must have occurred can be concluded from other paintings, popular illustrations, and common sense. Photographs of the children of the elite—from the sons of President Abraham Lincoln to those of Maj. Rutherford B. Hayes—show them in correct little Union uniforms. For the youngsters of the middle and lower classes, paper hats and pan-and-spoon drums evidently sufficed. Thomas Nast united these elements of high and low in a painting he executed in March 1863, which was made into a large colored lithograph by Currier & Ives the same year. In *The Domestic Blockade* the preciously beautiful children of the household, the boy in his perfect Zouave's uniform and his sister in republican white, have barricaded the kitchen and stand guard against the comical Irish maid, who holds a broom in her burly arms and wears ridiculously unfeminine brogans on her feet. The print is drawn with only modest skill: the bottle-cannons arranged in broadside on the table skirt would surely be rolling onto the floor as the boy places one foot on the same narrow band of wood (they hardly seem to sit solidly on the surface, as it is). But the lithograph evidently proved popular, for it soon inspired a sequel, *The Attack on the Home Guard,* also based on a Nast drawing.

These domestic scenes serve as a reminder of what military pictures do not adequately convey: the hidden rigidities of social class. In the Northern domestic images, class lines are drawn nearly as firmly as race lines in *The Burial of Latane.* Indeed, the dour ser-vant in Lilly Martin Spencer's painting stands in shadow behind the brightly lit mistress of the household and her cherubic children, and Nast's Irish servant girl is little more than a caricature in vividly depicted clothing.

Most painters thus obeyed the unwritten rules of Victorian genre painting on the home front, just as they obeyed the unwritten code of military glory when depicting the battle front. A rare exception, in a way, is E. D. Hawthorn's *Interior of George Hayward's Porter House,* painted in 1863. Artists did not often venture into drinking establishments—on their canvases, at any rate—and when they did, they were more likely to draw a moral or to depict comical dissolution. Hawthorn's painting, with its handsome portrait likenesses of drinking and smoking dandies and brightly uniformed militia officers, seems to pass no judgment. Of course, class barriers remain unbroken here, too, from the shoeshine boy to the pathetic girl beggar in the background; if lower-class persons were shown drinking—even the weak porter with its 4-percent alcohol content—they would surely have been somehow visually condemned.

It speaks well for nineteenth-century Americans that the most representative political painting from the war is

Carpenter's Emancipation Proclamation scene, with its earnest statesmen
situated in the plainest of offices, and
not pompous imitations of scenes of
European royal court life evident, for
example, in *The Republican Court in the
Days of Lincoln*, once, ironically, attributed to Carpenter, but, as it turns out,
actually painted by Peter Rothermel.

The Rothermel painting endeavored
to convert a wildly enthusiastic White
House reception into a frozen but dignified tableau of Washington Society. The
night before receiving from President
Abraham Lincoln his commission as
lieutenant general, Ulysses S. Grant was
welcomed to the executive mansion
at a thronged reception where he met

THE CONSECRATION, 1861 (1865)

George Cochrane Lambdin (1830–1896)

As a dashing Union officer prepares to depart for the front, his sweetheart blesses his dress sword with a tender kiss. In a more earthy vein, one recruit remembered that "every young fellow who went to war got a kiss from his 'best girl,' and as it was the first that many of us had ever enjoyed, it is not surprising that a last farewell was repeated over and over again before we actually took our departure." Any such scene would have shocked Victorian-era art patrons, who expected chaste images like this scene of sanctification. Yet one art critic of the day bluntly urged, "If it is not too late for George Lambdin to learn, he might be taught a few truths by Mr. Homer's…unsentimental treatment of masculine themes." One critic saw in this work symbols of "separation and non-fulfillment," with each character kissing "symbols of each others' sexuality."

Oil on canvas, 24 × 18 ½ inches. (Indianapolis Museum of Art; James E. Roberts Fund)

THE REPUBLICAN COURT IN THE DAYS OF LINCOLN (C. 1867)

Peter F. Rothermel (1817–1895)

*The night before receiving from Lincoln his commission as lieutenant general, Ulysses S. Grant attended a thronged
White House reception where he met Lincoln for the first time. As a recently unearthed advertising flyer for this picture admitted, the painting
was conceived not to recall realistically the boisterous White House welcome for Ulysses S. Grant, but rather to "give to the present generation and
to posterity, portraits of the prominent personages of the time, in the most pleasing manner possible." In Rothermel's static central grouping,
Grant presents his wife, Julia, to President Lincoln, while at right, Mrs. Lincoln fusses over General Winfield Scott—who most likely did not
attend the event, having retired and moved to West Point four years earlier.*

Oil on canvas, 23 × 27 inches. (The White House Collection)

IN THE HANDS OF THE ENEMY AFTER GETTYSBURG (1889)

Thomas Hovenden
(1840–1895)

A wounded Confederate is tended by a Union family in their Gettysburg home after the battle. Wounded Union troopers are also shown, but Hovenden made the injured Rebel—propped up beneath a portrait of Lincoln and an American flag—the central focus, which suggested that the home was the cradle of sectional reconciliation.

Etching. Signed lower left: *Hovenden, N.A./1889.*
(Library of Congress)

President Lincoln for the first time.

"It was quite a gathering," remembered Secretary of the Navy Gideon Welles. "Clapping of hands" erupted as Grant was first glimpsed, after which "all in the East Room joined in it as he entered. A cheer or two followed." Lincoln's private secretary recalled the crowd growing so thick that Grant, a small man, "was forced to mount a sofa from whence he could shake hands with those who pressed from all sides to see him." Welles found the scene altogether "rowdy and unseemly." But when Rothermel decided to immortalize the occasion in oils in the style of Daniel Huntington's dignified *Republican Court in the Days of Washington*, he made it look as staid and formal as a royal cotillion.[12]

Genre painting proved better adapted to peace than to war, for sentimentalism was the American genre painter's stock in trade, and war often proved too rough a subject. This was true even of excellent genre painters like Eastman Johnson. His war painting *The Wounded Drummer Boy*, discussed in a later chapter, did not mea-

sure up to his evocations of the home front, and even the latter seem flawed as well. Take, for instance, *The Letter Home.* This celebration of the work of the United States Sanitary Commission, an institution that brought the modern organizing imperative to charity, depicted a typical activity of the women who volunteered to aid the wounded—writing letters for the disabled or illiterate. But the painting, showing the wounded soldier's cot in a secluded bower, would fail to convey any impression of war, had Johnson not written "U.S. Sanitary Commission" on a nearby haversack and placed a couple of tents and a man in a kepi in the background. The Sanitary Commission helped organize charity and followed the rules devised by Florence Nightingale in the recent Crimean War, and there were hordes of wounded and sick to be organized and ministered to. More soldiers died of disease than were killed by enemy action, and before these afflicted men died, many of them lay in hospitals. *In hospitals*—not in cots scattered picturesquely about the woods and bushes near camps where they had caught the disease in the first place. Johnson's scene seems quite improbable.

Johnson's work grew stronger when he focused more closely on home and family. *The Pension Claim Agent*, finished in 1867, had the virtue of bringing to life a scene that must have been acted out in many a home after the war. By the end of the nineteenth century, veterans' benefits absorbed more than 40 percent of the federal budget. In truth, the number of veterans or dependents receiving such benefits in the period right after the war, when Johnson painted this work, lay below 200,000, but it reached nearly a million by the turn of the century. Pensions indeed formed an important aspect of daily life in post–Civil War America.[13]

HOME FROM ANDERSONVILLE (PHILADELPHIA, 1866)

William Sartain, after Joseph Noel Paton

"Blessed are they that suffer for righteousness' sake," this postwar engraving told its viewers with a biblical subtitle. But the principal character of the scene, who is supposed to be a repatriated prisoner from the notorious Confederate camp at Andersonville, looks positively beefy compared to the men who actually survived incarceration there, and were promptly photographed in their near-skeletal condition for a famous series of atrocity pictures. Such horrors, however suitable for the gathering places of bitter old veterans, were hardly appropriate for display on parlor walls. This domestic tableau, featuring its wounded veteran and grateful wife and mother, seemed ideal for such a purpose. The addition of the portrait of U. S. Grant helped orient viewers of this otherwise universal scene.

Mezzotint engraving, 13¾ × 19½ inches. (The Lincoln Museum)

RETURN FROM CRIMEA (LONDON, 1856)

Joseph Noel Paton

A veteran of the Scots Fusilier guards returns home from Crimean War service bearing a captured Russian helmet as a trophy, in one of the earliest of all artistic tributes to the common soldier, and later the inspiration for Sartain's print Home from Andersonville. *Sartain ill-advisedly copied the husky soldier from this print for his own depiction of an Andersonville prisoner. Queen Victoria so admired this scene that she purchased a copy of the original painting as a Christmas gift for Prince Albert.*

Oil on canvas. (The Royal Collection)

THE PENSION CLAIM AGENT (1867)

Eastman Johnson (1824–1906)

The war had hardly begun when Congress passed its first pension law for invalided Union soldiers. By war's end, veterans were eligible for payments ranging from eight dollars monthly for enlisted men to thirty dollars for high-ranking officers, the disabled receiving up to twenty-five dollars. In this tribute to the system, a pension claim agent interviews an amputee. When first exhibited in 1867, this canvas won from the critic Russell Sturgis praise as "both a memorial of the war, and of New England domestic life." He particularly praised the portraits of the veteran, "so calm about his own story"; the agent, "excited beyond reserve"; and the mother, "moved … more at her boy's suffering than by his services." The result, Sturgis said, was a "true realistic work."

Oil on canvas, 37½ × 25¼ inches. (The Fine Arts Museum of San Francisco)

A painter more disposed to criticize the social order, however, might not have depicted the agent with such a bright, attentive, helpful, avuncular countenance. The pension business was rife with possibilities for fraud. Some claims agents, who went to Washington to track down errant pensions for the poor and illiterate who lived far away, retained part of the claim as their pay. There were opportunities, of course, to retain more than their due. Some of the claimants proved to be no angels, either. Almost half the claims for veterans and about a third of those for dependents filed through 1885 were disallowed. The man in Johnson's painting might actually have lost his leg in a farming accident rather than in battle, and the sandy-whiskered agent might later have made off with much of the pension benefits due honest veterans. Still, the painting, with its presentation of rustic poverty consequent upon having a disabled head of household in a rural economy, can certainly be described as a successful genre scene.

Such genre painters—and their printmaking popularizers in the lithograph and engraving industry—proved especially adept at presenting what the art historian Christopher Kent Wilson has described as "the sentimental, narrative reunion of soldier and family." These works generally depicted common soldiers and rustic homes. It seems, to judge from the painters' world, that soldiers seldom returned *to* cities (though they might march *through* them in victory parades). Gilbert Gaul once painted such a scene, but it was executed in the early twentieth century, when many more Americans lived in cities than had during the Civil War. And the Civil War artists also ignored the opportunity to make the personal family reunion somehow a symbol of the national political reunion of North and South brought about by the Union soldiers' work. The titles of such pictures offer the clue: Joseph W. John's *Harvest Home: When the War Was Over; The Soldier's Return to His Home* (a lithograph offered in January 1866 as a premium from the *Philadelphia Inquirer*); *How We Won the War* (a John Sartain engraving after a picture by Christian Schussele) published in Philadelphia in 1865; and, more significant, *Home from Andersonville*, a William Sartain engraving, also published in Philadelphia in 1865. These titles suggest triumph and not reconciliation.[14]

Home from Andersonville provides another interesting reminder of the gulf that separated popular prints from the world of painting. Even for engravers as distinguished as the Sartains, and even when dealing with the more refined medium of engraving rather than lithography, popular prints remained more a business than an art. Sartain appropriated the image in *Home from Andersonville* from a painting by a British artist named Joseph N. Paton. Paton called his 1856 depiction of a Scots Fusilier Guard returned from the Crimean War to his cottage *Home;* in turn, it was engraved in mezzotint in England as *Return from the Crimea*. Sartain necessarily altered a few details to adapt the picture to the American scene. He removed the Scottish fishing gear, and the spiked Russian helmet the soldier brought home as a trophy. He hung a picture of General Grant on the cottage wall. He changed the form of the windowpanes.[15]

But Sartain failed to make enough changes for his engraving to embody a telling message. Andersonville had become a byword for cruel treatment of Union prisoners with the publication of sensationally gruesome photographs showing the emaciated and diseased condition of some of the inmates liberated from the notorious Confederate military prison in Georgia. Sartain's beefy soldier with his clothes in reasonably useful condition hardly resembled the skeletons in rags who came out of Andersonville.

In his commercial haste to produce a print, Sartain thus missed his chance to enrage his audience, and that, after all, was the point of the popular prints depicting Andersonville. Mostly ugly scenes with propaganda messages, these prints must have decorated soldiers' and sailors' hospitals and veterans' lodges. They were not intended, surely, for the "home" used so resonantly in Paton's title. It is interesting as well to note that

THE GUN FOUNDRY (1866)

John Ferguson Weir (b. 1841)

The bustling West Point Foundry supplied most of the Parrott guns for the Federal armies, and President Lincoln himself testified to its importance by visiting in June 1862 and personally inspecting the pouring pit depicted here. "A wonderful place," exclaimed a guest who arrived soon thereafter. "One can hardly worm his way through the piles of shot and shell." When this canvas was exhibited at the frothy 1867 Exposition Universelle *in Paris, a critic lauded it as a mythic work populated by workers he described as "Cyclops at their toil." That same year, the American critic Henry T. Tuckerman more perceptively saw it as a tribute to national economic transformation. "We know of no picture," he marveled, "which so deftly celebrates our industrial economy."*

Oil on canvas, 47 × 62 inches. Signed lower right: *John F. Weir/1866.*
(Putnam County Historical Society, Cold Spring, New York)

painters, who produced works meant to endure, generally eschewed the theme of Andersonville, with its brittle, short-range propaganda value. Of course, they were led to do so in part from self-interest, for paintings were expensive and, if sold to private patrons, needed to embody beauty. The possibility of painting political or social criticism was limited by the paucity of public galleries that, in modern times, display the controversial works ordinary people would not care to live with every day.

Even so, it remains striking how sectionally partisan were the depictions of Union soldiers' returns. Avoiding the use of the term "reunion" in their titles, these works were created by artists who were apparently not ready to consider themselves at one with the Southern people. The Union remained uneasy, and images of triumph or peace came more readily to mind than images of sectional reconciliation. Years would pass before significant change. Thus Thomas Hovenden's *In the Hands of the Enemy After Gettysburg*, copyrighted as an etching in 1889, may be a more important image than it seems at first glance. Though not a homecoming scene, it does show soldiers convalescing at home—in this case both Union and Confederate. Such blue-gray reconciliations in art were hard won and came— with the great outpouring of published Civil War reminiscences—only in the 1880s. By 1890, when the United Confederate Veterans began to take control of the movement to keep memories of the Confederacy alive, a new spirit reigned. As the historian Gaines Foster says, Southerners no longer sought to rejuvenate sectional battles. They emphasized "reconciliation and the comradeship of battle."[16]

The genius of Winslow Homer's *The Veteran in a New Field*, painted in 1865, becomes clear against this background of popular images and less imaginative paintings. As the critic Christopher Kent Wilson points out, Homer eschewed the reunion scene and instead offered a solitary figure, and he employed the symbolic device of the scythe to show that instead of doing the grim reaper's work, the veteran now turned to a harvest of abundance. The theme, an old and important one in American history, of Cincinnatus, the soldier returned to the plow and spurning a continuing military role that might endanger liberty and lead to Caesarism, is here dressed in plebeian colors. This is not General George Washington or General William Henry Harrison as a potential dictator returning to the plantation; it is the common soldier, returning in republican fashion to his farm, so that he does not become part of a standing army, the tool by which generals could rise to dictatorial power.

The nineteenth century seems to have found reassurance in this work. *Frank Leslie's Illustrated Newspaper* reproduced the painting as a woodcut in 1867, and lauded the message of "the stability of our political system" they saw in it. It seemed "simple and truthful."[17] But given the expanse of the field of wheat that faces the anonymous figure with his hat-shaded face, there remains, at least for the modern observer, something of that haunting sense so often found in Homer that the individual faces an engulfing and uncertain natural world. Everyday life *The Veteran in a New Field* does show, but an everyday genre painting it was not. And it spurned the sentimentalism that later would hobble the long-term appeal of the genre painters' Civil War works.

Return Home (c. 1907–9)

Gilbert Gaul (1855–1919)

Like Henry Mosler's Confederate veteran who comes home to discover his rural cabin shattered and abandoned, this soldier has returned to his conquered city home to find his fine brick dwelling reduced to rubble. Gaul's choice of urban ruin over pastoral was unusual among artists of the Civil War.

Oil on canvas, 32 × 44 inches. Signed lower left: *Gilbert Gaul*. (The Birmingham Museum of Art)

THE LOST CAUSE (c. 1868)

Henry Mosler (nineteenth century)

Conceived as a companion piece to his verdantly optimistic genre painting, Leaving for War, *this brown-hued scene of defeat and ruin made vivid the shock that awaited many Confederate veterans when they returned to their homes in 1865. Mosler was a Northerner who had traveled with Union armies in the West as an artist-correspondent for* Harper's Weekly. *The lone soldier returning to a crumbling cabin or modest house, his family gone and presumed dead, quickly became a widespread popular symbol of Confederate defeat and the Lost Cause.*

Oil on board, 30 × 48 inches. (Kentucky Historical Society)

THE VETERAN IN A NEW FIELD (1865)

Winslow Homer (1836–1910)

Some critics at first dismissed this deceptively simple composition as "hasty," "slight," and "slapdash," and others criticized its failure to equip the veteran with a modern "cradle" scythe, a technology developed during the war. Homer added this detail later, although at first he may have relied on the old "grim reaper" scythe intentionally, to symbolize the war's death toll. Harper's Weekly *later published a poem similarly depicting the "yellow harvest-field" as "cursed with a crimson yield." Perhaps as a result of its poor initial reception, Homer exhibited this canvas but little following the war, and, after failing to sell it at the Artists' Fund Society of New York in 1865, auctioned it off the following year. But modern scholars have lauded the painting as a powerful example "of Homer's vision, which sets him apart from his contemporaries."*

Oil on canvas, 24⅛ × 38⅛ inches. Signed lower left: *Winslow Homer 65;* and lower right: *W. H.*
(The Metropolitan Museum of Art; bequest of Miss Adelaide Milton de Groot, 1967)

[CIVILIANS ON WAGON
WITH FLAG CELEBRATING
LEE'S SURRENDER]
(c. 1865)

Artist unknown

A wagonload of exuberant Northerners races through the countryside to spread the news of Lee's surrender in this oil by an unknown artist. The scene presents both the exhilaration of victory—vivified in the characters on the porch who raise their arms in triumph—as well as the bitter aftermath of war, suggested by the gravesite in the left foreground. Surely not lost on the painter was the fact that the once-violated landscape, rendered with more skill than the men and horses, was now returned to the tranquil state in which he or she here portrays it.

Oil on canvas, 12 × 17 inches. (West Point Museum, U. S. Military Academy; photograph by Don Pollard)

THE HERO'S RETURN (c. 1860s)

Trevor McClurg (1816–1893)

A symbolic cross-section of the generations joyfully welcomes home the conquering—and only slightly wounded—hero in this genre scene romanticizing the veteran's return to family hearth. Wife, children, sisters, a brother, and a dog greet their loved one, and the table most of them encircle groans with simple but nutritious fare. The painting subtly declares that the war has been fought to preserve such homes, and not as clearly for the freedom of the black man, here relegated to the task of toting the soldier's gear in the shadows of the doorway. Not surprisingly, the painter also ignored challenges facing many veterans in readjusting to domestic life. One Iowa officer, for example, worried because war "benumbs all the tender feelings of men and makes them brutes."

Oil on canvas, 29½ × 41½ inches. (The Civil War Library and Museum, Philadelphia)

SEVEN

COME *and* JOIN US, BROTHERS

The White Artist and the Image of Blacks

Singing "John Brown's Body" and "The Battle Cry of Freedom" as they marched, black troops of the Fifty-fifth Massachusetts, many with caps perched on their bayonets in celebration, enter Charleston after its fall to Sherman on February 21, 1865. Amid the ruins of the city where the Civil War had begun, Charleston's black residents—those few who remained from a prewar slave population of 18,000— swarmed into the streets to greet their liberators. "Cheers, blessings, prayers and songs were heard on every side," a colonel remembered.

Pencil, oil, and wash on board, 14½ × 21¼ inches. (M. and M. Karolik Collection, courtesy Museum of Fine Arts, Boston)

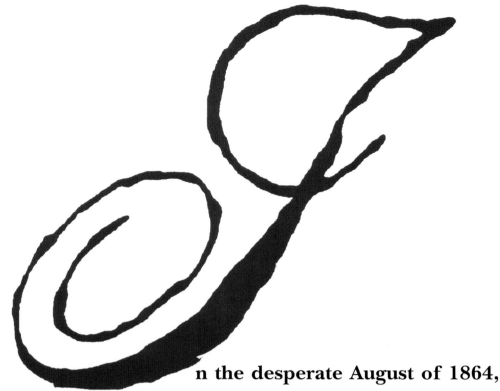

n the desperate August of 1864, President Abraham Lincoln summoned to the Executive Mansion the most famous black leader of the era, Frederick Douglass. While the governor of Connecticut waited impatiently in the anteroom after twice being announced to the president, Lincoln parleyed frankly with Douglass. He must have told his visitor how dim were the political prospects for the administration. This was an election year, after all, and as autumn approached, Lincoln found little comfort in news from the front. General Grant was bogged down in Virginia, suffering heavy casualties and still no closer to Richmond than the reviled McClellan had been two years earlier. General Sherman remained outside Atlanta, which the Confederates still held stoutly. It seemed to the president that he would not gain reelection, and that meant, in his mind, that the policy of emancipation would be doomed under the subsequent Democratic administration.

Lincoln was a practical man who knew that desperate situations required desperate remedies. So he asked Douglass to come up with a plan to spread the word to the slaves remaining on the plantations of the Confederacy that the Emancipation Proclamation had set them free. They must seize their chance for liberty before a new administration came to power. But this mission required a clandestine and dangerous scheme, for these plantations, of course, lay beyond Union control.

Douglass went home from his White House meeting and drafted a letter proposing that he employ black agents or "scouts" at two dollars a day to pass beyond Union lines, infiltrate the plantations, spread the word of emancipation, and organize and guide as many slaves as were willing to come north. As it turned out, the daring scheme never developed further, because General Sherman captured Atlanta and that news reversed the political fortunes of the administration.

Frederick Douglass remembered it, though, and in his reminiscences in later years he cited the plan as proof of Lincoln's sincerity in desiring emancipation. Douglass even described the scheme as being modeled "somewhat after the original plan of John Brown."[1]

What a remarkable development it was that Abraham Lincoln should have come to support a plan that could reasonably be described as resembling John Brown's. Less than five years before he met with Douglass on that fearful August day, Lincoln had insisted in a speech to a large audience, "John Brown is no Republican," and denied that any Republican had been implicated in Brown's plot. Lincoln characterized the Harpers Ferry raid of 1859 this way:

> *It was an attempt by white men to get up a revolt among slaves, in which the slaves refused to participate. In fact, it was so absurd that the slaves, with all their ignorance, saw plainly enough it could not succeed. That affair, in its philosophy, corresponds with the many attempts, related in history, at the assassination of kings and emperors. An enthusiast broods over the oppression of a people till he fancies himself commissioned by Heaven to liberate them. He ventures the attempt, which ends in little else than his own execution. Orsini's attempt on Napoleon, and John Brown's*

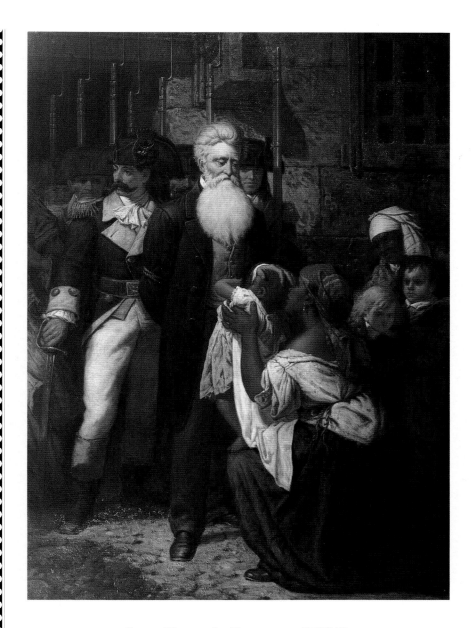

JOHN BROWN'S BLESSING (1867)

Thomas Satterwhite Noble (1835–1907)

Looking more like a patriarch of the church than a dangerous religious fanatic, white-bearded John Brown emerges from jail, a phalanx of bayonets behind him to symbolize his martyrdom by the state. As he blesses a black child, the cherubic white children (right) watch with a mixture of envy and disapproval. The colonial uniforms on the military guards recall Virginia's early history, but the black handlebar mustache seems incongruous in such garb.

Oil on canvas, 7 feet ¼ inch × 5 feet ¼ inch.
Signed lower right: *T. S. Noble 1867.* (The New-York Historical Society)

REVIEW OF MAINE AND RHODE ISLAND TROOPS (c. 1865)

James Walker (1819–1889)

Walker painted a number of military drill and parade scenes, most likely on commission from the regiments portrayed. This unusual example showed both white and black troops in the same parade. Thus the painting paid tribute to the first all-black heavy artillery regiment of the war, the Fourteenth Rhode Island, organized in June 1863. Parading through the streets of Providence two months later, they won warm praise from the local press, but Walker saw fit to portray these "noteworthy specimen[s]," as one paper described them, merely from the back, showing little of their faces, and making them pictorially subservient to the white comrades they accompany.

Oil on canvas, 16 × 21 inches. (The Corcoran Gallery of Art)

THOUGHTS OF LIBERIA, EMANCIPATION (1861)

Edwin White (1817–1877)

An aging slave bundled up against the harsh realities of bondage daydreams about emigrating in this dignified wartime genre painting. A poster on his door marked "HAYTI" suggests the subject ardently believes in colonization (Caribbean destinations were proposed by advocates as affordable alternatives to more distant African locations). In truth, most blacks had been born in the United States and were dubious. Frederick Douglass, who for a time flirted with the idea of colonization in Haiti, later spoke for millions of blacks when he said, "We are Americans…and shall rise or fall with Americans."

Oil on canvas, 17 × 21 inches. Signed left: *Edwin White/N.Y. 1861.* (The New-York Historical Society)

JOHN BROWN MEETING THE SLAVE MOTHER AND HER CHILD ON THE STEPS OF CHARLESTON [SIC] JAIL ON HIS WAY TO EXECUTION... (NEW YORK, 1863)

Currier & Ives, after
Louis L. Ransom
(1831–1927)

"Regarding them with a look of compassion"—in the words of the caption to this print adaptation of Louis Ransom's sympathetic painting—John Brown pauses before a slave family, and kisses a child as he is led down the courthouse steps and toward the gallows. All the incongruous details from the original remain, including the Revolutionary-era uniforms of the guards, so depicted to remind viewers of Virginia's eighteenth-century role in the fight for, not against, liberty.

Lithograph, 9 × 13 inches.
(The Lincoln Museum)

attempt at Harper's Ferry were, in their philosophy, precisely the same.[2]

Despised as an assassin in 1860 even by sincere antislavery men, John Brown enjoyed a different reputation later, and his image quickly changed with Civil War events. Of course, he had a "cult" following all along: an early and enthusiastic biographer, James Redpath; eloquent defenders and eulogists in Henry David Thoreau and John Greenleaf Whittier; and celebratory print portraits produced as early as 1859. It is significant that the popular printmakers Currier & Ives published an allegorical John Brown lithograph in 1863, the year of the Emancipation Proclamation. It was based on a painting by Louis Ransom.

Like some other key Civil War images, this one owed its inception to poetry—and to myth. An entirely fabricated story in the *New York Tribune* described John Brown's leaning over to kiss a black infant held up to him by its mother, as he was being led down the Charles Town courthouse steps on the way to his execution. In fact, Virginia authorities were so fearful of rescue attempts that people were banished from the streets of Harpers Ferry at the time Brown was to be led from the jail. But Whittier included the incident anyway in his poem "Brown of Ossawatomie":

*John Brown of Ossawatomie spake
    on his dying day
"I will not have to shrive my soul a
    priest in Slavery's pay.
But let some poor slave mother whom I
    have striven to free,
With her children, from the gallows-
    stair put up a prayer for me."*

*John Brown of Ossawatomie, they led
    him out to die;*

*And lo a poor slave mother with her
    little child pressed nigh.
Then the bold, blue eye grew tender,
    and the old harsh face grew mild,
And he stooped between the jeering ranks
    and kissed the negro's child.[3]*

Louis Ransom's *John Brown on His Way to Execution* represented the event not as a history painting but as an allegorical one. Known from its Currier & Ives print adaptation, Ransom's image includes an absurdly scowling Old World hussar, a neoclassical figure representing blind justice jammed into the lower left corner of the frame, and a figure in shadow, looking as though he may have reservations about the justice of Brown's fate, dressed in a tricorn hat with the number "76" on it, obviously representing the founding fathers who came from Virginia.[4]

Brown's image remained a matter of lively controversy throughout the rest of the century, and there was apparently enough demand for pictures of him that Currier & Ives later reissued their Ransom-inspired print in revised form, as *John Brown, the Martyr.* Only four figures remain from the original nine, and they are considerably altered. The ridiculous hussar now points the way to the scaffold, the slave mother raises her head to look up at Brown, and the child gazes up at him also.

Three years before Currier & Ives's reissue, Thomas Satterwhite Noble finished a canvas called *John Brown's Blessing.* Though Noble's painting had more of the superficial earmarks of a history painting than Ransom's, it too was a thoroughly confused image. Brown's guards are dressed as soldiers of the American Revolution, though there is nothing else of allegory or fantasy about the image. The slave mother is more effectively represented and looks like a person rather than a symbolic statue, but the black woman and two accompanying white children in the right background play no obvious role in the drama.

Thomas Hovenden's interpretation of the same scene, *The Last Moments of John Brown*, finished in 1884, was a triumph of history painting, and looking at its predecessors impresses us with the difficulty of the achievement. First, it qualifies as a true history painting: people are dressed in attire appropriate to the era. There are no hussars to represent tyranny, and no Continental soldiers to remind us of the distance Virginia had fallen from the heights of her libertarian leadership in the American Revolution. The soldiers appear to be men doing their job, not merely symbolic representatives of tyranny. The heaviest editorializing—aside from the sheer fact of the mythical event depicted in this affecting canvas—came in the representations of Brown's jailers. They look like ordinary middle-class men, curious about the historic event in which they participate. Brown's gesture and physical attitude are depicted with believable naturalism, and he seems dignified and fatherly but not biblical. The black woman and child are likewise superior to those painted by Ransom and Noble.

Hovenden's achievement seems especially remarkable when one considers that he did not even come to America (he was an orphan from Ireland) until 1863, and did not experience the impact of John Brown's raid when it was a news event. But in 1881 Hovenden had married a fellow artist whose father's farm had once served as a stop on the Underground Railroad. If this were not enough to stimulate his interest in black people, two years later came a lucrative and unusually specific com-

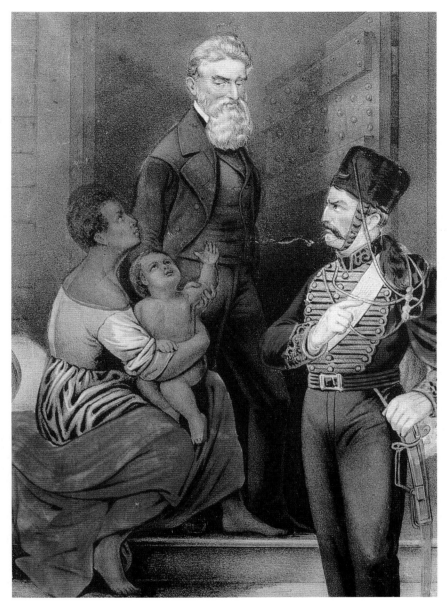

mission to paint John Brown. Hovenden's patron, New York manufacturer Robbins Battell, insisted that the scene be rendered in precisely the manner described by the *Tribune* and echoed by Whittier a generation earlier. "The incident of the kissing of the child must have occurred as stated and published at the time," Battell wrote to Hovenden. "You are familiar I suppose with Whittier's beautiful allusion to it.... It has probably occurred to you that you might represent the child in its mother's arms, extending one or both of its

SUNDAY MORNING IN VIRGINIA (1877)

Winslow Homer (1836–1910)

As a young teacher instructs her even younger students— possibly her own siblings—an elderly black woman sits nearby in lonely isolation, her opportunities for literacy long gone. This tribute to the quest for learning among emancipated Southern blacks reminded viewers of the lost generation of slaves whose minds, as well as their bodies, had been kept so long in bondage. "One of the most encouraging features attending the emancipation of the colored race," noted Harper's Weekly, *"is the eagerness to learn displayed from the earliest moments of freedom."*

Oil on canvas, 18 × 24 inches.
(Cincinnati Art Museum)

THE CHIMNEY CORNER (1863)

Eastman Johnson (1824–1906)

A black man struggles to comprehend the written word amid the discouraging ramshackle surroundings of his primitive cabin, in this poignant tribute to the educability of emancipated blacks. A modern art historian has noted that "the figure's dull expression, awkward way of grasping the book, and uncomfortable-looking position suggest some difficulty with the reading, but at the same time project an intense commitment."

Oil on board, 15½ × 13¼ inches.
(Munson-Williams-Proctor Institute Museum of Art, Utica, New York; gift of Edmund G. Munson, Jr.)

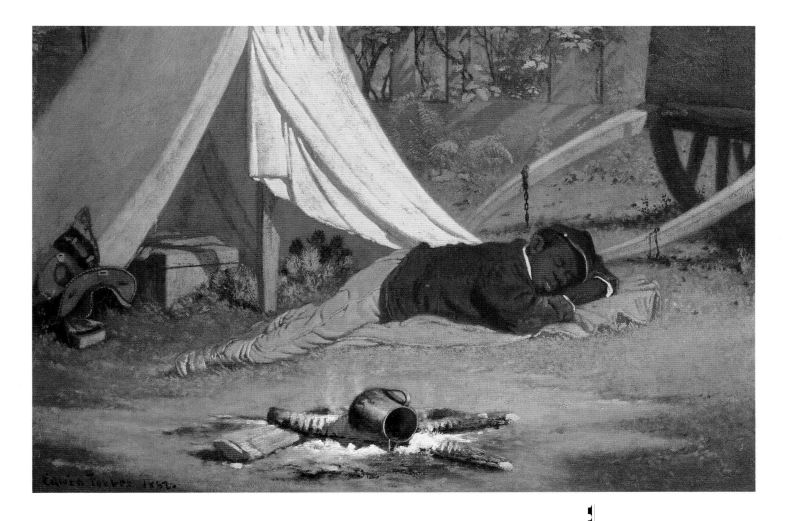

MESS BOY SLEEPING (1867)

Edwin Forbes (1839–1865)

As the Anglo-African *reported in 1861: "Five hundred men find employment each day in the Quartermaster's Department." All told, some 200,000 blacks served as cooks, teamsters, nurses, and laborers for the Union army. And as this affecting scene suggests, many were quite young. The mess boy depicted here has slept so long the coffeepot for which he is responsible has fallen into the now-doused fire.*

Oil on canvas, 14 × 20 ¼ inches. Signed lower left: *Edwin Forbes 1867*. (Wadsworth Atheneum, Hartford, Connecticut; the Ella Gallup Sumner and Mary Catlin Sumner Collection)

⌘ *R i g h t* ⌘

A WATCHED POT NEVER BOILS (1890)

Edwin Forbes (1839–1895)

The pencil drawing on which this etching was based also served as the model for Forbes's postwar painting Mess Boy Sleeping.

Etching, 6 × 8 inches. (The Lincoln Museum)

NEGRO LIFE AT THE
SOUTH, OR OLD
KENTUCKY HOME
(1859)

Eastman Johnson
(1824–1906)

*This tableau of workers at rest
and recreation reminded one
postwar Northern art critic of
"the 'good old times' before the
'peculiar institution' was
overturned—times that will
never again return." But
another observer saw in its
"dilapidated and decaying
negro quarters" a suggestion
of "the approaching destruction of the 'system' that they
serve to illustrate." Actually,
Johnson painted the scene not
in the South but in the backyard of his father's house in
Washington; family servants
served as models. When this
canvas was auctioned off in
1867, the "artists's masterpiece" fetched a staggering six
thousand dollars.*

Oil on canvas, 36 × 45¼ inches.
Signed: *E. Johnson/1859.*
(The New-York Historical Society)

little hands toward the man, with a wist-
ful look, which he pleasingly recognizes,
and is about to bend to kiss it." To make
certain the painter knew the details of
the story, Battell soon unearthed an old
copy of the 1859 *Tribune* article and for-
warded it to Hovenden as well.[5]

The artist followed his patron's
requirements to the letter. And Battell
was so pleased with the result that he
paid the artist six thousand dollars for
it—two thousand dollars more than
their agreed-upon price. The artist was
also rewarded with enthusiastic notices,
The New York Times proclaiming the
painting "the most significant and strik-

cution, the paper's editors pointed out
"that the subject of the picture…was
suggested by the gentleman who gave
the order for it, and the work was executed as a matter of business by the
artist…the historical accuracy of which
the artist probably knew nothing
about." Hovenden went on to produce
an 1885 etching, published in a limited
edition of one thousand copies by
George Gebbie of Philadelphia—who
offered it, appropriately enough,
together with the Whittier poem that
had helped inspire it in the first place.[6]

Thus Hovenden's enthusiasm for
Brown and sympathy for the blacks in

ing historical work of art ever executed
in the Republic." There were dissenters,
too. But when an old veteran of the
Richmond Howitzers wrote to the
Baltimore Sun to insist that Brown had
kissed no babies on the day of his exe-

his painting can be attributed to
the pressures of patronage. What is
astonishing is that Thomas Satterwhite
Noble, who, as a Kentuckian, had served in
the Confederate army, produced a work
separated from Hovenden's only by skill

A RIDE FOR LIBERTY—THE FUGITIVE SLAVES (C. 1862–63)

Eastman Johnson
(1824–1906)

In March 1862, Johnson observed a slave family fleeing toward the Union forces near Manassas, Virginia, and immortalized the incident in this vivid twilight scene, portraying the slave father, mother, and child as a latter-day Joseph, Mary, and Jesus escaping to Egypt. Customarily, blacks were depicted as docile, even cheerful in bondage. Now Johnson helped liberate them artistically by showing slaves as courageous masters of their own fate, capable of both initiative and humanity. That some audiences were ready for this change was evidenced by the fact that Johnson was commissioned to paint at least two copies of this work.

Oil on board, 22 × 26¼ inches. Signed
lower right: *E. J.*
(The Brooklyn Museum; gift of Miss
Gwendolyn O. L. Conkling)

and wisdom in conception, not by any obvious difference in sentiment about the subject.

And that may, in the end, illustrate the most important point that can reasonably be made about the appearance of black people in Civil War paintings: they may occupy only a marginal place but they usually gained honest or even sympathetic portrayal. Painting, it must be remembered, stood a step above the popular pictorial media, and the painters avoided, for whatever reasons—including personal political sentiments or pride in their ability to achieve formal results—caricature and overt character assassination. In some instances they achieved pictorial representations that were definitely exceptional within the climate of popular opinion and may even have constituted courageous image-making.

Certainly Eastman Johnson concoct-

ed a thrilling—one wants to say, anachronistically, nearly cinematic—image in *A Ride for Liberty: The Fugitive Slaves*. The son of a state government worker from Maine, Johnson achieved a "peculiar fame," in art critic Henry T. Tuckerman's words, for "his delineation of the negro." As Tuckerman saw it:

One may find in his best pictures of this class a better insight into the normal character of that unfortunate race than ethnological discussion often yields. The affection, the humor, the patience and serenity which redeem from brutality and ferocity the civilized though subjugated African, are made to appear in the creations of this artist with singular authenticity.[7]

Behind Tuckerman's racially charged and patronizing comments lay a gen-

shares the artist's exhilarating response to the scene, a response translated with skill and simplicity. Unlike L. M. D. Guillaume, for one, Johnson was capable of painting a believable image of a horse, and by giving the painting a low horizon, Johnson presented his escaping slaves almost as silhouettes. In other words, Johnson, who had already painted—in what is widely regarded as a proslavery image—*Negro Life at the South* (hence its nickname, *Old Kentucky Home*, after Stephen Foster's sentimental song), here created the artist's visual equivalent of abolitionist literature, an *Uncle Tom's Cabin* in oils. About all the viewer can surmise is the nobility of the woman, the innocence of the child, and the responsible seriousness of the husband and father determined to free himself and his family from the horrors of slavery. Like much antislavery propaganda, Johnson's painting aimed at the sentimental bull's-eye of the nineteenth-century American heart: the family. The blacks escape as a family unit, not as dislocated, unpredictable, hopeless, or dangerous individuals. And yet even modern critics can commend the painting for showing "black people as being energetic and forceful and, above all, as determining their own fate."[8] Here was finely crafted propaganda indeed.

uine respect for Johnson's skill at humanizing subjects whom most Americans, even its leading art critics, it would appear, were not accustomed to perceiving as anything but—again using the critic's word—"primitive."

In this line Johnson reached his artistic zenith with *A Ride for Liberty*, depicting, as the artist inscribed on the back of his canvas, "a veritable incident of the Civil War seen by myself at Centerville in the morning of McClelland's [*sic*] advance to Manassas, March 2, 1862." Even a modern viewer

The characters in Johnson's *Ride*, like the eager enlistee, soldier, and wounded veteran of Thomas Waterman Wood's heroic series, called *A Bit of War History*, are a long way from the subservient blacks of the John Brown paintings, and the moment at which it was painted, 1862 or 1863, was separated from the year of Brown's hanging, 1859, by what can only be described as an era. In between, most black people in the United States had been declared free, and the country began to turn its back on two and a half centuries of history to face a genuinely biracial future.

Paintings, oddly enough, had been biracial for a long time, even among painters from the great slave empire called the United States of America. From John Singleton Copley's *Watson and the Shark* (1778) and John Trumbull's *Battle of Bunker's Hill* (1786) to works by painters like Hovenden and Johnson, who appear to have been genuinely interested in black subjects in art, they had never been made invisible on American canvases. As subjects of Civil War art, though, blacks labored under special difficulties. Painting is an essentially retrospective medium, owing less to the inspiration of the moment than to painstaking effort. Civil War subjects blossomed in American painting mostly after the war was over. Many of them were painted after the end of Reconstruction, in the 1880s and 1890s, decades that marked what was probably the low point for the black image in the white mind. Painters may then have been painting Civil War subjects, but they were nevertheless men and women of their own times, and nothing in the culture brought to them consciousness of black achievements from the past.

Hand in hand with the pervasive and harsh racism that accompanied the failures of Reconstruction came the peculiar problem of black people in Civil War history: they stood as reminders of the political divisions that had led to the war. *Century Magazine*'s editors, for example, had realized that sectional subjects could boost circulation rather than threaten it with boycotts by one region or the other, as long as the political issues of the war were suppressed in favor of its military history. And because it seemed political, black military history was somewhat slighted. Thus, in Gen. Quincy A. Gillmore's article "The Army before Charleston in 1863," the death of Col. Robert Gould Shaw in the July 18 assault on Fort Wagner is mentioned (and a portrait of Shaw is reproduced) without acknowledging that Shaw led a black regiment, the Fifty-fourth Massachusetts, and was buried in a mass grave with his men.[9]

The pictorial record created in this postwar era was mixed but at least as creditable as the written one when it came to taking black history into account. Popular prints, for example, predictably ran the gamut from vulgar, racist caricature to fully representative acknowledgment of black achievements in the Civil War.

It must be kept in mind that the heyday of Civil War publishing and illustration in the late nineteenth century coincided with the depths of unashamed and public racism. In popular prints, the notorious landmark was Currier & Ives's "Darktown" print series. America's most prolific lithography firm turned out seventy-three different "Darktown" prints in the years 1884–1897. The broadest sort of saloon comic pictorials, the "Darktown" series included at least one print with a black veteran in it: *The Darktown Othello: I Mashed Her on de Dangers I Had Passed (Drivin' an Army Muell)*, printed in 1886. This lithograph dealt with a dangerous subject in late-nineteenth-century America—miscegenation—and showed the black man (who is identifiable as a Union veteran from the kepi resting on a porch rail) with a reasonably unexaggerated physiognomy as opposed to the scrawny, shoeless hayseed white Desdemona and her lazy corncob-pipe-smoking father. The black Civil War veteran, it seems, could bring out the best in even a vile series of pictures.[10]

For the more dignified prints designed for display in parlors rather than taverns, pool halls, and hotel basements, one would expect to find black

Opposite

THE LAST MOMENTS OF JOHN BROWN (c. 1884)

Thomas Hovenden
(1840–1895)

Commissioned to paint this fanciful scene by a wealthy New Yorker for a fee of four thousand dollars, Hovenden researched details of costume and architecture, making two visits to the scene and interviewing eyewitnesses to Brown's final moments. Although it was criticized for perpetuating the myth that Brown kissed a black child that day, this canvas was declared "a real addition to our limited gallery of historical art" by the New York Evening Post. *It showed Brown wearing the noose that would hang him, a detail Hovenden defended by insisting that "the rope was worn to the scaffold and placed on John Brown's neck before he left the jail."*

Oil on canvas, 48 × 38 inches.
(The Fine Arts Museum of San Francisco)

SLAVES ESCAPING THROUGH THE SWAMP (1863)

Thomas Moran (1837–1926)

A Union veteran who served in the deep South remembered that blacks fleeing into Union lines "in the search for freedom...were pursued by bloodhounds and often shot down like dogs when caught." To minimize the possibility of detection, fugitive slaves often made their way under cover of snake-filled swamps, where another eyewitness recalled seeing them "looking back over their shoulders as if expecting capture even there." This is the scene Moran portrayed in his wartime canvas, in which even nature itself seems to conspire to threaten the tiny figures.

Oil on canvas, 32½ × 43 inches. (Philbrook Art Center, Tulsa, Oklahoma; Laura A. Chubb Collection)

THE ARMED SLAVE
(c. 1865)

William Spang (active 1870s)

His rifle stacked symbolically against a nearby wall, with its bayonet fixed backward as a symbol of peace, this fierce-looking black soldier is armed for the new era with both a book for study and a cigar emblematic of the leisure inherent in freedom. Spang's daring portrait suggested a once-active warrior who had fought to win his liberty, now turned as determinedly to peaceful pursuits. "No people grow so rapidly in the right direction as Americans," exclaimed black veteran George Washington Williams. "What a wonderful revolution!"

Oil on canvas, 29½ × 23¼ inches. (The Civil War Library and Museum, Philadelphia)

PANEL FROM THE ARMY OF THE CUMBERLAND PANORAMA
(c. 1864–65)

William DeLaney Travis
(1839–1916)

Toting belongings hastily packed in knapsacks, slaves flee a Tennessee plantation house on a star-filled winter night to follow the Army of the Cumberland—seen marching in the distance—to freedom. Depictions of runaway slaves were rare, especially in panoramas and cycloramas.

Oil on cotton, 9 × 17 feet. (National Museum of American History, Smithsonian Institution)

**COME AND
JOIN US BROTHERS
(PHILADELPHIA,
PUBLISHED BY THE
SUPERVISORY
COMMITTEE FOR
RECRUITING COLORED
REGIMENTS,
c. 1863–65)**

P[ierre]. S. Duval

*One of the most compelling
pieces of political art of the
Civil War, this famous
recruiting poster presented an
attractive and inviting role
model to blacks considering
army service. In an 1863
article entitled "Why Should a
Colored Man Enlist?"
Frederick Douglass urged
blacks to join up not only "for
your own sake" but also for
the "more inviting, ennobling,
and soul enlarging work…of
making one of the glorious
band who shall carry liberty to
your enslaved people."
Douglass also believed that
with "an eagle on his button,
and a musket on his shoulder," there was "no power on
earth" that could deny black
veterans the full rights of
citizenship.*

Chromolithograph, 13¾ × 17¾ inches.
(Chicago Historical Society)

subjects simply avoided. That was the case certainly with Boston's Louis Prang, who assiduously avoided black subjects in his eighteen Civil War battle pictures. Only one black person, an unobtrusive sailor depicted on the deck of the *Kearsarge*, shows up in the entire series. By contrast, Kurz & Allison's series of thirty-six battle scenes gave considerable attention to black soldiers. A close look at their peculiarly land-bound *Battle Between the Monitor and Merrimac* reveals a small boat being launched by a black family (man, woman, and two children), apparently to help bring wounded sailors ashore. And a black man in a red shirt and straw hat aids a white Union infantryman in carrying a wounded sailor to the hospital. Kurz & Allison's *Storming of Fort Wagner*, illustrating the charge of the Fifty-fourth Massachusetts, remains the best extant depiction of that event in nineteenth-century art. Their *Battle of Olustee, Fla.*, printed in

1894, even celebrated a single regiment by name: the American flag in the center of the print carries a yellow streamer with "8th U.S. Col. Inf. Rt." written on it. And Kurz & Allison's depiction of the *Battle of Nashville* shows Confederate soldiers retreating and surrendering before black infantrymen who triumphantly mount their abandoned parapets, while white Union cavalrymen sweep around their flank.

Finally, and most astonishing of all, the Chicago lithographers included *The Fort Pillow Massacre* in their series. Discussions of this incident can still raise tempers in modern times. On April 12, 1864, Confederate soldiers under Gen. Nathan Bedford Forrest's command killed a substantial part of a Federal garrison in Tennessee; many of the Union dead were black soldiers who were apparently killed after they surrendered. Only the sort of print that could not comfortably be displayed in the dining room could memori-

Storming Fort Wagner (Chicago, 1890)

[Louis] Kurz & [Alexander] Allison

The New York Tribune *expressed the belief that the charge of black troops depicted here "made Fort Wagner such a name to the colored race as Bunker Hill had been for ninety years to the white Yankees." But no history painter emerged to create a canvas for these black heroes. This print particularly celebrated the regiment's white commander, Col. Robert Gould Shaw, by depicting the precise moment at which he was shot and killed. The charge took place at nightfall; a clear view such as this one would not have been possible.*

Chromolithograph, 22 × 28 inches. (The Lincoln Museum)

Robert Gould Shaw (1870)

Giovanni Fagnani
(1819–1873)

Oil on canvas, 27 × 24 inches. (The Union League Club of New York; photograph by Stan Wan.)

A Bit of War History: The Contraband (1866)

Thomas Waterman Wood

(1823–1903)

An escaped slave eagerly enters a provost marshal's office to enlist in the Union army, his simple pack and worn shoes testifying to his status as a "contraband"—a fugitive slave who seeks the protection of Federal forces invading the South. The first in a series of three paintings executed by Wood in Louisville to portray the various stages in the life of a black soldier, they offered "little value as far as their technical qualities are concerned," wrote a critic who saw the works in New York in 1867, adding, however, that "their best qualities consist of the clearness with which they tell their story, and the evident sympathy of the artist with his subject."

Oil on canvas, 28¼ × 20¼ inches.
Signed lower left: *T. W. Wood/1866.*
(The Metropolitan Museum of Art;
gift of Charles Stewart Smith, 1884)

alize such an action. Kurz & Allison's depiction of this rare atrocity from the Civil War showed black women and children being stabbed to death by Confederates, disarmed black prisoners in uniform being shot by Confederates in neat ranks and under orders from officers, and Gen. Nathan Bedford Forrest on a high bluff overlooking the whole grisly scene.

Leaving aside their *Monitor and Merrimac* view, where the role of blacks is marginal, one still finds that Kurz & Allison featured black soldiers in four of their thirty-six prints, more than ten percent of the series. And this was not a matter of incidental inclusion; on the contrary, the black soldiers are the focus of the action in three and crucial to the action in the fourth (Nashville).

Checking the coverage of these events in *Battles and Leaders* affords interesting comparisons. Olustee, for example, could be characterized by Union general Joseph R. Hawley, who wrote a brief comment for *Century*'s series, as no more than "one of the sideshows of the Great War." He shrewdly pointed out, however, that Union losses were nevertheless "about three times as great as those at Buena Vista," a famous battle in the Mexican War that helped make Zachary Taylor president. "I suppose," Hawley concluded resignedly of the Olustee battle, "it did help to whittle away the great rebellion."

Hawley's article provided comment on the description of Olustee given by the Confederate general Samuel Jones. Jones mentioned the Eighth U.S. Colored Infantry, stating that their "fire...was exceedingly effective," but added that the unit "fled and did not appear again as a regiment on the field." Hawley contested this characterization:

> *...Colonel Fribley's black men met the enemy at short range. They had reported to me only two or three days before; I was afterward told that they had never had a day's practice in loading and firing. Old troops, finding themselves so greatly overmatched, would have run a little and re-formed—with or without*

A BIT OF WAR HISTORY: THE RECRUIT (1866)

Thomas Waterman Wood (1823–1903)

*"His cares have now vanished," an observer wrote
of the recruit depicted in the second of Wood's portraits of a black soldier's rite of passage. "...We see him accepted, accoutred, uniformed,
and drilled, standing on guard at the very door where he entered to
enlist. This is the 'volunteer'...[who] looks younger, and, it is needless to say, happy and proud." But the same critic also pointed out
that "Mr. Wood's backgrounds are all very conventional in treatment,
being disagreeably and unnecessarily black, and injure rather than
improve the general effect of the picture." The artist apparently cared
little for such details: he did not bother to finish the American flag he
depicts hanging over the provost marshal's sign.*

Oil on canvas, 28¼ × 20¼ inches. Signed lower left: *T. W. Wood/1866.*
(The Metropolitan Museum of Art; gift of Charles Stewart Smith, 1884)

A BIT OF WAR HISTORY: THE VETERAN (1866)

Thomas Waterman Wood (1823–1903)

*Wood's final scene shows his black soldier, now an amputee,
returning a final time to the provost marshal's office to draw his pension and "additional bounty" for his injury. Writing in the year
the Wood series was first exhibited, the critic for the influential
American Art Journal thought them "excellent specimens of character drawing, good alike in color and expression, though somewhat
marred by an unpleasant feeling of hardness." But Wood had long
ago admitted, "To paint a picture which is not hard is something I
have never been able to do." Nevertheless, the postwar display of these
pictures evidently pleased audiences, for another critic acknowledged
in them "charms by which all who see them are attracted."*

Oil on canvas, 28¼ × 20¼ inches Signed lower left: *T. W. Wood/1866.*
(The Metropolitan Museum of Art; gift of Charles Stewart Smith, 1884)

orders. The black men stood to be killed or wounded—losing more than 300 out of 550.... [T]hey fell back and reorganized.[11]

As for the Fort Pillow massacre, it is mentioned in U. S. Grant's article for *Battles and Leaders* titled "Preparing for the Campaigns of '64," but in so gingerly a fashion as to leave in doubt exactly what happened and whether it violated the rules of war.

Forrest...fell back rapidly, and attacked the troops at Fort Pillow, a station for the protection of the navigation of the Mississippi River. The garrison consisted of a regiment of colored infantry and a detachment of Tennessee cavalry. These troops fought bravely, but were overpowered. I will leave Forrest in his dispatches to tell what he did with them. "The river was dyed," he says, "with the blood of the slaughtered for two hundred yards.... The approximate loss was upward of 500 killed, but few of the officers escaping. My loss was about 20 killed and about 60 wounded.... It is hoped that these facts will demonstrate to the Northern people that negro soldiers cannot cope with Southerners." Subsequently Forrest made a report in which he left out the part which shocks humanity to read.[12]

Battles and Leaders commissioned no illustration of the controversial event.

To move from the business of popular prints to the art of painting is to move to a generally dignified and feelingly crafted group of images. Their number is not great, nor is their emphasis particularly representative of what has come in modern times to constitute the important landmarks of the black experience in the Civil War. Francis B. Carpenter's great history painting aside, nothing notable, astonishingly enough, was ever crafted specifically to mark emancipation, and the charge of the Fifty-fourth Massachusetts at Fort Wagner, as well as the stolid bravery of the Eighth U.S. Colored Infantry at Olustee (which unit also lost its white colonel and took staggering losses in an all-but-useless battle) also lack their chronicling in a stirring history painting. In fact, no painting was ever produced to depict an event of the Civil War affecting or affected by black Americans that is the equal of the treatment of the prewar event, John Brown's hanging, by Thomas Hovenden. Nevertheless, considering the disastrous developments in racial thought at the time artists were most preoccupied by the war, one can say that the number of paintings is substantial, and the nature of their treatment of black themes surprisingly thoughtful and sensitive.

To be sure, neo-Confederate artists contributed to the developing "Sambo" image. *Confederate Camp During the Late American War*, published in London in 1871 and based on a painting by ex-Confederate soldier Conrad Wise Chapman, included four black figures, one of whom dozes against a tent (in a pose similar to Winslow Homer's depiction of black teamsters in a Union camp). He would almost certainly not have been dozing while Confederate soldiers cooked and performed other camp chores. Gilbert Gaul's slaves, who prop up the regime that enslaves them, are saved from caricature, but otherwise hold niches obviously dictated by ideology.

Not so the Northern depictions of black people in paintings. They are, at worst, ambiguous and opaque, and, at best, remarkably balanced for their

time. For example, *Thoughts of Liberia, Emancipation*, painted by Edwin White in 1861, defies simple explanation but surely deserves comment for its controversial theme and its lack of dogmatic storytelling in genre. *Slaves Escaping through the Swamp*, painted by Thomas Moran in 1863, perhaps in England, exemplifies the inability of the landscape painter to deal with political themes (as well as military), and the unlikely-looking swamp may owe its character to the fact that Moran, an Englishman who moved to Philadelphia and spent part of the Civil War studying art as a repatriate in London, probably never saw such a Southern landscape as he ventured to paint here.

Even Edwin Forbes's *Mess Boy Asleep*, completed in 1867 from an on-the-scene sketch, does not yield the easy interpretation that twentieth-century observers might see in it. Though the young black servant is sleeping, this figure likely represents an innocent, not a Sambo. At least one reminiscence of the war recalled such mess boys as "tough specimens" who, like Forbes's subject, slept "on the bare ground with anything or nothing over him as it happens."[13] Besides, Forbes was an enthusiastic antislavery partisan who retained his faith in the black race well beyond the war years and Reconstruction.

This has long been a matter of public record in Forbes's two-volume reminiscences entitled *Thirty Years After: An Artist's Story of the Great War Told, and Illustrated with Nearly 300 Relief-Etchings after Sketches in the Field, and 20 Half-Tone Equestrian Portraits from Original Oil Paintings*. This strangely neglected source, published in 1890 by Fords, Howard & Hulbert, is called "Army Sketch Book" on the outside cover, but that is misleading. Forbes's "sketch books," that is, the pencil sketches he

CONTRABAND OF WAR (1890)

Edwin Forbes (1839–1895)

Union soldiers question a "reliable contraband" at a remote campsite—clearly regarding the black man's report with attention and respect. Forbes testified that the intelligence received in the field from contrabands was almost always dependable and useful.

Etching, 7⅛ × 10⅜ inches. (The Lincoln Museum)

COMING INTO THE LINES (1879)

Edwin Forbes (1839–1895)

A family of escaping slaves, their dignity and determination evident even in the ludicrously crude wagon, crosses into the safe haven of Union lines as soldiers regard them curiously. The grandparents have apparently donned their best clothes for the trip to sanctuary. Forbes based this postwar etching on his on-the-spot pencil sketch.

Etching, 11 × 15 inches. (The Lincoln Museum)

THE LAST SALE OF SLAVES IN ST. LOUIS (1870 ARTIST'S COPY OF LOST 1865 ORIGINAL)

Thomas Satterwhite Noble (1835–1907)

Noble, an antislavery Confederate veteran, painted this scene to record the horror of the final slave auction in St. Louis, which he contended took place in 1865, and on the steps of the very courthouse where the Dred Scott Case was first tried. While well-dressed white men bargain and deal at left, the white-haired owner looks aside regretfully as the sale of a young mother and infant is conducted with crassly commercial enthusiasm by the conscienceless slave auctioneer. Even the depiction of the many hues of skin color constituted an antislavery state-ment, reminding spectators of the sexual exploitation of female slaves by their white masters. To the lost original, Noble added, for irony, a church spire and statues of liberty and justice. When the original canvas went on display in the U.S. Capitol, the progressive St. Louis Guardian declared, "Congress will now have an opportunity to compare a really admirable picture with some of the weak and indifferent apologies for art which now hang in the building."

Oil on canvas, 60 × 84 inches. Signed lower right: *T. S. Noble.* (Missouri Historical Society, St. Louis)

Winslow Homer (1836–1910)

A black woman stands in the doorway of her crude cabin, watching disconsolately as captured Union soldiers are led in procession toward the notorious Andersonville Prison, where thirteen thousand Federal soldiers died during the war. Homer gave the woman a quiet dignity he allowed less often in his early depictions of black men, and her expression reflects the frustration of seeing her potential liberators themselves in chains. When this painting was offered at auction in 1866, the New York Evening Post *hailed it as "full of significance." The canvas may have been inspired by the news that in July 1864 a Union cavalry force dispatched by General Sherman to liberate Andersonville had itself been captured, and six hundred of its men marched off to the compound as prisoners.*

Oil on canvas, 23 × 18 inches. Signed lower left: *Homer 65,* and lower right: *Homer 1866.* (The Newark Museum; gift of Mrs. Hannah Corbin Carter, Horace K. Corbin, Jr., Robert S. Corbin, William D. Corbin, and Mrs. Clementine Corbin Day, in memory of their parents, Hannah Stockton Corbin and Horace Kellogg Corbin) drew as a war correspondent, are now located in the Library of Congress. What the reader sees in the two oversized volumes of *Thirty Years After* are reproductions of reworked sketches.

Although Forbes's sketches and portfolios have been much praised and widely reproduced since the Civil War, the text of *Thirty Years After* has been overlooked as a source for army life in the war. The standard Civil War bibliography says of the work only that it contains "Excellent reproductions of Forbes' sketches of soldier life; extensive enough to cover many personal subjects." What the last phrase means is unclear, but it does not convey what it should: that *Thirty Years After* is a fine source for careful observations on the life of the common soldier, not only in pictures but also in words. The author of the biographical sketch of Forbes in the *Dictionary of American Biography* says of his reminiscences in *Thirty Years After* that they "were chatty and entertaining, but written solely as a vehicle for his remaining sketches."[14] That makes the work seem contrived and lightweight, but it is difficult to think of a comparably substantial work by any artist whose principal subject of interest was the American Civil War. Finally, in the landmark work on the common soldier in the Civil War, Bell Wiley's *Life of Billy Yank*, Forbes's original drawings in the Library of Congress and his *Life Studies of the Great Army*, a portfolio of forty etchings without text published in 1876, are praised in the bibliography, but *Thirty Years After* is not, and there do not appear to be any references to it in Wiley's footnotes.

Yet *Thirty Years After* is a book full of wise observations as well as good drawings, on subjects like sutlers, beef on the hoof, and doing a soldier's laundry. An earlier chapter mentioned its frank recreations of the sorrier side of life in camp and on campaign, right down to the execution of deserters. But it is also a decidedly pro-emancipation book, published, it should be remembered, at the nadir of race relations in U.S. history. His sketch of the "reliable contraband" is both frank and hopeful. It was a name given to the escaped slaves who brought intelligence about enemy movements to the Union soldiers, and it was, Forbes admitted, a name given them in jest. Though unfailingly eager to help, these slaves proved, some soldiers thought, quite ignorant of Confederate army movements and thus gave erroneous information. But Forbes insisted that the nickname should not be taken ironically. Rather, he said, "I do not know of a single instance when one of them proved false to a trust."

Forbes was not above a little contrivance in making his antislavery case, either. In the original pencil sketch of "Negro Refugees," the escaping slaves are shod. In the reproduction of the reworked sketch for *Thirty Years After*, bare feet increase the image of slave deprivation. That was abolition propaganda and not eyewitness journalism.

The ideological message in Forbes's work is made clear in "Sanctuary," the last picture in his book. In the accompanying text, the artist said of the freedmen: "they have kept good their promises, and the progress they have made is a full recompense for the sacrifice made for them and the protection they received." Not many white artists and creative writers were making such explicit and favorable calculations of the worth of the war in humanitarian achievement.

CHARGE OF THE 22ND NEGRO REGIMENT, PETERSBURG (1892)

Andre Castaigne (active 1885–1896)

"I never saw troops fight better, more bravely, and with more determination and enthusiasm," one of their white officers wrote of the black soldiers of the Twenty-second Negro Regiment. They are shown here on June 16, 1864, charging toward a Confederate position on the Dimmock Line before Petersburg. In terrain laid bare by Confederates who cut down trees along a ten-mile-long ditch, black troops captured three hundred prisoners that day. In re-creating the dramatic scene, Castaigne, who would win the Legion of Honor in his native France in 1899, added only the slightest hint of color on the otherwise monochromatic vista in the inspiring sight of the American flag.

Oil on canvas, 23½ × 30½ inches. Signed lower left: *Castaigne. 1892.* (West Point Museum, U.S. Military Academy)

EIGHT

ART
and the
COMMON
SOLDIER

⪼ Preceding Page⪻

REVEILLE ON A
WINTER MORNING
(N.D.)

Henry Bacon (1839–1912)

Drowsy soldiers emerge from their heated Sibley tents on a frigid winter morning, as an officer takes roll. An eyewitness to a similar winter reveille recalled "the men…emerging from their tents…their toilet in various stages of completion.… Here and there was a man just about half awake, having a fist at each eye, and looking as disconsolate and forsaken as men usually do when they get from the bed before the public at short notice." To a man, these soldiers look improbably handsome, and the winter sun looks too high for an early reveille. The painter may have been intent on suggesting America's bright awakening to national greatness.

Oil on canvas, 44 × 30½ inches. Signed lower left: *Henry Bacon.* (West Point Museum, U. S. Military Academy)

he artists who left the most memorable legacy of Civil War images painted the common soldier. Landscape entered their works only incidentally, and their canvases could hardly be classed as history paintings. Their works seem far removed from the grand

themes and manner of Benjamin West's *Death of General Wolfe.* Though they were figure painters, these artists did not produce genre scenes, because genre showed everyday life, and going off to the Civil War interrupted the everyday life of millions of American men who between 1861 and 1865 participated in something altogether extraordinary. Likewise, genre painting in the United States before the war was likely to focus on sentimental themes of home and family, perhaps pastoral ones of farm life and small-town society, or more robust nature studies of hunting, fishing, or trapping. Sentimentalism would not suffice to render this war.

These Civil War artists focused close-

ly on soldiers, and often did so without obvious flattery. They could not accurately be called history painters, because the action they depicted did not always bear the name of a famous battle. Even when a canvas carried the name of a particular engagement, the scene depicted was not necessarily one described by the press, the official records, or later diaries—as the death of a great general is. When they painted soldiers, their subjects did not necessarily wear the uniforms and carry the distinguishing marks of a recognizable regiment. Nor did their paintings usually feature identifiable generals, regimental flags, or famous heroes. Instead, these painters showed Americans the common soldier in the Civil War. "These subjects were all attempts to reproduce the daily life" of the troops, explained William Ludwell Sheppard of his own work, "apart from the great engagements that have been treated so often. Such paintings were received with great satisfaction by the old soldiers themselves," Sheppard recalled—perhaps because his postwar work always seemed to transform haggard Confederates into unrealistically, but appealingly, well-scrubbed troops. (Sheppard, who served in the elite Richmond Howitzers during the war, won later fame for illustrating a book called *Detailed Minutiae of Soldier Life in the Army of Northern Virginia*.) Understandably, these affectionate portraits have been regarded with similar nostalgic fondness by a broad audience ever since.[1]

To the artists, of course, their subjects were not "common" at all; they were uncommonly courageous. And it would probably be a mistake to attribute to the artists some consciously "democratic" ideal to give the common soldier his due and spurn the traditional depiction of glory, handed down from Benjamin West, with its focus on generals and other leaders. Nevertheless, Gilbert Gaul, William Ludwell Sheppard, Julian Scott, William Trego, and, in certain instances, others better known for different Civil War genres painted ordinary Civil War soldiers, either in combat or in camp, and many Americans still love them for having done so.

An especially remarkable achievement was that of William B. T. Trego, whose two hundred military paintings, many of them Civil War scenes, came from hands grotesquely misshapen and paralyzed by what was apparently a bout with polio in 1861, when he was two years old. Though his hand curved

NEWS FROM HOME (N.D.)

William Ludwell Sheppard
(1833–1912)

A Confederate cavalryman pauses over his campfire to read a comforting letter from home. Such letters generally cheered their recipients, just as the lack of correspondence occasionally infuriated them. "There is something wrong in the Post Office affairs somewhere," lamented one soldier cut off from reassuring mail from home, "and the villainous perpetrator of the deed ought to be found out, and no punishment too bad to be administered to him, not even the burning pit of H-ll."

Watercolor on paper, 11¼ × 8 inches. Signed lower right: *W. L. Sheppard/18 (?)*.
(Museum of the Confederacy, Richmond, Virginia; photograph by Katherine Wetzel)

THOMPSON'S HILL (1886)

Owen J. Hopkins (d. 1902)

Foraging by soldiers on both sides was a common wartime indulgence, one Union trooper recalling how "helpless women cried to see their small stock of poultry carried away." Here, in one such incident, a Federal soldier (right) carries away a scrawny chicken, while his comrades help themselves liberally to well water. Hopkins, who served under Gen. James A. Garfield with the Twenty-third Ohio Volunteer Infantry, probably witnessed this scene after the Thompson's Hill engagement near Port Gibson, Mississippi, in May 1863.

Oil on canvas, 24 × 36 inches. Signed lower right: *O. J. Hopkins/1886.* (The Ohio Historical Society)

LAYING THE BRIDGE AT FREDERICKSBURG (1887)

Thure de Thulstrup (1848–1930)

Confederate snipers open fire on Union troops as they struggle in the swollen waters opposite Fredericksburg to throw up pontoon bridges and maneuver boats across the Rappahannock River. Thulstrup's skillful work, probably based loosely on woodcuts in 1862 illustrated newspapers, combined a cityscape on the horizon, a well-composed (if a trifle too relaxed-looking) group in the foreground pontoon, a deftly handled perspective of the boats crossing the river, and the engineering interest of building a pontoon bridge.

Oil on canvas, 15 × 22 inches. Signed lower left: *Thulstrup 87*. (The Seventh Regiment Fund, Inc.)

backward and he had use of but two fingers, he somehow managed to paint by gripping the brush stiffly and moving his entire body. His legs were crippled too, and early study proved difficult, but Trego's father and mother were both painters and he was able to learn at home. He ignored much of Thomas Eakins's instruction at the Pennsylvania Academy of Fine Arts (premature application to oil technique, Trego thought, encouraged "carelessness about details") and worked on drawing before he tried painting, with the result that he developed what can perhaps best be described as an illustrator's style.

Born in Pennsylvania, Trego, after further study in Paris, eventually established a studio in suburban Philadelphia, where he continued to live with his parents. He collected military equipment and employed local people as models, posing them in the fields behind his house or in his studio, which was equipped with a place for these models to fall over as casualties might in a battle. He also contrived a dummy horse made

from a barrel, which men might mount to demonstrate the attitudes of riders.[2]

Trego drew illustrations, worked on commissioned history paintings of particular events (for which he studied published sources and interviewed participants), and painted other works. Most canvases, however, were posed in his backyard, not on historical terrain, and he rarely if ever employed models who had served in the war at the particular action portrayed. Instead Trego painted "batteries," "mortars firing," or "horse artillery"—phrases used in the titles of his works, suggesting no particular unit and no particular historical action. In his large, prizewinning 1882 canvas, *Battery of Light Artillery en Route*, Trego did not identify the specific battery in the title, and the unit's flag is depicted furled in the background mist. Nor did he indicate to what destination it was en route. The artillery must have been very light indeed, for the cannon in the painting is pulled through the mud by only a four-horse team. The weight of a cannon and limber was well over three thousand pounds, and six horses were customarily required to pull them. In another painting of Civil War infantrymen charging through low vegetation, no cap badges, cartridge-box emblems, or regimental flags are visible. Nevertheless, Trego did research his history paintings and struggled with the problem of great distances on Civil War battlefields. Scrupulous about details, he once asked an old general, "Did the enemy come near enough for the men in the front rank to see their hands?" Trego often chose to depict Civil War soldiers plain and simple. The historical point of such works, whatever artistic motive lay behind their composition and color, surely went beyond battle paintings. Accuracy, in terms of uniform color and style, was a goal shared with history painters; that is why Trego collected militaria in his studio. But surely another ideal besides accuracy was at work: a sense of obligation to show courage, determination, hard work, and sacrifice by ordinary American fighting men.

The word *glory* is inadequate to comprehend this ideal. Surely the coatless men with grimy hands shown laboring in their rolled-up shirtsleeves with a heavy black mortar did not exemplify military glory in the traditional artistic manner. Neither did the artillerymen struggling with their cannon on a muddy road. Likewise, *realism* is an inadequate term, for historical reality consists of individually identifiable persons, places, things, and events. To ignore cap badges, regimental flags, and idiosyncratic uniform details was to make the soldiers, in a way, ideal types—of soldiers, at the least, and maybe even of men in general.

Gilbert Gaul's work was more sentimental and more pro-Southern than Trego's, but he painted similar subjects

in a career that also had its tragedies, though none as pitiful as Trego's. (After Trego's parents died, in the early twentieth century, the crippled painter committed suicide.) Gaul was among the earliest of those Northerners (today's Civil War Round Tables boast many of them as members) who were, for inexplicable reasons, romantically drawn to identify with the Southern cause. Born in Jersey City, New Jersey, in 1866, he grew up with a military career in mind and graduated from a military preparatory academy, but decided not to join the navy because of poor health. Instead he moved to New York and studied art with J. G. Brown, an urban genre painter. After a trip to the West in 1876, Gaul began to paint military scenes.

In 1882, the same year that Trego painted his *Battery of Light Artillery en Route*, Gaul painted *Holding the Line at All Hazards*. His ragged, shirtsleeved, and occasionally sockless or shoeless Confederate infantrymen, one of whom has his head wrapped with a spotted bandanna, owe something to Gaul's mentor Brown, famous for his paintings of ragged New York shoeshine boys. But the canvas, though not as large or ambitious as Trego's, seems best compared to Trego's sort of military painting. Gaul pictured a nameless unit identified only by a Confederate battle flag and gray officers' uniforms. The infantrymen's youthful appearance, given emphasis by the unusual number of clean-shaven men pictured, seems striking. The painting aimed at showing the fierce concentration required in hazardous combat—much the same thing Trego depicted. Painters and illustrators, of course, had often depicted shoeless and ragged Confederates around their generals, but those soldiers had essentially taken the places of the much better-

Opposite

BATTERY OF LIGHT ARTILLERY EN ROUTE (1882)

William B. T. Trego (1859–1909)

An artillery battery threads its way over open countryside in one of Trego's best-known and most honored Civil War canvases. His meticulous attention to detail is much in evidence here in the concerned expression of the gray-bearded officer who glances backward to observe the trooper struggling to dislodge a fieldpiece from the mud. This canvas won the Toppan Prize at the Pennsylvania Academy of the Fine Arts in 1882.

Oil on canvas, 30¼ × 64⅛ inches. Signed lower right: *W. T. Trego/Philada 1882.* (Pennsylvania Academy of the Fine Arts, Philadelphia; gift of Fairman Rogers)

MILITARY DRILL SCENE (C. 1865)

James Walker (1819–1889)

The essence of military life from the downfall of knighthood to the twentieth century is showcased here. As a Union soldier from Pennsylvania, for example, wrote home to report: "The first thing in the morning is drill, then drill, then drill again. Then drill, drill, a little more drill. Then drill, and lastly drill. Between drills, we drill and sometimes stop to eat a little and have a roll-call."

Oil on canvas, 12½ × 17½ inches. (U. S. Military Academy, West Point Museum, U.S. Military Academy; photograph courtesy National Geographic Society)

Letters From Home (1861)

James Walker (1819–1889)

Union soldiers in the field cluster outside a tent to hear the latest news from home in this genre scene featuring the soldier "types" that artists enjoyed grouping together: young recruits, pipe-smoking professionals, and grizzled veterans. A Federal cavalry officer at the time described the arrival of newspapers in camp as one of the "remedial influences of army life." This handsome setting may be seen as a Union analogue to Virginia artist William Ludwell Sheppard's bleaker portrait of Confederates reading their own newspapers—in a desolate trench mockingly labeled "Spotswood Hotel." The Union gray uniforms in evidence here were not uncommon early in the war. Gray was a staple of the militias.

Oil on board, 12½ × 16 inches. Signed lower right: *J. Walker, 1861.*
(The Seventh Regiment Fund, Inc. Photograph courtesy The Metropolitan Museum of Art)

uniformed soldiers in European depictions of Napoleonic officers; they were props for the great men at center stage in the heroic canvases. Gaul's barefoot Confederates themselves constituted the focus of his paintings.

One year later Gaul painted *Union Troops at Cold Harbor* or *The Skirmish Line,* which employed a favorite technique of military painters of the era, from Lady Butler in Great Britain to Trego in Philadelphia: some of the blue-coated infantrymen face the viewer of the painting and seem to pour their fire directly into the gallery. Trego worked to learn how to paint horses coming directly at the viewer (the way the Fifth U.S. Cavalry is depicted in his famous painting of their charge at Gaines Mill), perhaps following the lead of Lady Butler's *Scotland Forever,* which depicted head-on the charge of the Scots Greys at Waterloo.

In the two Gaul canvases, viewers can already detect a central problem with his more complex works: the individual figures in them, though each is capably delineated, seem to bear little relationship to each other. His canvases thus have a muddled focus and an unsettling compositional scheme. They do not achieve the look of photographic candor, either. In the end they seem cluttered and a little unsatisfactory, as the viewer's eye wanders over them uneasily, seeking a place to rest. *Glorious Fighting,* for example, painted around 1885, employed the head-on perspective for a Confederate line of battle analogous to the Union one at Cold Harbor. Again, the composition is too ambitious, and some figures appear unrelated to others. The contemplative drummer boy, with his chin resting on his right hand, seems hardly engaged at all in the desperate struggle occupying the other figures. But, for all their faults, Gaul's paintings left no doubt about the artist's sentiments.

Gaul's mother was a Tennessean, and when he inherited a farm in that state from an uncle and established a residence there (in 1881), he reinforced his Southern sympathies. The sociology of his paintings was certainly affected by his sectional leanings. The officers look a class apart from the enlisted men in the Confederate army Gaul depicted, and the loyal slaves shown in these canvases, helping their Confederate enslavers, certainly did nothing to break racial barriers. *Faithful to the End,* for example, painted around 1906, shows a slave leading his wounded master, a Confederate officer, off a battlefield. And *Leaving Home,* a genre scene painted about a year later, includes, in its idealized vision of a Southern parlor, the mythical extended plantation family, with a concerned old male slave and a younger female wringing her hands while a boy holds the departing young officer's horse, visible through the open doorway.[3]

What was the point of these paintings? One can only speculate, for Gaul

left behind few written records, but *Between the Lines* offers a clue. In its vision of Confederate and Union soldiers, fraternizing across the lines, Gaul joined the editors of *Century* in a celebration of a manly white fraternity of courage and comradeship. The virtues celebrated, and this is surely true of Trego as well, were decidedly military ones, and such works might well be faulted as militaristic.

Indeed, Trego has been called "the American Detaille" after the French military painter and illustrator whose work seemed to aim at recovering French military glory from the humiliation of the Franco-Prussian War. Trego lived on the victor's side of the Mason-Dixon Line, however, and he had not the excuse of rebuilding shattered national confidence.

Surely some of these works were prompted by the land equivalent of navalism: militarism. Although the United States participated less in the end-of-century enthusiasm for war than did the European powers like Germany and France, it surely felt some of the same impulses. The Spanish-American War of 1898 and the growth of imperial ambitions brought renewed interest in improving the United States's armed forces, long kept weak by old antimilitary ideals and by the security of geographic isolation from Europe. Theodore Roosevelt's enthusiasm for military virtues colored the era, as did Elihu Root's army reforms. Changes in the armed forces helped military artists. Henry Ogden, for example, was employed by the Quartermaster's Department in 1890 to record the history of army uniforms (which he did in forty-four pictures) and continued to do, with government patronage, into the twentieth century. Civil War paintings to some degree benefited from,

≈ *Opposite* ≈

**HOLDING THE LINE
AT ALL HAZARDS
(1882)**

Gilbert Gaul (1855–1919)

In a thicket of trees piled with battle dead, Confederates protect their line heroically against Union attack. Gaul featured an artistic device familiar in the war landscapes of the 1860s—splashing the background with a highlight of red, the traditional symbolic color of blood, power, and action. But unlike landscapists, Gaul saw the war from the common soldier's perspective, focusing on such individual acts of courage as the trooper who here ignores his foot wound to maintain his rifle fire against the Federals. This painting won a gold medal from the American Art Association in 1888, and was included in Gaul's 1907 portfolio.

Oil on canvas, 32 × 44 inches. Signed lower left: *Gilbert Gaul.* (The Birmingham Museum of Art)

UNION SOLDIER CLEANING SWORD (N.D.)

Xanthus R. Smith

(1839–1929)

Sitting outside his tent, a Union soldier polishes his saber, in a rare land-based painting by this marine artist.

Oil on canvas, 4¾ × 5⅜ inches. (From the Tharpe Collection of American Military History)

THE NIGHT BEFORE THE BATTLE (1865)

James Henry Beard (1812–1893)

Oil on canvas, 30½ × 44½ inches. (Memorial Art Gallery of the University of Rochester; gift of Dr. Ronald M. Lawrence)

"THE MUD MARCH," FREDERICKSBURG CAMPAIGN, CIVIL WAR (N.D.)

Giovani Ponticelli (nineteenth century)

Following the bloody repulse of his attack on Fredericksburg, General Burnside ordered his army to cross the Rappahannock several miles upriver. But the demoralized, luckless troops were pelted by two days of rain and found themselves hopelessly mired in mud. New York Times *correspondent William Swinton reported that "an indescribable chaos of pontoons, wagons, and artillery encumber the road down to the river—supply wagons upset by the roadside, artillery stalled in the mud, ammunition trains mired by the way. Horses and mules dropped down dead, exhausted with the effort to move their loads through the hideous medium ... many of them buried in the liquid muck." For this unusually inglorious subject, Ponticelli included a lone Zouave so that his red cap could provide a focus in the center of the canvas along the otherwise dark mass of retreating soldiers.*

Oil on canvas, 26½ × 45½ inches. (West Point Museum, U. S. Military Academy)

CONFEDERATE CAVALRY SCOUTS IN THE WILDERNESS (N.D.)

Gilbert Gaul (1855–1919)

*Cavalry scouts gather around a warm campfire in the woods in this night scene. The painting
stresses individual portrait vignettes, not battle action, and the only clue to these soldiers' identification
with the cavalry—aside from the painting's title and the uniforms' trim—is the horse tied to a nearby tree.*

Oil on canvas, 25 × 30 inches. Signed lower left: *Gilbert Gaul.* (Collection of Jay P. Altmayer)

UNION TROOPS AT COLD HARBOR (THE SKIRMISH LINE) (1883)

Gilbert Gaul (1855–1919)

Union soldiers fire at the enemy in one of the skirmishes that preceded the Battle of Cold Harbor, in June 1864. Describing a skirmish line much like the one Gaul here portrayed, a Union private remembered: "The air was filled with a medley of sounds, shouts, cheers, commands, oaths, the sharp report of rifles, the hissing of shot," along with "groans and prayers." Commenting on the artist's work, Harper's Weekly noted, "Gilbert Gaul is not below his usual standard of excellence in his glimpse of a skirmish." The painting won a gold medal at the Appalachian Exposition in Knoxville, in 1910.

Oil on canvas, 29⅛ × 44 inches. Signed lower right: *Gilbert Gaul* (West Point Museum, U.S. Military Academy)

QUARTER GUARD OF THE CONFEDERATE FORCES AT DIASCUND BRIDGE, VIRGINIA, MARCH 10, 1863 (1874)

Conrad Wise Chapman (1842–1910)

A Confederate soldier stands lonely guard duty over his desolate outpost at the end of the bitter winter of 1862–63. John G. Chapman, the Confederate artist's father, made a fine etching from this scene years later but signed his son's name in the plate.

Oil and wash on paper, 7⅛ × 5 inches.
Signed lower right: *CWChapman/Roma 1874.*
(The Valentine Museum, Richmond, Virginia)

REBELS AT CAMP, LAS MORAS, TEXAS, 1861 (c. 1861)

Conrad Wise Chapman (1842–1910)

Before his assignment to Charleston, Chapman served the Confederacy in the West, where he observed and recorded more intimate scenes, like this one, with somewhat less success. In this hasty oil sketch, troopers huddle around a campfire, as a sentry, all but enveloped by the smoke, stands guard nearby. The cramped composition hardly rivals Gilbert Gaul's more professional-looking postwar depiction of a similar scene—but when Chapman painted this oil, he was only nineteen years old.

Oil on canvas, 8 × 8¾ inches. Signed lower right:
C. Chapman. (Gibbes Museum of Art, Charleston)

THE SCOUT'S RETURN (N.D.)

John Adams Elder (1833–1895)

*A Confederate "scout" returns to camp from a reconnaissance. A term with a different
meaning in that era, "scout" connoted both pathfinder and spy. Col. John Singleton Mosby, one such
specialist, insisted that "a scout is not a spy who goes in disguise, but a soldier in arms and
uniform who reconnoitres either inside or outside an enemy's fire." To Mosby, a scout's life was "full
of adventure, excitement, and romance."*

Oil on canvas, 21¾ × 27 inches. (Virginia Museum of Fine Arts, Richmond;
gift of Mrs. Hugh L. Macneil in memory of Mrs. Charles E. Bolling)

GLORIOUS FIGHTING
(c. 1885)

Gilbert Gaul (1855–1919)

This vivid depiction is filled with a roster of the stock characters of Gaul's war paintings: wounded troops fighting on despite their pain, a veteran inspiring younger comrades, and a proud flagbearer. Strangely, the drummer appears rather bored.

Oil on canvas, 32 × 44 inches. Signed lower left: *Gilbert Gaul.* (The Birmingham Museum of Art)

and even shared in, this new militaristic spirit.[4]

Another factor may well have been at work. The era's awareness of Darwinism, the idea that struggle and survival were humankind's lot, may have had something to do with the creation of these scenes of military combat on sometimes nameless fields by anonymous men.

The greatest of the painters of the common soldier, whose work naturally comes to mind at the mention of such Darwinian themes, was, of course, Winslow Homer. His Civil War works were well behind him by the waning of the century and the advent of militarism, but his Civil War paintings definitely foreshadowed Darwinian themes.

His background in journalistic illustration as an artist-correspondent for *Harper's Weekly* gave him an appreciation for depicting warfare beyond the heroic traditions of battle art—as well as plenty of eyewitness material to inform later paintings. Homer's reputation as a painter is so high—so much higher than that of anyone else who painted many Civil War works—that it may be difficult to think of him as in any way part of a tradition most often represented by illustrators, second-rate artists, and untutored veterans. Yet there were ways in which his experience resembled that of other Civil War painters.

Like most Civil War artists, even those of the war generation itself, Homer did not actually see much warfare up close. His mother commented in October 1861, while her son was acting as an artist-correspondent in Virginia, that he "scaled a parapet while out sketching...when they saw his book...the only wonder was that he was not shot his head popping up on such high places." Homer returned to Virginia in 1862, but an officer reported to Homer's brother that the artist "does not dare go to the front[,] having been an object of suspicion even before." Like other American painters in the era, Homer may have felt the lure of the historical that the war presented to American painters. His mother described him as "very happy & collecting material for future greatness."[5]

Yet others did the same thing and never came as close to greatness as Homer—quite the opposite, in fact. Edwin Forbes, for example, made hundreds of sketches as an artist-correspondent and later used them as material for his own polished etchings and paintings. Yet the closer his art came to the original battlefield sketch, the more it seems to be valued, and, with few exceptions, the higher his artistic aspiration in a later work, the lower the achievement and the less enthusiastic the work's reception. For somewhat different reasons the Confederate soldier-artist Conrad Wise Chapman also failed to realize fully the potential in his Civil War material, and some of his later work had to be aided by his artist father.

Before his family connections earned him reassignment to the comparative safety of Charleston harbor (where he created his landscapes), Chapman served in the thick of the action in the West, with the Third Kentucky Infantry. There he did prove occasionally to be a perceptive observer of camp life, producing several intimate scenes of the common soldier at rest, one of which became the model for a popular post-war lithograph. The painter, sculptor, and illustrator William Ludwell Sheppard, too, provided glimpses into the life of the Confederate fighting man, although his scenes seem more sentimentalized than Chapman's. The writer T. C. DeLeon believed that Sheppard's pictures "illustrate[d] both the details of the war, and the taste and heart of those who made it."[6]

Homer painted mostly genre pictures of military life, that is, scenes of everyday life in camp. They seem notable in part for their want of philosophic or ideal posturing. George C. Lamdin's contemplative officer outside his tent, for example, appears almost pretentious beside *The Briarwood Pipe*, a painting Homer finished in 1864. Comments on the Homer work often linger on the uniforms: the distinctive Zouave outfit with baggy Turkish pants, neatly trimmed short jacket, white puttees, and a soft cap of distinctly North African or Middle Eastern origin. And

CHARGING THE BATTERY (c. 1882)

Gilbert Gaul (1855–1919)

Bursting shells illuminate the night sky, dramatically silhouetting a Union force as it launches a charge against an enemy battery. This canvas was displayed at the National Academy of Design in 1882, where it was purchased on the opening day of its exhibition for a record $1,500. Later the painting won a bronze medal at the 1889 Paris Exposition. Notes to a photogravure adaptation declared that with this work Gaul's "originality asserted itself in method peculiarly his own."

Oil on canvas, 36 × 44 inches. (New-York Historical Society)

As an older Zouave grasps his home-whittled briarwood pipe, a young comrade works under his tutelage to finish carving his own handcrafted version. "A common occupation of a leisure hour," recalled a Vermont soldier, "is the carving of pipes from the roots … found in the woods here. It is a slow business." A critic of the day thought that Homer's sky in this canvas boasted "much delicacy in execution of color and would do credit to our best landscapists."

Oil on canvas, 16⅞ × 14⅞ inches. Signed lower left: *Homer 64.* (The Cleveland Museum of Art; Mr. and Mrs. William H. Marlatt Fund)

there lies in this preoccupation a nearly irresistible impulse to find something of nostalgic innocence about the work— on the assumption that the bright red pants proved impractical in battle because they made such vivid targets and must have been abandoned as the war grew more serious; the silly militia finery of antebellum gentlemen's units had to be shed, as in a reversal of the caterpillar's progress toward butterfly.

Some Zouave regiments did abandon their distinctive uniforms, though more out of difficulty in finding cloth to repair them after campaigning than from practicality in adjusting to battlefield conditions in modern warfare. And the Fourteenth New York State Militia, on the contrary, wore its red pants from 1861 until mustered out in 1864. After the Battle of Bull Run, in fact, the regiment was issued regulation blue pants for want of material to repair their red ones. The troops hated them and returned to red as soon as the government could supply the color. Likewise, the 114th Pennsylvania Volunteer Infantry, known as Collis' Zouaves, served from 1862 to the end of the war, having made arrangements for importing cloth from France to keep their distinctive uniforms mended. It should be remembered, too, that France retained her Zouave units in the Franco-Prussian War, five years after the American Civil War.[7]

In Homer's day, the Zouave uniform attracted less notice than it does today. When the painting was first spied by a critic visiting Homer's studio in January 1864, he noted only "a picture of camplife, representing a couple of soldiers seated on an old pine log, making brierwood pipes." Like all military painters, Homer needed models and he purchased one uniform from a musteredout Zouave veteran in New York.

The meaning of the uniform may thus have been different from what is sometimes imputed to it: that it represented an early period of relative innocence before the war became earnest and bloody. It is all but certain that the Zouave uniform was *not*, as has been said, "synecdochically identifiable with the whole Northern cause." There were Confederate Zouave units, too. And far from representing the lost innocence of the war's early months, the Zouave uniform may have connoted to a nineteenth-century viewer what it meant to the era's military men: primitive, allbut-uncontrollable fierceness in combat. French troops adapted the Zouave uniform from their North African wars, and it was French Zouaves, in part, who took Sebastopol in an assault in the Crimea, where red-coated British soldiers had failed before. This prestige carried across the sea to American military circles six years later. Thus Thomas Wentworth Higginson, a white abolitionist who became an officer in a black regiment, complimented his soldiers' fighting qualities by comparing them with Zouaves: "Nobody knows anything about these men who has not seen them in battle…. *There is a fierce energy about them beyond anything of which I have ever read,* unless it be the French Zouaves. It requires the strictest discipline to hold them in hand."[8] Moreover, the Zouave regiments may have carried some connotation of being elite units, not only in the fighting sense but also in the social sense. Some must have been old gentlemen's militia units. Thus the regimental history of Collis' Zouaves described the officers as "men of pride and culture."[9]

Whatever the uniform meant, Homer was attracted to it and went on to paint another Zouave picture called *Pitching Quoits,* a large canvas completed in 1865. Once again, it is difficult to read the theme of innocence and experience into this ambitious picture, though the temptation may be great. Soldiering is notorious for making "men" of innocent youths, and, on a grander symbolic scale, the Civil War was often interpreted as an innocent new nation's experience of Old World tragedy. The themes of innocence and experience certainly did engage Civil War painters, but they had readily available a more suggestive subject than Zouaves for exploring them visually: drummer boys. These underaged and overwise urchins provided subjects for Eastman Johnson, William Morris Hunt, Julian Scott, and Winslow Homer.

Surely no artist knew the impact of the experience of war on innocent youth better than Julian Scott, who had lied about his own age and enlisted at fifteen to become a fifer in the Third Vermont Infantry in 1861. Musicians and drummer boys were sent to the rear when combat was joined, but they nevertheless served, often in perilous situations, as stretcher bearers, attendants on the wounded, and buriers of the dead. In camp, except for sounding the orders of the day and performing at drill and ceremony, theirs was essentially the lot of servants: they cut soldiers' hair, drew water, and performed other unglamorous chores.[10]

Scott was subsequently "wounded slightly," first at Drewry's Bluff in May, and again at White Oak Swamp in June

(an engagement he would later paint), although he hastened to insist that the injuries were "hardly worth noting." Nonetheless he was shipped to a military hospital on David's Island. There, by chance, a rich New York businessman named Henry E. Clark arrived on a visit and, in the words of the nineteenth-century art historian Henry T. Tuckerman, "was struck with the spirit and expression of a soldier's figure

[Young Soldier] (c. 1864)

Winslow Homer (1836–1910)

*No doubt a study for part of an unexecuted larger painting, Homer's pensive
young recruit is nothing like the glamorous drummer boys romanticized by other artists.
Instead, this poignant portrait reveals an ordinary, understandably worried boy in an
oversized greatcoat, far too young for a man's war, and compelled to undertake such
decidedly unglamorous daily chores as cutting soldiers' hair, cleaning up camp, cooking,
and burying the battle dead.*

Oil, gouache, and pencil on canvas, 14⅛ × 7⅛ inches. (Cooper-Hewitt Museum, Smithsonian Institution's National
Museum of Design, New York; gift of Charles Savage Homer)

PITCHING QUOITS (1865)

Winslow Homer (1836–1910)

*The tedium of camp life could, in fair weather, be broken by sports and games.
Horseshoes, easily obtainable, as a reporter noted, from "the nearest cavalry or artillery range," were
popular, and so were their more genteel variant, quoits. Seeing this work in progress, the
New York* Leader's *art critic thought the scene of "sunburned and stalwart veterans . . . full of
action, life and power." But while the same critic lauded the finished work as "remarkably fine," he
could not help pointing out the incongruity of the Zouave uniforms in a modern camp—the "flaming
scarlet and blue," as he called them, "with which some departmental lunacy has clothed a large portion of our heroes." Still, the critic conceded, "You may go through many exhibition galleries without
seeing a human figure so full of real life and action," and he predicted that "Mr. Homer cannot draw
many such without finding himself famous."*

Oil on canvas, 26¾ × 55¾ inches. Signed lower right: *Winslow Homer NY/1865.* (Fogg Art Museum, Harvard University Art
Museums; gift of Mr. and Mrs. Frederic H. Curtiss)

traced in charcoal or chalk on the wall near the bed of one of the patients." The artist, Clark discovered, was a "Vermont boy" who, "having been wounded, amused himself with rough drawings of camp scenes, of which the specimen on the wall, coming thus accidentally under the eye of a judge of art, was found to indicate talent. The gallantry of the youth and his artistic tendencies gained him the warm friendship" of Clark, "who liberally provided for his education."[11]

Funded by his new patron, Scott traveled to New York at age seventeen and began to study under Emanuel Leutze. Armed with his newly acquired art education, Scott joined the staff of Gen. William F. "Baldy" Smith as an honorary aide-de-camp in 1864. This time Scott's avowed purpose was to make sketches of soldier life.

The experience served Scott well. Once peace was restored, he focused all his artistic attention on depicting the incidents of the war. As early as 1867, Tuckerman was noting that "Julian Scott has ever since the end of the war devoted himself assiduously to art," adding: "He is already an acknowledged draughtsman, and has made several authentic and effective illustrations of scenes in the hospital, the camp, and on the battlefield, from recollections and studies sketched on the spot."[12]

In 1870 his home state awarded him his first and probably his most prestigious major commission. He was chosen to create "a historical painting illustrating the Vermont troops in action, in some noted battle of the late war, to be hung in the State House, in commemoration of the valor of our soldiers." Scott

chose to portray the 1864 Battle of Cedar Creek. The most colorful event of the Cedar Creek experience was undoubtedly Sheridan's Ride, and certainly it became the most frequently portrayed, as well. But Scott saw war from quite another perspective than did those who populated their canvases with famous heroes of exalted rank. With rare exceptions, Scott focused on the more incidental aspects of army life, and when he depicted combat action, he did so almost always from the viewpoint of the common soldier. He took pains to paint them honestly and respectfully, as a traditional history painter would. To create an accurate depiction of Cedar Creek, for example, he returned to the scene of the battle to make topographical sketches, executed preliminary portraits of some of the key participants, and then in 1872 made an elaborate model oil of the entire scene, from which he finally painted a ten-by-twenty-foot finished copy that still hangs in the state capitol building. The entire project took four years. In the perceptive words of a modern Julian Scott student who assembled the only exhibition of his work in this century, the painter's viewpoint at once must have seemed liberating, for in this first major effort, the artist startlingly gave "prominence…to the men who did the fighting—a position previously assumed by the generals."[13]

But the composition, arranged essen-tially on the exciting diagonal, with red and gold atmospheric effects, proved a little too ambitious for Scott. He had difficulty placing a white horse in perspective between sensitively rendered Confederate prisoners in the foreground and the main group of Vermonters regrouping in the middle ground.

By all accounts, Scott early on enjoyed more commissions than he could handle, and was extremely successful. Some reports suggest that Scott's career began fading, however, in the late 1880s principally because he turned increasingly, and with disastrous results, to drink. He apparently lost his family as a consequence, and in 1890 was compelled to take a position with the national census as an illustrator.[14]

As late as 1893, however, he managed to win a commission from a Colonel Shepard of Shepard's Rifles, who offered one thousand dollars for a painting the artist described in a letter as "The Storming of Burnside's Bridge at Antietam by the Shepard Rifles." Surviving records show that Scott did receive a $250 advance, but asked for additional payments as the canvas was "approaching completion" early in 1893. Unfortunately, the original painting has long since vanished, although a photographer did expose a glass-plate negative of the finished work before it disappeared—murky modern prints of which offer only a hint of what it really looked like. What appears to be a large detail from this work *has* survived intact, with Burnside's bridge nowhere to be seen in it (hence its misidentification until recent times). To cloud the story even further, the principal figure in both the detail and the photograph of the lost painting is Col. Robert Potter of the Fifty-first New York, who in fact led the charge across the famous bridge in 1862. A photograph of Potter, the model

≈ *Opposite* ≈

THE FIRST VERMONT BRIGADE AT THE BATTLE OF CEDAR CREEK, OCTOBER 19, 1864 (1874)

Julian Scott (1846–1901)

As Confederate prisoners are led away in the left foreground, the First Vermont Brigade rallies. Scott was commissioned by his home state in 1870 to create "a historical painting illustrating the Vermont troops in action, in some noted battle of the late war, in commemoration of the valor of our soldiers." Scott chose Cedar Creek as his subject, and General Sheridan reportedly declared this finished work truthful, noting that it "made the boys as they were."

Oil on canvas, 10 × 20 feet. (Vermont State Museum; from *The Civil War: The Shenandoah in Flames;* photograph by Henry Groskinsky, © 1987 Time-Life Books, Inc.)

IN FRONT OF YORKTOWN

Winslow Homer (1836–1910)

Artist-correspondent Homer accompanied the Army of the Potomac during its ill-fated 1862 Peninsula campaign, sketching the troops in both daylight and in artistically ambitious nocturnal settings. In this, one of the first Civil War oil paintings he adapted from such studies, a small bank of Union pickets gathers before bivouac fire. Capt. D. P. Conyngham of the fabled Irish Brigade vividly recalled the sight of such men huddled "around camp-fires, some seated on logs, others reclining on the green pineboughs that served them for a couch." At night the natural treetop ceiling gave these settings "a most comfortable appearance . . . defining more strongly the dark figures grouped inside."

Oil on canvas, 13¼ × 19½ inches. Signed lower right: *Homer*. (Yale University Art Gallery; gift of Samuel R. Betts, B.A. 1875)

TROOPER MEDITATING BEFORE A GRAVE (1865)

Winslow Homer (1836–1910)

There is considerable romance in this simple mourning scene. In reality, few casualties found such formal, well-manicured final resting places. Many bodies were fated to be piled side by side in mass graves. As for the luxury of grief, one hardened veteran wrote home to confess: "I have seen so much…that in one sens [sic] of the word I have become hardened and it does not affect me but little to walk over the field of strife and behold its horrors." This canvas, owned by fellow Civil War artist Sanford Robinson Gifford, reveals Homer's constant search for broader philosophical meanings in military paintings.

Oil on canvas, 16⅛ × 8 inches. Signed lower right: *Homer.*
(Joslyn Art Museum; gift of Dr. Harold Gifford and Ann Gifford Forbes)

PLAYING OLD SOLDIER (1863)

Winslow Homer (1836–1910)

One of Homer's earliest oil paintings, this humorous genre scene—once called The Malingerer, *a less polite term for the period slang, "old soldier"—depicts a trooper showing his tongue to a field doctor, his eyes revealing, as the New York* Evening Post *noted, "an entire willingness to be considered ill" and excused from duty. "Art has gained some good even from 'the struggle,' " a critic for the New York Tribune observed of this painting, adding, "The head of the pretended invalid…is admirably painted, and the free, natural, wholesome handling…deserves the highest praise." The rumpled and casual soldiers owe much to Homer's stint as a wartime artist-correspondent, and differ markedly from the spruce and fierce-looking subjects of many Civil War paintings.*

Oil on canvas, 16 × 12 inches. Signed lower right: *Homer.* (Museum of Fine Arts, Boston; Ellen Kalleran Gardner Fund)

Hunt, one of the best known and most widely praised New England artists of his day, spent the Civil War years in Vermont, Rhode Island, and Massachusetts—painting, not fighting. It thus came as no surprise that his most famous Civil War painting made no attempt to portray a typical drummer boy realistically. Instead, Hunt attired his figure in clothes more reminiscent of the French Revolution than of the American Civil War, gave the child idealized features, and literally placed him on a pedestal to suggest his contributions to the Northern cause. Henry T. Tuckerman nevertheless declared this composition "one of the most popular and significant illustrations of the war for the Union."

Oil on canvas, 36 × 26 inches. Signed lower right: *WMHunt.* (Gift of Mrs. Samuel H. Wolcott; Museum of Fine Arts, Boston)

for the portrait in his painting, was found in Scott's studio after his death.[15]

There are several possible explanations for the tangled iconography of Scott's painting. He may have lost his funding from Colonel Shepard and altered his subject matter, focusing instead on the better-known and thus more commercially appealing Potter charge. Or he may have intended Potter as his subject all along. The surviving fragment may not be a detail at all. Whatever the case, Scott's final commission apparently failed. What succeeded are many fine works depicting not grand battlefields necessarily, or famous heroes, but common soldiers, including camp musicians like Julian Scott. Inevitably, however, most of these works, too, proved less than successful.[16]

Heaps of mythical nonsense were written about drummer boys during the Civil War, for example, so there should be little wonder that they also generated some quite unsatisfactory paintings: William Morris Hunt's barefoot Greek statue in rags, called *The Drummer Boy,* and Eastman Johnson's improbable picture *The Wounded Drummer Boy.* In the latter, the acrobatic pose of the soldier and the unlikely action (the drummer had no need to drum; he should have been helping the wounded) conspire to reveal in Johnson's depiction of common soldiers here the basic sentimentalism of this genre painter's approach to the Civil War. Contrast these depictions with what the sensible Edwin Forbes observed:

Painters of military pictures are fond of placing a broken drum in the fore-ground of their battle-scenes; but no representation could be more incorrect, for during a battle musicians and drummers are detailed to the rear for hospital service, and may often be found behind some fence enjoying a quiet cup of coffee.[17]

Scott was one of the rare drummers who did see serious action. At Lees Mills, Virginia, in April 1862, he repeatedly braved heavy enemy fire to wade into a creek several times to bring back wounded men who might otherwise have drowned. He won a Medal of Honor for it.

But Scott chose to ignore battle in his 1891 canvas called *Civil War Drummer Boys Playing Cards,* portraying the loss of

THE WOUNDED DRUMMER BOY
(c. 1862–65)

William Morris Hunt
(1824–1879)

Inspired by the same "incident of the war" that had moved Eastman Johnson to paint his more famous composition, Hunt's version depicted a young drummer lying prostrate before his discarded instrument, the skies above him symbolically gray. Like his other "drummer boy" painting, this canvas was first exhibited in Boston in 1879.

Oil on canvas, 14 × 19½ inches. Signed lower right: *WMH.* (Gift from Isaac Fenno Collection; Museum of Fine Arts, Boston)

THE WOUNDED DRUMMER BOY (1871)

Eastman Johnson (1824–1906)

Johnson observed firsthand this scene of bravery and brotherhood under fire, probably at the Battle of Antietam. In the words of the catalog issued for its first exhibition in 1872, "a drummer boy was disabled by a shot in the leg. As he lay upon the field he called to his comrades, 'Carry me and I'll drum her through.' They tied up his wound, a big soldier took him upon his shoulders, and he drummed through the fight." Although the canvas is encumbered by the soldier's acrobatic pose and by melodramatic portraiture that to modern eyes rob it of its potential power, in its day it was much admired. Henry T. Tuckerman called it "a vigorous work, full of spirit and expression" and commended its "simple and emphatic eloquence." The anecdote on which the painting was based was probably spurious, as drummers did not "drum through" battles. They were sent to the rear to act as stretcher bearers.

Oil on canvas, 40 × 39 inches.
(The Union League Club of New York)

A Break, Playing Cards
(Civil War Drummer Boys Playing Cards, 1891)

Julian Scott (1846–1901)

Drummer boys no older than children relax like men over a game of cards, as two of their older comrades look on, one amused, the other clearly disapproving. Complaining about such gambling among soldiers, one company musician wrote home to assail the "demoralizing influence the vices of army life have upon the minds of a great many," adding, "It sometimes seems to me that the Almighty wouldn't ever bless the efforts of our army to put down this rebellion while it is so depraved." If, for some, card playing could have such effects on soldiers, imagine the impact of seeing mere boys playing cards. Scott thus suggested innocence transformed too early into experience. Such transformations were sometimes said to have characterized the meaning of the Civil War for the young American republic.

Oil on canvas, 22 × 27 inches. Signed lower right: *Julian Scott/1891.* (West Point Museum, U.S. Military Academy)

REAR GUARD AT WHITE OAK SWAMP (1869)

Julian Scott (1846–1901)

Brig. Gen. William Smith (on horseback, saber drawn), directs the Vermont Brigade to fire at Confederate artillery while comrades struggle to turn a cannon toward the enemy in fighting on June 29, 1862. Confederates replied by firing "along their whole line with a crash that made the very earth tremble," a Union trooper recalled. The successful defense of this area preceded the Union victory at Malvern Hill the following day. Scott, who specialized in depicting common soldiers from his native Vermont, here made not the general but the strapping soldier at center the focus of this composition. He also employed the device of turning the action toward the viewer to heighten the drama. Scott sold this painting to New York's Union League Club in 1870 for one thousand dollars.

Oil on canvas, 45 × 70 inches. Signed lower right: *Julian Scott/1869.*
(The Union League Club of New York; photograph by Stan Wan)

innocence in the very activity of playing cards, a nearly universal pastime in camp, and one widely regarded as a vice. Although Scott's depictions of the three boys seated at cards might appear somewhat coy, the figure of the tallest boy, watching the game in his outsized military greatcoat, does convey the sadness of experience gained at too young an age and seems especially melancholy against the bleak yellow-gray sky.

Winslow Homer had earlier seen similar possibilities in the war's young drummers. *Sounding Reveille*, which he painted in 1865 and is sadly hidden away in a private collection, focused on these figures who loomed so large in soldiers' lives because they woke them for another wearying day each morning. In a study of a young soldier painted in 1864, some elements of which appear in *Sounding Reveille*, Homer also focused on a figure in an outsized military coat.

There exist other depictions of reveille to which to compare it, for waking up was a memorable part of the weary soldier's life and the idea held obvious symbolic possibilities for painters who might wish to suggest America's awakening to national greatness in the Civil War. Henry Bacon's *Reveille on a Winter Morning* employs, as a central figure, a drummer boy blowing on his hands to warm his fingers, but the handsome young soldiers depicted gathering in the snow before their tents seem impossibly handsome and lack the sad expressiveness of Julian Scott's drummers. Moreover, Bacon's bright scene suggests a more straightforwardly patriotic message than Homer's bleak reveille.

Homer surely held true to military experience in suggesting the early hour by his dusky palate—soldiers rose early and not at the bright banker's hour that seems to light Bacon's painting. In fact, Homer's camp scene, though lighted by myriad dots from flickering campfires, is nevertheless far bleaker in appearance than Bacon's cold winter morning. Winslow Homer's whole landscape seems almost brown and blighted.

Though he was capable of rendering beautiful scenery, it is interesting to note how far were Homer's concerns as a painter of the Civil War from those of the artists trained as landscapists. Although he sometimes chose the long horizontal canvas appropriate for a panorama, Homer was likely to render the landscape inhabited by Civil War soldiers as barren. In *Pitching Quoits*, the Zouaves stand on ground so hard and flat it is difficult to imagine where the logs and brush came from that were used to set up the soldiers' encampment. And *Rainy Day in Camp*, painted even later, in 1871, shows a bleakly cold landscape indeed, in which the great-coated Union cavalrymen cluster together for warmth. The sun may always have shone on Gifford's Seventh New York Regiment, but in the Civil War that Winslow Homer depicted, there was a variety of weather, some of it quite unpleasant. To some degree, the barren landscapes were surely literal renderings of Homer's observations near the battle front, for Civil War armies cut down virtual forests of trees—to build huts for winter quarters, to use as firewood for warmth and cooking, and to clear fire zones so that their weapons would be effective and the enemy could not approach under cover. The characters in *Prisoners from the Front* are so riveting to the eye that it is difficult for the viewer to take note of the landscape of tree stumps behind them. Likewise, the lone figure defiantly *Inviting a Shot before Petersburg, Virginia, 1864,* stands clad in brown, easily dominating a dull blue-gray sky in a logged-over landscape.

Escaping the arcadian conventions of the landscape painters helped Homer render warfare more convincingly on canvas. When Homer's landscape was not barren, it was darkly threatening and full of dangerous snipers, sharpshooters, and skirmishers. Ultimately, soldiers at war lived in a threatening and inhospitable environment. Thus the critic Marc Simpson is surely correct when he says that in these early works of Winslow Homer one sees not only accurate, homely details of everyday soldier's life, but also "glimmerings of the themes of mortality, isolation, and nature's adversity that would come to dominate his later art." Here, as historian Clive Bush has recognized, is an act of heroism clouded in irony: a soldier exposing himself to almost certain death, his figure silhouetted but not lit by the sky—his sacrifice therefore "not sanctioned by the light of divine glory." It is the quintessential death in a modern war: horrible, but not necessarily honorable. And it occurs in a landscape that a British visitor to wartime America saw as "a Valley of the Shadow of Death," marked by "its entire nakedness and desolation, and the knowledge that Man not Nature, had made the waste."[18]

Homer's career provides useful commentary on the problem of militarism in military paintings. Winslow Homer was not a great military painter, he was a great painter. His last Civil War canvas appears to have been completed in 1871, and then he moved on to paint other scenes that engaged his imagination and embodied the philosophical themes that interested him. Even the stimulus of *Battles and Leaders* commissions failed to revive his interest. Homer placed sketches in three of the four volumes, but this return to Civil War images in the 1880s otherwise left no mark on his enterprise, and neither did the battles in the West with Indians, European conflicts, or America's splendid little war at

Opposite

A RAINY DAY IN CAMP (1871)

Winslow Homer (1836–1910)

One of Homer's final Civil War paintings, this canvas succeeds in evoking great distances within its limited frame, and presents such technically accomplished highlights as the modest campfire around which the small group of cavalry officers gathers in their greatcoats; the distant puddles shimmering in the dim light; and the animals suffering the inclement weather alongside the soldiers. One camp musician remembered rainy days as producing "the greatest discomfort a soldier could have," including "wet clothes, shoes, and blankets; wet meat and bread; wet feet and wet ground."

Oil on canvas, 19¾ × 36 inches. Signed lower right: *Winslow Homer/1871*; lower left: *Homer.* (The Metropolitan Museum of Art; gift of Mrs. William F. Milton)

PRISONERS FROM THE FRONT (1866)

Winslow Homer (1836–1910)

The landscape that dominated much Civil War art is stripped away in this extraordinary tableau; all that remains are the opposing forces, and here they meet face-to-face in a confrontation that brilliantly summarizes the inevitable consequences of all war— conquest and capitulation. With symbolically discarded weapons at their feet, three highly individualized Confederate prisoners are brought under guard before a dignified young Federal officer. One Union veteran recalled seeing "such captured men" whose ragged "appearance told of their poverty." But Homer's Civil War masterpiece went beyond such general criticism of the backwardness of the Southern economy. For example, though he based his youthful captor on the war's celebrated "boy general," Francis C. Barlow, he refrained from depicting him as gloating over his catch; the ingenious originality of Homer's work was that it recorded captor and captives with more judicious impartiality. What was more, with adroit use of color, shape, and even headgear (or lack of it), he created distinctive portraits of archetypal prisoners. One period writer saw in them a "bewildered old man, perhaps a spy, with his furtive look"; a "'poor white,' stupid, stolid, helpless"; and a "reckless, impudent young Virginian." Agreeing, another observer believed the painting reflected the war's conflict between efficiency and enthusiasm, and the inevitable victory of efficiency. And yet, as another period observer conceded, the central Confederate was rendered as "a truly chivalric and manly figure," every inch the equal of the "composed, lithe, and alert" Barlow, whose own "air of reserved and tranquil power, are contrasted with the subdued eagerness of the foremost prisoner." Homer's "Homeric reminiscence," as one wag dubbed it at the time, elicited acclaim wherever it was exhibited. The New York Evening Post *called it "vital" and "vigorous," and the* New York Tribune *a "clever study of character." The picture proved a sensation at the 1867 Exposition Universelle in Paris, with the* London Art Journal *praising it for its "touch, character, and vigour." The greatest American art critic of the day, Henry T. Tuckerman, accurately summarized its impact when he asserted that same year that this canvas "won more praise than any genre picture by a native hand that has appeared of late years."*

Oil on canvas, 24 × 38 inches. Signed lower right: *Homer 1866.* (The Metropolitan Museum of Art; gift of Mrs. Frank B. Porter, 1922)

PUNISHMENT FOR INTOXICATION, OR IN FRONT OF THE GUARD-HOUSE (1863)

Winslow Homer (1836–1910)

Camp drunks could be sentenced to elaborate, painful punishment—buck-ing and gagging, marching inside barrels (known as "wooden overcoats"), carrying rocks or sand in backpacks— and, in the case of this soldier, standing under guard atop a small cracker box, holding a heavy log. One soldier subject-ed to this ignominy called the ordeal "the utterly useless and shoulder-chafing punishment of carrying a stick of cord-wood" until it grew "heavier and heavier as the sun rose higher and higher." Homer thought this early painting "about as beautiful and inter-esting as the button on a barn door," and reportedly his own brother bought it secretly from a shop to encourage him to keep painting. By the follow-ing year, an art critic noticing it on display at the National Academy turned to a friend and said in astonishment: "If this is the work of a new beginner, where on earth will he stop?"

Oil on canvas, 17 × 13 inches. Signed lower right: *Homer 1863.* (Canajoharie Library and Art Gallery, Canajoharie, New York)

With wounded and dead littering the field (and causing the artist problems with proportion), Catholic troops of the Irish Brigade kneel for a battlefield mass before the second day's fighting at Gettysburg. The chaplain shown here, William Corby, one eyewitness recalled, "stood upon a large rock in front of the brigade" and reminded them "of the high and sacred nature of their trust as soldiers and the noble object for which they fought." At the close of the brief sermon, "every man fell on his knees," and "stretching his right hand toward the brigade," Father Corby recited a general absolution—the scene that Wood captured in this stirring depiction. It was not unusual for chaplains to organize divine worship "preparatory to the general slaughter of battle," one soldier testified, but it was unusual for artists to depict such services, especially Catholic ones.

Oil on canvas, 72 × 102 inches. Signed lower right: *Paul Wood/1891.* (The Snite Museum of Art, University of Notre Dame; gift of the artist)

the end of the century. Homer apparently exhausted his firsthand material gathered during the Civil War, and, as far as he was concerned, as a painter, he had perhaps exhausted the larger themes he could explore in war art.

This is not to say that other painters, like Gaul, showed an immature infatuation with military glory, or, like Trego, a pathetic longing for a life of vigor and violence denied him by the bitter circumstance of physical handicap. It is not fair to club them with Homer's subsequent reputation. Julian Scott, for example, developed as a painter and was growing better, despite apparent bouts of alcoholism, before the stroke that sadly ended his artistic career at age fifty-one. Trego, likewise, showed great skill, and it was a tragedy for art when he committed suicide. Most of the painters mentioned in this book were not exclusively military artists anyhow; some painted only a military canvas or two among many others depicting more peaceful scenes, and their reasons for painting them surely varied.

Still, it is worthwhile to ask the question of purpose in examining any of these works. And when one does, one is sure to be struck by purposes that never occurred to the Civil War artists of the nineteenth century: themes unexplored, questions they refused to ask or answer.

Julian Scott, who had seen combat himself (and fearfully close-up), but at a much younger age than Homer, had certainly observed innocence changing to experience. But Scott was rarely able to explore such themes freely because he could not abandon commissions that required him to depict officers in particular moments of glory in their military careers. He did occasionally offer subjects that commanded attention for their homely accuracy, if not their sym-

bolic and philosophical renderings of soldiers or men at war. His sketch of two cavalrymen in camp thus employs a tree stump more as a convenient prop than as a symbol of nature or a report of the ravaging of the environment by nineteenth-century armies on the march and in camp. Likewise, the carefully drawn saddle, a model 1859 McClellan saddle, seems almost too perfectly visible, a prop from the artist's collection of military artifacts present as a proof of authenticity in research.[19] Still, the rather casual attitudes of the men seem convincing and perhaps a little less studied than some of Homer's frozen Zouaves or soldiers standing in poses reminiscent of French uniform prints. Yet the easy fraternity of Scott's charming sketch, though like the friendship in *The Briarwood Pipe*'s two smokers, was never destined to dissolve, as it did in Homer's bleaker canvases, into the "solitude" of struggle not simply against an enemy action, but against a hostile universe.

Thus, in Homer's Civil War works, considerable attention focuses on his oil sketch of a solitary cavalryman looking at a grave. If one stops to think about the idea of solitude in military art, one realizes immediately that solitude must have been one thing that soldiers could not get, no matter how much they desired it. The Civil War was fought by massed armies of tens of thousands of men who lived together in crowded cabins in winter quarters, or in tents on campaign, or in barracks while in training. They slept together, ate together, and often drilled and fought in close order, almost touching each other's elbows. Even generals could not find solitude, as they needed sentries, messengers, and staff officers; they had to be readily available in case news of an enemy movement needed to be com-

municated to them. Doubtless most soldiers knew the psychological solitude of fear of death, but that would have been difficult to represent on canvas—even if anyone had wanted to do so.

But fear, the opposite of the supreme Civil War virtue of courage, belonged to the realm of the cartoonist only. An occasional painting of a retreat—like the Mud March—was a rare gesture to fear in the grand medium of painting. Flight was rarely shown, and panic, never.

If artists of Civil War scenes always shied away from war's grimmest aspects, and the United States produced no Goya for its bloody conflict, nevertheless the art inspired by the war usually avoided the most genteel pieties. There are important conclusions about these works that can be arrived at only by looking at them as a mass. One of the most important is that, among artists, the war prompted little or no spiritual response. There are only two Civil War paintings of any fame that embrace religious scenes: Sanford Robinson Gifford's landscape of a religious service in camp and Paul Wood's *Absolution under Fire*, depicting a chaplain of the Irish Brigade conducting a mass before the second day's fighting at Gettysburg. Research has uncovered only four such popular prints, one of prayer in Stonewall Jackson's camp, Volck's "Cave Life in Vicksburg," one Union

Opposite

THE RESCUE OF THE COLORS (1899)

William B. T. Trego
(1859–1909)

A Bucks County, Pennsylvania, regiment lunges forward to recapture its battle flag during the Battle of Fair Oaks. Trego agreed to capture the moment on canvas for the unit's commander, Gen. William W. H. Davis, "at the lowest possible price ($400) as a favor to my native county." But a subscription effort failed, and the fee had to be paid by the wealthy Philadelphia merchant John Wanamaker. Trego's painting, which took a year to finish, was not fettered to the cavalier image of mounted officers grappling hand-to-hand over battle colors. Here, common soldiers do the fighting, while General Davis, his patronage notwithstanding, looks on helplessly (left), holding his wounded arm. Trego also included bloody casualties and bodies in rigor mortis (center), probably inspired by famous Civil War photographs. But his canvas lacks focus, and, ultimately, power.

Oil on canvas, 48¼ × 91 inches. Signed lower right: *Wm. T. Trego 1899.* (Mercer Museum, Bucks County Historical Society)

Protestant scene, and one Catholic.

This is remarkable in a country as driven by evangelical fervor as was nineteenth-century America. Religious revivals swept the Confederate armies, especially, while the Union ones were virtually deluged by religious materials provided by the U.S. Christian Commission. And chaplains were plentifully provided to minister to soldiers' spiritual needs in both armies. Yet many of the war's famous soldiers, the evangelical Stonewall Jackson and the austere Episcopalian Robert E. Lee aside, hardly presented a pious image. Though he never swore, U. S. Grant never belonged to a church, either, and was only baptized when an unscrupulous Methodist clergyman came to him while the general was dying of throat cancer and was too weak to resist. William T. Sherman, who experienced complicated and unhappy family conflicts because of his wife's Catholicism, likewise was given last rites only when unconscious and dying of pneumonia. There were Christian soldiers like O. O. Howard, and to think of the music inspired by the war is to think of *The Battle Hymn of the Republic.* But for the most part, painting seems rather secular by comparison.

In part, American military painting had little religiosity about it because invoking the symbols of one faith was sure to expose one's canvas to criticism from all the other faiths. And the country had no established church. Therefore, America's cycloramas do not resemble Poland's panorama celebrating the Battle of Racliwice, in 1794, with its scene of scythemen led into battle behind a banner suspended from a cross and its peasants praying before a huge wayside cross as Polish reinforcements march to engage the Russian armies.[20]

A more important factor, especially

in later American military paintings, may have been the rather secular nature of even their symbolic themes: experience over innocence, man against nature, and struggling for survival—ideas that do not lend themselves to easy iconographic spiritual formulas.

Among other subjects that the artists rarely painted were sailors. Ships are well represented in this book, but their crews are hard to find in nineteenth-century art. The rare depictions of them came from the brushes or pens of marine painters, who, after all, were not really figure painters but mainly artists of seascapes and vessels. This absence is

partly attributable to a factor David
Dixon Porter suggested in regard to
photography and the Civil War navy:
few artists, with camera or brush,
desired the harsh discipline and long
isolation of a cruise.

If one reflects on naval scenes, one
can see another important idea here.
When sailors were depicted, it was on
open decks, as in Overend's dramatic
view of the deck of the *Hartford* in the
Battle of Mobile Bay. One searches in vain
for canvases depicting the crews of ironclad vessels. Of course, the men on ironclad duty did not fight on decks in the
open air, but rather entirely inside their

cramped armored monsters. So small was
the two-gun turret of the *Monitor* that
there was barely space to reload the big
rifles, and as a result they could be fired
only at two-and-a-half-minute intervals at
best. And painters who shunned even the
salt air of the wooden vessels would have
been even less likely to ship on board one
of these hot, unseaworthy, and dangerously experimental machines. The result is
that artists missed an opportunity to
depict men in ways that might have
shown what the industrial revolution was
doing to warfare.

Few American artists were far enough
away from landscape traditions to feel

CARLISLE, PA., JULY 1, 1863 (1886)

Charles B. Cox (nineteenth century)

*As New York and Pennsylvania troops march through Carlisle toward Gettysburg,
Confederate shells strike a large gray house (center), shattering its chimney. The artist skillfully contrasted the frenzy overtaking the civilian population—women shouting from the upper floors of the
buildings and the excited child scampering in the street—with the calm of the soldiers, even as one of
them (to the right of the officer on the white horse) falls wounded into the arms of comrades. Cox
achieved a look of near-photographic candidness with the soldier stooping to pick up his comrade's cap,
the shattered streetlight, and the blood dripping over the curb.*

Oil on canvas, 33 × 17½ inches. Signed lower left: *Chas. B. Cox./1886.*
(First Regiment Infantry Museum, Upper Darby, Pennsylvania; from *The Civil War: Gettysburg;*
photograph by Larry Sherer, © 1985 Time-Life Books, Inc.)

CONFEDERATE PRISON SCENE, CIVIL WAR (1873)

Julian Scott (1846–1901)

An orderly brings meager rations to ragged Confederate prisoners cruelly crowded into a tiny cell, as a Union guard watches dispassionately. The fruit rinds and empty bottle littering the curbside suggest that onlookers may have been sadistically taunting these starving captives. Prisoners of war typically complained of poor and inadequate food and mistreatment by their guards. Many preferred seasoned veterans as guards to raw soldiers who had never seen action. "From soldiers who fight in the field," a prisoner at Johnson's Island explained, "better treatment is expected." Six years after painting this scene, artist Scott produced a far more sympathetic view of a Confederate guard in a similar setting, titling the work, The Compassionate Enemy.

Oil on canvas, 26¼ × 20½ inches. Signed lower right: *Julian Scott/1873.* (West Point Museum, U.S. Military Academy; photograph by Don Pollard)

CONFEDERATE CAMP DURING THE LATE AMERICAN WAR FROM THE ORIGINAL PAINTING BY C. W. CHAPMAN...

M. and N. Hanhart, after Conrad Wise Chapman

From his on-the-spot oil sketch, Chapman prepared an expanded scene including other groups of soldiers. The artist (who inserted a self-portrait into the scene; he can be seen leaning on his rifle at left) also revised his central group of card players; instead of three, there were now two, and one was depicted as a Lee-like elder statesman, perhaps in an effort to take the onus off their questionable activity. This scene was realistic, however, according to a veteran who pointed out that Confederates preferred to make camp in woods, not open fields, "and so the Confederate camp was not as orderly or as systematically arranged but the more picturesque."

Chromolithograph, 10⅜ × 15¼ inches. (The Valentine Museum, Richmond, Virginia)

⮞ *Above* ⮜

CAMP NEAR CORINTH, MISS., MAY 10, 1862 (1862)

Conrad Wise Chapman (1842–1910)

Confederate soldiers play cards—"throw the papers," as the pastime was then sometimes called—in the peaceful campsite, where Chapman served in the Third Kentucky Infantry. This oil sketch formed the basis of a larger camp scene turned into an etching by the artist's father and into a famous chromolithograph in London after the war. Chapman captured the Confederate preference for camps in woods rather than open fields by a lovely depiction of dappling shade.

Oil on board, 5½ × 9¼ inches. Signed lower left: *C W C.* (The Valentine Museum, Richmond, Virginia)

THE SENTRY (1892)

William Spang
(nineteenth century)

Using his small model, shown below, Spang created this larger-than-life Union sentry gripping his rifle tightly as he patrols a battle-ravaged landscape. This painting was commissioned by the Grant Chapter of the Grand Army of the Republic to decorate the organization's Philadelphia meeting hall. The open canteen shown spilling its contents in the right foreground suggests that action has recently taken place on this site, increasing the danger facing the sentry.

Oil on canvas, 7 feet 6 inches × 4 feet 10 inches. (U.S. Army Infantry Center, Fort Benning, Georgia)

THE SENTRY (N.D.)

William Spang
(nineteenth century)

Oil on canvas, 11×6¼ inches. (The Civil War Library and Museum, Philadelphia)

comfortable painting depictions of the machine age. And the opportunity that they lost in the case of the monitors can be seen, once again, in the work of Herman Melville. His *Battle-Pieces* included a near-nightmare poem called "In the Turret," which celebrated John L. Worden, the commander of the *Monitor* in its historic encounter with the *Merrimac* off Hampton Roads. But Melville saluted the commander's courage in a haunting way:

> *Your honest heart of duty, Worden,*
> *So helped you that in fame you*
> *dwell;*
> *You bore the first iron battle's burden*
> *Sealed as in a diving bell.*
> *Alcides, groping into haunted hell*
> *To bring forth King Admetus' bride,*
> *Braved naught more vaguely direful*
> *and untried.*

Melville went on to describe the dialogue in John Worden's head as he approached battle riveted in a "welded tomb" whose armor, instead of proving to be "the foeman's terror" might turn out to be a "monstrous error."[21] But no Civil War painting yet uncovered responded to the opportunity to show the nightmare of war within a machine-age "Og," as Melville described the *Merrimac*. In fact, Civil War painters were trained and were intellectually inclined as well to depict men and animals and nature, not metal and machines and technology. Although artillery gets some attention in Civil War art (in battle, it was located farthest to the rear, where the artists were as well),

it attracts notice as an arm of the service, not as a technological symbol. Trego, for example, depicted a four-horse team pulling a limber and cannon through the mud, but only the breech and elevating screw of the artillery piece itself are visible behind muddy carriage and struggling men and horses. He did give the ugly black mortars prominence in his other famous artillery picture, but, on the whole, Civil War painters did not often depict artillery with either loving accuracy or symbolic prominence.

In ignoring the impact of the machine on war, even painters of the Civil War as talented as Winslow Homer failed in any way to suggest the demise of individual courage as a significant battlefield factor. If they can thus be faulted for failing to find in this mid-nineteenth-century conflict those elements that led to the horrors of World War I and twentieth-century warfare in general, they can, on the other hand, be commended for rendering "their" war accurately. Ultimately, the Civil War was among the last of the old-fashioned conflicts in which courageous individual soldiers played the principal roles in bringing either victory or defeat—not large machines, not fast-moving vehicles, not even the economies that could produce such mechanical devices in overwhelming quantities. When the painters depicted courageous men with shoulder arms, well led, they were not as far from the truth of the Civil War as our age, still spiritually bruised by the imbecilic carnage of World War I and its hideous twentieth-century successors, might imagine.

Inviting a Shot Before Petersburg (Defiance, 1864)

Winslow Homer (1836–1910)

Noting that "it was almost certain death to show one's head above the works," two early memoirists recorded the story of "a sort of dare-devil fellow" who mounted the works one day "and catching his red cap from his head, swung it defiantly at the enemy." He was promptly shot in the head. Most soldiers, faced with similar danger, stayed deep in their trenches as long as they could, fully aware of the constant threat from sharpshooters aiming at them from a distance. This uncharacteristic painting, from the Confederate side of the lines, includes a caricature of a black man of the sort Homer would quickly outgrow; the image here owed something to the stock racist images Homer saw as a newspaper artist and creator of popular lithographs.

Oil on panel, 12 × 18 inches. Signed lower left: *Homer 1864*. (Detroit Institute of Arts; gift of Dexter M. Ferry)

ASSAULT ON CONFEDERATE WORKS (N.D.)

William E. Winner
(c. 1815–1883)

Winner, who specialized in religious scenes before the war, here brought almost evangelical fervor to his depiction of a brave Union assault against well-fortified enemy works. A Confederate who observed such a charge compared it to "ocean waves driven by a hurricane," describing Union troops "trampling…over dead and wounded, sweeping on as if by irresistible impulse, to dash and break and reel and die against the Confederate works, and stagger back like drunken men, broken and routed."

Oil on canvas, 26 × 33 inches. Signed lower left: *Winner.* (West Point Museum, U.S. Military Academy)

PICKET POST (N.D.)

Conrad Wise Chapman (1842–1910)

A bored-looking sentry— a self-portrait of Chapman—sits comfortably as dawn comes to a peaceful-looking Confederate camp, whose fellow soldiers (rear) seem even more nonchalant than their picket. Chapman's father produced an etched print based on the scene, locating the post at Diascund Bridge, Virginia, and dating it March 8, 1863.

Oil on canvas, 24 × 16 inches. (The Valentine Museum, Richmond, Virginia)

THE BATTLE OF FREDERICKSBURG (C. 1865)

Frederic Cavada (nineteenth century)

*Union forces launch their futile attack on the all-but-impregnable Confederate stronghold
atop Marye's Heights. Cavada, a Union lieutenant, depicted the action from just behind Federal
lines, where troops are already beginning to drop under the withering fire from above. Each
advancing brigade, Union general Darius Couch remembered, would "melt like snow coming down
on the ground." The oversized banners show how large flags loomed in soldiers' consciousness,
and lend a vividly patriotic air as well.*

Oil on canvas, 24 × 36 inches. Signed lower left: *Cavada.* (The Historical Society of Pennsylvania)

**HORSE ARTILLERY GOING INTO BATTLE, PETERSBURG, VIRGINIA, 1865
(FEDERAL ARTILLERY ATTACK, N.D.)**

William B. T. Trego (1859–1909)

*As buglers sound the charge, a battery of Union artillery gallops into action, providing Trego
with an opportunity to show his virtuosic ability to paint horses of many colors and from many different angles. The scene was reproduced as a black-and-white print in 1893.*

Oil on canvas, 24½ × 36½ inches. Signed lower right: *W. Trego.*
(West Point Museum, U.S. Military Academy; from *The Civil War: Pursuit to Appomattox;*
photograph by Henry Groskinsky, © 1987 Time-Life Books, Inc.)

MORTAR BATTERY FIRING (C. 1875)

William B. T. Trego (1859–1909)

Union forces hurl mortar shells toward distant Confederate targets in this compelling close-up view of a typical battery. "The mortars are fired without the gunner seeing the spot he aims at," artist-correspondent Alfred Waud observed of a similar scene, adding, "...as the shell is visible as it leaves the smoke till it falls into the doomed spot, it is very interesting to watch." Trego made it even more interesting by designing the composition as a series of dramatic, intersecting lines.

Oil on canvas, 24 × 20 inches. Signed lower left: *W. T. Trego.*
(West Point Museum, U.S. Military Academy;
photograph by Don Pollard)

BATTLE OF FREDERICKSBURG, OR COBB'S AND KERSHAW'S TROOPS BEHIND THE STONE-WALL (1886)

Allen Christian Redwood (1844–1922)

Redwood based this illustration, for Battles and Leaders of The Civil War, *on a grisly wartime photograph that showed casualties stacked against this stone wall atop Marye's Heights—but casualties not of Fredericksburg but of Chancellorsville the following spring, when the armies again fought over this ground. The bloodied figure at left, for example, is clearly visible in the original photograph, surprisingly reproduced in the same book. "I walked the battle-ground, and examined the heights beyond Marye's house," Union brigadier general Herman Haupt remembered. "My photographic artist, Captain [Andrew J.] Russell, was with me and secured several large photograph negatives—one very good one of the stone wall, with the rebel dead lying behind it."*

Watercolor and gouache on board, 11½ × 16½ inches. Signed lower left: *A. C. Redwood/1886.* (Courtesy Tharpe Collection of American Military History)

THE CHARGE (1887)

William B. T. Trego (1859–1909)

Sabers drawn and battle flag waving in the breeze, a company of Union cavalry charges forward in attack formation against an unseen enemy. These mounted units, undoubtedly the most romantic branch of the service—at least as far as artists were concerned—were anything but revered by infantrymen. One Illinois soldier called them "a positive nuisance," contending: "They won't fight, and whenever they are around they are always in the way of those who will fight."

Oil on canvas, 20 × 30 inches. Signed lower left: *W. T. Trego/87* (Fort Garland Museum, Fort Garland, Colorado; photograph courtesy Colorado Historical Society)

NEARING THE END (c. 1907–9)

Gilbert Gaul (1855–1919)

Against the ironically promising background of a blossoming Southern springtime, ragged, battle-weary Confederates ponder the latest disheartening war news while partaking of a meager breakfast in camp. "I have had nothing to eat for four days," a Virginia private noted around this time, adding, "I don't feel very hungry now but I know damned well I'm starving to death."

Oil on canvas, 32 × 44 inches.
Signed lower left: *Gilbert Gaul.*
(The Birmingham Museum of Art)

TAPS (c. 1907–9)

Gilbert Gaul (1855–1919)

A Confederate soldier lies dead on a war-torn field, his horse nearby, in this bathetic depiction of battle death. A Georgia soldier remembered observing "the dead lying around…horses & wagons & troops passing heedlessly along…. The stiffened bodies lie, grasping in death the arms they bravely bore, with glazed eyes and features blackened by rapid decay…." Painters like Gaul preferred depictions of perpetual sleep to medically detailed views of post-battle decomposition.

Oil on canvas, 32 × 44 inches. Signed lower left: *Gilbert Gaul.* (The Birmingham Museum of Art)

THE RETURN OF THE FLAGS OF THE IRISH BRIGADE, 1865 (1869)

Thomas Waterman Wood
(1823–1903)

This canvas, probably commissioned by the units portrayed, depicted members of the Sixty-third, Sixty-ninth, and Eighty-eighth New York Infantry of the Irish Brigade returning their battle flags at war's end. The journalist William Swinton would write of these solemn victory ceremonies: "If one army drank the joy of victory…it was a joy moderated by the recollection of the cost at which it had been purchased…. How terrible had been the struggle! How many hundreds of thousands of brave men had fallen before that result could be achieved!" To such battle-scarred veterans, their regimental flags, "bespattered with the life-blood of their heroic bearers," became sacred relics of the "devotion of their followers."

Oil on canvas, 30 × 37 inches. Signed: *T W. Wood, 1869.* (West Point Museum Collections, U. S. Army Signal Corps photograph)

❖ MINE EYES HAVE SEEN THE GLORY ❖

FURLING THE FLAG (1872)

Richard Norris Brooke (1847–1920)

*As news of surrender reaches these ragged Confederate soldiers—some wounded, others barefoot—
they tearfully roll up their beloved battle flag for the last time. Brooke skillfully represented a range of
"types" in this sentimental genre painting, from the grizzled veteran to the youthful drummer boy,
and the characters bear witness to the emotional moment with both mournful sadness and disbelief.
Brooke conceived the painting to represent "After sunset Appomattox, Confederates looking on with
emotion while the tattered battle flag is furled for the last time."*

Oil on canvas, 22 × 30 inches. Signed lower left: *R. N. Brooke/1872.* (West Point Museum, U.S. Military Academy)

THE GRAND PARADE OF GENERAL SHERMAN'S ARMY IN WASHINGTON (1881)

James E. Taylor (1839–1901)

Marching past exuberant crowds lining Pennsylvania Avenue—the same route
Union troops took on their way to war four years earlier—the victorious Union army parades through
Washington in May 1865. "Every house was decorated by flags," marveled General Sherman, and the
city "was full of strangers who filled the streets in holiday dress." To the victorious general,
it was "a splendid success, and a fitting conclusion to the campaign and the war." Walt Whitman,
who joined the throngs, agreed that it was "a magnificent sight." One elderly onlooker was so moved by
this spectacle that he declared, "They march like the lords of the world."

Watercolor on paper, 21 × 29 inches. Signed lower right: *James E. Taylor./July 1st 1881.* (The Ohio Historical Society)

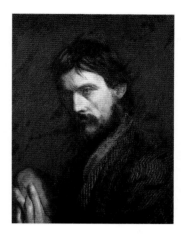

THE VETERAN (1884)

Thomas W. Eakins
(1844–1916)

To suggest the representative veteran, Eakins had one of his young students at the Pennsylvania Academy of the Fine Arts pose for this portrait. Deeply influenced by the poet Walt Whitman, Eakins preferred painting anonymous "democratic" types to actual war heroes.

Oil on canvas, 22¼ × 15 inches. (Yale University Art Gallery; bequest of Stephen Carlton Clark, B.A. 1903)

THE OLD VETERAN (N.D.)

William Spang (active 1870s)

His frame slightly stooped with the passage of time, a proud, old Union veteran stands at attention beneath a flag-festooned painting of General Grant, the stacked arms behind him symbolizing the return of peace. This scene records early uses of portraits of Civil War heroes like Grant: they decorated veterans' lodges, hospitals, and clubhouses. Spang, a Philadelphia artist, gave this picture an added touch of realism by modeling the Grant painting-within-the-painting on Anthony Lamor's Grant portrait at the local Union League Club.

Oil on canvas, 29½ × 24 inches. Signed lower left: *W. Spang./Phila./Pa.* (The Civil War Library and Museum, Philadelphia)

THE BATTLE OF THE CRATER (1869 COPY OF DESTROYED 1865 ORIGINAL)

John Adams Elder
(1833–1895)

To one onlooker, the underground mine that the Union detonated on July 30, 1864, to destroy Confederate entrenchments before Petersburg created "a mass without form or shape, full of red flames." After the smoke cleared, poorly led Federal forces, including black troops under Gen. Edward Ferrero, a former dance teacher, rushed the huge, smoldering crater only to be repulsed in a heroic defense by survivors of the blast. Elder portrayed this clash under a sulfurous sky as a blazingly red landscape just as a Confederate officer, John Wise, remembered it: "a scene of awful carnage." Rallying beneath a bullet-riddled flag supported by a shredded wooden staff, Confederates trapped the attackers inside the gaping crater and shot them down; more than 3,700 Federal casualties were counted, including some black troops said to have been killed after they surrendered. This painting was purchased by Gen. William Mahone, who led the successful repulse that day.

Oil on canvas, 38 × 61 inches. (Commonwealth Club, Richmond, Virginia; photograph by Dementi-Foster Studios, Richmond)

Acknowledgments

Our earlier books on Civil War–era iconography and photography typically (and conveniently) featured illustrations that were culled from a single, dominant collection, or at most, from several. Of course, we knew even before we set to work on *Mine Eyes Have Seen the Glory* that for this project we would instead be surveying hundreds of public and private repositories throughout the country. Nevertheless, neither our previous efforts nor our advance planning prepared us for the mountain of indebtedness we amassed along the way: to museum directors, curators, registrars, collectors, scholars, archivists, photo librarians, battlefield park rangers, friends, and family. This is our opportunity to acknowledge them.

Before we wrote a word of text for this book, there were the pictures—and our laborious, sometimes frustrating, but frequently rewarding two-year search for them. Needless to say, it would not have been possible to amass this collection without the significant contributions and boundless patience of dozens of specialists.

Among the chief contributors were experts who guided us through their collections at the very outset of our research. We owe them special thanks for both encouragement and inspiration: Russ A. Pritchard, executive director of the Civil War Library and Museum in Philadelphia; Joan Hendrix, coordinator of collections for the Union League of Philadelphia; Roger Friedman, Librarian of the Union League of New York; and Lisa Weilbacker, curator of the Seventh Regiment Collection in New York City.

Rex Scouten, curator of the White House, along with his assistant Lydia Tederick, provided early and crucial guidance, as well as fine illustrations. Jerry M. Bloomer, secretary to the board of the R. W. Norton Art Gallery in Shreveport, was most generous. And Robert M. Hicklin, Jr., a respected art dealer from Spartanburg, S.C., not only provided pictures and suggestions, he introduced us to the great private collector Jay P. Altmayer of Mobile, to whom we also owe thanks for his generosity (and the help of his able assistant, Gayle Dearman).

The New-York Historical Society provided pictures and expertise; we are especially grateful to Juliana Sciolla, vice-president for external relations, and Timothy Anglin Burgard, curator of paintings, drawings, and sculpture. In Richmond, our always dependable and congenial colleagues Malinda W. Collier and Corrine P. Hudgins, respectively registrar and manager of photographic services at the Museum of the Confederacy, helped us collect a superb archive of Southern images.

Robert J. Titterton supplied invaluable guidance on the life and career of the neglected artist Julian Scott, as did Leon Kramer of the Kramer Gallery in St. Paul. And at the Library of Congress's Prints and Photographs Division, where we spent countless hours in research, Bernard Reilly's expert staff, particularly Mary Ison, reference specialist for the Civil War collections, brought pictures that dazzled and inspired us—especially the long-ignored Battle of Gettysburg series by Edwin Forbes.

Three more people provided help that can only be called crucial; without them, this book could never have been produced. First is David Meschutt, curator of art at the West Point Museum, who threw open the files of that institution's magnificent Civil War art collection; Don Pollard, whose camera mastery captured the beauty of oil paintings at both West Point and in New York City; and John C. Weiser, director of photography and research for Time-Life, who granted us permission to use here some of the paintings first photographed for the Time-Life series on the Civil War.

In addition to Jay Altmayer, we thank private collectors who made their pictures available to us—frequently for first book publication—here: Edward M. Hageman; Sally Turner of the Sally Turner Galleries in Phoenix; Judge John E. De Hardit of Virginia; Louise Taper of Beverly Hills, California; and Jenny Long Murphy of Meredith Long & Co. in Houston. We are indebted, as well, to print experts Kenneth M. Newman of the Old Print Shop in New York; Lillian Brenwasser (and, of course, Barbara Fleischman) of the Kennedy Galleries in New York; and Donald Cresswell of the Philadelphia Print Shop.

Additional guidance came from P. Charles Lunsford of the Georgia Division of the Sons of Confederate Veterans; Evie Terrono, who provided useful information on wartime sanitary fairs; George Craig, guardian of General George H. Thomas's reputation; and Dan Weinberg of the Abraham Lincoln Book Shop in Chicago (both for ideas, suggestions, and as always, books).

For a scrupulous, valuable reading of the text we owe sincere thanks to the knowledgeable Peter Harrington, curator of the Anne S. K. Brown Military Collection at Brown University. And we are grateful to our friend John Y. Simon, executive director of the Ulysses S. Grant Association, for helping us find new information—and preventing us from making errors, as well—on the subject he knows better than anyone else. Frank J. Williams, president of the Abraham Lincoln Association, gave freely, as usual, of his expertise both historical and legal.

We are immeasurably grateful for the enthusiasm we found at Orion Books, especially for the hard work, scrupulous attention to detail, boundless optimism, and frequent forays for Japanese cuisine that we received from our editor, Steve Topping. Cressida Connolly, Lindsey Crittenden, and Joan Denman provided crucial help, too. Thanks also to Kay Schuckhart for her lively design and long hours. And our agent, Geri Thoma, has our eternal gratitude for introducing us to Steve in the first place—planting the seeds from which this book has blossomed.

In our respective offices (which each of us has since left to start new careers elsewhere), we thank Yvonne White (who typed the manuscript) and Ruth Cook at the Lincoln Museum in Fort Wayne, and their counterparts in New York: Jeff Schneider, for his research assistance, and also Janice Banks, Vince Lipani, and Amy Varney-Kiet. All of them kept the paper trail moving seamlessly and rapidly between cities during the long months it took to research, write, and rewrite this book. We will miss all of them enormously.

Chapter Notes and Sources

Introduction

1. Leslie Humm Cormier, "Correspondences Between Military Paintings by American Artists and their European Contemporaries," in *All the Banners Wave: Art and War in the Romantic Era, 1792–1851* (Providence: Department of Art, Brown University, 1982), 33; Simon Schama, *Dead Certainties (Unwarranted Speculations)* (New York: Alfred A. Knopf, 1991), 24–34.

2. The brief Mexican War inspired "few paintings." See Ronnie C. Tyler, "The Mexican War: A Lithographic Record," *Southwestern Historical Quarterly* 77 (July 1973), 2.

3. *The American Cyclopaedia and Register of Important Events of the Year 1865* (New York: D. Appleton & Co., 1866), 356–57.

4. *Union League . . . Annual Report (1980)*, original in the Union League Club of New York, p. 28; for records of sanitary fair art exhibitions see, for example, *Catalogue of Paintings, Drawings, Statuary, etc. . . . of the Art Department of the Great Central Fair* (Philadelphia: 1864), or *Catalogue of the Art Exhibition at the Metropolitan Fair* (New York: 1864); *Catalogue of the Art Exhibition at the Maryland State Fair* (Baltimore: 1864); Marc Simpson, *Winslow Homer: Paintings of the Civil War* (San Francisco: The Fine Arts Museum of San Francisco and Bedford Arts Publishers, 1988), 30–31.

5. *Harper's Weekly*, 3 May 1862, 274; *The Round Table* 2, no. 32 (23 July 1864), 90.

6. Estill Curtis Pennington, *The Last Meeting's Lost Cause* (Spartanburg, S.C.: Robert M. Hicklin, Jr., Inc., 1988), 39, 42.

7. Henry James, *The American Scene* (London: Chapman & Hall, 1907), 384–86.

8. Hennig Cohen, ed., *The Battle-Pieces of Herman Melville* (New York: Thomas Yoseloff, 1963), 9, 14; for record of 1865 N.A.D. exhibition, see *The American Cyclopaedia . . . of the Year 1865*, 357.

Chapter One

⌒ *War Comes to Arcadia* ⌒

1. Marc Simpson, *Winslow Homer: Paintings of the Civil War* (San Francisco: Fine Arts Museums of San Francisco, 1988), 259; Harold Holzer, Gabor S. Boritt, Mark E. Neely, Jr., *The Lincoln Image: Abraham Lincoln and the Popular Print* (New York: Scribners, 1984), 82.

2. Judith Seklowitz, "Sanford R. Gifford" (independent study ms., 1966, in Frick Art Reference Library), 10, 29; William Swinton, *History of the Seventh Regiment National Guard During the War of the Rebellion* (New York: Fields, Osgood Co., 1870), 155; Frederick H. Dyer, *A Compendium of the War of the Rebellion*, vol. 3 (Des Moines: Dyer Publishing, 1908), 1408; Ila Weiss, *Sanford Robinson Gifford (1823–1880)* (New York: Garland Publishing, 1977), 206; Thomas S. Cummings, *Historic Annals of the National Academy of Design* (Philadelphia: George W. Childs, 1865), 301.

3. Albert Bigelow Paine, *Th: Nast: His Period and His Pictures* (New York: Macmillan, 1904), 16, 78; *New York Times*, 20 April 1861.

4. Weiss, *Sanford Robinson Gifford*, 207.

5. Ibid., 208; Maureen Meister, "To All the Glories of France: The Versailles of Louis-Philippe," in *All the Banners Wave: Art and War in the Romantic Era, 1792–1851* (Providence: Department of Art, Brown University, 1982), 23–25.

6. *The Crayon*, vol. 7, no. 6 (June 1861), 134; John F. Weir, *A Memorial Catalogue of the Paintings of Sanford Robinson Gifford, N.A.*, (New York: Metropolitan Museum of Art, 1881), 8.

7. Weiss, *Sanford Robinson Gifford*, 208; Union League Club of New York art acquisition records; Chaplain William H. Brown quoted in James I. Robertson, Jr., *Soldiers Blue and Gray* (New York: Warner Books, 1988), 173; Russell Duncan, ed., *Blue-Eyed Child of Fortune: The Civil War Letters of Colonel Robert Gould Shaw* (Athens: University of Georgia Press, 1992), 147.

8. Weiss, *Sanford Robinson Gifford*, 210.

9. *New York Tribune*, 7 April 1863, 16 April 1864. The scene was undeniably dramatic; another artist, James E. Taylor, sketched a similarly vivid scene while "knocking about" Baltimore in August 1864. See James E. Taylor, *The James E. Taylor Sketchbook* (Dayton, Ohio: Morningside House, 1989), 216–18; John H. Hunt, *American Landscape: The World of the Hudson River School* (New York: Harry N. Abrams, 1987), 227.

10. Henry T. Tuckerman, *Book of the Artists: American Artist Life* (New York: James F. Carr, 1967 reprint of 1867 edition), 524–25; Weir, *A Memorial Catalogue*, 7.

11. Cummings, *Historic Annals of the National Academy of Design*, 304.

12. Edward D. C. Campbell, Jr., "The 'Eccentric Genius' of Conrad Wise Chapman," *Virginia Cavalcade* 37 (Spring 1988), 158–59; William H. Gerdts, *Art Across America: Two Centuries of Regional Painting, 1720–1920*, vol. 2 (New York: Abbeville Press, 1990), 55.

13. Campbell, "The 'Eccentric Genius' of Conrad Wise Chapman," 163; Jules Abels, *Man on Fire: John Brown and the Cause of Liberty* (New York: Macmillan, 1971), 309–10; Patricia L. Faust, ed., *The Historical Times Encyclopedia of the Civil War* (New York: Harper & Row, 1986), 52.

14. Campbell, "The 'Eccentric Genius' of Conrad Wise Chapman," 175; Peter M. Chaitin, ed., *The Civil War: The Coastal War, Chesapeake Bay to Rio Grande* (Alexandria, Va.: Time-Life Books, 1984), 99.

15. Alfred C. Harrison, Jr., "Bierstadt's *Bombardment of Sumter* Reattributed," *Magazine Antiques* 129 (February 1986), 419; see also T. Michael Parrish and Robert M. Willingham, Jr., *Confederate Imprints: A Bibliography of Southern Publications from Secession to Surrender* (Austin, Texas: Jenkins Publishing Co., c. 1984), 13–71, 530–34. See, in the Museum of the Confederacy, *The Attack on Charleston by the Yankee Iron Clad Fleet*, a small lithograph, "drawn on the spot" not by Key but by one "A. Grinevald."

16. Harrison, "Bierstadt's *Bombardment of Sumter* Reattributed," 420–21.

17. Ibid.

18. Tuckerman, *Book of the Artists*, 566; Harrison, "Bierstadt's *Bombardment of Sumter* Reattributed," 421; Gerdts, *Art Across America*, 56.

19. Richard J. Koke, *American Landscape and Genre Paintings in the New-York Historical Society*, vol. 2 (Boston: G. K. Hall, 1982), 128.

20. Frances L. Henry, "A Memorial Sketch: E. L. Henry, N.A., His Life and His Life Work," *New York State Museum Bulletin* No. 339 (September

1945), 319; David S. Bundy et al., *Painting in the South: 1564–1980* (Richmond: Virginia Museum of Fine Arts, 1983), 250.

21. For faulty identification of Henry's *Entraining for the Front*, see, for example, Donald Dale Jackson, *The Civil War: Twenty Million Yankees* (Alexandria, Va.: Time-Life Books, 1985), 90–91; also Robert Paul Jordan, *The Civil War* (Washington: National Geographic Society, 1969), 50–51; Elizabeth McCausland, "The Life and Work of Edward Lamson Henry, N.A., 1841–1919," *New York State Museum Bulletin* No. 339 (September 1945), 159 (Henry also retained an albumen photograph of the scene, called "A New York Regiment Leaving New Jersey for the Front, March, 1864," which Henry meant to portray; see McCausland, 163); Dyer, *A Compendium of the War of the Rebellion*, vol. 3, 1408.

22. Guy C. McElroy, *Facing History: The Black Image in American Art, 1710–1940* (San Francisco: Bedford Arts Publishers, 1990), 98; Bundy, *Painting in the South* 86, 250.

23. Henry, "A Memorial Sketch," 319.

24. Ibid., 319–20; Guy StClair, "American Paintings at the Union League Club, New York" (unpublished ms., Union League Club archives), 12; Henry, "A Memorial Sketch," 320.

25. John Russell Young, *Around the World with General Grant*, vol. 2 (New York: American News Co., 1879), 443.

26. James M. McPherson, *The Negro's Civil War* (Urbana: University of Illinois Press, 1982), 208–9.

27. *Presentation Address of the Ladies of the City of New York to the Officers and Men of the Twentieth U.S. Colored Troops* (New York: Whitehouse Printer, c. 1864), original broadside in the New-York Historical Society.

28. McCausland, "Edward Lamson Henry," 65, 66.

29. Ibid., 64; Peter Harrington, "War on Grand Scale," *Military History* (August 1992), 66–75.

30. *Harper's Weekly*, 13 May 1865, 291.

31. Charles E. Fairman, *Works of Art in the United States Capitol Building* (Washington: Government Printing Office, 1913), 76–77; *Art in the United States Capitol* (Washington: United States Government Printing Office, 1976), 146; Tuckerman, *Book of the Artists*, 493; *Master Index* to The Civil War (Alexandria, Va: Time-Life Books, 1987), 30–31.

32. Larry Freeman, *The Hope Paintings* (Watkins Glen, N.Y.: Century House, 1961), 8, 9, 19, 85, 88.

33. Ibid., 80.

34. Ibid., 24, 88.

35. Ibid., 23; Stephen W. Sears, *George B. McClellan: The Young Napoleon* (New York: Ticknor & Fields, 1988), 247.

36. Freeman, *The Hope Paintings*, 22.

37. Stephen W. Sears, ed., *The Civil War Papers of George B. McClellan: Selected Correspondence, 1860–1865* (New York: Ticknor & Fields, 1989), 85.

38. Nancy K. Anderson and Linda S. Ferber, *Albert Bierstadt: Art and Commerce* (New York: Hudson Hills Press, 1990), 23, 28–29, 65, 147.

39. Ibid., 80-81.

40. Ibid., 26, 28, 80, 141, 147, 167, 181.

41. U.S. War Department, *The War of the Rebellion: A Compilation of the Official Records of the Union and Confederate Armies*, series I, vol. 38, pt. 1 (Washington, D.C.: U.S. Government Printing Office, 1880–1901), 67. (Cited hereafter as *O.R.*)

42. *The American Cyclopaedia*, 356–57; Samuel Hynes, "The Death of Landscape," *Military History Quarterly* 3 (Spring 1991), 17–27.

Caption Sources

Page 2. Koke, *American Landscape and Genre Paintings*, vol. 3, 4; Henry T. Tuckerman, *Book of the Artists: American Artist Life* (New York: James F. Carr, 1967 reprint of 1867 edition), 489; David W. Dunlap, *On Broadway: A Journey Uptown Over Time* (New York: Rizzoli Books, 1990), 4–5, 92.

Page 3. Ila Weiss, *Sanford Robinson Gifford (1823–1880)* (New York: Garland Publishing, 1977), 212–13; Tuckerman, *Book of the Artists*, 527.

Page 4. Albert Bigelow Paine, *Th: Nast: His Period and His Pictures* (New York: Macmillan, 1904), 78; Koke, *American Landscape and Genre Paintings*, vol. 3, 4; *The New York Times*, 20 April 1861.

Page 5. Koke, *American Landscape and Genre Paintings*, vol. 2, 3–4.

Page 6. McCausland, "The Life and Work of Edward Lamson Henry," 159, 163.

Page 7. Williams, *The Civil War: The Artists' Record*, 133; Dorothy Miller, *The Life and Work of David G. Blythe* (Pittsburgh: University of Pittsburgh Press, 1950), 79, 86.

Page 9. Alfred Waud, "The Army of the Potomac," *Harper's Weekly* 6 (15 August 1862), 523; Augustus Woodbury, quoted in Williams, *The Civil War: The Artists' Record*, 68. The camp, located in "the villa and farm of" a Dr. Stone, was named for Secretary of War Simon Cameron; see *Atlantic Monthly* 18 (July 1861): 110.

Page 10. William Swinton, *History of the Seventh Regiment, National Guard, New York* (New York, 1870), 198; Tuckerman, *Book of the Artists*, 525, 527.

Page 12 (top). Freeman, *The Hope Paintings*, 29.

Page 12 (bottom). Freeman, *The Hope Paintings*, 30.

Page 13. Freeman, *The Hope Paintings*, 30–31; Ronald H. Bailey, *The Civil War: The Bloodiest Day* (Alexandria, Va.: Time-Life Books, 1984) 111; Yarnell and Gerdts, *National Museum...Catalogue*, vol. 3, 1787.

Page 14 (bottom). Richard E. Beringer et al., *Why the South Lost the Civil War* (Athens: University of Georgia Press, 1986), 16.

Page 15. Roy P. Basler et al., eds., *Collected Works of Abraham Lincoln*, vol. 6 (New Brunswick, N.J.: Rutgers University Press, 1953–55), 108.

Page 19. Freeman, *The Hope Paintings*, 24, 80, 85.

Page 20. Baltimore *Gazette*, 16 December 1865; Harrison, "Bierstadt's...Fort Sumter," 416–18.

Page 22. George C. Groce and David H. Wallace, *The New-York Historical Society's Dictionary of Artists in America, 1564–1860* (New Haven: Yale University Press, 1957), 414.

Page 23. Richard Wheeler, *Sword Over Richmond: An Eyewitness History of McClellan's Peninsular Campaign* (New York: Harper & Row, 1986), 126.

Page 24. McCausland, "The Life and Work of Edward Lamson Henry," 156.

Page 25. David S. Bundy et al., *Painting in the South: 1564–1980* (Richmond: Virginia Museum of Fine Arts, 1983), 86, 250; David King Gleason, *Virginia Plantation Homes* (Baton Rouge: Louisiana State University Press, 1989), 23–25.

Page 26. McCausland, "The Life and Work of Edward Lamson Henry," 164–65; Frances L. Henry, "A Memorial Sketch of E. L. Henry, 319–20; James G. Barber, *U. S. Grant: The Man and the Image* (Washington: National Portrait Gallery, 1985), 47, 76; Guy StClair, *American Paintings at the Union League Club, New York* (unpublished ms., Union League Club archives), 12.

Page 29 (top). McCausland, "The Life and Work of Edward Lamson Henry," 162; StClair, *American Paintings at the Union League Club*, 12.

Page 29 (bottom). StClair, *American Paintings at the Union League Club*, 12; *Presentation Address of the Ladies of the City of New York to the Officers and Men of the Twentieth U.S. Colored Troops* (New York: Whitehouse Printer, c. 1864), broadside in the New-York Historical Society.

Page 30. J. S. Fullerton, quoted in Wheeler, *Voices of the Civil War*, 368; Philip H. Sheridan, *Personal Memoirs*, vol. 1 (New York: Charles L. Webster & Co., 1888), 307.

Page 31. Jerry Korn, *The Civil War: The Fight For Chattanooga* (Alexandria, Va.: Time-Life Books, 1984), 128.

Page 33. James Y. Yarnell and William H. Gerdts, *The National Museum of American Art Exhibition Catalogue from the Beginning Through...1876* (Boston: G.K. Hall, 1986), vol. 5, 3500–3501.

Page 35. *Harper's New Monthly Magazine*, 1879, quoted in Nancy K. Anderson and Linda S. Ferber, *Albert Bierstadt: Art and Commerce* (New York: Hudson Hills Press, 1990), 80, 147, 167.

Page 39. John S. Bowman, ed., *The Civil War Almanac* (New York: Bison Books, 1982), 174; Bundy et al., *Painting in the South*, 246; *U.S. Army & Navy Journal* I (1863–64), 346.

Chapter Two

☞ *Life Imitating Art* ☜

1. Allan Nevins, *The War for the Union: The Organized War, 1863–1864* (New York: Scribner's, 1971); John Keegan, *The Mask of Command* (New York: Viking, 1987), 197; *Harper's Weekly*, 14 November 1863, 722.

2. Keegan, *The Mask of Command*, 208.

3. Harold Holzer, Gabor S. Boritt, Mark E. Neely, Jr. *The Lincoln Image: Abraham Lincoln and the Popular Print* (New York: Scribner's, 1984), 83.

4. Stephen W. Sears, *George B. McClellan: The Young Napoleon* (New York: Ticknor & Fields, 1988), 84.

5. Ibid., 101; Stephen W. Sears, ed., *The Civil War Papers of George B. McClellan: Selected Correspondence, 1860–1865* (New York: Ticknor & Fields, 1989), 85.

6. Ibid., 179; George B. McClellan, *Letter of the Secretary of War Transmitting Report of the Organization of the Army of the Potomac...under the Command of Maj. Gen. George B. McClellan* (Washington: U.S. Government Printing Office, 1864), 91.

7. Sears, *Civil War Papers of McClellan*, 257.

8. George B. McClellan, *McClellan's Own Story* (New York: Charles L. Webster, 1887), 327.

9. Sears, *Civil War Papers of McClellan*, 260.

10. Sears, *George B. McClellan*, 196.

11. Ibid., 215.

12. Sears, *Civil War Papers of McClellan*, 473.

13. Sears, *George B. McClellan*, 296–317.

14. Sears, *Civil War Papers of McClellan*, 476.

15. Proceedings of the New Jersey Historical Society, 3rd series (1918), 90.

16. Clifford Dowdey, ed., *The Wartime Papers of R. E. Lee* (New York: Bramhall House, 1961), 440.

17. Roy Meredith, *The Face of Robert E. Lee in Life and Legend* (New York: Fairfax Press, 1981), 66–67; William H. Gerdts, *Art Across America: Two Centuries of Regional Painting, 1710–1920*, vol. 2 (New York: Abbeville Press, 1990), 32–33; T. C. DeLeon, *Four Years in Rebel Capitals: An Inside View of Life in the Southern Confederacy, from Birth to Death* (Mobile: Gossip Printing Co., 1890), 301.

18. John Y. Simon, ed., *The Papers of Ulysses S. Grant*, vol. 9 (Carbondale: Southern Illinois University Press, 1982), 406.

19. Ibid., 542; *Galena Weekly Northwestern Gazette*, 26 January 1864.

20. Simon, *Grant Papers*, vol. 9, 542; P. J. Staudenraus, ed., *Mr. Lincoln's Washington: Selections from the Writings of Noah Brooks* (New York: Thomas Yoseloff, 1967), 288–89; *The Martial Face: The Military Portrait in Britain, 1760–1900* (Providence, R.I.: Brown University, 1991), 57–58, 83, 95.

21. DeLeon, *Four Years in Rebel Capitals*, 299–300.

22. Ibid.

23. Mosby to Pauline Mosby, n.d., and 21 November 1861, Mosby Papers, Virginia Historical Society (photocopies of originals in private hands).

24. Mosby to Pauline Mosby, 14 February 1861; 18 February 1863[?]; 3 February 1865, Virginia Historical Society.

25. Mosby to Pauline Mosby, 3 February 1865, Virginia Historical Society.

26. Richard Shelly Hartigan, *Lieber's Code and the Law of War* (Chicago: Precedent, 1983), 58; *O.R.*, series I, vol. 4, pt. 3, 509–10, 608.

27. Mosby to Pauline Mosby, June 1861, 10 August 1861, Virginia Historical Society.

28. Edmund Wilson, *Patriotic Gore: Studies in the Literature of the American Civil War* (New York: Oxford University Press, 1962), 312; Jeffrey D. Wert, *Mosby's Rangers* (New York: Simon and Schuster, 1990), 76; James M. McPherson, *Battle Cry of Freedom* (New York: Oxford University Press, 1988), 738.

29. Harold Holzer and Mark E. Neely, Jr., "Aristocratic Company: Colonel John S. Mosby and the French Artistes," *Virginia Cavalcade* 41 (Spring 1992), 148–57.

30. Annabel Shanklin Perlik, "Signed L. M. D. Guillaume: Louis Mathieu Didier Guillaume, 1816–1892" (M.A. thesis, George Washington University, Washington, D.C., 1979), 6, 35, 36, 44, 60.

31. Ibid., 71.

32. Ibid., 15–16; 61; Gerdts, *Art Across America*, vol. 2, 18–19.

33. Perlik, "Signed L. M. D. Guillaume," 70.

34. Ibid., 61.

35. Basil Gildersleeve, *The Creed of the Old South, 1865–1915* (Baltimore: Johns Hopkins University Press, 1915), 5.

36. *Southern Illustrated News*, 29 August 1863; Emily V. Mason, *Popular Life of Gen. Robert Edward Lee* (Baltimore: John Murphy & Co., 1874), 106–7; Mark E. Neely, Harold Holzer, and Gabor S. Boritt, *The Confederate Image: Prints of the Lost Cause* (Chapel Hill: University of North Carolina Press, 1987), 130.

37. Neely, Holzer, and Boritt, *The Confederate Image*, 14–15; C. Vann Woodward, ed., *Mary Chesnut's Civil War* (New Haven: Yale University Press, 1981), 84; Varina Howell Davis, *Jefferson Davis, Ex-President of the Confederate States of America: A Memoir*, vol. 2 (New York: Belford Co., 1890), 392.

38. A. L. Long, *Memoirs of Robert E. Lee* (London: Low, Marston, Searle, & Rivington, 1886), 132–33; Mason, *Popular Life of...Lee*, 106–7.

39. Gildersleeve, *The Creed of the Old South*, 5.

40. Lewis Art Gallery Supplement to 1875 Catalog, in Perlik, "Signed L. M. D. Guillaume," 89.

41. Ibid., 90.

42. Ibid., 84; Neely, Holzer, and Boritt, *The Confederate Image*, 69, 72; Ulysses S. Grant, *Personal Memoirs*, vol. 2 (New York: Charles L. Webster & Co., 1892), 490.

43. Francis B. Carpenter, *Six Months at the White House with Abraham Lincoln: The Story of a Picture* (New York: Hurd & Houghton, 1866), 20; Justin Turner and Linda Levitt Turner, eds., *Mary Todd Lincoln: Her Life and Letters* (New York: Knopf, 1972), 403; StClair, "American Paintings at the Union League Club," 7.

44. Tyler Dennett, ed., *Lincoln and the Civil War in the Diaries and Letters of John Hay* (New York: Dodd, Mead & Co., 1939), 197; Carpenter, *Six Months at the White House*, 73; *The New York Times*, 9 June 1866; Gideon Welles, *Diary of Gideon Welles, Secretary of the Navy Under Lincoln and Johnson*, vol. 1 (New York: Houghton Mifflin, 1911), 527, 549; Fred B. Perkins, *The Picture and the Men* (New York: A. J. Johnson, 1867), opp. 190.

45. Carpenter, *Six Months at the White House*, 11–12.

46. Francis B. Carpenter to Owen Lovejoy (typed manuscript), 5 January 1864, Lincoln Museum.

47. Carpenter, *Six Months at the White House*, 25, 27–28; Henry T. Tuckerman, *Book of the Artists: American Artist Life* (New York: James F. Carr, 1967 reprint of 1867 edition), 447–78.

48. Carpenter, *Diary* (unpublished manuscript in family collection); Henry J. Raymond, *The Life and Public Services of Abraham Lincoln* (New York: Derby and Miller, 1865), opp., p. 5.

49. Mark E. Neely, Jr., *The Fate of Liberty: Abraham Lincoln and Civil Liberties* (New York: Oxford University Press, 1991), 46–47; Nancy Rash, *The Paintings and Politics of George Caleb Bingham* (New Haven: Yale University Press, 1991), 189–215.

50. *Harper's Weekly*, 3 June 1865.

51. *Harper's Weekly*, 13 May 1865, 291.

52. *U.S. Army and Navy Journal, 1863–1864*, quoted in Hermann Warner Williams, *The Civil War: The Artists' Record* (Boston: Beacon Press, 1961), 24.

Caption Sources

Page 43. Wheeler, *Voices of the Civil War*, 187; Stephen W. Sears, *George B. McClellan: The Young Napoleon* (New York: Ticknor & Fields, 1988), 110, 202–3, opp. p. 260.

Page 47 (top). Burke Davis, *The Long Surrender* (New York: Random House, 1985), 21–22; Tucker Hill, *Victory in Defeat: Jefferson Davis and the Lost Cause* (Richmond: The Museum of the Confederacy, 1986), 2–3; *Portrait of President Jefferson Davis...*, descriptive label, from the collection of the Museum of the Confederacy.

Page 52. Ulysses S. Grant, *Personal Memoirs*, vol. 2 (New York: Charles L. Webster & Co., 1892), 539; Williams, *The Civil War: The Artist's Record*, 24–25; Nathaniel Hawthorne, "Chiefly About War Matters," *Atlantic Monthly* 10 (July 1862), 46.

Page 55. L. Moody Simms, Jr., "Edward Caledon Bruce: Virginia Artist and Writer," *Virginia Cavalcade* 23 (Winter 1974), 34; Edward D. C. Campbell, Jr., "The Fabric of Command: R. E. Lee, Confederate Insignia, and the Perception of Rank," *The Virginia Magazine of History and Biography* 98 (April 1990), 263–64.

Page 57. Simms, "Edward Caledon Bruce," 34; Edward D. C. Campbell, Jr., "The Fabric of Command: R. E. Lee, Confederate Insignia, and the Perception of Rank," *The Virginia Magazines of History and Biography* 98 (April 1990), 263–64.

Page 58. *Galena Weekly Northwestern Gazette*, 26 January 1864; P. J. Staudenraus, *Mr. Lincoln's Washington: Selections from the Writings of Noah Brooks, Civil War Correspondent* (New York: Thomas Yoseloff, 1967), 289.

Page 59. Jeffrey D. Wert, *Mosby's Rangers* (New York: Simon & Schuster, 1990), 31–32.

Page 60. John B. Jones, *A Rebel War Clerk's Diary at the Confederate States Capital*, vol.1 (Philadelphia: J. B. Lippincott & Co., 1866), 179.

Page 61. S. F. Chapman to Mrs. W. B. Palmer, 2 May 1919, and Joseph L. McAleer to S. F. Chapman, 13 April 1868, typescript copies in the collection of the Museum of the Confederacy; Holzer and Neely, "Aristocratic Company," 153–56.

Page 63. Wert, *Mosby's Rangers*, 31–32; S. F. Chapman to Mrs. W. B. Palmer, May 2, 1919, Museum of the Confederacy.

Page 64. Wert, *Mosby's Rangers*, 76; Joseph L. McAleer to S. F. Chapman, 13 April 1868, Museum of the Confederacy.

Page 66. Frank H. Alfriend, *The Life of Jefferson Davis* (Cincinnati: Caxton Printers, 1868), 305; C. Vann Woodward, ed., *Mary Chesnut's Civil War* (New Haven: Yale University Press, 1981), 84.

Page 67. A. L. Long, *Memoirs of Robert E. Lee* (London: Low, Marston, Searle, and Rivington, 1886), 263.

Page 68. *Illustrated London News*, 4 June 1864; T. C. DeLeon, *Four Years in Rebel Capitals: An Inside View of Life in the Southern Confederacy, from Birth to Death* (Mobile: Gossip Printing Co., 1890), 300–301.

Page 69. Richard B. Harwell, ed., *Confederate Reader* (New York: Longmans, Green & Co., 1957), 176; Wert, *Mosby's Rangers*, 31.

Page 70. Woodward, *Mary Chesnut's Civil War*, 143; Harwell, *The Confederate Reader*, 22; Mark E. Neely, Jr., Harold Holzer, and Gabor S. Boritt, *The Confederate Image: Prints of the Lost Cause* (Chapel Hill: University of North Carolina Press, 1987), 199.

Page 71. Thomas Connelly, *The Marble Man: Robert E. Lee and His Image in American Society* (Baton Rouge: Louisiana State University Press, 1977), 22–23.

Page 73. Francis B. Carpenter to Theodore Thornton Munger, 22 February 1864, Munger Papers, Yale University; Carpenter, *Six Months at the White House*, 19, 20, 29, 37. Fred B. Perkins, *The Picture and the Men* (New York: A. J. Johnson, 1867), 34. Carpenter, *Diary*; Charles Hamilton and Lloyd Ostendorf, *Lincoln in Photographs*, rev. ed. (Dayton, Ohio: Morningside Books, 1985), pp. 190–93.

Page 74. Carpenter, *Six Months at the White House*, 13, 27; advertising supplement, "Carpenter's Great National Picture," in endpapers of *Six Months at the White House*, after p. 360.

Page 76 (left). Carpenter, *Six Months at the White House*, 12, 37; advertising endorsements for the engraved adaptation in endpapers of Perkins, *The Picture and the Men*, opp. 190; anonymous letter to the New York *Sun*, 9 January 1909, clipping in the New-York Historical Society; Carpenter, *Diary*.

Page 76 (center). Carpenter, *Six Months at the White House*, 28; advertisements for Carpenter's "Great National Picture," in endpapers to Carpenter, *Six Months at the White House*; Perkins, *The Picture and the Men*, 136.

Page 76 (right). Carpenter, *Six Months at the White House*, 27; Tyler Dennett, ed., *Lincoln and the Civil War in the Diaries and Letters of John Hay* (New York: Dodd, Mead & Co., 1939), 272.

Page 77 (left). Perkins, *The Picture and the Men*, 175.

Page 77 (center). Perkins, *The Picture and the Men*, 159.

Page 77 (right). Carpenter, *Six Months at the White House*, 21, 28; David Donald, ed., *Inside Lincoln's Cabinet: The Civil War Diaries of Salmon Portland Chase* (New York: Longmans, Green & Co., 1954), 152; advertisement for Carpenter's "Great National Picture" in endpapers of *Six Months at the White House*.

Pages 78–79. Carpenter, *Six Months at the White House*, 9, 26, 353; Francis B. Carpenter to Theodore Thornton Munger, 22 February 1864, Munger Papers, Yale University; endpapers to Carpenter, *Six Months at the White House*; Henry G. Raymond, *Life, Public Services and State Papers of Abraham Lincoln* (New York: Derby & Miller, 1865), 763–64; Carpenter, *Diary*; Perkins, *The Picture and the Men*, 47–48; *The New York Times*, 13 February 1878; Holzer, Boritt, and Neely, "Francis B. Carpenter," 78.

Page 80. Michael Fellman, *Inside War: The Guerrilla Conflict in Missouri During the American Civil War* (New York: Oxford University Press, 1989), 95–96; Mark E. Neely, Jr., *The Fate of Liberty: Abraham Lincoln and Civil Liberties* (New York: Oxford University Press, 1991), 47–49; Michael Edward Shapiro et al., *George Caleb Bingham* (New York: Harry N. Abrams, 1990), 43; E. Maurice Bloch, *The Paintings of George Caleb Bingham: A Catalogue Raisonné* (Columbia: University of Missouri Press, 1986), 23–24.

Page 83. Miller, *The Life and Work of David G. Blythe*, 116.

Chapter Three

Victory Without the Gaud

1. Herman Melville, *Battle-Pieces and Aspects of the War* (New York: Harper & Bros., 1866), 61–62; John Keegan, *The Price of Admiralty: The Evolution of Naval Warfare* (New York: Viking, 1988), 47.

2. Ambrose Bierce, "The Ingenious Patriot," in *The Collected Works of Ambrose Bierce*, vol. 6 (New York: Gordian Press, 1966), 167–69.

3. J. R. Soley, *The Blockade and the Cruisers* (New York: Charles Scribner's Sons, 1883), 61; *Official Records of the Union and Confederate Navies in the War of the Rebellion*, series I, vol. 14 (Washington, D.C.: U.S. Government Printing Office, 1894–1922), 273. (Cited hereafter as *O.R., Navy*.)

4. Edmund Wilson, *Patriotic Gore: Studies in the Literature of the American Civil War* (New York: Oxford University Press, 1962), 479.

5. David D. Porter, *The Naval History of the Civil War* (New York: Sherman Publishing Company, 1886), iv.

6. Raphael Semmes, *Memoirs of Service Afloat During the War Between the States* (Baltimore: Kelly, Piet & Co., 1869), 748.

7. Ibid., 753.

8. Ibid.; *O.R., Navy*, series I, vol. 3, 80.

9. Semmes, *Memoirs*, 752.

10. *O.R., Navy*, series I, vol. 3, 59; C. Vann Woodward, ed., *Mary Chesnut's Civil War* (New Haven: Yale University Press, 1981), 623.

11. Thomas Buchanan Read, *A Summer Story: Sheridan's Ride and Other Poems* (Philadelphia: Lippincott, 1865), 97–99.

12. Joseph Adams Smith, *An Address Delivered Before the Union League of Philadelphia…January 20th, 1906* (Philadelphia: Joseph Adams Smith, 1906), 2–3; Dorothy E. R. Brewington, *Dictionary of Marine Artists* (Salem, Mass.: Peabody Museum, 1982), 360; Virginia E. Lewis, *Russell Smith, Romantic Realist* (Pittsburgh: University of Pittsburgh Press, 1956), 243. See also John Wilmerding, *American Marine Painting* (New York: Harry N. Abrams, 1987), 150–51.

13. *O.R., Navy*, series I, vol. 3, 60.

14. Ibid., series I, vol. 3, 650.

15. Ibid., series I, vol. 3, 650–51.

16. Bruce Catton, *The American Heritage Picture History of the Civil War* (New York: American Heritage Publishing Co., 1960), 168, 206–7; Maxwell Whiteman, *Gentlemen in Crisis: The First Century of the Union League of Philadelphia, 1862–1962* (Philadelphia: The Union League Club of Philadelphia, 1975), 76.

17. A. T. Mahan, *The Gulf and Inland Waters* (New York: Charles Scribner's Sons, 1883), 221.

18. Ibid., 244. Overend's painting enjoyed a reputation in Great Britain through a black-and-white print published in London in September 1884 by the Fine Art Society and copyrighted by Max Jacoby & Co. The print bears a Lincoln remarque. A copy hangs in the U.S. Navy Museum in Washington, D.C.

19. Welles, *Diary*, vol. 2, 153.

20. Ibid., vol. 2, 66.

21. Ibid., vol. 2, 67.

22. Ibid., vol. 2, 67.

23. John M. Ellicott, *The Life of John Ancrum Winslow, Rear-Admiral, United States Navy* (New York: G. P. Putnam's Sons, 1902), 275.

24. Keegan, *Price of Admiralty*, 101, 169–70.

Caption Sources

Page 86. Williams, *The Civil War: The Artists' Record*, 184; William C. Davis, ed., *The Image of War*, vol. 2 (New York: Doubleday, 1982), 269.

Page 88. Williams, *The Civil War: The Artists' Record*, 184; Davis, *The Image of War*, vol. 2, 269.

Page 89. Geoffrey C. Ward et al., *The Civil War: An Illustrated History* (New York: Alfred A. Knopf, 1990), 125.

Page 92. Frederic A. Conningham, *Currier & Ives Prints: An Illustrated Check List* (revised edition, New York: Crown, 1970), 276.

Page 99. Kathleen Adler, *Manet* (Topsfield, Mass.: Salem House, 1986), 107–10.

Page 100. Joseph Foster, *The Presentation of the Portraits of General William Whipple…and of David Glasgow Farragut, Admiral, United States Navy, November 20th, 1891, by Storer Post No. 1, Grand Army of the Republic, Department of New Hampshire* (Portsmouth, N.H.: 1891; microfilm, New York Public Library).

Page 102. J. A. Smith, *Address Delivered Before the Union League*, 26.

Page 105. John McIntosh Kell, "Cruise and Combats of the *Alabama*," Buel and Johnson, *Battles and Leaders of the Civil War*, vol. 4, 608.

Page 109. Williams, *The Civil War: The Artists' Record*, 192; Tony

Gibbons, *Warships and Naval Battles of the Civil War* (New York: Gallery Books, 1989), 158–59.

Page 111. Welles, *Diary*, vol. 1, 249; James M. McPherson, *Battle Cry of Freedom* (New York: Oxford University Press, 1988), 587.

Page 112. Joseph T. Woodward, *Historic Record and Complete Biographic Roster, 21st Maine Volunteers* (Augusta, Maine: privately published, 1907), 18.

Page 115. John M. Morgan, quoted in Otto Eisenschiml and Ralph G. Newman, *Eyewitness: The Civil War as We Lived It* (New York: Grosset & Dunlap, 1956), 360.

Page 117. Ketchum, *American Heritage Picture History of the Civil War*, 195.

Chapter Four

⇌ *Glory* ⇌

1. Gerald F. Linderman, *Embattled Courage: The Experience of Combat in the American Civil War* (New York: Free Press, 1987), 271; Harold E. Mahan, "The Arsenal of History: *The Official Records of the War of the Rebellion*," *Civil War History* 29 (March 1983), 5–10; Stephen Davis, "A Matter of Sensational Interest": The *Century* 'Battles and Leaders' Series," *Civil War History* 27 (December 1981), 338–39.

2. Davis, "A Matter of Sensational Interest," 341–48.

3. Linderman, *Embattled Courage*, 266–82.

4. William T. Sherman, *Personal Memoirs of Gen. W. T. Sherman*, 3rd edition, vol. 2 (New York: Charles L. Webster, 1890) 55, 60.

5. *O.R.*, series I, vol. 38, pt. 1, 74; Sherman, *Personal Memoirs*, vol. 2, 61.

6. Ibid., vol. 2, 60.

7. *The New York Times*, 10 June 1930; Katherine McClinton, *The Chromolithographs of Louis Prang* (New York: Clarkson N. Potter, 1973), 36, 148.

8. McClinton, *Chromolithographs of Louis Prang*, 151; Larry Freeman, *Louis Prang: Color Lithographer, Giant of a Man* (Watkins Glen, N.Y.: Century House, 1971), 87; Charlotte Adams, *Catalogue of an unusual collection of water-colors and oil paintings purchased…by L. Prang & Co.* (New York: American Art Association, 1892), 3, 5, 77, 81.

9. Herman Melville, *Battle-Pieces and Aspects of the War* (New York: Harper & Bros., 1866), 174.

10. Dennis A. Walters and Ken Raveill, *The Battle of Atlanta*, souvenir booklet (Atlanta: Thomas Warren Enterprises, n.d.), 26–27.

11. Rachel Sherman Thorndike, ed., *The Sherman Letters* (New York: Charles Scribner's Sons, 1894), 220, 223.

12. James G. Barber, *U. S. Grant: The Man and the Image* (Washington: National Portrait Gallery, 1985), 49–50; *A Brief History of P. H. Balling's Original Oil Painting of General Ulysses S. Grant "In the Trenches Before Vicksburg"* (New York: Herman Linde, n.d.; advertising brochure in the New York Public Library Collection).

13. Ole Peter Hansen Balling, "An Artist's Close-up View of Lincoln, Grant and Sherman," *Civil War Times* 3 (October 1964), 17–18.

14. William S. McFeely, *Grant: A Biography* (New York: W. W. Norton, 1981), 18–19; Balling, "An Artist's Close-up View," 14, 16.

15. Balling, "An Artist's Close-up View," 14.

16. Ibid., 16, 18.

17. *A Brief History of P. H. Balling's Oil Painting*; Henry T. Tuckerman, *Book of the Artists: American Artist Life* (New York: James F. Carr, 1967 reprint of 1867 edition), 493; *National Portrait Gallery Illustrated Checklist* (Washington: National Portrait Gallery, 1987), 346.

18. *A Brief History of P. H. Balling's Oil Painting*; Balling, "An Artist's Close-up View," 15.

19. *A Brief History of P. H. Balling's Oil Painting*.

20. Ibid.

21. Margaret Coons, "A Portrait of His Times: John Elder's paintings reflect people and events during a critical period in Virginia history," *Virginia Cavalcade* 16 (spring 1967), 14–21.

22. Ibid.: T. C. DeLeon, *Four Years in Rebel Capitals, An Inside View of Life in the Southern Confederacy, from Birth to Death* (Mobile: Gossip Printing Co., 1890), 300.

23. Coons, "A Portrait of His Times," 21; Estill Curtis Pennington, *The Last Meeting's Lost Cause* (Spartanburg, S.C.: Robert M. Hicklin, Jr., Inc., 1988), 17.

24. Mark E. Neely, Jr., Harold Holzer, and Gabor S. Boritt, *The Confederate Image: Prints of the Lost Cause* (Chapel Hill: University of North Carolina Press, 1987), 133; Pennington, *The Last Meeting's Lost Cause*, 13–15, 28–29.

25. J. William Jones, *Personal Reminiscences of General Robert E. Lee* (New York: Appleton, 1875), 275; Pennington, *The Last Meeting's Lost Cause*, 17.

26. Pennington, *The Last Meeting's Lost Cause*, i, 21, 39, 47.

27. Ibid., 21.

28. Gaines M. Foster, *Ghosts of the Confederacy: Defeat, The Lost Cause, and the Emergence of the New South* (New York: Oxford University Press, 1987), 88–89.

29. DeLeon, *Four Years in Rebel Capitals*, 300.

30. Charles Bracelen Flood, *Lee: The Last Years* (Boston: Houghton Mifflin, 1981), 219; David B. Dickens, "Frank Buscher in Virginia: A Swiss Artist's Impressions," *Virginia Cavalcade* 38 (Summer 1988), 11–13.

31. Flood, *Lee: The Last Years*, 222; Dickens, "Frank Buscher in Virginia," 11.

32. *O.R.*, series III, vol. 5, 500; Roy P. Basler, et al., eds., *Collected Works of Abraham Lincoln*, vol. 8 (New Brunswick, N.J.: Rutgers University Press, 1953–55), 73–74.

33. *O.R.*, series I, vol. 43, pt. 1, 32.

34. *Personal Memoirs of P. H. Sheridan, General United States Army*, vol. 2 (New York: Charles L. Webster & Co., 1888), 66–69.

35. Ibid., 71–73.

36. Ibid., 75–76.

37. Ibid., 78–79.

38. Ibid., 80–81.

39. Ibid., 82.

40. Ibid., 83.

41. Harvey S. Ford, "Thomas Buchanan Read and the Civil War: The Story of 'Sheridan's Ride,'" *The Ohio State Archeological and Historical Quarterly* 56 (September 1947), 226; James F. Murdoch, *Patriotism in Poetry and Prose: Being Selected Passages from Lectures and Patriotic Readings* (Philadelphia: Lippincott, 1864), 86.

42. Smith, "Letters of Thomas Buchanan Read," 80; Ford, "Thomas Buchanan Read," 215–16; *The New York Times*, 12 May 1872; Thomas Buchanan Read, ed., *The Female Poets of America* (Philadelphia: E. H. Butler & Co., 1852), v, 382.

43. Ford, "Thomas Buchanan Read," 217; Earl Schenck Miers, ed., *Lincoln Day by Day: A Chronology*, vol. 3 (Washington: Lincoln Sesquicentennial Commission, 1960), 158; Murdoch, *Patriotism in Poetry and Prose*, 7, 83–84.

44. Ford, "Thomas Buchanan Read," 217–18; Miers, *Lincoln Day by Day*, vol. 3, 162, 164; Stewart Sifkis, *Who Was Who in the Civil War* (New York:

Facts on File, 1988), 411; Murdoch, *Patriotism in Poetry and Prose*, 114–16.

45. Ford, "Thomas Buchanan Read," 220; Harvey S. Ford, ed., *John Beatty: Memoirs of a Volunteer, 1861–1863* (New York: W. W. Norton, 1946), 169.

46. Ford, "Thomas Buchanan Read," 223–25.

47. Ibid., 225; *The New York Times*, 12 May 1872.

48. Ford, "Thomas Buchanan Read," 225–26.

49. Ibid., 226; Thomas Buchanan Read, *A Summer Story: Sheridan's Ride, and Other Poems* (Philadelphia: Lippincott, 1865), 97–99; Hennig Cohen, *The Battle-Pieces of Herman Melville* (New York: Thomas Yoseloff, 1963), 110, 223, 251–52; Murdoch, *Patriotism in Poetry and Prose*, 86.

50. Melville, *Battle-Pieces*, 117.

51. Maxwell Whiteman, *Paintings and Sculpture at the Union League of Philadelphia* (Philadelphia: The Union League, 1978), 35.

52. Ford, "Thomas Buchanan Read," 226; Records of the West Point Museum; Murdoch, *Patriotism in Poetry and Prose*, 85.

53. Cohen, *The Battle-Pieces of Herman Melville*, 111, 251.

54. Ford, "Thomas Buchanan Read," 226–27; *The New York Times*, 12 May 1872.

55. *The New York Times*, 12 May 1872; Charles Dudley Warner et al., eds., *A Library of the World's Best Literature Ancient and Modern* (New York: The International Society, 1897), vol. 30, 12,095.

56. *O.R.*, series I, vol. 43, pt. 1, 562–63.

57. Ibid.

58. Linderman, *Embattled Courage*, esp. 17–19, 36–47.

Caption Sources

Page 120. "Images of Cincinnati," *The Cincinnati Historical Society Bulletin* 38 (winter 1980).

Page 121. Jones, *A Rebel War Clerk's Diary*, vol. 1, 64; Joseph E. Johnston, *Narrative of Military Operations* (New York: D. Appleton, 1874), 54; C. Vann Woodward and Elizabeth Muhlenfeld, eds., *The Private Mary Chesnut: The Unpublished Civil War Diaries* (New York: Oxford University Press, 1984), 105.

Page 123. W. C. King and W. P. Derby, *Camp-Fire Sketches and Battle-Field Echoes of '61–'65* (Springfield, Mass.: King, Richardson & Co., 1889), 285, 349.

Page 124 (top). *The New York Times*, 19 April 1861.

Page 124 (bottom). Cohen, *Battle-Pieces of Herman Melville*, 132; Robertson, *Soldiers Blue and Gray*, 7.

Page 125. Ruth Painter Randall, *Colonel Elmer Ellsworth* (Boston: Little, Brown, 1960), 258; Winfred Porter Truesdell, *Catalog Raisonné of the Portraits of Col. Elmer E. Ellsworth* (Champlain, N.Y.: The Print Connoisseur, 1927), 20.

Pages 128–29. John B. Bachelder, *Descriptive Key to the Painting of Longstreet's Assault* (New York: John B. Bachelder, 1870), 49, 54, 55, and end-paper endorsements; gallery notes for exhibition of the painting at Boston Five Cents Savings Bank, n.d.

Page 131. Sherman, *Memoirs*, vol. 2, 101.

Page 132. Thomas, *Bold Dragoon*, 128, 285–86.

Page 133. General John Imboden, quoted in Walton Rawls, ed., *Great Civil War Heroes and Their Battles* (New York: Abbeville Press, 1985), 226–27; Burke Davis, *They Called Him Stonewall: A Life of Lt. Gen. T. J. Jackson, C.S.A.* (New York: Rinehart & Co., 1954), opp. p. 150, 328.

Page 135. Grant, *Memoirs*, vol. 2, 78–79; Wheeler, *Voices of the Civil War*, 371–72.

Page 136 (left). Belle Becker Sideman and Lillian Friedman, eds., *Europe Looks at the Civil War* (New York: Orion Press, 1960), 33; William B. Hesseltine, ed., *Three Against Lincoln: Murat Halstead Reports the Caucuses of 1860* (Baton Rouge: Louisiana State University Press, 1960), 121.

Page 137. Shelby Foote, *The Civil War: A Narrative*, vol. 1 (New York: Random House, 1958–74), 644; Guy StClair, *American Paintings at the Union League Club*, 14.

Page 138. *A Brief History of P. H. Balling's Original Oil Painting of General Ulysses S. Grant "In The Trenches Before Vicksburg."*

Page 140 (left). Letter, Scott to Shepard, 3 February 1893, typescript in the collection of Robert J. Titterton, Morrisville, Vermont.

Page 140 (right). Grant, *Memoirs*, vol. 2, 78–79; Wheeler, *Voices of the Civil War*, 371–72.

Page 141 (top). Noah André Trudeau, *Bloody Roads South: The Wilderness to Cold Harbor, May–June, 1864* (Boston: Little, Brown, 1989), 131; Gary W. Gallagher, ed., *Fighting for the Confederacy: The Personal Recollections of General Edward Porter Alexander* (Chapel Hill: University of North Carolina Press, 1989), 514–15.

Page 141 (bottom). Staudenraus, *Mr. Lincoln's Washington*, 210; Richard Wheeler, *Witness to Gettysburg* (New York: New American Library, 1987), 168; Joseph Ripley Ward, *History of the George G. Meade Post No. 1, Dept. of Pa., GAR* (Philadelphia: privately printed, 1889), 102.

Page 142. Ole Peter Hansen Balling, "A Close-up View of Lincoln, Grant, and Sherman," edited by Richard Seldon Creamer, *Civil War Times* 3 (October 1964), 13–18; *National Portrait Gallery Permanent Collection Illustrated Checklist* (Washington: Smithsonian Institution Press, 1987), 344–45.

Page 144. Wheeler, *Voices of the Civil War*, 60; Grant, *Memoirs*, vol. 1, 316–18.

Page 145 (top). Freeman Cleaves, *Rock of Chickamauga: The Life of General George H. Thomas* (Norman, Oklahoma; University of Oklahoma Press, 1949), 227; Charles E. Fairman, *Works of Art in the United States Capitol Building* (Washington, D.C.: U.S. Government Printing Office, 1913), 58.

Page 146. *The James Taylor Sketchbook* (Dayton, Ohio: Morningside House, 1989), 4, 592; McPherson, *The Negro's Civil War*, 145; Philip H. Sheridan, *Personal Memoirs*, vol. 2 (New York: Charles L. Webster & Co., 1888), 137–39.

Page 148. Cornelia Peake McDonald, quoted in Katharine M. Jones, *Heroines of Dixie: Confederate Women Tell Their Story of the War* (Indianapolis: Bobbs-Merrill, 1955), 145; Mary Anna Jackson, *Life and Letters of General Thomas J. Jackson* (New York: Harper & Bros., 1892), 427–28; Jeffrey D. Wert, "The Valley Campaign of 1862, Part II," *Virginia Cavalcade* 34 (Summer 1985), 38.

Page 149 (top). McPherson, *Battle Cry of Freedom*, 342.

Page 149 (bottom). Ibid., 429.

Page 151. Woodward, *Mary Chesnut's Civil War*, 116, 226, 521; Roy Meredith, *The Face of Robert E. Lee in Life and Legend* (New York: Fairfax Press, 1980), 86. Annabel Shanklin Perlik, "Signed L. M. D. Guillaume: Louis Mathieu Didier Guillaume, 1816–1892" (M.A. thesis, George Washington University, Washington, D.C., 1979), 113–114.

Page 152. Estill Curtis Pennington, *The Last Meeting's Lost Cause* (Spartanburg, S.C.: Robert M. Hicklin, Jr., Inc., 1988), 12, 16–19, 24–25, 39.

Page 155. Wheeler, *Voices of the Civil War*, 391.

Page 156. Charles Royster, ed., *Memoirs of General W. T. Sherman* (New York: Library of America, 1990), 812–17; Barber, *U. S. Grant: The Man and the Image*, 48; George P. A. Healy, *Reminiscences of a Portrait Painter* (Chicago: A. C. McClurg & Co., 1894), 70; Marie de Mare, *G. P. A. Healy:*

American Artist (New York: David McKay, 1954), 238–242. (Marie de Mare was Healy's granddaughter.)

Page 157. John S. Barnes, "With Lincoln from Washington to Richmond in 1865," *Appleton's Magazine* 11 (June 1907), 749; Harold Holzer, "I Myself Was At the Front," *Civil War Times Illustrated* 29 (January/February 1991), 34–35.

Page 159. W. Springer Menge and J. August Shimrak, eds., *The Civil War Notebook of Daniel Chisholm* (New York: Orion Books, 1989), 74; Thomas A. Lewis, *The Shenandoah in Flames: The Valley Campaign of 1864* (Alexandria, Va.: Time-Life Books, 1987), 152; Mary Sheridan to Col. L. E. Schenck, 18 November 1949, copy in U.S.M.A.

Page 161. Thomas A. Lewis, *The Guns of Cedar Creek* (New York: Dell, 1988), 236; George A. Forsyth, *Thrilling Days in Army Life* (New York: Harper & Bros., 1906), 141.

Page 163. James H. Rodabaugh, "Charles T. Webber," *Museum Echoes* (Bulletin of the Ohio Historical Society) 27 (August 1954), 59, 61.

Page 165. Burke Davis, *Sherman's March* (New York: Random House, 1980), 9; accession files in the library of the Union League Club of New York.

Page 166. Neely, Holzer, and Boritt, *The Confederate Image*, 69; Grant, *Memoirs*, vol. 2, 489.

Page 167. Andres J. Cosentino and Henry H. Glassie, *The Capital Image: Painters in Washington, 1800–1915* (Washington, D.C.: Smithsonian Institution Press, 1983) 89, 244, 253; Carl Bersch to Angelica Bode, April 16, 1866, and Gerda Vey (Bersch's granddaughter) to Bruce Catton, April 9, 1960; copies in the Ford's Theatre collection; research notes by Frank Hebblethwaite, Museum Technician, Ford's Theatre NHS, Washington; A. B. Faust, "Carl Bersch—Artist and Portrait Painter," unidentified clipping (August 1944) in Ford's Theatre collection.

Page 168. Key to Bachelder's painting, with *Brief Sayings of Eminent Men*, copy in the Chicago Historical Society.

Chapter Five

⌁ *The Theater of War* ⌁

1. *Descriptive Catalogue of the Cycloramas "Storming of Missionary Ridge" and "Battle Above the Clouds"* (Atlanta, n.d.), original in New York Public Library, 1–10.

2. Germain Bapst, *Essaie sur l'Histoire des Panoramas et des Dioramas* (Paris: Imprimerie Nationale, 1891), 7–9.

3. *The Martial Face: The Military Portrait in Britain, 1760–1900*, exhibition catalog (Providence, R.I.: Brown University [1990]), 56.

4. Dennis A. Walters and Ken Raveill, *The Battle of Atlanta*, souvenir booklet (Atlanta: Thomas Warren Enterprises, n.d.), 26–27.

5. *Souvenir Cyclorama of the Battle of Gettysburg* (Boston, 1885[?]); Dean S. Thomas, *The Gettysburg Cyclorama* (Gettysburg, Pennsylvania: Thomas Publications, 1989).

6. Abner Doubleday, *Chancellorsville and Gettysburg* (New York: Charles Scribner's Sons, 1882), 189, 195.

7. *Shiloh, Panorama Exhibited in Chicago* (n.d., catalog in the Chicago Public Library); Richard Wheeler, *Voices of the Civil War* (New York: Penguin Books, 1990), 91.

8. Peter Harrington, *Images of War, 1700–1914: The British at War in Art* (unpublished manuscript).

9. Robert W. Johannsen, *To the Halls of the Montezumas: The Mexican War in the American Imagination* (New York: Oxford University Press, 1985), 221–22; an original "Myrioptioon" is in the collection of Louise and Barry Taper of Beverly Hills, Ca.

10. Files of the National Museum of American History, Smithsonian Institution; James Street, Jr., *The Civil War: The Battle for Tennessee* (Alexandria, Va.: Time-Life Books, 1985), 100.

11. Allan Peskin, "The Civil War: Crucible of Change," Ohio Historical Society *Timeline* 3 (June–July 1986), 16.

12. Mark Thistlethwaite, "Peter F. Rothermel: A Forgotten History Painter," *Magazine Antiques* 111 (November 1983).

13. Ibid.; Basil L. Gildersleeve, *The Creed of the Old South, 1865–1915* (Baltimore: Johns Hopkins University Press, 1915), 18–19; Tuckerman, *Book of the Artists*, 437.

14. *Forbes Historical Art Collection of Battles, Incidents, Characters and Marches of the Union Armies* (1881 catalog in the Prints and Photographs Division, U.S. Library of Congress), 6, 17.

15. Jacob Edward Kent Ahrens, "Edwin Forbes" (M.A. thesis, University of Maryland, 1966), 52.

16. *Descriptive Catalogue of the Cycloramas "Storming of Missionary Ridge" and "Battle Above the Clouds,"* inside cover.

17. Thomas, *The Gettysburg Cyclorama*, 19.

18. Freeman, *The Hope Paintings*, 25, 34.

19. Ibid., 22.

20. Ibid., 9, 80.

21. Ibid., 44.

22. Ibid., 22.

23. Ibid., 22, 80.

24. Ibid., 91, 95.

Caption Sources

Page 174. Sherman, *Personal Memoirs*, vol. 2, 82.

Page 177. Ronald H. Bailey, *The Civil War: Battles for Atlanta* (Alexandria, Va.: Time-Life Books, 1985), 84.

Page 184. Grant, *Memoirs*, vol. 1, 353–54.

Page 185. Junius Henri Browne, quoted in Wheeler, *Voices of the Civil War*, 91.

Page 186 (bottom). Wheeler, *Witness to Gettysburg*, 226.

Page 188 (top). Photograph files, Library of Congress; Thompson, *The Image of War*, 125.

Page 188 (bottom). Eisenschiml and Newman, *Eyewitness*, 500.

Page 190. Wheeler, *Voices of the Civil War*, 310–11.

Page 191 (top). Frederic E. Ray, *Alfred Waud: Civil War Artist* (New York: Viking, 1974), 135–136.

Page 191 (bottom). Thompson, *The Image of War*, 125.

Page 194 (top). Donald E. Kloster, curator of the Division of Armed Forces History, National Museum of American History, to Harold Holzer, 25 March 1991; James Street, Jr., *The Civil War: The Struggle for Tennessee* (Alexandria, Va.: Time-Life Books, 1985), 100.

Page 196. Gordon files, Henry Ford Museum & Greenfield Village, in Sarah Innis to Harold Holzer, 6 June 1991.

Page 197. McPherson, *Battle Cry of Freedom*, 541.

Page 198. Wheeler, *Witness to Gettysburg*, 240; "Opinions of the Press on the Cyclorama of the Battle of Gettysburg," reprinted in Dean S. Thomas, *The Gettysburg Cyclorama* (Gettysburg, Pa.: Thomas Publications, 1989), 21–24.

Page 199. Wheeler, *Voices of the Civil War*, 313, 322.

Page 200. Ibid., 318, 320.

Page 202. Wheeler, *Witness to Gettysburg*, 243; Thomas, *The Gettysburg Cyclorama*, 243.

Page 204. Wheeler, *Witness to Gettysburg*, 217.

Chapter Six

⋟ *Peaceful Genres* ⋞

1. Hermann Warner Williams, Jr., *The Civil War: The Artists' Record* (Boston: Beacon Press, 1961), 222.

2. Otto Eisenschiml and Ralph G. Newman, *Eyewitness: The Civil War as We Lived It* (New York: Grosset & Dunlap, 1956), 323–24, 451.

3. Maris A. Vinovskis, ed., *Toward a Social History of the American Civil War: Exploratory Essays* (Cambridge: Cambridge University Press, 1990), vii, 1–30.

4. Drew Gilpin Faust, *The Creation of Confederate Nationalism: Ideology and Identity in the Civil War South* (Baton Rouge: Louisiana State University Press, 1988), 69–71.

5. Emily J. Salmon, "*The Burial of Latane:* Symbol of the Lost Cause," *Virginia Cavalcade* 29 (Winter 1979), 122, 124.

6. Frank Moore, ed., *Rebel Rhymes and Rhapsodies* (New York: George P. Putnam, 1864).

7. Richard Grant White, ed., *Poetry Lyrical, Narrative, and Satirical of the Civil War* (New York: American News Company, 1866); Frank Moore, *Anecdotes, Poetry and Incidents of the War: North and South, 1861–1865* (New York: privately printed, 1866); Francis F. Browne, ed., *Bugle Echoes: A Collection of Poems of the Civil War, Northern and Southern* (New York: White, Stokes, & Allen, 1886), 114–16.

8. Faust, *The Creation of Confederate Nationalism*, 69–71.

9. T. C. DeLeon, *Four Years in Rebel Capitals: An Inside View of Life in the Southern Confederacy, from Birth to Death* (Mobile: Gossip Printing Co.), 300.

10. Bell Irvin Wiley, *The Life of Billy Yank: The Common Soldier of the Civil War* (Baton Rouge: Louisiana State University Press, 1952), 358–59.

11. William H. Gerdts, *Art Across America: Two Centuries of Regional Painting, 1710–1920* (New York: Abbeville Press, 1990) vol. 1, 237; Robin Bolton-Smith and William H. Truettner, *Lilly Martin Spencer, 1822–1902: The Joys of Sentiment* (Washington: Smithsonian Institution Press, 1973), 42, 179; Ann Byrd Schumer, "Aspects of Lilly Martin Spencer's Career in Newark, New Jersey," *Proceedings of the New Jersey Historical Society* 77 (October 1959), 244–48.

12. Welles, *Diary*, vol. I, 538–39; Helen Nicolay, *Lincoln's Secretary: A Biography of John G. Nicolay* (New York: Longmans, Green & Co., 1949), 195.

13. Maris A. Vinovskis, "Have Social Historians Lost the War? Some Preliminary Demographic Speculations," in Vinovskis, *Toward a Social History of the American Civil War*, 23–27.

14. Christopher Kent Wilson, "Winslow Homer's *The Veteran in a New Field:* A Study of the Harvest Metaphor and Popular Culture," *American Art Journal* 17 (Autumn 1985), 9–10.

15. Matthew Paul Lalumia, *Realism and Politics in Victorian Art of the Crimean War* (Ann Arbor, Michigan: UMI Research, 1984), 96-97.

16. Gaines M. Foster, *Ghosts of the Confederacy: Defeat, the Lost Cause, and the Emergence of the New South* (New York: Oxford University Press, 1987), 103.

17. Wilson, "Winslow Homer's *The Veteran in a New Field*," 11.

Caption Sources

Page 208. Whiteman, *Paintings and Sculpture at the Union League of Philadelphia*, 5, 22–23, 124; Maxwell Whiteman, *Gentlemen in Crisis: The First Century of the Union League Club of Philadelphia, 1862–1962* (Philadelphia: The Union League, 1975), 128; Charles Eberstadt, *Lincoln's Emancipation Proclamation* (New York: Duschnes Crawford, 1950), 38.

Page 209. Buel and Johnson, *Battles and Leaders*, vol. 3, 71.

Page 211. Wheeler, *Voices of the Civil War*, 210.

Page 212. Robertson, *Soldiers Blue and Gray*, 103–4; *American Paintings in the Museum of Fine Arts, Boston*, vol. 1, 175.

Page 213 (left). Charles G. Coffin, *The Boys of '61* (Boston: Estes & Lauriat, 1884), 83.

Page 213 (right). Robertson, *Soldiers Blue and Gray*, 78; Patricia Hills, *The Genre Painting of Eastman Johnson: The Sources and Development of His Styles and Themes* (New York: Garland Publishers, 1977), 92, 96.

Page 214. Jones, *Heroines of Dixie*, 229.

Page 216. Bell I. Wiley, ed., *A Southern Woman's Story: Life in Confederate Richmond by Phoebe Yates Pember* (St. Simons Island, Ga.: Mockingbird Books, 1974), 4, 28–29, 116.

Page 217 (top). Robert H. Bremmer, *The Public Good: Philanthropy and Welfare in the Civil War Era* (New York: Alfred A. Knopf, 1980), 45, 52.

Page 217 (bottom). Annette Taper, ed., *The Brother's War* (New York: Times Books, 1988), ix; Hills, *The Genre Painting of Eastman Johnson*, 82–83.

Page 218. Neely, Holzer and Boritt, *The Confederate Image*, ix–xi; Turnbull Bros. advertising sheet, The Museum of the Confederacy, Richmond.

Page 221 (top). Robin Bolton-Smith and William H. Truettner, *Lilly Martin Spencer: The Joys of Sentiment* (Washington: Smithsonian Institution Press, 1973), 76, 209.

Page 221 (bottom). Conningham, *Currier & Ives Prints*, 78, 120; Gale Research, *Currier & Ives: A Catalogue Raisonné*, vol. 2 (Detroit: Gale Research, 1984), 179.

Page 222. Koke, *American Landscape and Genre Paintings*, vol. 2, 119–20.

Page 224. Advertising flyer for Rothermel's *The Republican Court in the Days of Lincoln* (New York: Russell's American Steam Printing House, n.d.).

Page 225. Lois Hall, ed., *Poems and Songs of the Civil War* (New York: Fairfax Press, 1990), 226–27; J. P. Cannon, *Inside of Rebeldom: The Daily Life of a Private in the Confederate Army* (Washington, D.C.: National Tribune Co., 1900), 20; Marc Simpson, *Winslow Homer: Paintings of the Civil War* (San Francisco: Fine Arts Museums of San Francisco, 1988), 257; Olive Bush, *The Dream of Reason: American Consciousness and Cultural Achievement from Independence to the Civil War* (New York: St. Martin's Press, 1977), 156–57.

Page 227 (left). Lalumia, *Realism and Politics in Victorian Art of the Crimean War*, 96–97.

Page 228. Bremmer, *The Public Good, Philanthropy and Welfare in the Civil War Era* (New York: Alfred A. Knopf, 1980), 145; Hills, *The Genre Painting of Eastman Johnson*, 83–84.

Page 230. Robert V. Bruce, *Lincoln and the Tools of War* (Indianapolis: Bobbs-Merrill, 1956), 187–88; Carol Troyen, "Innocents Abroad: American Painters at the 1867 *Exposition Universelle*, Paris," *American Art Journal* 16 (Autumn 1984), 10; Tuckerman, *Book of the Artists*, 488; Simpson, *Winslow Homer: Paintings of the Civil War*, 256.

Page 233. Bruce W. Chambers, *Art and Artists of the South* (Columbia: University of South Carolina Press, 1984), 36.

Page 234. Simpson, *Winslow Homer Paintings of the Civil War*, 22, 217–21; Nicolai Cikovsky, Jr., "A Harvest of Death: *The Veteran in a New Field*," ibid., 84, 93; *Frank Leslie's Illustrated Newspaper*, 13 July 1877, 268; Christopher Kent Wilson, "Winslow Homer's *The Veteran in a New Field*: A Study of the Harvest Metaphor and Popular Culture," *American Art Journal* 17 (Autumn 1985), 17.

Page 235 (bottom). Cyrus F. Boyd, *The Civil War Diary of Cyrus F. Boyd, 15th Iowa* (Iowa City: Iowa State Historical Society, 1953), 42.

Chapter Seven

⮞ *Come and Join Us, Brothers* ⮜

1. Frederick Douglass, *Life and Times of...Written by Himself* (New York: Pathway Press, 1941 reprint of 1847 edition), 394.

2. Roy P. Basler et al., eds., *Collected Works of Abraham Lincoln*, vol. 3 (New Brunswick, N.J.: Rutgers Univ. Press, 1953–55), 541.

3. Albert Boime, *The Art of Exclusion: Representing Blacks in the Nineteenth Century* (Washington: Smithsonian Institution Press, 1990), 141–43.

4. Ibid., 130–31.

5. Natalie Spassky et al., *American Paintings in The Metropolitan Museum of Art*, vol. 2 (New York: Metropolitan Museum of Art, 1985), 540–43.

6. Ibid.

7. Henry T. Tuckerman, *Book of the Artists: American Artist Life* (New York: James F. Carr, 1967 reprint of 1867 edition), 467, 470.

8. Boime, *The Art of Exclusion*, 115.

9. Buel and Johnson, *Battles and Leaders of the Civil War*, vol. 4, 58–60.

10. *Currier & Ives: A Catalogue Raisonné*, 149–65.

11. Buel and Johnson, *Battles and Leaders of the Civil War*, vol. 4, 78–80.

12. Ibid., vol. 4, 107–8.

13. Hermann Warner Williams, Jr., *The Civil War: The Artists' Record* (Boston: Beacon Press, 1961), 90.

14. Allen Nevins, James I. Robertson, Jr., and Bell I. Wiley, eds., *Civil War Books: A Critical Bibliography*, vol. 2 (Baton Rouge: Louisiana State Univ. Press, 1967), 13.

Caption Sources

Page 238. Benjamin Quarles, *The Negro in the Civil War* (New York: Da Capo Press, 1988), 325–28; Joseph T. Glatthaar, *Forged in Battle: The Civil War Alliance of Black Soldiers and White Officers* (New York: Free Press,

1990), 13; McPherson, *The Negro's Civil War*, 236–.37.

Page 239. Mary Noble Welleck Garretson, "Thomas S. Noble and His Paintings," New-York Historical Society *Quarterly Bulletin* 5 (October 1940), 118.

Page 240. Quarles, *The Negro in the Civil War*, 185–86.

Page 241. Basler, *Collected Works of Lincoln*, vol. 5, 372; McPherson, *The Negro's Civil War*, 82.

Page 244 (top). Peter H. Wood and Karen C. C. Dalton, *Winslow Homer's Images of Blacks: The Civil War and Reconstruction Years* (Austin: University of Texas Press, 1988), 85–89.

Page 244 (bottom). Boime, *The Art of Exclusion*, 106, 117–18.

Page 245. McPherson, *The Negro's Civil War*, 143.

Page 246. Koke, *American Landscape and Genre Paintings*, vol. 2, 232–34; Boime, *The Art of Exclusion*, 109–10.

Page 247. McElroy, *Facing History*; Hills, *The Genre Painting of Eastman Johnson*, 80.

Page 249. Spassky et al., *American Paintings in The Metropolitan Museum of Art*, vol. 2, 542.

Page 250. Williams, *The Civil War: The Artists' Record*, 232–33; Hugh Hanover, *The Image of the Black in Western Art*, vol. 4, part 1 (Cambridge: Harvard University Press, 1987), 207–8.

Page 251 (left). Quarles, *The Negro in the Civil War*, 345.

Page 252. David W. Blight, *Frederick Douglass' Civil War: Keeping Faith in Jubilee* (Baton Rouge: Louisiana State University Press, 1989), 159, 161.

Page 253. McPherson, *The Negro's Civil War*, 191.

Page 254. Spassky et al., *American Paintings in The Metropolitan Museum of Art*, vol. 2, 195–98; Tuckerman, *Book of the Artists*, 488–89.

Page 255 (left). Tuckerman, *Book of the Artists*, 488–89.

Page 255 (right). Spassky et al., *American Paintings in The Metropolitan Museum of Art*, vol. 2, 198.

Page 257 (bottom). Williams, *The Civil War, The Artists' Record*, 236.

Page 259. McPherson, *Battle Cry of Freedom*, 755; Simpson, *Winslow Homer: Paintings of the Civil War*, 181–82.

Page 261. Foote, *The Civil War: A Narrative*, vol. 3, 430–31; William C. Davis, *The Civil War: Death in the Trenches* (Alexandria, Va.: Time-Life Books, 1984), 116–17; E. Benezit, *Dictionnaire Critique et Documentaire des Peintres, Sculpteurs, Dessinateurs et Graveurs*, vol. 2 (Paris: Librairie Grund, 1976).

Chapter Eight

⮞ *Art and the Common Soldier* ⮜

1. Ulrich Troubetzkoy, "W. L. Sheppard: Artist of Action," *Virginia Cavalcade* 11 (Winter 1961–62), 20; "Other Southern Subjects: The Artwork of William Ludwell Sheppard," *Virginia Cavalcade* 42 (Summer 1992), 23.

2. Helen Hartman Gemmill, "William B. T. Trego: The Artist with Paralyzed Hands," *Antiques Magazine* 134 (November 1983), 994–1000.

3. James F. Reeves, *Gilbert Gaul* (Huntsville, Ala.: Huntsville Museum of Art, 1975), 7–9; see also George Parsons Lathrop, "An American Military Artist," *The Quarterly Illustrator* 1 (October–December, 1893), 234–40; and Jeanette L. Gilder, "A Painter of Soldiers," *The Outlook*, 2 July 1898, 570–73.

4. Alfred Vagts, *A History of Militarism: Civilian and Military* (revised edition, Meridian Books, 1959), 388–89, 453; Marvin Pakula, ed., *Uniforms of the United States Army* (New York: Thomas Yoseloff, 1960).

5. Marc Simpson, *Winslow Homer: Paintings of the Civil War* (San Francisco: The Fine Arts Museum of San Francisco and Bedford Arts Publishers, 1988), 18, 20.

6. Mark E. Neely, Jr., Harold Holzer, and Gabor S. Boritt, *The Confederate Image: Prints of the Lost Cause* (Chapel Hill: University of North Carolina Press, 1987), 204; T. C. DeLeon, *Four Years in Rebel Capitals: An Inside View of Life in the Southern Confederacy, from Birth to Death* (Mobile: Gossip Printing Co., 1890), 300.

7. John R. Elting and Michael J. McAfee, eds., *Military Uniforms in America*, volume 3; *Long Endure: The Civil War Period, 1852–1867* (Novato, Calif.: Presidio Press, 1982), 60, 74.

8. Leon F. Litwack, *Been in the Storm So Long: The Aftermath of Slavery* (New York: Knopf, 1980), 69–70.

9. Elting and McAfee, *Military Uniforms in America*, 74.

10. Bell Irvin Wiley, *The Life of Billy Yank: The Common Soldier of the Civil War* (Baton Rouge: Louisiana State University Press, 1952), 196–298.

11. Robert J. Titterton, *Julian Scott: A Return to Johnson* (Johnson, Vermont: Dibder Gallery, Johnson State College, 1989), 1, 16; Joseph B. Mitchell, *The Badge of Gallantry: Recollections of Civil War Congressional Medal of Honor Winners* (New York: Macmillan, 1968), 96; Henry T. Tuckerman, *Book of the Artists: American Artist Life* (New York: James F. Carr, 1967 reprint of 1867 edition), 493.

12. Tuckerman, *Book of the Artists*, 493; Robert J. Titterton, "A Soldier's Sketchbook," *Civil War Times Illustrated* 30 (September–October 1991), 56–58.

13. Titterton, *Julian Scott*, 2, 7.

14. Ibid., 6–8.

15. Typescript of Julian Scott letter to Colonel Shepard, courtesy of Robert J. Titterton; Ronald H. Bailey, *The Bloodiest Day: The Battle of Antietam* (Alexandria, Va.: Time-Life Books, 1984), 127.

16. Titterton, *Julian Scott*, 1.

17. Edwin Forbes, *Thirty Years After: An Artist's Story of the Great War* (New York: Howard & Hulbert, 1890) vol. 1, 21.

18. Simpson, *Winslow Homer: Paintings of the Civil War*, 15; Clive Bush, *The Dream of Reason: American Consciousness and Cultural Achievement from Independence to the Civil War* (New York: St. Martin's Press, 1977), 158–60.

19. Randy Steffen, *The Horse Soldier, 1776–1943, vol. 2: The Frontier, the Mexican War, the Civil War, the Indian Wars, 1861–1880* (Norman, Okla.: University of Oklahoma Press, 1978), 60.

20. Jozef Piatek and Malgorzata Dolistowska, *Panorama Raclawicka* (Wroclaw: 1988).

21. Herman Melville, *Battle-Pieces and Aspects of the War* (New York: Harper & Brothers, 1866), 56; Earl J. Hess, "Northern Response to the Ironclad: A Prospect for the Study of Military Technology," *Civil War History* 31 (June 1985), 138–39

Caption Sources

Page 264. John D. Billings, *Hardtack and Coffee; or, the Unwritten Story of Army Life* (Boston: G. M. Smith & Co., 1887); Robertson, *Soldiers Blue and Gray*, 74.

Page 265. Robertson, *Soldiers Blue and Gray*, 109.

Page 266. Benjamin Borton, *On the Parallels; or, Chapters in Inner History: A Story of the Rappahannock* (Woodstown, N.J.: The Monitor-Register Press, 1903), 39–40.

Page 267. Wheeler, *Voices of the Civil War*, 211–12.

Page 269. Gemmill, "William B. T. Trego," 994.

Page 270. Oliver W. Norton, *Army Letters, 1861–1865* (Chicago: O. L. Deming, 1903), 28.

Page 271. Willard Glazier, *Three Years in the Federal Cavalry* (New York: 1870), 32; Robertson, *Soldiers Blue and Gray*, 16.

Page 273. Reeves, *Gilbert Gaul*, 13; Gertrude Grace Sill, *A Handbook of Symbols in Christian Art* (New York: Collier Books, 1975), 29; Ernest L. Waitt, *History of the Nineteenth Regiment Conn. Volunteers in the War for the Union* (Norwich, Conn.: The Committee, 1885), 242.

Page 274. Robertson, *Soldiers Blue and Gray*, 57–58.

Page 275. Wheeler, *Voices of the Civil War*, 247.

Page 277. Theodore Gerrish, *Army Life: A Private's Reminiscences of the Civil War* (Portland, Maine: Hoyt, Fogg & Donham, 1882), 177; *Harper's Weekly*, 6 April 1889.

Page 278 (top). *Conrad Wise Chapman, 1842–1910: An Exhibition…in the Valentine Museum* (Richmond: The Valentine Museum, 1962), 77.

Page 279. Williams, *The Civil War: The Artists' Record*, 103.

Page 280. Reeves, *Gilbert Gaul*, 13.

Page 281. Koke, *American Landscape and Genre Paintings in the New-York Historical Society*, vol. 2, 128; Reeves, *Gilbert Gaul*, 11.

Page 282. George G. Benedict, *Army Life in Virginia: Letters From the 12th Vermont Regiment …* (Burlington: Free Press Association, 1895), 67–68; Simpson, *Winslow Homer: Paintings of the Civil War*, 172.

Page 285. *The New York Times*, 30 October 1864; Simpson, *Winslow Homer: Paintings of the Civil War*, 214.

Page 287. Robert J. Titterton, *A Return to Johnson* (Johnson, Vt.: Dibder Gallery, Johnson State College, 1989), 2–7.

Page 288. Christopher Kent Wilson, "Marks of Honor and Death: *Sharpshooter* and the Peninsular Campaign of 1862," in Simpson, *Winslow Homer: Paintings of the Civil War*, 30.

Page 289 (left). Simpson, *Winslow Homer: Paintings of the Civil War*, 231; Robertson, Soldiers Blue and Gray, 226.

Page 289 (right). Simpson, *Winslow Homer: Paintings of the Civil War*, 152.

Page 290. Tuckerman, *Book of the Artists*, 450.

Page 291 (top). *American Paintings in the Museum of Fine Arts, Boston*, vol. 1, 159.

Page 291 (bottom). *Catalogue of the 47th Annual Exhibition of the National Academy of Design, 1871* (New York: National Academy, 1872), No. 205; Tuckerman, *Book of the Artists*, 468.

Page 292. Robertson, *Soldiers Blue and Gray*, 81.

Page 293. F. Colburn Adams, quoted in Wheeler, *Voices of the Civil War*, 147; StClair, *American Paintings at the Union League Club, New York*, 14; accession record in the library of the Union League Club of New York.

Page 295. Simpson, *Winslow Homer: Paintings of the Civil War*, 267; C. W. Bardeen, *A Little Fifer's War Story* (Syracuse: C. W. Bardeen, 1910), 153.

Page 296. Williams, *The Civil War: The Artists' Record*, 194; Simpson, *Winslow Homer: Paintings of the Civil War*, pp. 247–58; Tuckerman, *Book of the Artists*, 491; Julian Grossman, *Echo of a Distant Drum: Winslow Homer and the Civil War* (New York: Harry M. Abrams, 1974), 117.

Page 297. Robertson, *Soldiers Blue and Gray*, 98; Simpson, *Winslow Homer: Paintings of the Civil War*, 161–64.

Page 298. Wheeler, *Witness to Gettysburg*, 201; Williams, *The Civil War: The Artists' Record*, 55–56; Benedict Maryniak, "'Their Faith Brings Them,'" *Civil War Magazine* (March–April 1991), 55.

Page 300. Gemmill, "William B. T. Trego," 997–98.

Page 303. Reid Mitchell, *Civil War Soldiers: Their Expectations and Their Experiences* (New York: Viking, 1988), 45–47.

Page 304 (left). Neely, Holzer, and Boritt, *The Confederate Image*, 209.

Page 304 (right). Carlton McCarthy, *Detailed Minutiae of Soldier Life in the Army of Northern Virginia 1861–1865* (Richmond: Carlton McCarthy & Co., 1884), 204.

Page 307. Williams, *The Civil War: The Artists' Record*, 82; Simpson, *Winslow Homer: Paintings of the Civil War*, 187.

Page 308 (left). John B. Lindsley, ed., *The Military Annals of Tennessee: Confederate* (Nashville: J. M. Lindsley & Co., 1886), 219.

Page 309. William C. Davis, ed., *The Image of War*, vol. 3: *The Embattled Confederacy* (New York: Doubleday, 1982), 75.

Page 311 (top). Ray, *Alfred Waud*, 156.

Page 311 (bottom). Davis, ed., *The Image of War*, vol. 3: *The Embattled Confederacy*, 322–23.

Page 312. James A. Connolly, *Three Years in the Army of the Cumberland* (Bloomington: Indiana University Press, 1959), 333.

Page 313 (top). Robertson, *Soldiers Blue and Gray*, 71.

Page 313 (bottom). Robertson, *Soldiers Blue and Gray*, 225.

Page 314. William Swinton, quoted in Wheeler, *Voices of the Civil War*, 464–65; George H. Allen, *Forty Six Months with the Fourth Rhode Island Volunteers in the War of 1861 to 1865...* (Providence, R.I.: J. A. & R. A. Reid, 1887), 14.

Page 315. Richard Norris Brooke, *Record of My Work* (manuscript, 1978; copy in West Point Museum collection).

Page 316. Sherman, *Memoirs*, vol. 2, 376; Allan Peskin, "The Civil War: Crucible of Change," Ohio Historical Society *Timeline* 3 (June–July 1986), 15; Whitman, *Specimen Days*, in Van Doren, ed., *The Portable Walt Whitman*, 473.

Page 317 (right). Elizabeth Johns, *Thomas Eakins: The Heroism of Modern Life* (Princeton, N. J.: Princeton University Press, 1983P, 148–49, 152.

Page 319. Margaret Coons, "A Portrait of His Times: John Elder's paintings reflect people and events during a crucial period in Virginia History," *Virginia Cavalcade* 16 (Spring 1967), 17, 19; Richard Wheeler, *On Fields of Fury: From the Wilderness to the Crater—An Eyewitness to History* (New York; HarperCollins. 1991), 281, 285.

Index

Page numbers in italic refer to illustrations.